Norms of protection

Norms of protection: Responsibility to protect, protection of civilians and their interaction

Edited by Angus Francis, Vesselin Popovski and Charles Sampford

**United Nations
University Press**

TOKYO · NEW YORK · PARIS

The views expressed in this publication are those of the authors and do not necessarily reflect the views of the United Nations University.

United Nations University Press
United Nations University, 53-70, Jingumae 5-chome,
Shibuya-ku, Tokyo 150-8925, Japan
Tel: +81-3-5467-1212   Fax: +81-3-3406-7345
E-mail: sales@unu.edu   General enquiries: press@unu.edu
http://www.unu.edu

United Nations University Office at the United Nations, New York
2 United Nations Plaza, Room DC2-2062, New York, NY 10017, USA
Tel: +1-212-963-6387   Fax: +1-212-371-9454
E-mail: unuony@unu.edu

United Nations University Press is the publishing division of the United Nations University.

Cover design by Andrew Corbett
Cover photograph by Dieter Telemans/Panos Pictures

Printed in the United States of America for the Americas and Asia
Printed in the United Kingdom for Europe, Africa and the Middle East

ISBN 978-92-808-1218-3
e-ISBN 978-92-808-7187-6

Library of Congress Cataloging-in-Publication Data

Norms of protection : responsibility to protect, protection of civilians and their
interaction / edited by Angus Francis, Vesselin Popovski and Charles Sampford.
    p. cm.
 Includes bibliographical references and index.
 ISBN 978-9280812183 (pbk.)
 1. Humanitarian intervention. 2. Responsibility to protect (International law)
I. Francis, Angus. II. Popovski, Vesselin. III. Sampford, C. J. G. (Charles J. G.)
KZ6369.N67   2012
341.6′7—dc23   2012031156

Endorsements

"Norms of Protection is a valuable contribution to the growing literature on the Responsibility to Protect (R2P). It ably addresses the question of how R2P relates to the earlier yet still developing doctrine of civilian protection. This is far more than an academic or conceptual matter. Confusion over which norm should apply under which circumstances has muddled strategy and practice in capitals and the Security Council alike. The authors do not claim to have all the answers, but they surely have provided the essential place to start the debate. The sooner we can clarify doctrine, the sooner these human protection norms will become both policy and practice. In that spirit, I am pleased to recommend this timely and important volume."
Edward C. Luck, *Dean and Professor, The Joan B. Kroc School of Peace Studies, The University of San Diego*

"Since the end of the Cold War, efforts to protect civilians from violence and war have become, deservedly, one of the highest priorities for the United Nations and its Member States. Whilst the number of casualties from conflicts has continued to decrease over the past century, unfortunately the proportion of civilian casualties – killed, maimed and often deliberately targeted – has continued to rise. The genocides of Rwanda and Srebrenica (among others) led ultimately to the norm of the Responsibility to Protect (R2P), unanimously agreed by world leaders in 2005, aimed at decisively preventing four specific crimes against humanity. Ahead of agreement on R2P, however, the UN Security Council in 1999 began mandating peacekeeping missions to protect civilians from the threat of violence. Since that time the Council has included the Protection of Civilians (POC) as a central task in more than 10 UN peacekeeping missions. This volume provides valuable insights into the two related norms of R2P and PoC, including from an Asian perspective. It is essential reading for those concerned in understanding and enhancing civilian protection mechanisms."

Michael Smith, *Founding Executive Director, Australian Civil-Military Centre*

"No contemporary problem requires more rigorous analysis of real-world dilemmas than the responsibility to protect and the protection of civilians. This book is essential reading for both scholars and practitioners at this critical juncture in the history of international efforts to come to the rescue of affected populations caught in the cross hairs of violence and war."

Thomas G. Weiss, *Director, Ralph Bunche Institute for International Studies, The CUNY Graduate Center*

Contents

Contributors

Lina A. Alexandra is a researcher in the Department of Politics and International Relations, Centre for Strategic and International Studies (CSIS), based in Jakarta, Indonesia.

Edwin Bikundo is a lecturer at the School of Criminology and Criminal Justice at Griffith University in Brisbane, Australia.

Hugh Breakey is a Research Fellow at the Institute for Ethics, Governance and Law at Griffith University, Australia.

Helen Durham is a Senior Fellow at the Melbourne Law School and Strategic Adviser, International Law for the Australian Red Cross.

Angus Francis is Senior Lecturer in international and refugee law and Program Leader of the Human Rights and Governance Program at the Queensland University of Technology Faculty of Law, Australia.

Andrew Garwood-Gowers is an Associate Lecturer at the Faculty of Law at Queensland University of Technology, Australia.

Annie Herro is a PhD candidate at the Centre for Peace and Conflict Studies of the University of Sydney, Australia.

Hitoshi Nasu is a Senior Lecturer in law at the Australian National University.

Vesselin Popovski is Senior Academic Programme Officer, Head of Peace and Security Studies at the United Nations University Institute for Sustainability and Peace (UNU-ISP), Tokyo.

Charles Sampford is Foundation Dean and Professor of Law and Research Professor in Ethics, Griffith University, Brisbane, Australia, and Director of the Institute for Ethics, Governance and Law.

Kavitha Suthanthiraraj is a PhD candidate at the School of Social Science and International Studies of the University of New South Wales, Australia.

See Seng Tan is Deputy Director and head of research at the Institute for Defence and Strategic Studies, S. Rajaratnam School of International Studies, Nanyang Technological University, Singapore.

Phoebe Wynn-Pope is an independent consultant specializing in international law and humanitarian affairs with a particular focus on responsibilities of the international community working in conflict zones.

Foreword

Global governance is defined as the sum of norms, laws, policies and institutions that define, constitute and mediate international relations between and among people, society, market and the state – the wielders and objects of the exercise of international public power. It advances (and sometimes retreats) by filling (or widening) five analytical gaps: knowledge, norms, policies, institutions and compliance.

Over the past decade and a half, concerned citizens – in the language of Angus Francis and Charles Sampford in their scene-setting Introduction, "engaged academics and reflective practitioners" – have joined mandated and non-governmental organizations in becoming exercised about a much more acute empirical gap, namely the protection gap. The frequency and deadly consequences of armed conflict rise and fall on the ebb and tide of history and mercifully over the last fifteen years they have waned from a peak in the mid-1990s. But that statistical decline in the numbers and lethality per battle and per year is little solace to innocent civilians killed by intent or when caught in the crossfire, starved into submission or death, ethnically cleansed, displaced from their homes, villages and communities, and in other brutal fashion terrorized and brutalized. Moreover, unlike the nonlinear movement on the number and lethality of wars, there seems to have been more or less a linear progression over the last two centuries in the increasing proportion of civilians being killed in armed conflict, whether in the violence of war directly, or from conflict-related hunger and disease.

The angry and bitter debate in the late 1990s over the so-called chal-

lenge of humanitarian intervention highlighted a triple policy dilemma –
that is, a threefold protection gap – of complicity, paralysis or illegality. If
we have the means to stop mass killings underway or imminently threatened but chose to look the other way, we are not the moral equivalent of
the perpetrators of the atrocities, but we are part-complicit through our
deliberate act of omission. The Rwanda genocide in 1994 clearly fits this
description. If we insist that any effective international action to protect
populations at risk of mass atrocity must be formally authorized by the
United Nations Security Council, then the practical effect of this is to
surrender the agenda to the obstructionist obduracy of any one of the
five veto-wielding permanent members of the Council, as has been the
case in Syria in 2011–2012, or indeed to the apathy and indifference of
the Council as a whole: no draft resolution on Rwanda was submitted
and vetoed in 1994. But if we accept therefore that effective intervention
by one power or a coalition of states is justified, as with the intervention
by the North Atlantic Treaty Organization in Kosovo in 1999, then we are
endorsing action that under existing UN Charter law is illegal.

Since those conscience-shocking scenes from Rwanda, the Balkans and
East Timor in the 1990s in particular, several efforts have been launched
to strengthen the protection gaps in global governance. With respect to
knowledge gaps: What are the causes of atrocity crimes and contributing
factors behind them? Can we identify early warning signs? Who are the
actors best placed to respond quickly and effectively to avert or halt
atrocities? On normative gaps: How can old, outdated and ineffectual
norms be replaced by robust new powerful ones? Who are the norm entrepreneurs, brokers, champions, carriers and spoilers? On policy gaps:
What policy remedies work best? By whom can they be adopted? On
institutional gaps: Do we need new institutions or can existing ones be
adapted, reformed and improved to be made fit for purpose? How can
the division of labour between them be optimally allocated to avoid
duplication and institutional infighting? Most crucially, what are the
compliance gaps and how can they best be filled to ensure predictable,
credible and reliable protection?

One answer to these series of questions came through the work of the
International Commission on Intervention and State Sovereignty which
published its path-breaking report The Responsibility to Protect (R2P) in
2001. The core elements of its ideas were adopted unanimously at the
summit of world leaders at the United Nations in 2005. The 2005 Outcome Document with four atrocity crimes added clarity, rigour and specificity, limiting the triggering events to war crimes, genocide, crimes
against humanity and ethnic cleansing, and so realigning the emerging
political norm to existing categories of international legal crimes. In 2009,
Secretary-General Ban Ki-moon's Three Pillars formulation further re-

fined the ideas into a well-received three-part agenda. Civil society organizations have been engaged in a vigorous process of norm socialization and crystallisation. The annual General Assembly debates since 2009 have helped to forge a shared understanding and consolidate global consensus on R2P.

Yet, as the resort to Pillar Three external military intervention in Libya in 2011 showed, R2P remains a subject of debate and some confusion conceptually, contested normatively, and controversial politically. That is no reason to run away from it. On the contrary, it merely heightens the importance of and need for such books as this one to clarify the concept, affirm the norm, and draw attention to the need to consolidate shared understandings. R2P is no more self-guaranteeing than any other type of external intervention. It is not a magical formula by means of which good intentions can guarantee good policy outcomes in distant foreign lands. The risks of unintended and perverse consequences remain as only too real. There is no humanitarian crisis so grave that it cannot be made worse by an outside military intervention. Hence the due diligence imperative: on an informed assessment, are we reasonably confident of doing more good than harm?

In the meantime, the protection of civilians (POC), whose emergence on the agenda of international policy coincides chronologically with that of R2P, has been markedly less contentious, to the point where its advocates and actors fear contagion from the more politicized R2P. One of the great merits of this book is the detailed and sophisticated exposition of the points of convergence, overlap, tension and divergence between R2P and POC. This is done, with skill and care, on the normative, institutional and operational dimensions.

I have been involved in this project as an adviser from conceptualization to completion. It is enormously gratifying to see it brought to fruition and publication. The civilian protection agenda that encompasses both POC and R2P requires mutually supportive collaboration among military, police, political and humanitarian actors from national governments, regional organizations, international organizations and civil society. It ranges from conflict prevention and management to conflict resolution and post-conflict peacebuilding and reconciliation. It will require further conceptual refinement, norm development, and institutional capacity building. With roots in international, human rights, humanitarian and refugee laws, and based in empathy for the weak and vulnerable that is common to all cultures, both POC and R2P can meet concerns about abuses and misappropriations. But in order to do so, they must be thoroughly and dispassionately studied: mere exhortations to better behaviour will never prove enough of an incentive to secure compliance with global norms.

Our common humanity demands an acceptance of a duty of care by all of us who live in zones of safety towards all those who are trapped in zones of danger. In the vacuum of responsibility for the safety and security of the marginalized, stigmatized and dehumanized out-groups at risk of mass atrocities, both POC and R2P provide points of entry – sometimes different, sometimes the same – for the international community to take up the moral, political, institutional and military slack. This collection of essays should help to point the way forward.

Ramesh Thakur
Canberra
August 2012

Acknowledgements

This book came about as a result of an already well-developed collaboration between the Institute for Ethics, Governance and Law[1] headquartered in Brisbane, and the United Nations University in Tokyo. The two academic partners, jointly with the Australian Civil-Military Centre, developed the idea for a new book project aimed at unpacking and mapping the relationship between two norms of protection – responsibility to protect (R2P) and protection of civilians (POC) – and to identify gaps, overlaps and areas of complementarity. We submitted a grant application to the Australian Government's Responsibility to Protect Fund,[2] and were successful.

The content of the book was shaped at a workshop in Sydney, kindly hosted by Professor Ben Saul and the Sydney Centre for International Law, at which a group of experts from academia and practice deliberated on the relationship between R2P and POC and the ways in which R2P might add value to the POC agenda (and vice versa). We also elaborated what needs to be done in order to support states, international organizations and regional arrangements in building capacities to take part in protection operations, focusing especially on the Asia-Pacific region. The chapters in this collection do justice to the workshop's rich and engaging discussions on these fundamentally important questions.

A number of individuals at the partner institutions played a crucial hand in making this collection – and the project more generally – a reality. At the United Nations University: Johanna Stratton, Mark Notaras, Stephanie Dietrich and Katalin Kekesi. At the Institute for Ethics,

Governance and Law and its affiliated institutions: Valentin Hadjiev, Carmel Connors, Tanya Butkovsky and Gail Fellows. We would also like to acknowledge and thank the three regional institutions that supported the Sydney workshop through their involvement and who later hosted follow-up regional workshops on our behalf in Kuala Lumpur, Manila and Jakarta, respectively: the Institute of Strategic and International Studies in Malaysia; the Institute for Strategic and Development Studies in the Philippines, and the Centre for Strategic and International Studies in Indonesia.

Our especial thanks go to Major General Michael G. Smith AO (Retd), Executive Director of the then Asia-Pacific Civil-Military Centre of Excellence (now the Australian Civil-Military Centre), who saw the importance of the project and has steadfastly supported it from inception to completion, including playing a key role in the Sydney workshop and the regional workshops, as well as providing his expert comments on the project's other main output (*Enhancing Protection Capacity: Policy Guide to the Responsibility to Protect and the Protection of Civilians in Armed Conflicts*). Thanks also are due to the staff of the ACMC, especially Jeni Whalan and Olivia Cribb, who contributed to ACMC's involvement in the project.

The project has benefited immeasurably from the encouragement and insights of Professor Ramesh Thakur, one of the principal authors of the R2P Report in 2001. Professor Thakur acted as the senior adviser on the project and has given his time and expertise most generously in pursuit of the project's key activities and outputs, most notably the Sydney workshop and the series of regional workshops on R2P and POC, at both of which Professor Thakur was a keynote speaker and contributor. We could not have achieved this book without his valuable guidance.

Angus Francis, Vesselin Popovski and Charles Sampford

Notes

1. IEGL is a joint initiative of the United Nations University, Griffith University, the Australian National University, Queensland University of Technology, the O. P. Jindal Global University in Delhi and the Center for Asian Integrity in Manila.
2. This fund is provided through AusAID and is administered by the Regional R2P Centre based at the University of Queensland.

Introduction

Angus Francis and Charles Sampford

With intra-state conflict replacing inter-state conflict across the globe (Orchard, 2010: 38), "civilian-based civil wars" (Ferris, 2011) are exposing vulnerable populations to war crimes, ethnic cleansing and acts of genocide. The UN Secretary-General has highlighted the growing threats to women and children caught up in armed conflicts, as well as dangers faced by civilians forced to mix with combatants and armed elements in camps for refugees and the internally displaced. The vulnerability of civilians in conflict has been exacerbated by some governments' reluctance to accept international assistance and the increasing number of attacks on humanitarian workers and UN staff (UNSG, 1999).

In the early 1990s, the international community's reaction to this "crisis of protection" revolved around three main responses. The first was normative developments in humanitarian assistance through the intergovernmental legislative framework of the UN General Assembly (UNGA), the Economic and Social Council (ECOSOC) and the UN Security Council (UNSC). The second saw the evolution in organizational mechanisms for humanitarian coordination, such as the Inter-Agency Standing Committee (IASC). And third, there was an expansion of military and civil actors involved in the provision of humanitarian assistance and the protection of civilians.

However, a series of humanitarian tragedies in the 1990s (Somalia 1992–1994; Rwanda 1994; Srebrenica 1995; Kosovo 1999) demonstrated the failure of the international community to protect civilians in the context of complex emergencies involving multiple issues of access, internal

Norms of protection: Responsibility to protect, protection of civilians and their interaction,
Francis, Popovski and Sampford (eds),
United Nations University Press, 2012, ISBN 978-92-808-1218-3

displacement, security of humanitarian workers and the relationship between civil and military actors. These events also undermined, to a large extent, the reaching of any consensus among UN members on the criteria for and means of intervention.

Since that time the UN Secretary-General, the UNSC, UN agencies and other humanitarian actors have renewed their efforts to ensure the effective protection of civilians from armed conflict. Among the strategies employed has been a human-rights-based approach to protection coupled with new protection endeavours, including: promotion of the protection of civilians (POC) in UN peacekeeping operations; greater inter-agency cooperation in the coordination of humanitarian responses to crisis situations; and promoting the responsibility to protect (R2P) principle as an overarching protection norm.

The emergence of POC as a core directive of humanitarian efforts

Explicit reference to the protection of civilians emerged in the UNSC from the late 1990s (Ferris, 2011). Over the last decade or more, POC has been endorsed in a series of reports by the UN Secretary-General to the Security Council (S/1999/957, S/2001/331, S/2002/1300, S/2004/431, S/2005/740, S/2007/643, S/2009/277), four UNSC resolutions (Res. 1265 in 1999; 1296 in 2000; 1674 and 1738 in 2006) as well as at least eight presidential statements (1999/6, 2002/6, 2002/41, 2003/27, 2004/46, 2005/25, 2009/1, 2009/9). A number of UNSC mandates have also incorporated POC – Afghanistan (UNAMA), Central African Republic (MINURCAT), Côte d'Ivoire (UNOCI), Darfur (UNAMID), Democratic Republic of Congo (MONUC), Haiti (MINUSTAH), Liberia (UNMIL) and Sudan (UNMIS).

These and other UN documents contain a range of recommendations for the better protection of civilians in conflicts, including: broadening the mandate of peacekeeping operations to allow troops to protect civilians under imminent threat of violence; protection of particularly vulnerable groups (women, children, refugees and internally displaced persons (IDPs) and humanitarian workers); closing gaps in existing international law; conflict prevention; confidence-building; humanitarian access; targeted sanctions; stressing the multidisciplinary nature of peacebuilding; cooperation with regional actors; separation of combatants and armed elements from civilians in IDP and refugee camps; disarmament and demobilization; and intervention in cases of genocide, crimes against humanity and war crimes (UNSC Res. 1265/1999, 1296/2000, 1674/2006, 1738/2006; UNSG S/1999/957, S/2001/331, S/2004/431).

Furthermore, as part of these initiatives, UN bodies have sought to entrench the protection of civilians in conflict in the obligations of parties under international humanitarian, human rights and refugee law. UN bodies have repeatedly called upon states which are not a party to the major treaties of international humanitarian, human rights and refugee law to ratify those instruments. Once ratified, all states are called upon to take steps to implement these instruments within their jurisdictions through appropriate legislative, judicial and administrative measures.

Convergence of POC and UN reform

The emergence of POC has coincided with reforms to the UN humanitarian system. This process identified protection as a gap in humanitarian efforts and instigated institutional mechanisms to ensure that protection of civilians was a core component of humanitarian responses. Principals of the IASC established the "cluster approach" in 2005 whereby responsibilities are assigned to lead agencies in order to provide a more effective response to humanitarian emergencies, particularly those involving mass internal displacement. The Global Protection Cluster, chaired by the UN High Commissioner for Refugees, is the main forum at the global level for coordination of protection in humanitarian action (IASC, 2007). The development of the protection cluster is recognition that refugee flows, internal displacement and humanitarian crises can occur in complex emergencies where the state is unable or unwilling to protect civilians. The response must involve the combined efforts of an array of actors at national, regional and international levels.

The IASC has been instrumental in defining civil-military collaborations for the protection of civilians in conflict, which have increased in importance as the mandates of UN protection missions increasingly cover POC in conflict. The Global Protection Cluster approach and the principles and practices associated with POC are converging, as evident in the joint leadership of the protection cluster granted to UNHCR and the UN's peacekeeping mission in the Democratic Republic of Congo (MONUC) (Murthy, 2007). The Protection Cluster in the DRC involved the participation of a number of international protection actors – UNHCR, MONUC, UNICEF, the Office for the Coordination of Humanitarian Affairs (OCHA), the International Committee of the Red Cross (ICRC) and international NGOs – alongside civil-military actors (Murthy, 2007).

The parallel emergence of the R2P principle

The responsibility to protect (R2P) principle arose alongside POC, beginning with the report of the International Commission on Intervention and State Sovereignty (ICISS, 2001). The ICISS report turned humanitarian intervention on its head – shifting the focus from the rights of states (rights to intervene vs rights to territorial integrity) to the rights of individuals and the responsibility of states and, ultimately, the international community to protect those rights. Rather than the subject having to demonstrate fidelity to his sovereign, the state had to justify itself to its citizens (Sampford, 2009). This approach of emphasizing human rights, primary state responsibility and international backup brings what was previously called "humanitarian intervention" into line with other areas of international law.

The emergence of the R2P principle raises the issue of how POC and R2P interrelate. In keeping with the general move toward a more coordinated approach to the UN humanitarian system addressed in the Global Protection Cluster and elsewhere, the Report of the UN Secretary-General issued on 12 January 2009 entitled "Implementing the responsibility to protect" outlines a three-pillar strategy for operationalizing the R2P principle that adopts a cross-sectoral approach. This approach embraces other protection agenda (UNSG, 2009). This is reflected in the Report's "narrow but deep" approach to the R2P principle's implementation: "while the scope [of the R2P principle] should be kept narrow, the response ought to be deep, employing the wide array of prevention and protection instruments available to Member States, the United Nations system, regional and subregional organizations and their civil society partners" (ibid., para. 10(c)). The Report concludes by underscoring the need to forge "a common strategy" (ibid., para. 68).

Despite these initiatives many states suspect that R2P is just a means of legitimating military intervention[1] – a suspicion that has been accentuated by some of the traditional complaints about humanitarian intervention; the use of ICISS to justify the intervention in Iraq by an ICISS author; and unfortunate concentration on non-consensual intervention rather the prevention, reaction and rebuilding emphasized by the ICISS report. Accordingly, while R2P and POC have wide formal UN endorsement and support in international humanitarian law, human rights law and refugee law, this ongoing resistance to R2P emphasizes the importance of exploring its relationship with POC.

Developments in Libya and Côte d'Ivoire and the actions of the UNSC have given new significance to the relationship between R2P and POC. In both cases – though in different ways and under different types of Security Council mandates – robust international military force was used against belligerents in order to protect civilians. In Libya, Resolution 1973 (UNSC, 2011b) (preceded by Res. 1970 (UNSC, 2011a)) authorized the use of force to prevent Gaddafi's troops attacking his people; the objective of the international action was expressly to protect the lives of

Libyan civilians. The Secretary-General (UNSG, 2011) did not shy away from expressing the overall resolution in terms of the R2P.

Additionally the recent use of robust force by the French in Côte d'Ivoire, authorized by the Secretary-General under the Protection of Civilians mandate in UNSC Resolutions 1933 (UNSC, 2010a), 1962 (UNSC, 2010b) and 1975 (UNSC, 2011c), extends the ever-growing links between POC and R2P. In Côte d'Ivoire robust military action was authorized without the Secretary-General requiring a special mandate beyond the initial Protection of Civilians clauses of prior Security Council resolutions. This use of force had a decisive influence on domestic authority and regime change – and this proved true also in Libya. Even as the principles are applied in one context, however, they may be resisted in another. At the time of writing, the attacks of the Syrian government on its own civilians have precipitated Security Council attention and a Presidential Statement, but no resolutions have been forthcoming.

To consider the relationship between R2P and POC, and their relationship with other protection norms, a research team from the Institute for Ethics, Governance and Law (IEGL,[2] through two of its affiliated centres[3]), the United Nations University (UNU) and the Australian Civil-Military Centre (ACMC) brought together engaged academics and reflective practitioners in November 2010. The project was funded by the Australian Responsibility to Protect Fund with support from ACMC, UNU and IEGL itself.

Dr Hugh Breakey, an IEGL Research Fellow, conducted an extensive review of the current literature on R2P and POC, covering relevant Security Council resolutions, Secretary-General Reports, international humanitarian and human rights law, and studies and reports on the operation of R2P and POC in humanitarian crises and with regard to peacekeeping operations. The full review is available on the IEGL and ACMC websites and is summarized in Chapters 1 to 3. In addition, the research team engaged in a series of interviews and roundtable discussions conducted by Dr Vesselin Popovski and Dr Angus Francis in Geneva and New York with key practitioners in the protection operations of UN intergovernmental bodies and NGOs. There followed an academic practitioner workshop in Sydney to flesh out and "road test" the ideas being developed, and leading to drafts of the essays in this volume. The project team has since facilitated capacity-building workshops throughout the Asia-Pacific region, engaging with policymakers, peacekeepers, humanitarians and civil society stakeholders on their understandings of and interaction with R2P and POC.

As well as this edited collection, the project is producing a *Guide to R2P and POC* aimed at enhancing the ability of governments, regional and international organizations and civil society to protect civilians from conflict-related grave harm and mass atrocity crimes.

Themes

Building on prior work linking R2P and POC (APCR2P, 2009; Bergholm and Badescu, 2009; Holt and Berkman, 2006; Hunt, 2009; LaeGreid, 2008; Strauss, 2009), this book explains the relationships in law, practice and political theory between R2P and POC and other relevant humanitarian norms and identifies ways in which R2P can add practical, legal and normative value to the POC agenda and vice versa. Chapters 1 and 2 define in turn R2P and POC, tracing their respective histories, contemporary content and structure, overlap, gaps, areas of controversy and legal status. Just as R2P may be usefully divided into its "three pillars", Breakey argues that the different roles and perspectives of key POC actors – combatants, peacekeepers, UN actors and humanitarians – give rise to four distinct but mutually reinforcing protection norms.

Chapters 3 and 4 investigate the links between R2P and POC, beginning with Breakey's survey and critique of current understandings in the literature of the connection between the two norms, before turning to Francis and Popovski's report of practitioners' perspectives on the nature and interrelations between R2P and POC. This report is based on interviews with key actors and stakeholders in Geneva and New York, including Assistant Secretaries-General Edward Luck and Francis Deng and other key protection actors (the Department of Peacekeeping Operations (DPKO), OCHA and UNHCR). In Chapter 5, Charles Sampford then places the international norms of R2P and POC in their historical and cultural context. He argues that both are rooted in empathy and common humanity that are found in all cultures and religions and the claims by all leaders to protect their followers, and suggests that one way of strengthening R2P and POC is to look for "congruent" values within local cultures and religions and relate R2P and POC to them. He argues that concerns about the overreach and abuse of R2P (and POC) norms are legitimate and that similar concerns lay at the heart of the Westphalian system. However, he argues that these concerns can be addressed through international law and international institutions.

Chapter 6 by Hitoshi Nasu, Chapter 7 by Andrew Garwood-Gowers and Chapter 8 by Annie Herro and Kavitha Suthanthiraraj deal with the operationalization of R2P and POC. Nasu weighs the extent to which the mandating of peacekeeping operations to protect civilians may facilitate the process of operationalizing the R2P principle in practice. While seeing POC in this manner as a vehicle for R2P, Nasu warns of the difficulties R2P's robust use of force may create for peacekeepers. Like Nasu, Garwood-Gowers sees peacekeeping forces as a crucial tool of R2P, but in his chapter he focuses particularly on what he sees as the signature contribution of R2P – its *preventive* aspect. Peacekeeping forces, regional organizations and UN organs are all considered in their capacities for developing improved early-warning mechanisms, which would in turn facilitate (with host state consent) preventive deployments of peacekeepers.

Picking up a thread touched upon by both Nasu and Garwood-Gowers – the limitations on the capacity of contemporary peacekeeping operations for swiftly deploying robust and well-equipped forces – Herro and Suthanthiraraj examine the prospects for a UN Emergency Peace Service. While not new, the idea of a ready-reaction UN force capable of timely and effective deployment promises to resolve ongoing gaps in civilian protection. Herro and Suthanthiraraj consider how the norms of R2P and (especially) POC might contribute to the realization and nature of such a force.

Chapter 9 by Helen Durham and Phoebe Wynne-Pope, Chapter 10 by Edwin Bikundo and Chapter 11 by Angus Francis develop the legal aspects and interrelations of R2P and POC and other humanitarian norms. Durham and Wynne-Pope begin by tracing the ways international humanitarian law (the Geneva Conventions and Additional Protocols) and the Genocide Convention give legal authority to key aspects of R2P's first two pillars. Importantly, they argue that Article 89 of Additional Protocol I requiring states to take collective action to prevent war crimes is stronger than that found in paragraph 139 of the *World Summit Outcome Document* – thus highlighting the need for R2P advocates not to overlook or ignore existing international legal obligations.

Taking a broader viewpoint, in his chapter Bikundo argues that recent developments in international law and Security Council action (especially with regard to Libya) suggest the emergence of the protection of civilians as the pre-eminent norm in the international legal regime. POC, on this footing, governs and shapes all legitimate use of force, and R2P is understood as a key means for furthering this overarching POC agenda. Turning to the application of R2P to refugee law and policy, Francis welcomes the R2P focus on the prevention of atrocity crimes, but gives a cautious appraisal of the extent to which military intervention improves prospects for at-risk communities. While "in-country" protection of displaced persons remains an obvious focus of contemporary measures, it should not obscure the necessity for planning and realizing the protection opportunities that can be afforded by neighbouring states.

In the next chapters, the role of regional capacities and perspectives on R2P and POC is gauged, with a specific focus on the Asia-Pacific region. In Chapter 12, Lina Alexandra considers what institutional capacities in

Indonesia and ASEAN might be utilized or enhanced to promote R2P, and what steps need to be taken to develop the capacity of states and regional organizations to react to mass atrocity crimes. While noting the capacities and gaps of current government and regional organs, Alexandra highlights one preventive mechanism often overlooked: the engagement of local civilian movements to stop and prevent further violence. In Chapter 13, See Seng Tan delves deeply into the notion of "sovereignty as responsibility" underpinning R2P as it is emerging in the region. He notes particularly the practice and concern for providing for one's population and the population of neighbouring states (the "responsibility to provide") as a potential entry point for the type of regional support envisaged by R2P.

In the final chapter, Vesselin Popovski reflects on the interaction of R2P and POC as two norms of protection that have been developing and interacting over the last decade. Both are deeply rooted in the empathy that human beings have for the suffering of others. Both have achieved high-level endorsement: R2P from the 2005 Global Summit and POC from Security Council resolutions – with 2011 seeing them both used in UNSC Resolution 1973 on Libya. Both raise concerns because of the sometimes sorry history of attempts by outsiders to protect civilians – concerns that did not start with claims of rights to humanitarian intervention in Kosovo but are based on similar seventeenth-century European concerns that were central to the development of Westphalian traditions of sovereignty and non-interference. The two norms are developing, sometimes in parallel, sometimes diverging and sometimes converging – with varying degrees of institutionalization and acceptance. This process is likely to continue for some time with crises, successes and failures enhancing or retarding that development.

Our hope is that this collection will be of use to those involved in this process: policymakers and actors (national, regional and UN); practitioners with protective roles (force commanders, military trainers and strategists and humanitarian actors); academics and researchers (in international relations, law, political theory and ethics); and NGO officials and other civil society R2P and POC advocates.

Notes

1. See Adebajo and Fakier (2007), Bellamy (2008, 2009), Benjamin (2007), Bessler and Seki (2006) and Newman (2009).
2. IEGL is a joint initiative of the United Nations University (UNU), Griffith University and Queensland University of Technology (QUT) in association with the Australian National University (ANU), the Center for Asian Integrity and O. P. Jindal Global University.

3. The Law and Justice Research Centre at QUT and the Key Centre for Ethics, Law, Justice and Governance at Griffith University.

REFERENCES

Adebajo, A. and Y. Fakier (2007) *Africa's Responsibility to Protect: Policy Advisory Group Seminar Report*. Cape Town: Centre for Conflict Resolution.

APCR2P (2009) The Responsibility to Protect and the Protection of Civilians: Asia-Pacific in the UN Security Council, Update No. 1. Brisbane: Asia-Pacific Centre for the Responsibility to Protect.

Bellamy, A. (2008) "The Responsibility to Protect and the Problem of Military Intervention", *International Affairs* 84(4): 615–639.

Bellamy, A. (2009) *Responsibility to Protect: The Global Effort to End Mass Atrocities*. Cambridge: Polity.

Benjamin, D. (2007) "Changing Norms in International Humanitarian Law: From Non-Intervention to R2P", *ISA 50th Annual Convention "Exploring The Past, Anticipating The Future"*. New York Marriott: ISA. 6 July 2007. [Online] Available at: ⟨http://www.allacademic.com/meta/p314010_index.html⟩.

Bergholm, L. and C. Badescu (2009) "The Responsibility to Protect and the Conflict in Darfur: The Big Let-Down", *Security Dialogue* 40(3): 287–307.

Bessler, M. and K. Seki (2006) "Civil-Military Relations in Armed Conflicts: A Humanitarian Perspective", *Liaison: A Journal of Civil-Military Humanitarian Relief Collaborations* 3(3): 4–10.

Ferris, E. (2011) *The Politics of Protection*. Washington, DC: The Brookings Institution.

Holt, V. and T. Berkman (2006) *The Impossible Mandate? Military Preparedness, the Responsibility to Protect and Modern Peace Operations*. Washington, DC: The Henry L. Stimson Center.

Hunt, C. (2009) *Protection of Civilians and the Responsibility to Protect: Perspectives and Precedents in the Asia-Pacific*, Program on the Protection of Civilians. Brisbane: Asia-Pacific Centre for the Responsibility to Protect.

IASC, Inter-Agency Standing Committee (2007) *Protection Cluster Working Group: Mission Statement and Terms of Reference*, 21 March. [Online] Available at: ⟨http://www.unhcr.org/refworld/docid/4ae9acb71a3.html⟩.

ICISS, International Commission on Intervention and State Sovereignty (2001) *The Responsibility to Protect*. Ottawa: IDRC.

LaeGreid, T. (2008) *Protecting Civilians from Harm: A Humanitarian Perspective*, NUPI Report No. 6 2008.

Murthy, J. (2007) "Mandating the Protection Cluster with the Responsibility to Protect: A Policy Recommendation Based on the Protection Cluster's Implementation in South Kivu, DRC", *Journal of Humanitarian Assistance* 5 (Oct).

Newman, M. (2009) "Revisiting the 'Responsibility to Protect'", *Political Quarterly* 80(1): 92–100.

Orchard, P. (2010) "The Perils of Humanitarianism: Refugee and IDP Protection in Situations of Regime-Induced Displacement", *Refugee Survey Quarterly* 29(1): 38–60.

Sampford, C. (2009) "The Potential for a Post-Westphalian Convergence of 'Public Law' and 'Public International Law'", in J. Farrall and K. Rubenstein, eds. *Sanctions, Accountability and Governance in a Globalised World.* Cambridge: Cambridge University Press, 53–71.

Strauss, E. (2009) "A Bird in the Hand Is Worth Two in the Bush: On the Assumed Legal Nature of the Responsibility to Protect", *Global Responsibility to Protect* 1(3): 291–323.

UNSC (2010a) *UN Security Council Resolution 1933 (2010): The Situation in Côte d'Ivoire*, S/RES/1933, 30 June 2010.

UNSC (2010b) *UN Security Council Resolution 1962 (2010): The Situation in Côte d'Ivoire,* S/RES/1962, 20 December 2010.

UNSC (2011a) *UN Security Council Resolution 1970 (2011): Peace and Security in Africa,* S/RES/1970, 26 February 2011.

UNSC (2011b) *UN Security Council Resolution 1973 (2011): The Situation in Libya,* S/RES/1973, 17 March 2011.

UNSC (2011c) *UN Security Council Resolution 1975 (2011): The Situation in Côte d'Ivoire,* S/RES/1975, 30 March 2011.

UNSG (1999) *Report to the Security Council on the Protection of Civilians in Armed Conflict,* S/1999/957, 8 September 1999.

UNSG (2009) *Implementing the Responsibility to Protect,* A/63/677, 12 January 2009.

UNSG (2011) "Statement by the Secretary-General on Libya", 17 March 2011.

1

The responsibility to protect: Game change and regime change

Hugh Breakey

In the short span of years since its inception the concept of the Responsibility to Protect (R2P) has had a substantial yet controversial impact on international relations and efforts to protect populations from atrocities. This chapter overviews the nature and history of R2P before turning to consider the major critiques of the principle. It deals in detail with the important objection that R2P is a vehicle for regime change – a critique that has assumed a new urgency in the fallout over the NATO military action in Libya in 2011. This chapter argues that members of the UN Security Council (UNSC), and of the international community more generally, need to be realistic about the ways military intervention for protective purposes will inevitably have implications for incumbent regimes, but at the same time be sensitive to the ways protective intervention can be operationally separated from the deliberate pursuit of regime change.

The first four sections will be useful to those unfamiliar with R2P. These describe in turn the core idea of R2P, its first formulation in the eponymous report of the International Commission on Intervention and State Sovereignty (ICISS, 2001), the specific version affirmed in 2005 by the General Assembly in the *World Summit Outcome Document* (WSOD) and in 2006 by the UNSC in Resolution 1674, and its utilization and development since that point. Sections 1.5 and 1.6 respectively survey the ethical, legal and institutional justifications for R2P and the major critiques of the principle, and flag the larger literature on these topics. In section 1.7, the most substantive section, the central contemporary challenge to R2P – the relationship between R2P military operations to

Norms of protection: Responsibility to protect, protection of civilians and their interaction,
Francis, Popovski and Sampford (eds),
United Nations University Press, 2012, ISBN 978-92-808-1218-3

protect populations and regime change – is analysed in depth. Section 1.8 concludes this chapter.

1.1 The core idea of R2P

There is a core concept of R2P – a central theme on which different variations are possible. This core has three elements. The first is a shift in the understanding of sovereignty from "sovereignty as control" to "sovereignty as responsibility" (ICISS, 2001: 13–14). That is, sovereignty is no longer to be understood as a right to perform whatever domestic activities the state authority desires. To the contrary, the very reason for sovereignty is at base the protection of the people's most fundamental rights from egregious acts of violence: sovereignty is no longer a defence for atrocity.

The second element of R2P's core is that if the state proves unwilling or unable to fulfil its responsibilities, then the responsibility to protect its citizenry shifts to the international community as a whole. While the state has the primary responsibility for protecting its citizens, members of the international community have a backup responsibility, requiring them to protect or help protect those populations – including, if need be, by using military force. In this way R2P aims to displace the controversial "right of humanitarian intervention", and refocus attention on the needs of the vulnerable rather than the entitlements of interveners.

The third element dictates the manner in which interventions or interferences with states may occur, namely, with great weight given to the importance of a principled and multilateral response consistent with international law. In the contemporary international milieu this makes the United Nations in general – and the UNSC in particular – the primary agent for international decision-making and authorization regarding sanctions and interventions.

This broad core concept of R2P can then be specified in different ways, in particular in the manner ICISS presented in their 2001 Report and in the further specified (and somewhat diluted) form that UN member states accepted at the 2005 World Summit. It is by reference to this core concept of R2P that it can be claimed that, for instance, the Constitutive Act of the African Union, and perhaps the Genocide Convention, embody R2P, even as they differ in various specifics regarding the assignation of obligation and authorization for intervention (ICR2P, 2009; UNSG, 2009). So too, this core concept may be used to refer to actions taken in cases prior to the ICISS Report, such as the peace enforcement operation in East Timor (Martin, 2004). Naturally, each of these three conceptual elements can be found in political theory and international relations prior to their exposition and consolidation in the work of ICISS.

1.2 R2P in 2001

This section describes the history that led to the development of R2P in 2001 by ICISS, and the nature and structure of the R2P principle that ICISS advanced.

1.2.1 Developments prior to the ICISS report

Throughout the 1990s the international community – and the United Nations in particular – was faced with an array of humanitarian crises, including genocide, ethnic cleansing, mass internal displacement of populations and the subsequent humanitarian disasters arising from these atrocities. Many factors played a role in the character of these catastrophes and their increase in number, and the perceived need that the international community should do something about them (Frohardt, Paul and Minear, 1999; Roberts, 2000; Weiss, 2007). In some cases (e.g. Somalia and Sierra Leone) the United Nations sanctioned military intervention for human protection purposes. In others (e.g. Kosovo) non-sanctioned intervention occurred. And in still others (e.g. Rwanda and Bosnia/ Herzegovina) no effective intervention took place. By the decade's end, the tension between intervention and sovereignty was a major topic of legal, political and philosophical debate (Bellamy, 2009; IICK, 2000; Sampford, 1997; UN, 1999; UNSG, 1999). UN Secretary-General Kofi Annan (2000) explicitly invoked a "moral duty" of the UNSC to act on behalf of the international community when faced with crimes against humanity. While he did not himself solve the dilemma posed by the apparently conflicting principles of humanity and sovereignty, Annan (ibid: 48) placed it before the General Assembly in telling terms:

> But to the critics I would pose this question: if humanitarian intervention is, indeed, an unacceptable assault on sovereignty, how should we respond to a Rwanda, to a Srebrenica – to gross and systematic violations of human rights that offend every precept of our common humanity?

The initial reaction of the General Assembly to Annan's position on intervention, however, was frosty at best (Roberts, 2000). Against this turbulent background the Canadian government authorized the setting up of the International Commission on Intervention and State Sovereignty – ICISS.

1.2.2 R2P 2001 content

The ICISS Report – *The Responsibility to Protect* – was released in 2001. The R2P concept it advanced was organized in terms of three key struts: the responsibilities to prevent, react and rebuild.

The *responsibility to prevent* imposed upon states and the international community the obligation to prevent large-scale loss of life through mass violence. The primary responsibility to prevent violence to its population fell on the sovereign state, but even in this early preventive stage the international community had responsibilities. ICISS (2001) envisaged the responsibility to prevent as addressing the root causes of conflicts – including poverty, repression and inequality – as well as direct prevention. Responsibilities to engage in diplomacy and mediation were also emphasized, as was developing effective early-warning mechanisms.

The second strut, the *responsibility to react*, is triggered when attempts at prevention fail. While it included non-interventionist measures such as targeted sanctions, the core of the responsibility to react lay in direct military intervention. Drawing on and paralleling prior work on the subject, in particular from the Just War tradition (IICK, 2000; Weiss, 2007), ICISS put forward six criteria for legitimating intervention against the consent of the state in question, including *just cause* (involving as triggers ethnic cleansing and the large-scale loss of life as a result of state action, neglect or incapacity), *right intention, last resort, proportional means* and *reasonable prospects*. With the sixth criterion – *right authority* – ICISS placed the UNSC as the primary legitimating authority for intervention, but envisaged the possibility of other multilateral avenues.

The *responsibility to rebuild* required that, post-intervention, a state was not left in a condition where it would swiftly return to hostilities and renewed threats to civilians. Central here was the disarmament, demobilization and reintegration of local armed forces and the safe return of refugees.

1.2.3 From 2001 to 2005

The ICISS Report was not born into propitious circumstances for a rethinking of sovereignty. Released at around the same time as the attacks of 9/11 in the US and the subsequent "Bush doctrine", its success was anything but inevitable. Nevertheless, R2P steadily attracted endorsement from key actors.[1] The influential 2004 Secretary-General's High-Level Panel report affirmed the central thrust of the ICISS report (McClean, 2008; Molier, 2006; UNHLP, 2004), as did Annan's *In Larger Freedom* (UNSG, 2005). Through the determination of the Secretary-General and other advocates, R2P became a key topic at the 2005 UN

Millennium Summit, and eleventh-hour negotiations (and not a little intrigue) led to R2P's affirmation in the WSOD (Bellamy, 2009; Feinstein and de Bruin, 2009; Strauss, 2009).

1.3 R2P in 2005

1.3.1 The World Summit Outcome Document

R2P was historically affirmed in Paragraphs 138–140 in the WSOD, giving rise to the now authoritative version of R2P (UNGA, 2005). The paragraphs read:

> Responsibility to protect populations from genocide, war crimes, ethnic cleansing and crimes against humanity
>
> 138. Each individual State has the responsibility to protect its populations from genocide, war crimes, ethnic cleansing and crimes against humanity. This responsibility entails the prevention of such crimes, including their incitement, through appropriate and necessary means. We accept that responsibility and will act in accordance with it. The international community should, as appropriate, encourage and help States to exercise this responsibility and support the United Nations in establishing an early warning capability.
>
> 139. The international community, through the United Nations, also has the responsibility to use appropriate diplomatic, humanitarian and other peaceful means, in accordance with Chapters VI and VIII of the Charter, to help to protect populations from genocide, war crimes, ethnic cleansing and crimes against humanity. In this context, we are prepared to take collective action, in a timely and decisive manner, through the UNSC, in accordance with the Charter, including Chapter VII, on a case-by-case basis and in cooperation with relevant regional organizations as appropriate, should peaceful means be inadequate and national authorities are manifestly failing to protect their populations from genocide, war crimes, ethnic cleansing and crimes against humanity. We stress the need for the General Assembly to continue consideration of the responsibility to protect populations from genocide, war crimes, ethnic cleansing and crimes against humanity and its implications, bearing in mind the principles of the Charter and international law. We also intend to commit ourselves, as necessary and appropriate, to helping States build capacity to protect their populations from genocide, war crimes, ethnic cleansing and crimes against humanity and to assisting those which are under stress before crises and conflicts break out.
>
> 140. We fully support the mission of the Special Adviser of the Secretary-General on the Prevention of Genocide.

Other parts of the WSOD were also pertinent to R2P: Paragraph 133 committed member states to support efforts aimed at addressing the causes of refugee movement; Paragraphs 97–105 on the Peacebuilding Commission give substance to the *responsibility to rebuild*; Paragraphs 92–93 on peacekeeping include consideration of rapid deployment and improved policy capacities; and the paragraphs on the Rule of Law (119–120, 134) align with R2P's attempt to deal with atrocity crimes in a settled, principled manner, rather than through Kosovo-style exceptionalism.

1.3.2 Content of the WSOD rendering of R2P

The content of the now-authoritative WSOD version of R2P differed in several ways from that advanced by ICISS.

1 *Intervention can only occur with an explicit UNSC mandate.* Unlike the ICISS version of R2P, the WSOD made no mention of regional bodies or other avenues to authorizing intervention. Any envisaged R2P intervention could *only* happen with authorization by the UNSC (UNGA, 2005). This change was central to Weiss's (2007: 116–117) famous characterization of the WSOD conceptualization as "R2P lite". Still, the WSOD does not *explicitly rule out* the legitimacy of other types of authorization – even unilateral action remains a possible action *outside* of the R2P aegis (Bellamy, 2006; Stahn, 2007).

2 *The use of the ICISS' criteria for UNSC deliberations on the use of force was not adopted.* Strauss (2009: 296) explains the negotiations process:

> The draft paragraph on the responsibility to protect was completely altered by the amendments and the clause urging the five permanent members of the Security Council not to veto action aimed at halting or preventing genocide or ethnic cleansing was deleted.

3 *R2P's scope was limited to the four specific atrocity crimes.* The WSOD's (UNGA, 2005: 138) specific list of atrocities – "genocide, war crimes, ethnic cleansing and crimes against humanity" – is narrower than ICISS's human-caused "large-scale loss of life". Similarly, the trigger for reaction shifted from states being "unwilling and unable" to protect to their "manifest failure" to do so (Bellamy, 2006). Such alterations created a toe-hold for delegates to later deny that the member states had committed to R2P at all, rather than just to protect civilians from specific crimes (Evans, 2008).

4 *The responsibility to react was weakened.* The section of the WSOD on the use of coercive force by the international community has several caveats (acting "on a case-by-case basis and in cooperation with relevant regional organizations as appropriate" and with "preparedness" rather than "responsibility") compared to the stronger language deter-

mining state responsibilities to their own population (Bellamy, 2009; Luck, 2010a).

1.4 Utilization and development since 2005

Since its affirmation in 2005, R2P has assumed a key place in international relations and discourse.

1.4.1 R2P in the Security Council

After substantial further negotiations (Leitenberg, 2006; Strauss, 2009), the UNSC (2006a) historically affirmed the WSOD version of R2P in Resolution 1674 – a thematic resolution on the protection of civilians in armed conflict. After repeating its affirmation of R2P in Resolution 1706 (UNSC, 2006b) regarding Sudan, allusions to R2P became for a period more subtle and mediated, until the UNSC (2009) again endorsed the principle in Resolution 1894. R2P language was widely used by key actors with regard to Resolution 1973 (UNSC, 2011) authorizing military action in Libya (Obama, 2011; Rudd, 2011). While the resolution noted the responsibility to protect only in terms of the Libyan state responsibilities, and not as a reason for international action, the Secretary-General (UNSG, 2011a) did not shy away from expressing the overall resolution in R2P terms, and there is now a widespread consensus that Resolution 1973, for better or worse, was an "R2P Resolution". For this reason, the political fallout from the operationalization and interpretation of Resolution 1973 shapes much of the current debate on R2P (see 1.7 below).

1.4.2 R2P in international affairs

R2P has played a growing role in international relations, being used by innumerable NGOs, committees and civil society institutions (Holt and Berkman, 2006). It was invoked in the UN-commissioned report into the Darfur crisis (UNHRC, 2007) and in international legal arguments concerning state culpability under the Genocide Convention (Rosenberg, 2009), and its language may be found in "peace support operations" documents and guidelines (Wills, 2004). International diplomatic action taken in Kenya in 2007 to quell post-election violence occurred against a backdrop of R2P invocations by influential actors (Evans, 2008; UNSG, 2009). In general, R2P frames the discourse around which discussions of sovereignty and international action must now take place (Serrano, 2010).

Even so, R2P's popularity has waxed and waned over the years. Shortly after its 2005 adoption the mood at the United Nations was characterized as one of "buyer's remorse" (Evans, 2008: 288). From 2007 to 2010, R2P's stocks seemed to have risen (Bellamy, 2010; Luck, 2010b). The 2009 General Assembly Plenary Debate reaffirmed R2P and was widely taken to be a success in the face of some concerted opposition (ICR2P, 2009; Luck, 2010a; UNSG, 2010). The debate was followed by the General Assembly's first resolution on R2P (2009). The successes and failures of the 2011 intervention into Libya have refigured the playing field again, and focus and debate since that time has surrounded the operationalization of R2P's military aspect. Whatever the outcome of this debate, there is little doubt that R2P has changed the discourse – and perhaps the substance – of international relations with respect to the protection of populations from atrocities.

1.4.3 R2P in Secretary-General reports: The "three pillars"

Secretary-General Ban Ki-moon's 2009 Report, *Implementing the Responsibility to Protect,* has been significant in clarifying, concretizing and building consensus around R2P. "The task ahead," as he (UNSG, 2009: 2) expressed it, "is not to reinterpret or renegotiate the conclusions of the World Summit but to find ways of implementing its decisions in a fully faithful and consistent manner." The report fleshed out the bare bones of the WSOD paragraphs with a "three pillars" approach:

Pillar One: The protection responsibilities of the state. Drawing on the first three sentences of WSOD Paragraph 138, Pillar One delineates the responsibilities of the state to: (i) inculcate appropriate social values; (ii) build institutions facilitating protection; and (iii) consider the use of various learning devices and training capacities.

Pillar Two: International assistance and capacity-building. Drawing on the final sentences of WSOD Paragraphs 138 and 139, Pillar Two describes the duties of the international community to persuade individual states to perform their Pillar One duties and to help them build capacities to do so. This latter can include such measures as providing a UN or regional presence, supporting states against violent insurgencies, granting development assistance, aiding states' security sectors, and building mediation and dispute resolution capacities. Early warning and assessment are also key Pillar Two responsibilities (UNSG, 2010).

Pillar Three: Timely and decisive response. Drawing on the first sentence of WSOD Paragraph 139, Pillar Three outlines the *pacific* measures available to the international community in response to states in breach of their Pillar One responsibilities (including fact-finding investigations, alerting authorities to their legal responsibilities, public advocacy, and imposing sanctions and arms embargoes). Drawing on the second sentence of Paragraph 139, Pillar Three also includes the duties of individual states, the UNGA, the Secretariat and the UNSC with regard to the *coercive use of force* in such cases.

Two further reports on R2P by the Secretary-General appeared in 2010 and 2011, describing and developing R2P early-warning and atrocity-risk assessment capacities (2010) and the R2P role of regional and sub-regional organizations (2011b).

1.4.4 Norm, principle or concept?

Alex Bellamy (2009: 4–7) emphasizes the importance of the WSOD affirmation of R2P by speaking of the R2P *concept* prior to 2005, and the R2P *principle* after the summit, with this latter term connoting that R2P had acquired a shared understanding and sufficient consensus to mobilize action. Prior to 2005, with no univocal endorsement of R2P, the concept required further development and elaboration before it could serve as a shared basis for action.

Even so, it is perhaps worth distinguishing the separate status of each of the pillars of R2P.[2] If a "norm" is understood to be a shared expectation of appropriate behaviour by actors with a given identity, then Pillar One duties of the state to protect their own people, with their substantial basis in international law (see section 1.5.3 below), warrant this appellation. The Pillar Two duties of the international community and the Pillar Three responsibilities of the UNSC, on the other hand, are far less determinate, and it is at least questionable whether the WSOD shifted them fully from "concept" to "principle". Still, the three Secretary-General reports on R2P have substantially developed Pillar Two, and despite ongoing concerns regarding the operationalization of military interventions under Pillar Three, UNSC practices and expectations about those practices are arguably contributing to its determinacy. While they are by no means yet norms, this chapter will thus follow Bellamy in describing Pillars Two and Three as principles.

1.5 Justifications

This section outlines the key normative, institutional and legal justifications for R2P. The wide and overlapping breadth of these many bases is an important feature of R2P. Each of the sources noted below have different operational, jurisdictional and doctrinal limitations, so each fills gaps and adds weight to the others, creating a larger web of justificatory bases for protection.

1.5.1 Normative justifications

A manifest source of moral justification for a protective norm such as R2P is by appeal to universal human rights. The use of human rights to obligate military intervention for protection purposes is a common thread in the ethics literature, with theorists advancing Lockean, Kantian and other rights-based justifications for the practice (Bagnoli, 2006; Shue, 2004; Ward, 2006). For their part, in arguing that human rights law is increasingly "without borders", ICISS (2001: 8) cited Article 1.3 of the founding 1945 UN Charter and the 1948 Universal Declaration of Human Rights, and noted the universal reach of international criminal tribunals. The WSOD sealed this link with human rights by placing R2P under its "human rights" rubric.

A second and related ethical justification is "human security". In the 1990s this concept had arisen to juxtapose "narrow national security". In focusing solely on the security of states this latter norm appeared to lose sight of the reason why national security was itself to be valued – because of its capacity to protect individuals and societies from harm. In prioritizing the security of people over states, human security had attained considerable currency in international affairs, and it was well placed to serve as a normative basis for R2P (ICISS, 2001; Newman, 2009; Popovski, 2010).

A third source of moral authority for R2P is the idea of "sovereignty as responsibility". This is the key idea noted earlier, that to hold sovereignty over a population is to be responsible for the protection of that population; the protection of the citizenry is *the reason why* sovereignty is given and respected. The recent impetus for "sovereignty as responsibility" was the work of Francis Deng on internally displaced persons (IDPs).[3] Of course, the great contract theorists of the early Enlightenment – Hobbes, Rousseau and Locke – had put forward just this view of the state, understanding it as being formed instrumentally by the agreement of free persons in order to protect their prior natural rights (Locke, 1947; Ward, 2006). The ICISS's innovation was that when the state fails in its duty to protect its citizens' rights, rather than the responsibility to protect those rights reverting back to the citizens – as would occur in a Lockean right of revolution, for example – instead the obligation to protect moves upward and outward to the international community.

1.5.2 Precedents, practices and institutions

R2P may be defended in terms of the place of sovereignty in the institutions of the United Nations and the past practice of the United Nations and its member states. The UN Charter has resources both for and against military intervention for human protection purposes. Against are the crucial non-interventionist Articles 2(4) and 2(7). In favour are the Charter's human rights mandates in the Preamble and Articles 1(2), 1(3) and 55, and the discretionary powers it vests in the UNSC in Articles 39, 42 and 51 (Roberts, 2004). ICISS (2001: 13) drew upon these latter, arguing that sovereignty must assimilate with the fundamental mandate of the United Nations itself: "to save succeeding generations from the scourge of war".

ICISS also looked to the prior practices of states and the United Nations, arguing such practices were suggestive of an emerging principle of R2P, and later commentators have followed this lead (Deng, 2010; Popovski, 2004–5). A preliminary list of cases of military intervention for humanitarian purposes would include the UNSC in Somalia and Northern Iraq, ECOWAS in Liberia and NATO in Kosovo.[4] A variety of earlier UN practices, reports and statements also carried an R2P drift, including *inter alia* UNSC statements of states' responsibilities to police and prosecute atrocity crimes, UNSC statements of the role of the international community in protection capacity-building,[5] the protection obligations implicit in UN peacekeeping operations and their relationship to the norm of non-interference,[6] and the use of R2P themes and language in the peace support operations doctrine of various countries (Wills, 2004).

In all, as Thakur and Weiss (2009: 27) observe, ICISS's version of sovereignty as responsibility "is a less radical departure from established precept and practice than it appears. The authority of the state is nowhere regarded as absolute."

1.5.3 Law

Perhaps the most important and controversial question of justification is the status of R2P in law. ICISS argued for the grounding of aspects of R2P in international human rights law (IHRL), international humanitarian law (IHL) and the Genocide Convention, and later commentators have pursued the potential of these and other avenues.

In terms of IHRL, the prospects for grounding the First Pillar of R2P are very strong; human rights law plainly imposes protection responsibilities on states in regard to their own populations (Rosenberg, 2009). More ambitiously, some commentators argue that IHRL can support and specify some of the duties imposed on the international community (McClean, 2008; Nasu, 2009). Gierycz (2010: 266) in particular develops the ways R2P can "be recognized as an opportunity to give force to the implementation of the underlying human rights instruments". While IHRL has application with respect to R2P Pillars One and Two, however, it offers little support for Third Pillar military intervention for human protection purposes (Roberts, 2004).

A further legal avenue for justifying R2P is IHL – especially the Fourth Geneva Convention of 1949 and the Second Additional Protocol of 1977. Article 1 common to the four Geneva Conventions seems promising in this light: "The High Contracting Parties undertake to respect and to ensure respect for the present Convention in all circumstances" (ICRC, 1949: Art. 1), as does Additional Protocol Article 89: "In situations of serious violations of the Conventions or of this Protocol, the High Contracting Parties undertake to act jointly or individually, in co-operation with the United Nations and in conformity with the United Nations Charter" (ICRC, 1977: Art. 89). These and related IHL instruments justify both First Pillar and (though somewhat more controversially; Focarelli, 2010) even some Second Pillar R2P duties (Fleck, 2006; Strauss, 2009). However, as with IHRL, any direct application of the Geneva Conventions to Third Pillar duties would be highly controversial (Fleck, 2006; Henckaerts, 2005; Ryniker, 2001). Still, Wills (2004) argues that duties of intervention may be at least suggested in the key articles; however, she emphasizes that any response must be specified and legitimized by other legal mechanisms, particularly the UN Charter.

The most common avenue for the legal bulwarking of R2P is by appeal to the *Convention on the Prevention and Punishment of the Crime of Genocide* (UNGA, 1948), whose Art. 1 provides that "The Contracting Parties confirm that genocide, whether committed in time of peace or in time of war, is a crime under international law which they undertake to prevent and to punish", and whose Art. 8 specifies, "Any Contracting Party may call upon the competent organs of the United Nations to take such action under the Charter of the United Nations as they consider appropriate for the prevention and suppression of acts of genocide ...". Strauss (2009: 317) argues that the Genocide Convention thus supports "a general obligation of states to prevent the commission of acts contrary to certain norms of general international law". Still, the matter is controversial, with other commentators more sceptical of the reach and significance of the Genocide Convention – especially if it is taken to require positive state duties to act against third-party violators and even to legitimize military intervention (de Waal, 2007; Ward, 2007; Welsh, 2004; Wills, 2004). Focarelli (2010) suggests that, while the text of the Genocide Convention might conceivably open a space for third-party duties of genocide prevention, state practice (in the form of inaction in the face of known genocide) tells decisively against such an obligation. A further limitation on the Genocide Convention's relationship to R2P is its precise requirements on the nature of the victims and the specific intentions of the perpetrators. The effect of these demanding requirements is to exclude atrocities like the genocide in Cambodia from the application of the Convention, and to pose formidable obstacles to proving the crime of genocide in law in any particular case (Evans, 2006).

Even with these limitations in mind, the Genocide Convention gives legal force to at least some R2P obligations. Of particular significance is the 2007 Judgment of the International Court of Justice (ICJ) on the Crime of Genocide (*Bosnia and Herzegovina* v. *Serbia and Montenegro*). While the ICJ eschewed consideration of a general duty to prevent genocide (and so of R2P; Gattini, 2007), the judgment was not unsupportive of R2P thinking. The ICJ did not constrain responsibility to sovereign borders but to "a capacity to effectively influence", and the court explicitly invoked positive duties and due diligence in preventing genocide.[7] From this platform, commentators have argued that the judgment of the ICJ can be used to fill out key areas of ambiguity in R2P (Arbour, 2008; McClean, 2008), while Rosenberg (2009) suggests that R2P implies that the same principles and processes applicable to genocide should also apply to the wider category of crimes against humanity.

This overview of IHRL, IHL and the Genocide Convention does not exhaust the legal avenues for justifying various aspects of R2P. For instance, the obligations imposed by the International Law Commission's Articles on State Responsibility (ILC, 2001) (especially Art. 41(1)) have substantial similarities to the general idea of R2P, though they are more limited in scope and narrower in assigning duties – most pertinently in not authorizing military force (Stahn, 2007; Strauss, 2009). However, as Stahn (2007: 116) emphasizes, the ILC "acknowledged that it is open to question whether general international law at present prescribes a positive duty of cooperation and conceded that in that respect Article 41(1) 'may reflect the progressive development of international law'", rather than the law as it currently stands.

1.6 Critiques of R2P

Unsurprisingly, given its refiguring of state sovereignty, R2P has been subject to a wide range of important criticisms.

1.6.1 Vagueness and ambiguity

A consistent challenge levelled at R2P is its ambiguity (Bellamy, 2006). Some apparent ambiguities have been largely resolved: these include the scope of R2P, the temporal sequence of R2P's duties and the legal status of the international community's duties. As regards the first, it was questioned in the context of Myanmar and Cyclone Nargis whether R2P was applicable to natural disasters. R2P theorists have argued that this situation does not fall within the ambit of the stipulated four atrocity crimes (Caballero-Anthony and Chng, 2009; Haacke, 2009). R2P must, it is urged, stay focused on imminent large-scale crimes, as trying to solve everything leads to solving nothing (Evans, 2008; UNSG, 2009). Even so, R2P's scope is not univocally settled, with commentators considering its application to Chechnya, Georgia, Lebanon, North Korea, Kyrgyzstan, Syria and Zimbabwe, just to name a few. As regards the second question of *when* R2P duties arise, Ban Ki-moon's (UNSG, 2009: 12) report determines that there is "no set sequence for moving from one [Pillar] to another, especially in a strategy of early and flexible response". As regards the third issue, it is widely held that Third Pillar duties – especially of military intervention – are not advanced by R2P as legal duties (as observed in section 1.5.3 above). Rather they are only moral or "political" obligations (ICR2P, 2009: 8; Luck, 2008: 5).

Ambiguities remain, however. One vexing question regards the question of *who in particular* holds the duties that are imposed on the international community (Wills, 2004). While some attempts have been made to specify this aspect of R2P legally (Arbour, 2008) and morally (Pattison, 2008; Tan, 2006), the question remains pivotal:

> It is the lack of clarity about who will lead international action, and when, that is the biggest drawback in the current formulation of R2P, for it threatens to set up a mismatch between the expectations of individuals being oppressed on the one hand, and the capabilities and willingness of outside actors to provide for security on the other. (Welsh, 2006: 43–44)

A second ambiguity lies in the potential depth and breadth of the international community's Second Pillar responsibilities – with commentators worrying that these responsibilities are unworkably broad (Molier, 2006; Nasu, 2009). Several authors (McClean, 2008; Nasu, 2009; Popovski, 2010; Strauss, 2009) have located resources from other realms of law, policy and theory that serve to specify aspects of this responsibility, and the Secretary-General's 2009 Report on the implementation of R2P goes some way towards concretizing the diffuse responsibilities into tractable tasks. Bellamy (2009) seeks to constrain the Second Pillar by emphasizing direct preventive measures rather than more mediated structural prevention, and focusing only on the four atrocity crimes rather than armed conflict in general. Still, as Hehir (2010: 228) ripostes, "one may well wonder whether preventing 'genocide, war crimes, ethnic cleansing and crimes against humanity' can reasonably be prefixed with the word 'only' ".

1.6.2   R2P as hollow rhetoric

These last two ambiguities – regarding the extent of the international community's duties, and who in particular holds them – seem to combine with the "political, not legal" status of such duties to leave ample room for states to avoid their Second and Third Pillar responsibilities, or to only undertake them at their discretion (Durch, 2010: 6; Focarelli, 2008: 202). This then opens the worry that R2P is for the international community more about grandiose speech-making than problem-solving, of the sort unlikely to create the political will needed to alter foreign policy (Chandler, 2007; Glennon, 2006; Hehir, 2010; Leitenberg, 2006). It is also open to a critic to consider whether actual troop and resource allocations to UN civilian-protection missions, and the political will to support them, substantiate or belie member states' acceptance of a weighty political duty. The case of Darfur will loom large in such an adjudication (Bergholm and Badescu, 2009; Breau, 2007; Traub, 2010), though it would need to be juxtaposed with NATO's 2011 intervention in Libya. In any case, most theories of international norm development would predict rhetorical flourish to precede costly action. As time passes, nations and institutions are increasingly entrapped by their prior asseverations and modify their preferences in the light of previously stated commitments (Finnemore and Sikkink, 1998; Johnstone, 2003).

1.6.3   R2P and the Security Council

While to some extent allaying concerns about unilateralism, R2P's use of the UNSC to authorize coercive force has created controversy in its own right. As ICISS Commissioner Ramesh Thakur (2010: 18) describes:

> The legitimacy of the UNSC as the authoritative validator of international security action suffers from a quadruple legitimacy deficit: performance, representational, procedural and accountability. Its performance legitimacy suffers from two strikes: an uneven and a selective record. It is unrepresentative from almost any point of view. Its procedural legitimacy is suspect on grounds of a lack of democratisation and transparency in decision-making. And it is not answerable to the General Assembly, the World Court, the nations or the peoples of the world.

Such concerns with the role of the UNSC are not new (Ayoob, 2004), but they attained a new urgency in the last decade when humanitarians were faced with the narrowly self-interested machinations of members of the UNSC, for instance in application to the Darfur genocide (Bellamy, 2005; Bergholm and Badescu, 2009; Grono, 2006; Traub, 2010). In the 2009

General Assembly discussions of R2P, 35 governments called for restrictions on the Permanent Five's veto when dealing with atrocity crimes (ICR2P, 2009) and many international theorists have proffered ways of augmenting or replacing the UNSC decision-making on such matters (Dastoor, 2009; Johnstone, 2003; Leitenberg, 2006; Peters, 2009). However, it is questionable whether UNSC adoption of guiding criteria would improve matters (Bellamy, 2008). Optimists may think that recent UNSC decision-making with regard to Libya (UNSC, 2011) illustrates some improvements on this front, but such claims would need to be balanced with, for example, the intransigence of Russia with respect to violence in Syria (particularly its veto on 4 February 2012).

1.6.4 The "nothing new" critique

Some commentators have argued that R2P contributes "nothing new" to international affairs. After all, the UNSC has always had the discretionary authority to intervene in internal conflicts that pose a danger to international peace and security, and it had previously shown its willingness to view R2P-type situations in just this way (Chomsky, 2009; Hehir, 2010). In response, the following points describing the specific value added by R2P may be made.

First, it is one thing in law and policy to have a variety of actions and statements intermittently occurring over the last 20 years. It is quite another, as a result of a lengthy and inclusive discourse and plebiscite, to explicitly concretize and endorse a specific principle underlying such actions (Luck, 2008; Nanda, 2006).

Second, the grouping together of the four crimes was significant. Ethnic cleansing, war crimes and crimes against humanity are now deemed to be worthy of inclusion alongside the established crime of genocide (Luck, 2008; Rosenberg, 2009).

Third, while various aspects of R2P were present in IHL, IHRL and prior UNSC resolutions, R2P broadens the gamut of "tools, actors, and procedures" that can be called upon to protect civilians, in particular through its preventive agenda (Luck, 2008: 3).

Fourthly and finally, prior to 2005 it was possible to argue that the UNSC had overstepped its bounds in holding that internal mass violations of human rights constituted a threat to international peace and security – and that the UNSC had therefore "arrogated to itself" the right to authorize intervention into domestic conflicts (Ayoob, 2002: 225; Cohen, 2004: 23). Since 2005 and the unanimous and explicit endorsement of the UNSC's role in authorizing military action, it is much less plausible to argue that the UNSC as a matter of principle does not have the authority to rule on such matters.

1.6.5 R2P as Trojan horse

Perhaps the longest-standing critique levelled at R2P, and the main impediment to action on its behalf, is the view that R2P is a "Trojan horse" – a rhetorical vehicle for self-interested invasions by powerful international actors (Chavez, 2005; Chomsky, 2009: 4). In 2009 several member states and the President of the UNGA charged that R2P was effectively a vehicle for "redecorated colonialism" (ICR2P, 2009: 3, 7). A more subtle version of this challenge argues that R2P's disrespect for traditional sovereignty and the norm of non-interference contributes to a general environment of unilateralism (Chandler, 2004; Falk, 2006). In response, proponents of R2P have emphasized its multilateralism (ICR2P, 2009) and the severe limitations on its scope (Luck, 2008).

Perhaps, however, these charges of unilateralism and colonialism – in an era of globalization that is "post-imperial" (Peters, 2009: 532) – have overshadowed the more subtle and trenchant challenge to R2P, namely, that it allows world powers to intervene only if they have strategic interests at stake. At the 2005 debate on R2P, as Focarelli (2008: 202) describes, a number of member states (especially from the Non-Aligned Movement) stressed:

> that the responsibility to protect doctrine was formulated in a way that lets major powers discretionally decide whether and where to intervene. As the strongest states have a power, not an obligation to intervene, these states predicted that interventions will only be made by the strongest to further their interests and values.

This criticism sharpened with the fallout from the UN-authorized military intervention in Libya in 2011, and the alleged use of R2P and Resolution 1973 as a cloak for regime change by Western powers. This concern looms as a pivotal issue in moving R2P forward, and the following section explores it in some depth.

1.7 R2P and regime change

While a variety of important issues regarding the interpretation and operationalization of Resolution 1973 arose, including the scope of the arms embargo, the lack of information and explanation filtering back to UNSC members and the collateral damage to civilians caused by NATO actions, it is the association between R2P action and regime change that has proved most controversial (Gerber and Porter, 2012). This issue lies at the heart of the influential Brazilian Concept Note, *Responsibility while*

Protecting (Government of Brazil, 2011), which declares: "There is a growing perception that the concept of the responsibility to protect might be misused for purposes other than protecting civilians, such as regime change." Similarly, the Indian Permanent Representative to the UNSC (Puri, 2012) objected to the swift process from UNSC resolution, to military operations, to arming the rebels, as "three quick steps to regime change. That's not what R2P is all about."

In order to evaluate how R2P Pillar Three military operations can and cannot be disentangled from regime change, however, it is necessary to have a clear understanding of precisely what is meant by regime change, and the implications of various sorts of protective military operations for the viability of the incumbent regime. This section develops these issues, and sketches possible ways forward.

"Regime change" can refer to:

1 *Jurisdictional change* in geopolitical boundaries. The de facto state authority no longer reaches to certain parts of the country – such as "safe zones" – because these are now controlled by non-state forces (aided by, for example, no-fly zones created by interveners), intervening forces or peacekeeping forces.

2 *Institutional change*. Changes are made to the structure and limitations on the organs of government to ensure the executive no longer has the powers it once had to harm civilians. For example, it may be limited by the presence of human rights monitors, peacekeepers, independent courts or empowered civil society actors.

3 *Power-sharing change*. The executive power is shared between the incumbent and minority/opposition figures in a (perhaps transitional) parliamentary system or unity government.

4 *Total regime change*. The executive figures in authority are replaced. New state authority rests in hands altogether different from the previous regime.

Importantly, one actor can differ from others in what they mean by "regime change". For instance, in a situation such as Libya in 2011, most of the international community may desire both *institutional* and *power-sharing change*, but the incumbent regime may view both results as tantamount to externally imposed regime change. Certainly the UN Special Envoy to Libya understood the Gaddafi regime to view such outcomes in this way (Al-Khatib, 2012).

While it is *total regime change* that is the gravest concern, all four changes in a regime's status can be worrisome interferences when imposed by forces outside the country, especially if they are politically motivated by objectives unrelated to civilian protection. In this respect, the concern is not limited to the type of change created by the intervener, but the biased and self-interested reasons for precipitating that change.

While in the wake of Libya many commentators and policymakers have been keen to conceptually divorce R2P Pillar Three from regime change, in fact any military intervention for protective purposes that protects civilians against state or state-sponsored actors will have substantial consequences for the viability of the incumbent regime.

Consider what might be termed the "*most restrained*" Pillar Three intervention possible in a context like Libya, where international ground forces are explicitly excluded by the UNSC mandate. In the most restrained intervention of this type, intervening air forces use force only to ensure a no-fly zone and to defeat forces *actually in the process of* attacking or besieging safe zones and protected civilian objects (such as Benghazi, and later Misuratah). Even this type of operation involves at least temporary *jurisdictional change*. If a state is wilfully slaughtering its civilians in certain areas, then the primary purpose of the operation is to alter the balance of power so that the state no longer can or will do so. Such a change, moreover, has consequences for stronger forms of regime change.

First, the mission will only depart when civilian protection in safe zones can be guaranteed by indigenous institutions. Plainly, the unchanged regime cannot be left in charge of the endangered civilians without secure constraints on its actions toward them. The price the indigenous regime will have to pay for removal of the de facto partition created by the intervention will usually be some combination of *institutional* or *power-sharing change*.

Second, a state authority usually massacres its own civilians to the point of risking international intervention only when it perceives this as necessary for it to hold onto or consolidate its power. Even the most restrained protective intervention, therefore, prevents the regime doing what it perceived it needed to do in order to guarantee its survival. The very act of keeping alive people the regime wanted dead allows protesters to speak out, information and evidence on state brutality to surface, and the opposition to organize and galvanize unmolested. All these increase the likelihood of *institutional, power-sharing* and even *total regime change*.

Third, weakening the state authority through the creation of no-fly zones, and the robust protection of large-scale safe areas and civilian objects, can alter the strategic topography of the military theatre, effectively sheltering rebel troops, defensive structures and lines of supply. Such shifts may make the regime's military defeat – issuing in *total regime change* – comparatively much more likely. Such a result occurred in Côte d'Ivoire in 2011, where UN-authorized helicopter attacks on heavy weapons that had been used against civilian populations effectively cleared a path for the military defeat of the forces of ex-President Gbagbo (UNSG, 2011c).

It may be, however, that such a restrained operation is not tenable. The intervening force may judge that they cannot protect civilians without local indigenous ground military forces – *rebel forces* – defending civilian areas. If so, then civilian protection is irrevocably linked to the prospects of the rebel force as a defensive unit.

This would not be a surprising state of affairs. The US *Mass Atrocity Response Operation (MARO) Handbook* contains only two strategic approaches that do not involve troops on the ground. The first, *containment*, includes no-fly zones and air strikes, but is effective only when perpetrator forces are readily identifiable and targetable, and in any case "is unable to provide direct protection to vulnerable civilians" (Sewall, Raymond and Chin, 2010: 74–79). The only remaining strategy is *partner enabling*, where the interveners are fully enrolled as support actors to local forces. As one of the earliest analyses of military strategies for civilian protection observed: "the only sure way to defend the victims from further attacks is with ground forces" (Hinote, 2008: 16).

Thus, in a case where the rebel forces are at risk of being overrun – and NATO clearly believed this to be the situation at least in the early days of the Libyan intervention (Majoor, 2012) – then civilian protection may necessitate strengthening the overall position of rebel troops by proactively weakening the state forces' ability to defeat or outlast them. In such a situation – of *military support for partner defence* – the topography of the military theatre is tilted further towards the military defeat of the regime.

Finally, the intervening forces may take a longer-term view of civilian protection. If the regime is not genuinely open to *institutional* or *power-sharing changes* then the question becomes how may the environment be altered to ensure civilian protection by the only reliable mechanism for doing so in the long term: functioning and trustworthy state institutions. The status quo itself – a partitioned state protected through international force – may be inimical to long-term civilian protection. It risks precipitating quasi-occupation, permanent territorial division, interminable full-scale civil war and even the anarchy of a failed state. All these concerns were evident in the 14 April statement by Obama, Cameron and Sarkozy (2011) which called for Gaddafi's removal. In such a situation, the best long-term course for protecting civilians, and the most viable exit strategy for intervening forces, may be *military support for partner offensives*, where the interveners effectively function as air support for the advancing rebel forces.

To summarize, even the *most restrained* operation implies temporary *jurisdictional change*, and has geopolitical effects making *institutional, power-sharing* and *total regime change* more probable. *Military support for partner defence* makes these forms of regime change more likely again. In both scenarios, protection of civilians causes regime change. The situation in *military support for partner offensives* is different; here regime change causes protection of civilians – it is a means to the end.

With all this in mind, where does the major source of the dispute over the "regime change" interpretation of Resolution 1973 lie? Presumably few members could in principle object to the changes created by the "most restrained" military operation considered above. It is impossible to robustly protect civilians without these sorts of knock-on effects. Presumably too, if the NATO strategic evaluation of the profound threat to rebel forces and the vital role these forces played in ensuring local civilian protection was correct, then a strategy of *military support for partner defence* seems to fall within the UNSC mandate, provided that any risks to civilians were proportional to the protection objectives achieved. Plausibly, the central controversy occurred with the decision and explicit declaration by Obama, Sarkozy and Cameron that long-term protection required Gaddafi's removal, and the subsequent use by NATO of military support for the rebels' offensives (including the new dangers for civilians in Tripoli which this strategy created). Questions could be raised about the correctness of their judgement, the swiftness with which it was made and publicized, and whether Resolution 1973 vested the NATO leaders with discretion over such a long-term question of protection, or whether this could have been a matter for the UNSC to determine in a further resolution. With respect to the question of authority, it is arguable that the NATO leaders ignored what UNSC members Brazil and India referred to as the "two-track" nature of Resolution 1973, especially the calls for a ceasefire in its opening operative paragraph (Puri, 2012; Viotti, 2012). Arguably, the stabilization of the situation in Libya created by NATO's *military support for partner defence* could have at that point set the scene for attempts at a genuine ceasefire, renewed dialogue and a political resolution of the conflict. Whatever the prospects for such a dialogue, the position taken by the NATO leaders precluded attempts at such a resolution. Those who question the correctness, timing and authority of NATO's decision will suspect that it was made on the basis of political interests tangential to the protection of civilians.

In terms of proposals for moving forward, then, it is worth emphasizing that the term "necessary" in "all necessary measures" has both an enabling and a constraining connotation. When rebel militaries are the only force standing between an atrocity-bent army and massive civilian populations, then defensive military support of the rebels is unquestionably necessary, irrespective of whether this will have consequences for regime change (though, of course, not irrespective of the dangers such a strategy might create for other civilians). Here the term "necessary" enables such a use of force. Equally though, when a situation is stabilized, military overthrow of the regime by rebel forces may not be the exclusive – or even the best – path to long-term civilian protection. Here the term "necessary" has a constraining force; political solutions may once again be worth a concerted effort.

In conclusion, it is important to be realistic about the strong causal relationships between military operations to protect civilians against state forces and regime change – but equally to be respectful of the ways the two concepts are not synonymous. This section has argued that even the most constrained protective operations have implications for regime change, and that strategic necessity may well involve directly supporting the defensive integrity of non-perpetrator forces. However, support for rebels' regime-changing offensives – while it cannot be ruled out as a potential long-term means to resolving the conflict, removing international forces and protecting civilians – is not an irremovable part of the use of force to protect civilians; at least, not until other means have been exhausted.

1.8 Conclusion

This chapter has traced the R2P principle from its inception by ICISS in 2001, through its affirmation by the General Assembly in 2005 and the UNSC in 2006, to its present position in the wake of the 2011 Libyan intervention. Its consideration of the controversial relationship between military intervention for protection purposes and regime change has argued that attention to the specific ways protective action impacts on regime change may guide both authorizers and interveners to an increasingly shared understanding of "all necessary measures".

Notes

1. See Bellamy (2009), Thakur (2003), Thakur (2002), Weiss (2007) and Task-Force (2005).
2. See Stahn (2007). For more detail and technical specification on this issue, see Chapter 3 of this volume, section 3.3.3.
3. See Deng (1993). Deng was not specifically cited in the ICISS Report, however.
4. For critical arguments on this matter see McClean (2008), Roberts (2004) and Focarelli (2008).
5. E.g. UNSC (2000, 2011).
6. As understood by, e.g., UN Secretary-General Hammarskjold (Wills, 2009), and the reports on Rwanda and Srebrenica (UN, 1999; UNSG, 1999).
7. See Barbour and Gorlick (2008) and Arbour (2008); though note Carvin (2010).

REFERENCES

Al-Khatib, Abdel-Elah, Special Envoy of the UN Secretary-General for Libya (2012) "R2P in Practice – Policy Approaches since 2005: Libya", *R2P: The Next Decade*. New York: Stanley Foundation. 18 January 2012. [Online] Available at: ⟨http://fora.tv/2012/01/18/R2P_in_2022#fullprogram⟩.

Annan, Kofi (2000) *We the Peoples: Millennium Report to the General Assembly*. New York: United Nations.

Arbour, Louise (2008) "The Responsibility to Protect as a Duty of Care in International Law and Practice", *Review of International Studies* 34(3): 445–458.

Ayoob, Mohammed (2002) "Humanitarian Intervention and International Society", *Global Governance* 7: 225–230.

Ayoob, Mohammed (2004) "Third World Perspectives on Humanitarian Intervention and International Administration", *Global Governance* 10(1): 99–118.

Bagnoli, Carla (2006) "Humanitarian Intervention as a Perfect Duty", in Terry Nardin and Melissa Williams, eds. *Nomos XLVII: Humanitarian Intervention*. New York: New York University, 117–140.

Barbour, Brian, and Brian Gorlick (2008) "Embracing the 'Responsibility to Protect': A Repertoire of Measures Including Asylum for Potential Victims", *International Journal of Refugee Law* 20(4): 533–566.

Bellamy, Alex (2005) "Responsibility to Protect or Trojan Horse? The Crisis in Darfur and Humanitarian Intervention after Iraq", *Ethics and International Affairs* 19(2): 31–53.

Bellamy, Alex (2006) "Whither the Responsibility to Protect? Humanitarian Intervention and the 2005 World Summit", *Ethics and International Affairs* 20(2): 143–169.

Bellamy, Alex (2008) "The Responsibility to Protect and the Problem of Military Intervention", *International Affairs* 84(4): 615–639.

Bellamy, Alex (2009) *Responsibility to Protect: The Global Effort to End Mass Atrocities*. Cambridge: Polity.

Bellamy, Alex (2010) "The Responsibility to Protect – Five Years On", *Ethics and International Affairs* 24(2): 143–169.

Bergholm, Linnea, and Cristina Badescu (2009) "The Responsibility to Protect and the Conflict in Darfur: The Big Let-Down", *Security Dialogue* 40(3): 287–307.

Brazil, Government of (2011) *Concept Note: Responsibility While Protecting: Elements for the Development and Promotion of a Concept,* A/66/551; S/2011/701, 11 November 2011.

Breau, Susan (2007) "The Impact of the Responsibility to Protect on Peacekeeping", *Journal of Conflict and Security Law* 11(3): 429–464.

Caballero-Anthony, Mely, and Belinda Chng (2009) "Cyclones and Humanitarian Crises: Pushing the Limits of R2P in Southeast Asia", *Global Responsibility to Protect* 1: 135–155.

Carvin, Stephanie (2010) "A Responsibility to Reality: A Reply to Louise Arbour", *British International Studies Association* 36: 47–54.

Chandler, David (2004) "The Responsibility to Protect? Imposing the Liberal Peace", *International Peacekeeping* 11(1): 59–81.

Chandler, David (2007) "The Security–Development Nexus and the Rise of 'Anti-Foreign Policy'", *Journal of International Relations and Development* 10(4): 362–386.

Chavez, Hugo (2005) "Speech at 70th UN General Assembly", New York. Sept. 15, 2005 [Online] Available at: ⟨http:www.embavenez-us.org/news.php?nid =1745⟩.

Chomsky, Noam (2009) "Statement by Professor Noam Chomsky to the United Nations General Assembly Thematic Dialogue on the Responsibility to Protect." 23 July 2009.

Cohen, Jean (2004) "Whose Sovereignty? Empire Versus International Law", *Ethics and International Affairs* 18(3): 1–24.

Dastoor, Neville F (2009) "The Responsibility to Refine: The Need for a Security Council Committee on the Responsibility to Protect", *Harvard Human Rights Journal* 22: 25–62.

Deng, Francis (1993) *Protecting the Dispossessed: A Challenge for the International Community*. Washington, DC: Brookings Institution.

Deng, Francis M. (2010) "From 'Sovereignty as Responsibility' to the 'Responsibility to Protect'", *Global Responsibility to Protect* 2: 353–370.

de Waal, Alex (2007) "No Such Thing as Humanitarian Intervention: Why We Need to Rethink How to Realize the "Responsibility to Protect" in Wartime", *Harvard International Review*, 1–4.

Durch, William J. (2010) "Cross-Cutting Issues in Protection of Civilians for UN Peace Operations", *Challenges of Protecting Civilians in Multidimensional Peace Operations*. Canberra: International Forum for the Challenges of Peace Operations. 27 April, 2010.

Evans, Gareth (2006) "Crimes against Humanity: Overcoming Indifference", *Journal of Genocide Research* 8(3): 325–339.

Evans, Gareth (2008) "The Responsibility to Protect: An Idea Whose Time Has Come ... And Gone?", *International Relations* 22(3): 283–298.

Falk, Richard (2006) "International Law and the Future", *Third World Quarterly* 27(5): 727–737.

Feinstein, Lee, and Erica De Bruin (2009) "Beyond Words: US Policy and the Responsibility to Protect", in Richard Cooper and Juliette Kohler, eds. *Responsibility to Protect: The Global Moral Compact for the 21st Century*. New York: Palgrave Macmillan.

Finnemore, Martha, and Kathryn Sikkink (1998) "International Norm Dynamics and Political Change", *International Organisation* 52(4): 887–917.

Fleck, Dieter (2006) "International Accountability for Violations of the Ius in Bello: The Impact of the ICRC Study on Customary International Humanitarian Law", *Journal of Conflict and Security Law* 11(2): 179–199.

Focarelli, Carlo (2008) "The Responsibility to Protect Doctrine and Humanitarian Intervention: Too Many Ambiguities for a Working Doctrine", *Journal of Conflict & Security Law* 13(2): 191–213.

Focarelli, Carlo (2010) "Common Article 1 of the 1949 Geneva Conventions: A Soap Bubble?", *European Journal of International Law* 21(1): 125–171.

Frohardt, Mark, Diane Paul and Larry Minear (1999) *Protecting Human Rights: The Challenge to Humanitarian Organizations, Occasional Papers 35.* Providence, RI: The Watson Institute.

Gattini, Andrea (2007) "Breach of the Obligation to Prevent and Reparation Thereof in the ICJ's Genocide Judgment", *European Journal of International Law* 18(4): 695–713.

Gerber, Rachel and Keith Porter (2012) "Policy Memo: R2P the Next Decade." New York: Stanley Foundation. 1 February 2012. [Online] Available at: ⟨http://www.stanleyfoundation.org/resources.cfm?id=475⟩.

Gierycz, Dorota (2010) "The Responsibility to Protect: A Legal and Rights-Based Perspective", *Global Responsibility to Protect* 2: 250–266.

Glennon, Michael J. (2006) "The Emerging Use-of-Force Paradigm", *Journal of Conflict & Security Law* 11(3): 309–317.

Grono, Nick (2006) "Briefing – Darfur: The International Community's Failure to Protect", *African Affairs* 105(421): 621–631.

Haacke, Jürgen (2009) "Myanmar, the Responsibility to Protect, and the Need for Practical Assistance", *Global Responsibility to Protect* 1(2): 156–184.

Hehir, Aidan (2010) "The Responsibility to Protect: 'Sound and Fury Signifying Nothing'?", *International Relations* 24(2): 218–239.

Henckaerts, Jean-Marie (2005) "Study on Customary International Humanitarian Law: A Contribution to the Understanding and Respect for the Rule of Law in Armed Conflict", *International Review of the Red Cross* 87(857): 175–212.

Hinote, Clint (2008) "Campaigning to Protect: Using Military Force to Stop Genocide and Mass Atrocities". Available at: ⟨http://www.hks.harvard.edu/cchrp/maro/pdf/Clint_Hinote_Campaigning_to_Protect_Third%20Draft.pdf⟩.

Holt, Victoria, and Tobias Berkman (2006) *The Impossible Mandate? Military Preparedness, the Responsibility to Protect and Modern Peace Operations.* Washington, DC: The Henry L. Stimson Center.

ICISS, International Commission on Intervention and State Sovereignty (2001) *The Responsibility to Protect.* Ottawa: International Development Research Centre.

ICRC (1949) *Convention (IV) Relative to the Protection of Civilian Persons in Time of War.* Geneva. 12 August 1949.

ICRC (1977) *Protocol Additional to the Geneva Conventions of 12 August 1949, and Relating to the Protection of Victims of International Armed Conflicts (Protocol I).* Geneva: International Committee of the Red Cross. 8 June 1977.

ICR2P, International Coalition for the Responsibility to Protect (2009) *Report on the General Assembly Plenary Debate on the Responsibility to Protect*, 15 September 2009.

IICK (2000) *The Kosovo Report: Conflict, International Response, Lessons Learned.* New York: The Independent International Commission on Kosovo.

ILC, International Law Commission (2001) "Articles on Responsibility of States for Internationally Wrongful Acts", *Report of the International Law Commission on the Work of Its Fifty-Third Session.* UN GAOR: A/56/10.

Johnstone, Ian (2003) "Security Council Deliberations: The Power of the Better Argument", *European Journal of International Law* 14(3): 437–480.

Leitenberg, Milton (2006) "Beyond the 'Never Agains'," *Asian Perspective* 30(3): 159–165.

Locke, John (1947) *Two Treatises of Government*. New York: Hafner.

Luck, Edward (2008) *The United Nations and the Responsibility to Protect*. Muscatine, IA: The Stanley Foundation.

Luck, Edward (2010a) "A Response", *Global Responsibility to Protect* 2: 178–183.

Luck, Edward (2010b) "The Responsibility to Protect: Growing Pains or Early Promise?", *Ethics and International Affairs* 24(4): 349–365.

Majoor, Frank, Permanent Representative of the Netherlands to NATO (2012) "Statement During R2P in 2022 Panel", in *R2P: The Next Decade*. New York: Stanley Foundation, 18 January 2012. [Online] Available at: ⟨http://fora.tv/2012/01/18/R2P_in_2022#fullprogram⟩.

Martin, Ian (2004) "International Intervention in East Timor", in Jennifer Welsh, ed. *Humanitarian Intervention and International Relations*. Oxford: Oxford University Press, 142–162.

McClean, Emma (2008) "The Responsibility to Protect: The Role of International Human Rights Law", *Journal of Conflict and Security Law* 13(1): 123–152.

Molier, Gelijn (2006) "Humanitarian Intervention and the Responsibility to Protect after 9/11", *Netherlands International Law Review* LIII: 37–62.

Nanda, Ved P. (2006) "The Protection of Human Rights under International Law: Will the UN Human Rights Council and the Emerging New Norm 'Responsibility to Protect' Make a Difference?", *Denver Journal of International Law and Policy* 35: 353–378.

Nasu, Hitoshi (2009) "Operationalizing the 'Responsibility to Protect' and Conflict Prevention: Dilemmas of Civilian Protection in Armed Conflict", *Journal of Conflict & Security Law* 14(2): 209–241.

Newman, Michael (2009) "Revisiting the 'Responsibility to Protect'," *Political Quarterly* 80(1): 92–100.

Obama, Barack (2011) "Weekly Address: President Obama Says Mission in Libya Succeeding", Washington, DC: The White House. 27 March, 2011 [Online] Available at: ⟨http://www.whitehouse.gov/the-press-office/2011/03/26/weekly-address-president-obama-says-mission-libya-succeeding⟩.

Obama, Barack, David Cameron and Nicolas Sarkozy (2011) "Libya's Pathway to Peace", *International Herald Tribune*, 14 April 2011 [Online] Available at: ⟨http://www.nytimes.com/2011/04/15/opinion/15iht-edlibya15.html?_r=4&ref=global⟩.

Pattison, James (2008) "Whose Responsibility to Protect? The Duties of Humanitarian Intervention", *Journal of Military Ethics* 7(4): 262–283.

Peters, Anne (2009) "Humanity as the *A* and Ω of Sovereignty", *European Journal of International Law* 20(3): 513–544.

Popovski, Vesselin (2004–5) "Sovereignty as Duty to Protect Human Rights", *UN Chronicle* 41(4): 16–18.

Popovski, Vesselin (2010) "Responsibility to Protect", in Malcolm McIntosh and Alan Hunter, eds. *New Perspectives on Human Security*. Sheffield, UK: Greenleaf, 204–219.

Puri, Hardeep Singh, Permanent Representative of India to the United Nations (2012) "Interview: R2P", New York: Stanley Foundation. 18 January 2012 [Online] Available at: ⟨http://www.youtube.com/watch?v=OP7QOQ5Aqoo&feature =youtu.be⟩.

Roberts, Adam (2000) "The So-Called 'Right' of Humanitarian Intervention", *Yearbook of International Humanitarian Law* 3(3): 3–51.

Roberts, Adam (2004) "The United Nations and Humanitarian Intervention", in Jennifer Welsh, ed. *Humanitarian Intervention and International Relations*. Oxford: Oxford University Press, 71–97.

Rosenberg, Sheri P. (2009) "Responsibility to Protect: A Framework for Prevention", *Global Responsibility to Protect* 1(4): 442–477.

Rudd, Kevin (2011) "Security Council Heeds Lessons from Rwanda and Balkans", *The Australian*, 19 March 2011 [Online] Available at: ⟨http://www.theaustralian.com.au/news/world/security-council-heeds-lessons-from-rwanda-and-balkans/story-e6frg6ux-1226024272337⟩.

Ryniker, Anne (2001) "The ICRC's Position on 'Humanitarian Intervention',", *International Review of the Red Cross* 482: 527–532.

Sampford, Charles (1997) "The Four Dimensions of Rights and Their Means of Protection", in Charles Sampford and B. Galligan, eds. *Rethinking Human Rights*. Sydney: Federation Press.

Serrano, Monica (2010) "Implementing the Responsibility to Protect: The Power of R2P Talk", *Global Responsibility to Protect* 2: 167–177.

Sewall, Sarah, Dwight Raymond and Sally Chin (2010) *Mass Atrocity Response Operations: A Military Planning Handbook*. 4.30 ed. Cambridge, MA: Harvard Kennedy School and US Army Peacekeeping and Stability Operations Institute.

Shue, Henry (2004) "Limiting Sovereignty", in Jennifer Welsh, ed. *Humanitarian Intervention and International Relations*. Oxford: Oxford University Press, 11–28.

Stahn, Carsten (2007) "Responsibility to Protect: Political Rhetoric or Emerging Legal Norm?", *American Journal of International Law* 101(1): 99–120.

Strauss, Ekkehard (2009) "A Bird in the Hand Is Worth Two in the Bush: On the Assumed Legal Nature of the Responsibility to Protect", *Global Responsibility to Protect* 1(3): 291–323.

Tan, Kok-Chor (2006) "The Duty to Protect", in T. Nardin and M. Williams, eds. *Nomo–s XLVII: Humanitarian Intervention*. New York: New York University, 84–116.

Task-Force, US (2005) *American Interests and United Nations Reform*. Washington, DC: United States Institute of Peace.

Thakur, Ramesh (2002) "Intervention, Sovereignty and the Responsibility to Protect: Experiences from ICISS", *Security Dialogue* 33(3): 323–340.

Thakur, Ramesh (2003) "In Defence of the Responsibility to Protect", *International Journal of Human Rights* 7(3): 160–178.

Thakur, Ramesh (2010) "Law, Legitimacy and United Nations", *Melbourne Journal of International Law* 11(1): 1–26.

Thakur, Ramesh, and Thomas G. Weiss (2009) "R2P: From Idea to Norm – and Action?", *Global Responsibility to Protect* 1(1): 22–53.

Traub, James (2010) *Unwilling and Unable: The Failed Response to the Atrocities in Darfur*, Occasional Paper Series. New York: Global Centre for the Responsibility to Protect.

UN (1999) *Report of the Independent Inquiry into the Actions of the United Nations During the 1994 Genocide in Rwanda*, S/1999/1257/Annex, 16 December 1999.

UNGA (1948) "Convention on the Prevention and Punishment of the Crime of Genocide, 9 December 1948" Geneva: United Nations. 9 December 1948 [Online] Available at: ⟨http://www.un.org/ga/search/view_doc.asp?symbol=a/res/260(III)⟩.

UNGA (2005) *Resolution 60/1: World Summit Outcome Document*, A/Res/60/1, 16 September 2005.

UNGA (2009) *Resolution Adopted by the General Assembly: The Responsibility to Protect*, A/RES/63/308.

UNHLP, High-Level Panel on Threats, Challenges and Change (2004) *A More Secure World: Our Shared Responsibility*, A/59/565, December 2004.

UNHRC, United Nations Human Rights Council (2007) *Implementation of General Assembly Resolution 60/251 of 15 March 2006 Entitled "Human Rights Council": Report of the High-Level Mission on the Situation of Human Rights in Darfur Pursuant to Human Rights Council Decision S-4/101*, A/HRC/4/80, 9 March 2007.

UNSC (2000) *UN Security Council Resolution 1325 (2000): On Women and Peace and Security*, S/RES/1325, 31 October 2000.

UNSC (2001) *UN Security Council Resolution 1366 (2001): On the Role of the Security Council in the Prevention of Armed Conflicts*, S/RES/1366, 30 August 2001.

UNSC (2006a) *UN Security Council Resolution 1674 (2006): Protection of Civilians in Armed Conflict*, S/RES/1674, 28 April 2006.

UNSC (2006b) *UN Security Council Resolution 1706 (2006): Reports of the Secretary-General on the Sudan*, S/RES/1706, 31 August 2006.

UNSC (2009) *UN Security Council Resolution 1894 (2009): Protection of Civilians in Armed Conflict*, S/RES/1894, 11 November 2009.

UNSC (2011) *UN Security Council Resolution 1973 (2011): The Situation in Libya*, S/RES/1973, 17 March 2011.

UNSG (1999) *Report of the Secretary General Pursuant to General Assembly Resolution 53/55: The Fall of Srebrenica*, A/54/549, 15 November 1999.

UNSG (2005) *Report of the Secretary-General: In Larger Freedom: Towards Development, Security and Human Rights for All*, A/59/2005, 21 March 2005.

UNSG (2009) *Report of the Secretary-General: Implementing the Responsibility to Protect*, A/63/677, 12 January 2009.

UNSG (2010) *Report of the Secretary-General: Early Warning, Assessment and the Responsibility to Protect*, A/64/864, 14 July 2010.

UNSG (2011a) "Statement by the Secretary-General on Libya", 17 March 2011. [Online] Available at: ⟨http://www.un.org/apps/sg/sgstats.asp?nid=5145⟩.

UNSG (2011b) *Report of the Secretary-General: The Role of Regional and Sub-Regional Arrangements in Implementing the Responsibility to Protect*, A/65/877–S/2011/393, 27 June 2011.

UNSG (2011c) "Statement by the Secretary-General on the Situation in Côte d'Ivoire", 4 April 2011. [Online] Available at: ⟨http://www.un.org/apps/sg/sgstats. asp?nid=5185#⟩.

Viotti, Maria Luiza Ribeiro, Permanent Representative of Brazil to the United Nations Security Council (2012) "R2P in 2022: Responsibility While Protecting", *R2P: The Next Decade*. New York: Stanley Foundation, 18 January 2012. [Online] Available at: ⟨http://fora.tv/2012/01/18/R2P_in_2022#fullprogram⟩.

Ward, Lee (2006) "Locke on the Moral Basis of International Relations", *American Journal of Political Science* 50(3): 691–705.

Ward, Lee (2007) *Toward a New Paradigm for Humanitarian Intervention*, Public Policy Paper No. 50, The Saskatchewan Institute of Public Policy.

Weiss, Thomas G. (2007) *Humanitarian Intervention*. Cambridge: Polity.

Welsh, Jennifer (2004) "Taking Consequences Seriously: Objections to Humanitarian Intervention", in Jennifer Welsh, ed. *Humanitarian Intervention and International Relations*, Oxford: Oxford University Press, 52–68.

Welsh, Jennifer (2006) "The Responsibility to Protect: Securing the Individual in International Society?", in Oliver Jütersonke and Keith Krause, eds. *From Rights to Responsibilities*. Geneva: Programme for Strategic and International Security Studies (PSIS), 23–44.

Wills, Siobhán (2004) "Military Interventions on Behalf of Vulnerable Populations: The Legal Responsibilities of States and International Organizations Engaged in Peace Support Operations", *Journal of Conflict and Security Law* 9(3): 387–418.

Wills, Siobhán (2009) *Protecting Civilians: The Obligations of Peacekeepers*. Oxford: Oxford University Press.

2

The protection of civilians in armed conflict: Four concepts

Hugh Breakey

For thousands of years, myriad cultures across the globe have developed principles aiming to protect unarmed populations from violence at the hands of the armed. Since the Fourth Geneva Convention of 1949 such efforts have fallen under the rubric of the *Protection of Civilians* (POC). This chapter details the nature of POC in the contemporary context. It argues that while all POC actors have a broadly shared understanding of the core concerns of POC – the basic rights of non-combatants and the types of violence that threaten them – the different perspectives, resources and powers possessed by separate types of POC actors make those actors develop distinct POC roles and responsibilities.

Over its four main sections, this chapter distils four separate versions of POC, reflective of the different perspectives and means brought by the four types of agent who are centrally concerned with POC. In brief:

Combatant POC. Directed to combatants in armed conflicts, *combatant POC* is the principle: "We must not harm or unduly risk harm to non-combatants." Dictated by the Geneva Conventions and Additional Protocols, these legal obligations constrain the actions, weapons and tactics used in armed conflicts in order to reduce the harm inflicted on civilians and wounded soldiers.

Peacekeeping POC. Directed to peacekeeping forces that have protection mandates, *peacekeeping POC* is the principle: "Taking responsibility for peace enforcement in an area necessarily involves taking responsibility for the protection of civilians in that area." These duties require peacekeeping operations to ensure a reasonable level of protection

Norms of protection: Responsibility to protect, protection of civilians and their interaction,
Francis, Popovski and Sampford (eds),
United Nations University Press, 2012, ISBN 978-92-808-1218-3

from mass violence (commensurate with the operation's capacities and mandate) to local civilians.

Security Council POC. Directed to the UN Security Council (UNSC) and Secretariat, *Security Council POC* is the concept that: "Where feasible, basic rights should be protected from large-scale violation." This very broad concept presents as a substantial but unspecified requirement to respond, through prevention, response and capacity-building, to widespread, systemic human-inflicted suffering.

Humanitarian POC. Directed to humanitarian actors such as the Red Cross, United Nations High Commissioner for Refugees (UNHCR) and Oxfam, *humanitarian POC* is the concept that: "Where possible, and acting within all relevant constraints, humanitarian organizations at work in a region should aim to contribute through peaceful means to the protection from violence and deprivation of local civilians." Such measures may include *inter alia* advocacy, visitations of prisons and camps, aid to sick, wounded or vulnerable persons, denunciation of rights violations and war crimes, ensuring a humanitarian presence and proactively using presence to discourage attacks, providing information to civilians on areas of risk and safety and so on.

As will be seen, in many ways these principles are dissimilar – requiring quite distinct actions from different sorts of actors, each of whom have diverging resources and objectives. Even so, their separateness from each other should not be overplayed. In many cases there will be operational overlap and interaction among them. For instance, the UNSC may decide, prompted by *Security Council POC* considerations, to undertake a protective mission that will be bound by the positive role-based *peacekeeping POC* duties as well as the perennial constraints of *combatant POC*. Part of the mission's mandate will include facilitating the work of humanitarian actors, as these undertake their own *humanitarian POC* tasks. Such overlap is likely to increase in the future as coordination and mutual support between protection actors become entrenched. That said, it is also true that the different protection agendas can work at crosspurposes. For instance, the more robust the use of force for *peacekeeping POC* purposes, the more the neutrality of associated humanitarian actors can be compromised, undermining the prospects for *humanitarian POC* (Lie, 2008).

As well as operational overlap, the four perspectives on POC share a common conceptual scope. All four aim to protect the basic rights of non-combatants from the direct threats arising in situations of widespread violence. A useful way of conceptualizing the interrelationship of the four understandings of POC is by analogy to the three pillars of the responsibility to protect (R2P). The three pillars of R2P each focus on the same narrow set of threats to human rights (the four atrocity crimes), but they each pick out different actors in different situations with different means and acting under different constraints. So, too, each of the POC concepts focuses on the ways large-scale and systemic conflict can impinge on basic human security rights, but each addresses itself to different actors under different circumstances, with different means at their disposal.

Like the R2P pillars too, each of the four concepts of POC has a different status in policy and law. In international affairs, a *norm* is generally understood to be a shared expectation of appropriate behaviour by actors with a given identity. With its clear status as legally obligatory, and its determinacy derived from the canon of international humanitarian law (IHL), *combatant POC* is the only version of POC that is unquestionably a norm. *Peacekeeping POC* is perhaps approaching the status of a norm (though not a legal norm), as ongoing attempts are being made both in the direction of improving protection and of managing unrealistic expectations of protection. At present, however, it is perhaps best to view *peacekeeping POC* as being a *principle*, with peacekeepers' goals, capacities and tasks with respect to protection becoming settled through the recent developments in doctrine, training, methods and institutionalization, but not yet concretized to the point where the principle has become a norm. *Security Council POC* and *humanitarian POC*, however, are considerably more plastic and amorphous, and there is genuine debate as to what they do and should require. If "principle" connotes a shared understanding that can function as a basis for action (Bellamy, 2009: 6), then the looser term "concept" may be more apt in this application. (For a more technical discussion of this point, see Chapter 3, section 3.3.3.) Hence this chapter will speak of the *norm* of *combatant POC*, the *principle* of *peacekeeping POC*, and the *concepts* of *Security Council* and *humanitarian POC*, with the proviso that these categorizations are somewhat vague, and that progressions and shifts can occur over time as roles and responsibilities become increasingly settled or contested. (Collectively this chapter will refer to the four as "concepts" – this being the term with the most minimal commitments.)

While the account given here of the specific content of the four conceptualizations of POC is new, the idea that POC may mean different things to different actors is well known (Lie, 2008). Holt and Berkman (2006) identify no fewer than six POC concepts, most of which are grouped here under the rubrics of *combatant POC* and *peacekeeping POC*. In a pithy Policy Brief, the Global Centre for the Responsibility to Protect (GCR2P, 2011) distinguishes a "broad" definition of POC, incorporating IHL and in a "subsidiary role" the work of humanitarians, from a "narrow" definition applicable to the UNSC. Bonwick (2006) and Lae-Greid (2008) likewise distinguish the protection activities undertaken by humanitarian actors from the POC concept found in UNSC decision-making and UN peacekeeping. For their part the Department of Peace-keeping Operations (DPKO) and Department of Field Support (DFS) explicitly acknowledge wider concepts of POC held by humanitarian and other actors, before distinguishing their own understanding of the concept specific to peacekeeping (DPKO/DFS, 2010a). At other times elements of all four perspectives on POC may be grouped together: an example is in the Office for the Coordination of Humanitarian Affairs' (OCHA, 2010) document "OCHA on Message: Protection". Reflecting OCHA's broad role of coordinating between disparate protection agents – combatants, peacekeepers, humanitarians and the UNSC – OCHA's concept of protection reflects and consolidates aspects of all four different perspectives.

2.1 Combatant POC

Combatant POC is the Protection of Civilians in Armed Conflicts norm as it is found in the *jus in bello* constraints of Just War Theory and in IHL – especially the Fourth Geneva Convention of 1949 and the Second Additional Protocol of 1977 – but extending to other instruments and institutions, including the decisions of the International Criminal Court and the Rome Statute (Barbour and Gorlick, 2008).

Combatant POC is for the greater part a prohibition on directly targeting, disproportionately affecting or exposing to risk civilians and civilian objects. Its oft-noted core concepts are of distinction, proportionality and limitation.

2.1.1 Combatant POC: Normative foundations

The normative basis for *combatant POC* could be founded on any number of ethical viewpoints, including human rights and utility, and versions of it can be found in innumerable cultures and religions throughout history (Durham, 2008; Popovski, Reichberg and Turner, 2009). It makes an explicit appearance, and receives perhaps its most comprehensive treatment, in the part of Just War Theory that relates to conduct within wars – *jus in bello* (Walzer, 2000). It was from such normative fundaments that the contemporary laws of war, as captured in the Geneva Conventions and related instruments, were constructed (Slim, 2008).

2.1.2 Combatant POC: Substance and content

This section details the content of *combatant POC* as found in the Geneva Conventions (especially the Fourth Convention; ICRC, 1949), the Additional Protocols (especially the Second Protocol; ICRC, 1977) and customary international humanitarian law. The fundamental guarantees for civilians are summarized in Common Article Three of the Geneva Conventions and Article Four of the Second Protocol, while the content of customary international humanitarian law is described in the 2005 International Committee of the Red Cross (ICRC) study (Henckaerts, 2005; Henckaerts and Doswald-Becks, 2005). For expository ease, where possible this section refers the particular duties to the Rules enumerated in the 2005 ICRC study.

Combatant POC negative duties. The core and greater part of *combatant POC* is constituted by negative duties – that is, duties of the form "thou shalt not ...". These duties prohibit certain specific types of actions. In most moral systems negative duties are concerned with prohibiting actions that harm others, and *combatant POC* is no exception. *Combatant POC* prohibits military actions that target or endanger civilians and civilian objects. The principle is thus very wide in scope, including protections against the targeting of civilians (Rules 1–10), murder, sexual assault and exploitation (Rules 87–105), forced displacement (Rules 129–133) and the destruction and removal of cultural property and private property (Rules 38–41, 49–52). As well as these prohibitions on directly targeting civilians, combatants are also restrained by laws against indiscriminate and disproportional attacks that risk harm to civilians as combatants pursue their military objectives (Rules 11–14).

Furthermore, in both the normative and legal literature on *combatant POC*, these constraints extend beyond prohibitions on directly harming civilians to include, for instance, prohibitions on destroying civilian infrastructure (e.g. electricity and sanitation facilities) and blockading civilian supplies of food, medical supplies and humanitarian aid.[1]

Combatant POC positive duties. Not all the laws of war are negative duties ("thou shalt *not* ..."), however. The "we" in *combatant POC*'s "we must not harm ..." is to be read expansively as implying "all those on our side" and arguably even all those under our influence or supply. As such, *combatant POC* includes positive actions such as requiring that state organs and force commanders educate and train their armed forces in their POC responsibilities, and police their behaviour (Rules 139–144, 158). *Combatant POC* can also include positive duties of aid to the wounded, sick or shipwrecked in specific circumstances, and for ensuring the proper care and education of children caught in conflict situations (ICRC, 1977: Art. 4, 8). In situations of occupation or internment, such positive duties become more substantial, as the authority is required to take on responsibilities for the well-being of those whose liberty it is constraining (ICRC, 1949: Sect. 3–4).

Some of *combatant POC*'s duties, however, fall into a conceptually murky space between negative and positive duties. These duties are those that require combatants to distinguish themselves from civilians (Rule 106) and to avoid placing military objects alongside civilian objects (Rules 23–24). Rather than proscribing direct harm to civilians, these duties create a larger context by which it becomes possible for an opposing force to continue to use military means to pursue its war objectives without being forced to target civilians. Rules regarding the investigation and prosecution by states for war crimes (Rules 157–161), and of states using their influence to stop violations (Rule 144), also fall into this same category of contributing to an environment where violations of rights are indirectly prevented.

It is a contested question whether *combatant POC* includes positive duties to actively protect civilians in war *from third parties*. Article One common to the four Geneva Conventions (ICRC, 1949) appears a potential source of proactive protection with its requirement that "The High Contracting Parties undertake to respect *and to ensure respect* for the present Convention in all circumstances" (emphasis added). However, this requirement of ensuring respect is usually understood to refer to combatants under a contracting party's direction or control (Rule 139) and there are substantial problems with interpreting it more expansively as a duty to ensure respect by engaging with *third-party violators* of the Conventions (Focarelli, 2010). Still, the matter is controversial, with some commentators suggesting there is in certain contexts at least a moral force – and perhaps even an incipient legal force – arising from Common Article One requiring combatants to actively protect civilians.[2] For our purposes here, such positive duties of direct protection against third-party violations are understood to fall on the margins of the concept – and outside the basic core of *combatant POC*.

In sum therefore, *combatant POC* is constituted by the precept: "We must not harm or unduly risk harm to non-combatants." *Combatant POC* imposes negative duties on combatants not to directly harm civilians or civilian objects, positive duties not to use war methods that create environments that would profoundly risk harm to civilians, and positive duties of state organs and commanders to ensure troops are educated and trained to fulfil their POC duties.

2.2 Peacekeeping POC

Peacekeeping POC is the civilian protection principle found in robust peacekeeping, peacebuilding and peace enforcement literature, especially as regards UN operations. For expository ease the familiar term "peacekeeping" is used to refer to all these operations, but it must be emphasized that the term is not thereby limited to traditional peacekeeping operations, and includes the wide variety of modern peacekeeping missions that are deployed into situations where there is precious little peace to keep (DPKO, 2008). Central *peacekeeping POC* texts are the UN and Independent Reports on Rwanda (International Panel, 2000; UN, 1999) and Srebrenica (UNSG, 1999a), the seminal Brahimi Report (2000), the more recent reports building upon Brahimi (DPKO, 2009; DPKO/DFS, 2011; Jones, Gowan and Sherman, 2009), and the recent work of authors such as Victoria Holt (Holt and Berkman, 2006; Holt and Smith, 2008; Holt, Taylor and Kelly, 2009) and Siobhán Wills (Wills, 2004, 2009).

2.2.1 Peacekeeping POC: Normative structure

Peacekeeping POC is a conditional obligation. It does not oblige a state or an international body to engage in protection operations. Rather, *peacekeeping POC* requires only that *if* a body does engage in such operations, *then* it is morally bound to perform them to a certain standard. Specifically, a peacekeeping operation with a protection mandate is duty-bound to provide a certain level of basic security to local civilians. An analogy might be drawn to more well-known fiduciary, role-based or special obligations. There is no duty to become a company director, for instance, but *having attained that status* one is in many jurisdictions ineluctably bound by legal constraints regarding one's behaviour in that role.

Wills (2004: 418) sums up the conditional nature of *peacekeeping POC*: "The idea that states or international organisations that intervene on humanitarian grounds do have responsibilities is accepted by the United Nations and Western powers." Many other commentators have similarly asserted such a conditional duty (Breau, 2007), including Kofi Annan (UNSG, 2004). The influential Brahimi Report (2000: 1) declared: "when the United Nations does send its forces to uphold the peace, they must be prepared to confront the lingering forces of war and violence with the ability and determination to defeat them". Recent peacekeeping military doctrines from a variety of countries make similar decrees (Wills, 2004) and the ICRC likewise holds that if the UNSC elects to involve itself in armed intervention, then its duty is to make certain it provides adequate resources and facilities in order to provide protection and remove the underlying causes that were threatening the peace in that case (Ryniker, 2001).

There are three sets of considerations that determine the minimum standards of protection that must be met by a protective peacekeeping operation. The first is that the protective body must fulfil its mission mandate. Thus the abiding focus throughout the *peacekeeping POC* literature is on how UN organs, in concert with other relevant parties, can best expedite UNSC mission mandates. Wills (2009) uses R2P language to distinguish between two broad sorts of protective mandates that apply to peacekeeping missions. The more minimal *general R2P* requires the peacekeeping operation to meet discrete mission objectives and establish sufficient security to allow humanitarian organizations to operate effectively. The more onerous *mission R2P* obtains when the operation's primary specified task is the physical protection of civilians, and requires a more substantial and systematic approach to protection. Since peacekeeping missions are inevitably limited by their capacities and the need to respect the protection responsibilities of the host state, carefully qualified caveats must be placed on POC mandates in both cases. As Holt, Taylor and Kelly (2009: 75) explain:

> The Council has consistently used caveats to offer useful limits for what peacekeeping missions could do for civilian security. Protecting civilians "within capabilities and areas of deployment" and with "respect to the responsibilities" of the host state should help avoid creating unrealistic expectations.

This claim gestures towards the second minimum standard: the seemingly natural expectations of relevant agents as to what counts – irrespective of mission mandate caveats – as an appropriate standard of protection. As innumerable commentators have noted, international observers, UN bodies, host governments and local civilians at risk have expectations about the level of protection that is called for, and which would legitimize the operation in their eyes (Holt, Taylor and Kelly, 2009; Mayall, 2004; UN, 1999; Wills, 2004, 2009). While it is crucial to deal with the local population's unrealistic expectations of protection (DPKO/DFS, 2011), there are limits to how far such expectations can be managed (Durch, 2010). Indeed, peacekeepers themselves have intuitive ideas of what is encompassed within their protective roles (Holt, Taylor and Kelly, 2009; Wills, 2004). The influential Brahimi Report (2000: 11) explicitly linked authorization, principles and expectations:

> Peacekeepers – troops or police – who witness violence against civilians should be presumed to be authorized to stop it, within their means, in support of basic United Nations principles and, as stated in the report of the Independent Inquiry on Rwanda, consistent with "the perception and the expectation of protection created by [the operation's] very presence".

Johnstone and Bah (2007: 3) aptly express this conjunction of expectancy and obligation as a "normative expectation". Doubtless it is a contentious matter exactly what this minimum standard requires, but as a minimum it would include requiring protection from mass violence (including sexual violence) in the immediate vicinity of the peacekeeping operation and not abandoning civilians in the peacekeeping force's immediate care to the depredations of waiting genocidaires.

The third minimum level is more controversial, but is potentially the most significant inasmuch as it seeks to establish a legal standard for *peacekeeping POC*. Apposite here are the positive duties of protection imposed by IHL and international human rights law on states and actors who hold power over a territory. Of particular relevance are the laws of occupation in the Fourth Geneva Convention and earlier instruments. These laws set down basic levels of security that an occupying force must provide for the local population. Such laws have previously been applied by peacekeeping operations, and with some notable success: for example, by Australian peacekeeping forces in Somalia (Wills, 2009). Such laws may be considered an independent and third minimum standard, or alternatively as a way of filling out and delineating the proper content of UN mission mandates and civilian expectations. Even if such laws do not impose weighty duties on peacekeepers, as a general matter IHL still helps to define the scope of POC and the objectives to which best practice should aspire (DPKO/DFS, 2010a; Oswald, Durham and Bates, 2010).

There are thus three (possibly cross-cutting) minimum standards determined by the *peacekeeping POC* principle. An operation fulfils its *peacekeeping POC* duties when it fulfils all three minimum standards.

Before concluding this section, it must be noted that the above-noted *normative* claims can be set aside, leaving *peacekeeping POC* as an instrumental concept. On this footing, *peacekeeping POC* literature becomes essentially a "how-to" manual for effective protection of civilians. Just as a medical treatise on first aid need not adopt normative pretensions (although the healing of others is, by and large, a moral thing to do), so too, the objectives set down by *peacekeeping POC* are goals that can be achieved well, poorly, or not at all. As such the *peacekeeping POC* literature can be read as advice and recommendations on the best ways of succeeding in achieving the goals set forth by *peacekeeping POC* without taking any stance as to whether any moral responsibilities are at stake. This position is implied in the *Building on Brahimi* report (Jones, Gowan and Sherman, 2009: 1), which declares at the outset that "The paper is not normative or prescriptive. It sets out a series of politically charged challenges and choices, but aims to be as objective as possible in its assessments."

2.2.2 Peacekeeping POC: Substance and content

Peacekeeping POC is broad-ranging, both in terms of the aspects of human well-being it aims to promote, and the types of action it might use in order to effect that promotion. *Peacekeeping POC* can thus refer to:

the physical protection of humanitarian personnel, as well as responsibilities such as facilitating the provision of humanitarian assistance, preventing sexual and gender-based violence, assisting in the creation of conditions conducive to the return of internally displaced persons and refugees, and addressing the special protection and assistance needs of children. (Holt, Taylor and Kelly, 2009: 19)

Added to this may be the broader concerns appearing in the Brahimi Report (2000: 8–9) regarding peacebuilding and disarmament, demobilization and reintegration of combatants. Institutional and bureaucratic issues such as improved coordination and cooperation between protection actors are a common target of *peacekeeping POC* reform agendas (Holt and Smith, 2008), while tasks of monitoring, reporting, assessments of risks and mine action can accomplish protection objectives (DPKO/DFS, 2010a: 13). And there are also specifically military understandings of how protection of civilians may be accomplished; while peacekeeping operations are not capable of engaging in the age-old protective practice of war-fighting and defeating evil-doers (Holt and Berkman, 2006), both preventive deployments and the more robust "peace enforcement" operations allow more direct measures to be taken to protect civilians (UNSG, 2009a; Lie, 2008). Within all these categories are myriad military strategies and context-specific factors for best achieving protection results (Holt and Smith, 2008; de Waal, 2007). The DPKO and DFS *Draft Operational Concept* (2010a) groups together these several modes of effecting civilian protection under three tiers: (i) implementation of the political process and peace agreement; (ii) protecting civilians from physical violence; and (iii) establishing a protective environment.

Despite this wide-ranging ambit, Holt, Taylor and Kelly (2009: 6) observe that "in its simplest form, the Council intends the instruction to 'protect civilians' to ensure that peacekeepers help prevent and halt acts of extreme violence". While other tasks and objectives are significant, it is typically upon the provision of basic safety against imminent large-scale violence that a peacekeeping mission is judged (hence the three minimum standards noted in the previous subsection centre on such protection) (DPKO/DFS, 2010a; Oxfam, 2011). The use of force to protect civilians is also one of the most complex and challenging tasks a peacekeeping operation can undertake, so such protection assumes the primary focus in operational documents such as the DPKO/DFS *Lessons Learned Note on POC* (DPKO/DFS, 2010b).

Peacekeeping POC does not itself press bodies such as the UNSC into action (de Carvalho and Lie, 2009): that is the preserve of the following concept, *Security Council POC*. However, *peacekeeping POC* does constrain the actions of bodies such as the UNSC. Demanding, as it does, that if protective action is taken it must be effective, *peacekeeping POC* requires of the UNSC that it be clear in its mandate about what protection activities must be performed, based on an accurate grasp of facts on the ground, and the causes and nature of threats to civilians (Holt and Smith, 2008; OCHA, 2011; UNSG, 2010; UNSC, 2000, 2009). Furthermore, the mandate must be able to be realistically fulfilled, given the resources and authority granted the protective peacekeeping operation – especially the legal capacity to use coercive force, as with a Chapter VII mandate (Brahimi, 2000; Holt and Smith, 2008; Holt, Taylor and Kelly, 2009). In this way the obligations of *peacekeeping POC* prevent the UNSC from ensuring a fit between mandate and resources by simply scaling back the mandate: "situating the estimate", as it is put in military terms (Dallaire, 2003: 56; Williams and Bellamy, 2007: 10). In a classic statement of *peacekeeping POC*, and the conditional duties it imposes on the United Nations, the report on *The Fall of Srebrenica* (UNSG, 1999a: 504) says:

> When the international community makes a solemn promise to safeguard and protect innocent civilians from massacre, then it must be willing to back its promise with the necessary means. Otherwise, it is surely better not to raise hopes and expectations in the first place, and not to impede whatever capability they may be able to muster in their own defence.

Peacekeeping POC prescribes similar constraints on troop-contributing countries. While not itself demanding involvement in the missions, *peacekeeping POC* responsibilities extend into member states, ensuring that the troops and capacities they provide to UN operations are appropriately trained and supported, and not legally restricted by domestic instruments or policies from performing the necessary protection activities (Brahimi, 2000; Holt and Smith, 2008).

In sum, then, *peacekeeping POC* is a conditional duty that falls upon peacekeepers when they undertake peace support operations in a region, requiring that they fulfil basic security and rights protection for local civilians.

2.3 Security Council POC

Security Council POC is the protection principle found in Secretary-General reports to the UNSC, and in the resolutions of the Council itself. While *combatant POC* places mostly *negative* constraints on actors, and *peacekeeping POC* imposes *conditional* duties on actors once they have committed to peace operations, *Security Council POC* serves as a direct reason for *positive* action: for applying diplomatic pressures, sanctions, accountability, monitoring and – ultimately – military force in order to protect civilians from widespread, systemic, human-inflicted suffering. Overall therefore, *Security Council POC* is very broad indeed. Though it would perhaps be too much to claim that *Security Council POC* includes R2P in the specific forms that ICISS or the *World Summit Outcome Document* rendered that principle, thematically it is suggestive of just such a commitment (APCR2P, 2008). However, *Security Council POC* extends well beyond R2P to more wide-ranging issues of civilian targeting in war (concerns with *combatant POC*), effective protection in cases of UNSC-mandated peacekeeping and much more – including concerns for refugees, arms limitations, child recruitment, demilitarization of civilian camps, and so on.

2.3.1 Security Council POC: Legal and institutional fundaments

Security Council POC is grounded legally and institutionally in a variety of ways. Legally, the scope of *Security Council POC* is found in IHL and international human rights law – especially in the context of the rights of women, children and other vulnerable groups (OCHA, 2011; UNSG, 1999b). UNSC involvement in POC matters is most directly grounded through appeal to the Council's mandate under the UN Charter: in Resolutions 1265 (UNSC, 1999) and 1296 (UNSC, 2000) the Council noted that the targeting of civilians could lead to threats to international peace and security, thus moving POC squarely within its purview under Art. 24 of the Charter (UNSG, 1999b). The most recent aide memoire opens with the telling assertion that "Enhancing the protection of civilians in armed conflict is at the core of the work of the United Nations Security Council for the maintenance of peace and security" (OCHA, 2011: 7). Given the United Nations' purpose to affirm fundamental human rights and save successive generations from the scourge of war, *Security Council POC* may be linked more largely with the United Nations' very *raison d'être*. In his first report on POC, Kofi Annan declared that the protection of civilians is "fundamental to the central mandate of the Organization" (UNSG, 1999b: 68). As the Council increasingly framed its decisions and resolutions in terms of POC, the Secretaries-General made due reference to these as precedent (UNSG, 2004). In its biannual Open Debates on the topic, Council members regularly endorse the importance of POC to the function of the Council (UNSC, 2011a).

2.3.2 Security Council POC: Content

The subjects of the Secretary-General's concerns are wide-ranging, including all civilians subject (or, as with refugees, previously subject) to any forms of widespread and systematic armed violence. "Armed conflict" is not viewed narrowly in the reports; Annan (UNSG, 1999b) cited concern with "mutilations in Sierra Leone, genocide in Rwanda, ethnic cleansing in the Balkans or disappearances in Latin America ...". The UNSC followed Annan's lead on the breadth of POC, with both the Council and the Secretary-General making particular reference to IDPs, refugees, women, and children (OCHA, 2011; UNSG, 1999b, 2001; UNSC, 1999). The Secretary-General reports increased their scope over the years as new concerns arose; Ban Ki-moon's 2010 Report discussed the increasing threats posed by improvised explosive devices, drones, and military and security companies, and highlighted further areas of human concern – such as housing, land and property issues (UNSG, 2010).

Security Council POC has a wide arsenal of actions at its disposal to respond to large-scale violence against civilians. Annan's first thematic report on POC included the activities of prevention, peace-making, peacekeeping and peace building, and he explicitly made mention of intervention under Chapter VII of the UN Charter (UNSG, 1999b). One long-standing role of the Council when responding to crises is to call for parties to observe international humanitarian law (i.e. to observe *combatant POC*) and to promote accountability for violations by setting up ad hoc courts or referring situations to the International Criminal Court.[3] *Security Council POC* responses may also include sanctions, arms embargoes, separation of civilians and combatants, ensuring access for humanitarian aid, establishing safe zones, monitoring and reporting, protection of refugees and counteracting hate media (UNSG, 1999b, 2001, 2004). Since 1999, UNSC mandates for peace operations evince a marked progression towards giving POC an increasingly central role, and in authorizing coercive force under Chapter VII of the Charter (OCHA, 2011; UNSG, 2010) – though the case of Darfur is arguably an exception to this trend. A recent instance is the UN-authorized French military action in Côte d'Ivoire against former president Gbagbo (UNSC, 2010; UNSG, 2011). In cases where peacekeeping operations are not possible, *Security Council POC* can authorize more direct and offensive force against regimes – as occurred in Libya (UNSC, 2011c). Further, Council willingness to act is not limited to *reaction*. The UNSC explicitly highlights the significance of preventive measures that may be undertaken by the United Nations, including dispute resolution, preventive military and civilian deployment, and avenues for fact-finding (UNSC, 1999, 2009). The strategic toolkit at the disposal of the UNSC continues to expand. In his last two reports Ban Ki-moon lists strategies including coordination with protective humanitarian actors, involvement with the civilian population's self-protective strategies, facilitating engagement with non-state actors, potential constraints on arms trading, improvements in and expansions of reporting, fact-finding and commissions of enquiry, protection within refugee and IDP camps and the safe return, including to appropriate property/land entitlements, of refugees and IDPs (UNSG, 2009b, 2010).

Arguably, there is one difference between the POC principle used by the Secretary-General and the concept understood by the UNSC, namely, that the Council is more circumspect in its use of terms such as "responsibility". To be sure, the UNSC is straightforward regarding its responsibility for the maintenance of peace and security, but its language regarding its civilian protection agenda is often of "concern", "willingness" and "intentions" rather than "responsibility" or "obligation", and it emphasizes its scope for discretion when it speaks of proceeding on a "case-by-case" basis (Bassiouni, 2009). Still, the Council's commitment to R2P in Resolution 1674 (UNSC, 2006) implies some movement toward shouldering a responsibility in this regard, and its most recent thematic resolution on POC (UNSC, 2009: Preamble) adopts a stronger tone, accepting for instance the "enduring need" for the Council to strengthen the protection of civilians.

2.3.3 Security Council POC's relationship to other POC principles

In some ways, *Security Council POC* functions as a facilitating principle, evincing awareness of all the concerns in the remaining POC principles, and considering any and all ways that the powers of the UN Secretary-General and the UNSC can further these existing POC practices. This facilitative relationship is particularly clear in Ban Ki-moon's 2009 Report, where he describes five "core challenges" to POC (UNSG, 2009b: 26–73). These challenges all involve the enhancement and facilitation of POC practices governed by the other POC principles. Challenges One, Two and Five revolve around IHL and *combatant POC*. Challenge One considers ways that the United Nations can *ex ante* motivate compliance with IHL, while Challenge Two moves to consider how this may be done with specifically non-state actors. Challenge Five focuses on *ex post* IHL accountability, and the various measures available – criminal courts, tribunals, commissions – for ending impunity. Challenge Three focuses on improving and better-resourcing peacekeeping operations (ensuring *peacekeeping POC* commitments are met), while Challenge Four requires ensuring the protection of humanitarian actors and their access to relevant areas (*humanitarian POC*, to which we will presently turn). In this way, *Security Council POC* protects civilians from large-scale assaults to their basic rights, not only by its own direct actions, but also by supporting the protection roles of peacekeepers, combatants and humanitarians.

Some theorists have insisted that "POC addresses the role and function of a peacekeeping *already agreed to* or an on-going mission. As a concept, POC does not provide a rationale for intervention" (de Carvalho and Lie, 2009: 4). Such a stipulation amounts, however, to a categorical denial of the existence of *Security Council POC*, and is simply impossible to align with the actions, resolutions, statements and institutional mandate of the UNSC in particular, and of the United Nations more generally.

2.4 Humanitarian POC

Humanitarian POC is the protection concept at work in humanitarian action. It appears in the work of mandated organizations that have a particular role enshrined in law or institutionalized in the functioning of the United Nations – such as the ICRC and the UNHCR, respectively. It arises also in the work of non-mandated NGOs and charities, such as Oxfam and Amnesty International. While shifts over the years in response to changing geopolitical environments and the perceived needs on the ground of vulnerable persons are discernible in the POC concerns and activities of both sorts of organization, the mandated agencies tend to have a more stable and less flexible POC arsenal, reflective of their fixed legal and institutional status.

The concept has been in flux over the last decade, undergoing considerable and ongoing development. Throughout most of the latter half of the twentieth century, humanitarian protection was understood in two ways. First, "traditional protection" involved – through persuasion, reporting and sometimes (and more controversially) denunciation – advocating on behalf of vulnerable persons, aiding the development of legal instruments and protective policies, and getting states to ratify and act upon such instruments (Forsythe, 2001; O'Callaghan and Pantuliano, 2007). Second, "relief protection" provided sustenance to those in need of it, protecting people's rights to these necessities of life, and by doing so making them less vulnerable to coercion and exploitation by others (Bonwick, 2006; Forsythe, 2001; Shue, 1980). Recently, however, for some organizations the humanitarian understanding of POC has expanded. Confronted with such cases as the placard around the neck of an Iraqi child in 1991 – reading "We don't need food. We need safety" – and the "well-fed dead" of Bosnia, many humanitarian actors have sought to expand and prioritize their protection activities (IASC, 2002; O'Callaghan and Pantuliano, 2007; Slim and Bonwick, 2005). This enlarged concept of civilian protection is *humanitarian POC*.

2.4.1 Humanitarian POC: Normative foundations

The normative foundations for *humanitarian POC* are explicitly rights-based. In 1999 a wide array of humanitarian and human rights agencies brought together by the ICRC reached a consensus that protection includes "all activities aimed at ensuring full respect for the rights of the individual in accordance with the letter and the spirit of the relevant bodies of law, i.e. human rights law, international humanitarian law and refugee law" (Caverzasio, 2001: 19; O'Callaghan and Pantuliano, 2007: 7–8). Consistent with this vision, comprehensive accounts of rights – including rights to safety, dignity and integrity – are invoked as the basis for humanitarian protection (IASC, 2002; Oxfam, 2005; Slim and Bonwick, 2005).

2.4.2 Humanitarian POC: Substance and content

Humanitarian POC responds to threats to rights in the form of large-scale personal violence, deprivation, dispossession and forced or restricted movement. These threats may arise in various contexts, including situations of armed conflict, protracted social conflict, post-conflict, natural disasters and famine (IRRC, 1988; Slim and Bonwick, 2005). Different humanitarian actors will often have different purviews – focusing on different contexts or persons of concern. However, expansion in scope to ensure the protection of hitherto unprotected groups is not uncommon, even by mandated organizations (Forsythe, 2001).

Given the (unarmed, peaceful) actors involved, there is in *humanitarian POC* little or no *direct* prevention or protection – as might require the use of coercive force. Still, imaginative and willing humanitarian actors have steadily unearthed a diverse array of protection activities open to them. A common approach to categorizing these different protection activities is the "egg framework" – so called because the different spheres of action surround a common centre, but repose at different distances from it, hence making the model appear as the cross-section of an egg (IASC, 2002: 11–12; Slim and Bonwick, 2005: 42–43). The most central and immediate type of protection activity – closest to the victims themselves – is *responsive action* aiming to prevent or alleviate threats and harms. Next in centrality and immediacy is *remedial action*, aimed at assisting and supporting people after violations of their rights. Finally, on the outermost shell, there is *environment-building*, where institutions and cultures are structured to increase civilian protection. In each of these three domains different strategies may be employed. The traditional protection activities of advocacy, persuasion, reporting and denunciation, as well as dissemination of information about IHL and human rights law, remain significant in all three spheres, as does the relief protection of providing vital aid (Frohardt, Paul and Minear, 1999; IASC, 2002; Oxfam, 2005; Slim and Bonwick, 2005). But *humanitarian POC* incorporates a raft of further strategies, including:[4]

- the strategic and proactive use of the *presence* of humanitarian actors, including accompaniment of civilians, as a way of discouraging attacks;
- the support and *empowering of local populations* in crafting and executing strategies to avoid and resist threats, and minimize risks in daily activities;
- the *creation of safe areas* (where safety is created through secrecy or an unwillingness of belligerents to brazenly attack humanitarian buildings or areas);
- the creation and dissemination of *information*, especially regarding early warning, areas of safety or danger, conditions for return of refugees and IDPs, location of resources, and so on;
- aiding in the *transport or evacuation* of civilian populations away from threats, or back to their (now safe) homes;
- *engagement with all parties* to the conflict, at all levels of authority, aiming to persuade actors to temper violence against civilians and to locate and empower those individuals most amenable to doing so;
- the *structure and design* of aid facilities and programmes to enhance civilian safety, including by the strategic distribution of humanitarian assistance, well-digging, providing fuel-efficient stoves and so on.

A further element of *humanitarian POC* is to ensure that humanitarian activities, whether of fact-finding, assistance in relocation, negotiating, providing provisions and the like, are not themselves contributing to – or are not capable of being manipulated in ways that lead them to contribute to – the harm of civilians (Oxfam, 2005; Slim and Bonwick, 2005). Such unwanted consequences may occur in many ways – by legitimating the political status of evil-doers, by motivating harmful activities as a way of ensuring provision and control of aid, by reducing community empowerment to find their own solutions, and so on. Whether it requires proactive new strategies, or revisiting familiar ones, Frohardt, Paul and Minear (1999: 55) note that effective protection activities are all:

> based upon concepts that have been applied elsewhere: international presence, clear-eyed analysis of the perpetrators' modus operandi, anticipation of vulnerability to abuse, issuance of clear instructions and guidelines, and education of vulnerable populations in self-protection and risk avoidance.

As noted earlier, the variation and flux within *humanitarian POC* differentiate it from more stable and determinate principles such as *peacekeeping POC* and *combatant POC*. One important reason for this variation is the different constraints on action adopted by different humanitarian organizations. Some, for instance, cleave to strong principles of neutrality and impartiality which require that they do not condemn parties to a conflict, or even make public their own reports on that party's (lack of) conformance to IHL. Others find public condemnations worth employing. Arguably, variation on such matters is itself helpful to the protection cause, as it allows some humanitarian organizations to speak out and raise awareness of risks to civilians while others are able to continue working in the theatre because of their policy of silence.

2.5 Conclusion

This chapter has detailed the protection of civilians as seen through the perspectives of four different types of actor – the UNSC and Secretariat, peacekeepers, combatants and humanitarians. Across all these perspectives, the core concerns of POC remain the same – the protection of the basic rights of non-combatants, as specified in IHL, from threats caused by large-scale violence. However, each of these four types of actor has different capacities and limitations that they each must assimilate with their commitment to protect. These factors give rise, this chapter has argued, to four distinct concepts of POC: the primarily negative duties of *combatant POC*, the role-based responsibilities of *peacekeeping POC*, the aspirational and universal concerns of *Security Council POC*, and the ever-growing toolkit of pacific strategies at work in *humanitarian POC*.

Notes

1. See Downes (2008), Walzer (2000), Henckaerts (2005: 203–204) and Barber (2009).
2. See Wills (2004, 2009). This question is taken up later in this volume in the chapter by Durham and Wynn-Pope.
3. Ad hoc courts were set up for the former Yugoslavia (UNSC, 1993) and Rwanda (UNSC, 1994). Referrals to the ICC have occurred, e.g. in Darfur (UNSC, 2005) and Libya (UNSC, 2011b).
4. This list takes strategies from Slim and Bonwick (2005), Frohardt, Paul and Minear (1999), Oxfam (2005), Oxfam (2009), Bonwick (2006), Forsythe (2001), O'Callaghan and Pantuliano (2007), IASC (2002) and Mahony (2006).

REFERENCES

APCR2P (2008) *The Responsibility to Protect and the Protection of Civilians: Asia-Pacific in the Security Council.* Brisbane: Asia Pacific Centre for the Responsibility to Protect.

Barber, Rebecca (2009) "Facilitating Humanitarian Assistance in International Humanitarian and Human Rights Law", *International Review of the Red Cross* 91(874): 371–397.

Barbour, Brian and Brian Gorlick (2008) "Embracing the 'Responsibility to Protect': A Repertoire of Measures Including Asylum for Potential Victims", *International Journal of Refugee Law* 20(4): 533–566.

Bassiouni, Cherif (2009) "Advancing the Responsibility to Protect through International Criminal Justice", in R. H. Cooper and J. V. Kohler, eds. *Responsibility to Protect: The Global Moral Compact for the 21st Century*. New York: Palgrave Macmillan.

Bellamy, Alex (2009) *Responsibility to Protect: The Global Effort to End Mass Atrocities*. Cambridge: Polity.

Bonwick, Andrew (2006) "Who Really Protects Civilians?", *Development in Practice* 16(3): 270–277.

Brahimi, Lakhdar (2000) *Report of the Panel on UN Peace Operations*, A/44/305-S/2000/809, 21 August 2000.

Breau, Susan (2007) "The Impact of the Responsibility to Protect on Peacekeeping", *Journal of Conflict and Security Law* 11(3): 429–464.

Caverzasio, S. G. (2001) *Strengthening Protection in War: A Search for Professional Standards*. Geneva: International Committee of the Red Cross.

Dallaire, Romeo (2003) *Shake Hands with the Devil: The Failure of Humanity in Rwanda*. New York: Carroll & Graf.

de Carvalho, Benjamin and Jon H. S. Lie (2009) *Challenges to Implementing the Protection of Civilians Agenda*, NUPI Report 2009, May, 2009.

de Waal, Alex (2007) "Darfur and the Failure of the Responsibility to Protect", *International Affairs* 83(6): 1039–1054.

Downes, Alexander (2008) *Targeting Civilians in War*. London: Cornell University Press.

DPKO (2008) *The Capstone Doctrine: United Nations Peacekeeping Operations Principles and Guidelines*, 18 January 2008.

DPKO (2009) *A New Partnership Agenda: Charting a New Horizon for UN Peacekeeping*, July, 2009.

DPKO/DFS (2010a) *Draft Operational Concept on the Protection of Civilians in United Nations Peacekeeping Operations*, 2010.

DPKO/DFS (2010b) *Lessons Learned Note on the Protection of Civilians in United Nations Peacekeeping Operations: Dilemmas, Emerging Practices and Lessons Learned*, 2010.

DPKO/DFS (2011) *Framework for Drafting Comprehensive Protection of Civilians Strategies in UN Peacekeeping Operations*, 20 January 2011.

Durch, William J. (2010) "Cross-Cutting Issues in Protection of Civilians for UN Peace Operations", *Challenges of Protecting Civilians in Multidimensional Peace Operations*. Canberra: International Forum for the Challenges of Peace Operations. 27–29 April, 2010.

Durham, Helen (2008) "The Laws of War and Traditional Cultures: A Case Study of the Pacific Region", *Commonwealth Law Bulletin* 34(4): 833–841.

Focarelli, Carlo (2010) "Common Article 1 of the 1949 Geneva Conventions: A Soap Bubble?", *European Journal of International Law* 21(1): 125–171.

Forsythe, David P. (2001) "Humanitarian Protection: The International Committee of the Red Cross and the United Nations High Commissioner for Refugees", *International Review of the Red Cross* 843: 675–697.

Frohardt, Mark, Diane Paul and Larry Minear (1999) *Protecting Human Rights: The Challenge to Humanitarian Organizations, Occasional Papers 35*. Providence, RI: The Watson Institute.

GCR2P (2011) *Policy Brief: The Relationship between the Responsibility to Protect and the Protection of Civilians in Armed Conflict (Update)*, Global Centre for the Responsibility to Protect, 9 May 2011.

Henckaerts, Jean-Marie (2005) "Study on Customary International Humanitarian Law: A Contribution to the Understanding and Respect for the Rule of Law in Armed Conflict", *International Review of the Red Cross* 87(857): 175–212.

Henckaerts, Jean-Marie and Louise Doswald-Becks (2005) *International Committee of the Red Cross: Customary International Humanitarian Law*. New York: Cambridge University Press.

Holt, Victoria, and Tobias Berkman (2006) *The Impossible Mandate? Military Preparedness, the Responsibility to Protect and Modern Peace Operations*. Washington: The Henry L. Stimson Center.

Holt, Victoria, and Joshua Smith (2008) *Halting Widespread or Systematic Attacks on Civilians: Military Strategies & Operational Concepts*. Washington: Henry L. Stimson Center.

Holt, Victoria, Glyn Taylor and Max Kelly (2009) *Protecting Civilians in the Context of UN Peacekeeping Operations: Successes, Setbacks and Remaining Challenges*. New York: DPKO, UNOCHA.

IASC, Inter-Agency Standing Committee (2002) *Growing the Sheltering Tree: Protecting Rights through Humanitarian Action, Programmes and Practice Gathered from the Field*. Geneva: UNICEF.

ICRC (1949) *Convention (IV) Relative to the Protection of Civilian Persons in Time of War*. Geneva. 12 August 1949.

ICRC (1977) *Protocol Additional to the Geneva Conventions of 12 August 1949, and Relating to the Protection of Victims of Non-International Armed Conflicts (Protocol II)*. Geneva: International Committee of the Red Cross. 8 June 1977.

International Panel (2000) *Rwanda: The Preventable Genocide: Special Report of the International Panel of Eminent Personalities to Investigate the 1994 Genocide in Rwanda and the Surrounding Events*, 7 July 2000.

IRRC (1988) "ICRC Protection and Assistance Activities in Situations Not Covered by International Humanitarian Law", *International Review of the Red Cross* 262: 9–37.

Johnstone, Ian, and Alhaji Bah (2007) *Peacekeeping in Sudan: The Dynamics of Protection, Partnerships and Inclusive Politics*. Vol. Occasional Paper. New York: NYU Center on International Cooperation.

Jones, Bruce, Richard Gowan and Jake Sherman (2009) *Building on Brahimi: Peacekeeping in an Era of Strategic Uncertainty*. New York: NYU Center on International Cooperation.

LaeGreid, Turid (2008) Protecting Civilians from Harm: A Humanitarian Perspective, NUPI Report No. 6 2008.

Lie, Jon H. S. (2008) *Protection of Civilians, the Responsibility to Protect and Peace Operations*, NUPI Report No. 4, 2008.

Mahony, Liam (2006) *Proactive Presence: Field Strategies for Civilian Protection*. Geneva: Centre for Humanitarian Dialogue.

Mayall, James (2004) "Humanitarian Intervention and International Society: Lessons from Africa", in Jennifer Welsh, ed. *Humanitarian Intervention and International Relations*. Oxford: Oxford University Press, 120–141.

O'Callaghan, Sorcha, and Sara Pantuliano (2007) *Protective Action: Incorporating Civilian Protection into Humanitarian Response*, HPG Report 26, December 2007.

OCHA (2010) *OCHA on Message: Protection*, Version 1, June 2010.

OCHA (2011) *Aide Memoire: For the Consideration of Issues Pertaining to the Protection of Civilians in Armed Conflict*. 4th ed. New York: United Nations.

Oswald, Bruce, Helen Durham and Adrian Bates (2010) *Documents on the Law of UN Peace Operations*. New York: Oxford University Press.

Oxfam (2005) *Protection into Practice*. Oxford: Oxfam.

Oxfam (2009) *Improving the Safety of Civilians: A Protection Training Pack*.

Oxfam (2011) *"We Are Entirely Exploitable": The Lack of Protection for Civilians in Eastern DRC*, Oxfam Briefing Note, 28 July 2011.

Popovski, Vesselin, Gregory Reichberg and Nicholas Turner, eds. (2009) *World Religions and the Norms of War*. New York: United Nations University Press.

Ryniker, Anne (2001) "The ICRC's Position on 'Humanitarian Intervention'," *International Review of the Red Cross* 482: 527–532.

Shue, Henry (1980) *Basic Rights: Subsistence, Affluence and US Foreign Policy*. Princeton, NJ: Princeton University Press.

Slim, Hugo (2008) *Killing Civilians: Method, Madness, and Morality in War*. New York: Columbia University Press.

Slim, Hugo, and Andrew Bonwick (2005) *Protection: An ALNAP Guide for Humanitarian Agencies*. London: Overseas Development Institute.

UN (1999) *Report of the Independent Inquiry into the Actions of the United Nations During the 1994 Genocide in Rwanda*, S/1999/1257/Annex, 16 December 1999.

UNSC (1993) *UN Security Council Resolution 827 (1993): Tribunal (Former Yugoslavia)*, S/RES/827, 25 May 1993.

UNSC (1994) *UN Security Council Resolution 955(1994): Establishment of an International Tribunal and Adoption of the Statute of the Tribunal*, S/RES/955, 8 November 1994.

UNSC (1999) *UN Security Council Resolution 1265 (1999): Protection of Civilians in Armed Conflict*, S/RES/1265, 17 September 1999.

UNSC (2000) *UN Security Council Resolution 1296 (2000): Protection of Civilians in Armed Conflict*, S/RES/1296, 19 April 2000.

UNSC (2005) *UN Security Council Resolution 1593 (2005): Reports of the Secretary-General on the Sudan*, S/RES/1593, 31 March 2005.

UNSC (2006) *UN Security Council Resolution 1674 (2006): Protection of Civilians in Armed Conflict*, S/RES/1674, 28 April 2006.

UNSC (2009) *UN Security Council Resolution 1894 (2009): Protection of Civilians in Armed Conflict,* S/RES/1894, 11 November 2009.

UNSC (2010) *UN Security Council Resolution 1933 (2010): The Situation in Côte d'Ivoire,* S/RES/1933, 30 June 2010.

UNSC (2011a) November 2011 Meeting: Protection of Civilians in Armed Conflict, S/PV.6650, 9 November 2011.

UNSC (2011b) *UN Security Council Resolution 1970 (2011): Peace and Security in Africa,* S/RES/1970, 26 February 2011.

UNSC (2011c) *UN Security Council Resolution 1973 (2011): The Situation in Libya,* S/RES/1973, 17 March 2011.

UNSG (1999a) *Report of the Secretary General Pursuant to General Assembly Resolution 53/55: The Fall of Srebrenica,* A/54/549, 15 November 1999.

UNSG (1999b) *Report to the Security Council on the Protection of Civilians in Armed Conflict,* S/1999/957, 8 September 1999.

UNSG (2001) *Report of the Secretary-General to the Security Council on the Protection of Civilians in Armed Conflict,* S/2001/331, 30 March 2001.

UNSG (2004) *Report of the Secretary-General to the Security Council on the Protection of Civilians in Armed Conflict,* S/2004/431, 28 May 2004.

UNSG (2009a) *Report of the Secretary-General: Implementing the Responsibility to Protect,* A/63/677, 12 January 2009.

UNSG (2009b) *Report of the Secretary-General to the Security Council on the Protection of Civilians in Armed Conflict,* S/2009/277, 29 May 2009.

UNSG (2010) *Report to the Security Council on the Protection of Civilians in Armed Conflict,* S/2010/579, 11 November 2010.

UNSG (2011) "Statement by the Secretary-General on the Situation in Côte d'Ivoire", 4 April, 2011. [Online] Available at: ⟨http://www.un.org/apps/sg/sgstats.asp?nid=5185#⟩.

Walzer, Michael (2000) *Just and Unjust Wars: A Moral Argument with Historical Illustrations.* 3rd ed. New York: Basic Books.

Williams, Paul, and Alex Bellamy (2007) "Contemporary Peace Operations: Four Challenges for the Brahimi Paradigm", *International Peacekeeping* 11(1): 1–28.

Wills, Siobhán (2004) "Military Interventions on Behalf of Vulnerable Populations: The Legal Responsibilities of States and International Organizations Engaged in Peace Support Operations", *Journal of Conflict and Security Law* 9(3): 387–418.

Wills, Siobhán (2009) *Protecting Civilians: The Obligations of Peacekeepers.* Oxford: Oxford University Press.

3

The responsibility to protect and the protection of civilians in armed conflict: Overlap and contrast

Hugh Breakey

This chapter investigates the overlap and contrast between the responsibility to protect (R2P) and the protection of civilians (POC), keeping in mind the different versions of these principles detailed in the preceding two chapters: the three pillars of R2P and the four POC concepts. Section 3.1 affirms two widely acknowledged differences between R2P and POC – R2P's narrow scope and deep response – before section 3.2 outlines two important similarities between them: their shared basis in human rights and the cross-cutting parallels between R2P pillars and POC concepts. Section 3.3 turns to more controversial terrain. It argues that the alleged limitation of POC to "armed conflict" is far less significant than commonly supposed and that POC's status as a humanitarian principle – with primary concerns for impartiality and neutrality – is not fully applicable to all POC concepts. Subsection 3.3.3 applies Abbott and Snidal's analytic categorization of soft laws to R2P and POC, illustrating the similarities and differences between each of the principles. Section 3.4 assesses the usefulness of differentiating peacekeeping operations (PKOs) on the basis of R2P and POC, and advances one model of how this may be done.

I list below the seven principles under consideration.

R2P Pillar One: Pillar One describes the protection duties of a state to its own population, requiring that it not commit (or facilitate the commission of) atrocity crimes upon them, and that it protect them against atrocities committed by third parties.

Norms of protection: Responsibility to protect, protection of civilians and their interaction,
Francis, Popovski and Sampford (eds),
United Nations University Press, 2012, ISBN 978-92-808-1218-3

R2P Pillar Two: Pillar Two outlines the responsibilities of the international community to help states that are willing but unable to meet their Pillar One protection responsibilities to build capacities and institutions enabling them to do so.

R2P Pillar Three: Pillar Three outlines the responsibilities of the international community to use both military and non-military measures against states that are manifestly failing in their Pillar One responsibilities, in order to protect civilians under threat of atrocity crimes. At the limit this may include military intervention for protective purposes.

Combatant POC: Dictated primarily by the Geneva Conventions and Additional Protocols, the legal obligations of *combatant POC* constrain the actions, weapons and tactics used in armed conflicts in order to ensure that combatants do not harm or unduly risk harm to civilians and soldiers *hors de combat.*

Peacekeeping POC: This principle requires PKOs with protection mandates to ensure a reasonable level of protection from mass violence (commensurate with the operation's capacities and mandate) to local civilians, and to work with the host state towards a more peaceful and secure larger environment.

Security Council POC: The broad concept of *Security Council POC* presents as a substantial but unspecified requirement to the UN Security Council (UNSC) and Secretariat to respond, through prevention, response and capacity-building, to widespread, systemic human-inflicted suffering.

Humanitarian POC: Used by humanitarian actors such as the Red Cross and Oxfam, *humanitarian POC* details how civilians may be protected from large-scale violence through exclusively non-military measures such as advocacy, relief, visitation, denunciation of rights violations and war crimes, ensuring a humanitarian presence, providing information to civilians on areas of risk and safety, and so on.

To anticipate one recurrent conclusion of the forthcoming argument, when making comparisons between R2P and POC it is important to be clear about which pillar of R2P, or which of the four POC concepts, is under consideration. This is because the properties of each distinct principle can be quite different, and it is an error to suppose that a property of one POC principle, for instance, will be shared by all members of the POC family. For example, R2P is widely seen to be intrinsically more controversial than POC. But this claim depends pivotally on which POC principle we are considering. None of the concepts of *combatant POC, peacekeeping POC* or *humanitarian POC* can be associated with the highly contentious "right of humanitarian intervention". Indeed, one can be a firm advocate of these forms of civilian protection while strongly adhering to the international principle of non-interference – an example is Lakhdar Brahimi, who penned the seminal text on *peacekeeping POC*, yet was wary of military interventions for protective purposes (Bellamy, 2009). *Security Council POC*, on the other hand, can involve the use of non-consensual measures and even military force against unwilling states, as was seen recently in UNSC Resolution 1973 and the subsequent direct military action taken against Libya (UNSC, 2011c). *Security Council POC* is thus worthy of the same level of controversy in this connection as R2P's third pillar.

3.1 Two differences

This section considers two differences between R2P and POC – R2P's narrow scope and its depth of response.

3.1.1 R2P is narrow in scope – applying only to the four atrocity crimes

R2P, as authoritatively expressed in the 2005 *World Summit Outcome Document* (WSOD), is strictly limited to the four "atrocity crimes" of genocide, crimes against humanity, war crimes and ethnic cleansing (UNGA, 2005: 148–149). All three pillars of R2P therefore have a narrow scope, applying only in relation to these four specific crimes, particularly as they occur in the context of widespread violence and civil unrest (Scheffer, 2009). POC, as many commentators have observed, has a broader ambit (GCR2P, 2011; Lie, 2008; Strauss, 2009). All four POC principles respond not only to the threats to life and limb characterized by atrocity crimes, but also to the less extreme threats posed by the targeting of civilians in war, sexual assault and exploitation, forced displacement, application of starvation strategies, the deliberate blocking of urgent humanitarian aid and more (Brahimi, 2000; OCHA, 2011; UNSC, 1999). *Combatant POC* is particularly broad in scope, prohibiting even isolated and discrete actions performed by small groups and even individuals acting alone (Henckaerts, 2005). In contrast, the remaining POC concepts place emphasis on large-scale and systemic violations of rights.

This difference in scope is in many ways the pivotal distinction between R2P and POC; it is the crux that shapes their other differences. Because R2P is narrower in scope, focusing only upon the most egregious violations of basic bodily rights, the responses it demands can be more determinate, more demanding and more peremptory.

3.1.2 R2P is deep in response – the preventive dimension

As Ban Ki-moon noted in his 2009 Report to the Security Council, R2P is "narrow and deep" (UNSG, 2009: 10(c)). That is, while its *scope* is tightly focused on the four atrocity crimes, the *responses* it can call for are diverse and multifaceted. One particular way this is so is in R2P's preventive dimension – that is, its focus on preventing atrocity crimes from happening in the first place. To be sure, POC is not disinterested in prevention. After all, *combatant POC* plainly includes duties that contribute to a larger environment that itself facilitates civilian security – such as through requirements that soldiers identify themselves as combatants and do not use human shields. Likewise *peacekeeping POC* imposes tasks on peacekeepers to prevent conflict in several ways, including by monitoring ceasefires and demilitarizing safe zones, as well as facilitating political processes leading to a larger peace. *Security Council POC* has an even wider arsenal of actions that can be used to prevent conflicts escalating, and the outermost layer of *humanitarian POC's* "egg model" includes myriad environment-building actions aimed to indirectly protect civilians (IASC, 2002: 11–12). All that said, however, since the very beginnings of R2P there has been a consistent awareness that when it comes to atrocity crimes, prevention is better than reaction (ICISS, 2001). This feature of R2P was built upon by Ban Ki-moon in his "Three Pillars" approach to R2P, where only one part of the Third Pillar deals with response; the remaining pillars of R2P are centrally concerned with prevention. In that report the Secretary-General (UNSG, 2009) listed a variety of measures required for the prevention of R2P crimes, and he expanded on one of these in particular – early warning capacities – in his 2010 Report (UNSG, 2010). Arguably, the narrowness of scope of R2P makes such prevention viable, at least in comparison to POC, where the prevention of armed conflict in general is too broad an aspiration to give rise to determinate and tractable tasks.[1]

3.2 Two important similarities

3.2.1 R2P, POC and human rights

Both R2P and POC share a basis in human rights. Regarding R2P, the original ICISS report (2001) emphasized the central role human rights play in justifying R2P. In particular, the refiguring of "sovereignty as control" to "sovereignty as responsibility" rejects the idea that sovereignty holds any intrinsic value in itself (2001: 14). Instead, sovereignty is justified only insofar as it is an effective tool for the protection of the basic human rights of its population. While the ICISS report drew upon Francis Deng's (1993) work on internally displaced persons (IDPs) that gave rise to the contemporary vision of "sovereignty as responsibility", in terms of political theory the idea is much older, and is tightly linked to human rights. As noted in Chapter 1, the great contract theorists of the early Enlightenment – Hobbes, Rousseau, Kant and Locke – put forward just this view of the state, understanding it as being formed instrumentally by the agreement of free persons as a crucial vehicle for protecting their prior natural rights (Locke, 1947; Ward, 2006). The 2005 *World Summit Outcome Document* followed suit on this matter, placing its treatment of R2P under the rubric of human rights rather than security.

Regarding POC, the influential International Committee of the Red Cross (ICRC) definition of protection – used by the Office for the Coordination of Humanitarian Affairs (OCHA, 2010) and endorsed by the Inter-Agency Standing Committee (IASC, 2002) – places human rights at its centre, holding protection to be "all activities aimed at obtaining full respect for the rights of the individual in accordance with the letter and spirit of the relevant bodies of law" (Caverzasio, 2001: 19). Similarly, Secretary-General reports and Security Council resolutions on the protection of civilians frequently appeal to rights and human rights law, especially in the context of women, children and other vulnerable groups (OCHA, 2011; UNSG, 1999b). For its part *combatant POC* developed primarily out of the Just War theory of natural law – the tradition that itself set the groundwork for early natural rights thought, especially that of influential theorists such as John Locke (Buckle, 1991; Mitsis, 2003).

POC and R2P thus have a shared basis in human rights and, as we will see in the next section, this gives rise to a set of cross-cutting similarities between their various parts.

3.2.2 Cross-cutting parallels between the three pillars of R2P and the four principles of POC

Different normative principles can aim to protect human rights in different ways. They may do so, (i) by prohibiting direct violations of the right, (ii) by requiring protection of the right against direct violations from third parties and (iii) by requiring agents to contribute to the building of social institutions and larger structural environments that indirectly protect the right (CESCR, 1999; IASC, 2002; Shue, 1980). The three pillars of R2P can be mapped onto this structure, with R2P Pillar One centrally concerned with prohibitions on harm, while Pillars Two and Three focus on institution-building and (though more rarely) direct protection against third-party violation, depending on context. Given that POC, like R2P, is also based on the protection of human rights, it will come as no surprise that its four principles similarly use these three distinct means of protection. While each of the four principles has elements that work in each category of obligations, *combatant POC* is centrally concerned with prohibitions on direct rights violations. *Humanitarian POC* places indirect protection and environment-shaping at the centre of its area of concern. Both *peacekeeping POC* and *Security Council POC* concern themselves with direct protection against third-party violations and with structural protections through institution-building.

Interestingly, this means that different elements of R2P and POC have strong cross-cutting similarities. For instance, in terms of the nature of the obligations they impose, R2P Pillar One and *combatant POC* have more in common with each other than with the other principles in their immediate rubric. Both centre on prohibitions on harming civilians – on "thou shalt nots": agent-centred, deontological, negative obligations, in technical terms. Both are constituted in international law, with *combatant POC* determined by international humanitarian law (IHL) and R2P Pillar One by IHL, international human rights law, occupation law and the Genocide Convention (Stahn, 2007). Likewise, there are structural parallels between R2P Pillar Three and *Security Council POC*, with both dealing with the various Security Council options in response to widespread and systemic violence, particularly state-sponsored violence, and dealing in depth with ways the Security Council can achieve direct protection of rights against third-party threats. There are also strong links between R2P Pillar Two and *peacekeeping POC* (and to some extent *humanitarian POC*), as these principles put forward positive duties to directly and indirectly protect civilians from assault in contexts where there is (at least some) state consent. These cross-cutting similarities are after all to be expected; as each larger principle (R2P and POC) establishes rights-promoting duties on similar agents with similar means and objectives, it is not surprising that parallels across the principles arise.

Despite these cross-cutting similarities, grouping the principles under the larger rubrics R2P and POC makes sense. As noted in section 3.1, it is the initial *scope* that is the crux of each rights-respecting principle, and determines the ambit and nature of the responses that may be deployed to protect the right from the threats described in its scope.

3.3 Controversial aspects

3.3.1 POC is narrower than R2P as it applies only to situations of armed conflict

One of the most widely asserted distinctions drawn between R2P and POC is that the latter only applies in the context of armed conflict (GCR2P, 2011; Strauss, 2009). One might think the constraint here is not just obvious but apodictic; after all, the acronym POC usually stands in for the longer phrase "the protection of civilians *in armed conflict*". R2P, on the other hand, contains no such restraint – potentially allowing it to have a broader ambit. Moreover, this enlarged purview of R2P may be important, allowing it to cover widespread and systemic violence as it occurs in the context of civil unrest rather than traditional armed conflict, for example, in crucial cases like the early stages of the genocides in Rwanda and Darfur, or of state repression that reaches the pitch of atrocity.

However, there is controversy here, and any straightforward distinction between the principles on this basis is difficult to substantiate. To be sure, the scope of *combatant POC*, as defined in the Geneva Conventions and Additional Protocols (note especially Protocol II, Art. 1(2)), is indeed limited to armed conflict. Even here, however, there are complexities. First, Common Article Three of the Conventions is widely understood to contain a hard core of fundamental rights that, in overlapping the non-derogable human rights norms, constitutes a "minimum standard" of humanitarian treatment that has widespread application, even to civil strife outside of armed conflict (Gasser, 1988; *IRRC*, 1988b). Second, the requirements for violence to be characterized as "armed conflict" are not especially demanding, requiring only the presence of two sides that each hold territory and have a military command structure, the involvement of UN actors in the fighting (e.g. peacekeepers acting in defence of their mandate) or the presence of international elements using force (Kolb and Hyde, 2008). On these bases, the situations of Rwanda, Srebrenica, Darfur and the Democratic Republic of Congo (DRC) all count as armed conflicts. Third, pursuant to Common Article Two of the Geneva Conventions, any even partial occupation of territory by an external force triggers application of the Conventions, even if there is no armed resistance to that occupation. In all, with the possible exception of Common Article Three, *combatant POC* is indeed limited in law to situations of armed conflict and occupation, but the definitions of these are not demanding.

When attention is turned to the three remaining POC principles, however, there is no such limitation. For their part, peacekeeping forces can operate in situations where there is no ongoing armed conflict, for instance as part of a preventive deployment, or when a situation has stabilized as part of a peace agreement. While such peacekeepers will be limited by their means and mandate, there is no provision to be found in the peacekeeping literature or in Council resolutions that they should not protect endangered civilians unless the larger situation amounts to armed conflict. To the contrary, the Brahimi Report (2000: 11) declares without qualification:

Peacekeepers – troops or police – who witness violence against civilians should be presumed to be authorized to stop it, within their means, in support of basic United Nations principles and, as stated in the report of the Independent Inquiry on Rwanda, consistent with "the perception and the expectation of protection created by [an operation's] very presence".

William Durch (2010: 2) speaks directly to the issue in question, holding that *peacekeeper POC* applies to a "broad spectrum of circumstances, including generalized violence and post-conflict situations that may not qualify as 'armed conflict'."

This same broad scope applies to *Security Council POC*. The Secretary-General (1999b: 2) asserted the breadth of this principle in his very first report to the Council on POC, declaring it to include "mutilations in Sierra Leone, genocide in Rwanda, ethnic cleansing in the Balkans or disappearances in Latin America". For its part, the Security Council's avowed rationale for concerning itself with civilian protection – that is, the capacity of volatile situations to threaten international peace and security (UNSC, 1999, 2000) – is plainly not limited to traditional armed conflict. Rwanda serves as an all-too-illustrative example of the capacity of atrocity crimes to spill over and foment conflict in neighbouring countries. Consistent with this rationale, in affirming its intention to ensure that peacekeeping missions would be given sufficient resources and mandates to protect civilians, the UNSC (2000: 13) in Resolution 1296 spoke simply of protecting civilians under "imminent threat of physical danger", with no provision regarding armed conflict. Since then the Council has been willing to take action in regions on the basis of civilian protection – such as Darfur and the DRC – without evincing any regard to whether such regions were experiencing violent civil unrest rather than "armed conflict" legally construed. Even state repression can count as a POC concern for the Council, if it rises to a sufficient threshold of violence. In the November 2011 Council Open Debate on POC (UNSC, 2011b), seven Council members included Syria as a prime POC concern, as did the UN High Commissioner for Human Rights and the Assistant Secretary-General for Humanitarian Affairs who briefed the Council, despite the fact that the Syrian crisis was understood to be one of state repression and not armed conflict. While there was of course dispute as to whether Syria should be an object of Council action, no Council member objected to Syria's inclusion on the basis of it not being a situation of armed conflict. Indeed, Gabon and Colombia explicitly noted the importance of protecting civilians in peacetime and in situations of violent and systematic state repression respectively, while Brazil (UNSC, 2011b: 14–15, 25) averred that "there is the imperative need to prevent violence against civilians in the conduct of hostilities – I would even venture to say to prevent violence against non-combatants in general ...". In the previous meeting in May, Liechtenstein (UNSC, 2011a: 33) had expressly stated that the question of when an armed conflict begins "has no bearing on whether action is needed".

Finally, in *humanitarian POC* the concern is with large-scale personal violence, deprivation, dispossession and displacement, irrespective of whether these occur in traditional armed conflict, post-conflict, or merely in the context of widespread civil strife (Slim and Bonwick, 2005). The ICRC, in particular, could not be more emphatic that their humanitarian purview and their traditional protection activities extend beyond armed conflict and into "internal disturbances and tensions" (*IRRC*, 1988a, 1988b). Their 2008 definition of protection holds that:

> For the ICRC, protection, in the broadest sense, aims to ensure that authorities and other actors respect their obligations and the rights of individuals in order to preserve the lives, security, physical and moral integrity and dignity of those affected by armed conflicts *and/or other situations of violence*. [Emphasis added] (ICRC, 2008: 9)

In all, the qualification regarding "armed conflict" may limit *combatant POC* from applying to cases such as state repression where R2P applies, but the remaining POC principles will apply in all cases where R2P atrocity crimes are being committed.

3.3.2 *POC is a humanitarian principle, evincing neutrality and impartiality*

In a similar vein to the limitation of "armed conflict", it is sometimes claimed that POC is a humanitarian principle, governed by traditional humanitarian constraints such as neutrality and impartiality (OCHA, 2011; Strauss, 2009). R2P, on the other hand, necessarily involves taking a stand against evil-doers, and so is not neutral in this sense.

Again, however, it is not easy to distinguish ways in which POC is neutral or impartial and R2P is not. The laws of *combatant POC*, for example, apply impartially to all combatants, but in the same way the prohibitions of R2P Pillar One apply impartially to all state sovereigns and authorities. Likewise, *Security Council POC* parallels R2P Pillar Three in prescribing a deliberate and determined stand against aggressors against civilians – as recent examples in Libya and Côte D'Ivoire attest. The question of the neutrality and impartiality of *peacekeeping POC* and *humanitarian POC* are, however, a little more subtle, and must be dealt with in turn.

As regards *peacekeeping POC*, in his 1999 report on the fall of Srebrenica, the Secretary-General explicitly decried the errors of judgement
"rooted in a philosophy of impartiality and non-violence wholly unsuited
to the conflict in Bosnia" (1999a: 499). The following year the Brahimi
Report (2000: 9) followed suit, advancing a non-traditional understanding
of impartiality:

> Impartiality for such operations must therefore mean adherence to the princi-
> ples of the Charter and to the objectives of a mandate that is rooted in those
> Charter principles. Such impartiality is not the same as neutrality or equal
> treatment of all parties in all cases for all time, which can amount to a policy of
> appeasement.

Many other influential authors explicitly distance PKOs from the neutrality prized by humanitarian actors (DPKO/DFS, 2008; Holt and Berkman, 2006). In the last analysis, while it is true that PKOs will often be
required to ensure military forces on the ground do not perceive and
treat them as a "third belligerent" – as peacekeepers cannot fight wars –
it is equally true that R2P Pillar Two missions (see section 3.4 below) will
have to factor in this constraint.

Turning to *humanitarian POC*, the situation is more complex again.
Humanitarian neutrality may refer to: (i) *non-discrimination* in who will
receive relief, assistance and humanitarian protection; (ii) not being an
agent of state policy or of one particular political or religious stand-
point; (iii) not *contributing to* one military-political outcome rather than
another; and/or (iv) *not speaking out* against a particular side on the
basis of its breaches of IHL or international human rights law (IASC,
2002). R2P itself is neutral in sense (i), and arguably also in sense (ii),
though its Pillar Two support for states may amount in principle to
privileging incumbent state sovereigns over insurgents. R2P is not, however, committed to being neutral in senses (iii) or (iv), so there are important ways in which humanitarian action is neutral where R2P is
not. Even here, however, the distinction between the two is not straightforward, as the more humanitarian organizations prioritize *humanitarian
POC*, the more they will find themselves in conflict with these stronger
versions of neutrality. If a humanitarian organization endeavours in any
way to protect a local group of civilians from slaughter, for instance,
in a situation where one party to the conflict has the deaths of this
group as a settled war aim (consider Rwanda or Srebrenica), then the
humanitarian organization is *ipso facto* violating neutrality in sense (iii)
by deliberately acting against the war objectives of one party to the
conflict.

In all, while *humanitarian POC* may in certain cases be able to uphold strong senses of neutrality and impartiality, for the most part R2P and POC are neutral and impartial in much the same ways.

3.3.3 POC and R2P have a different status in law

R2P and POC may be differentiated on the basis of their status in law. For instance, POC might be deemed well-established in law, given the customary and treaty status of the Geneva Conventions, for example. Conversely, R2P is often described as a "political principle" or "soft law". The problem with such swift characterizations, however, is that different parts of each larger principle may have very different connections to international law. As Carsten Stahn (2007: 110) notes, the UN High-Level Panel's 2004 description of R2P as an "emerging principle" was both over-optimistic and over-pessimistic. R2P's First Pillar is well-grounded in international law; a state wilfully defaulting on its responsibility to protect its own population is likely to be in breach of a wide set of international laws. The application of international law to the positive responsibilities of the international community with respect to R2P Pillar Two and Pillar Three, however, is much more controversial (Stahn, 2007: 118–120).

In their analysis of soft law in international affairs, Abbott and Snidal advance a three-dimensional taxonomy for categorizing the legal status of international obligations (2000). This section applies this taxonomy to R2P and POC. The point is not to give a definitive legal judgment regarding each principle – each one of the suggested renderings below contains controversial elements – but merely to illustrate as a general matter how each principle might plausibly differ in legal status from others in its group.

Abbott and Snidal describe three separate dimensions of each international principle. First there is the question of whether the principle is recognized as being a *legal obligation* (as distinct from merely a moral or political one). The second dimension is the *preciseness* of the principle, while the third gauges whether states have been willing to *delegate* authority to external institutions (for instance to an international court) to police and adjudicate the principle. Abbott and Snidal use the letters O, P and D respectively to refer to these three dimensions, viz., legal *O*bligation, *P*reciseness, and external *D*elegation. Capital letters indicate high levels on the dimension, lower-case letters indicate moderate levels, and subscript letters indicate low levels.[2] Thus if a principle has its three dimensions rated as [o, P, $_d$], for example, then it has at least some status as a legal obligation [o], its requirements are very precise [P], but there is little or no external delegation of authority for adjudicating it [$_d$].

Using this notation, *combatant POC* is [O, P, d]. The Geneva Conventions and Additional Protocols unquestionably dictate legal obligations, they have a high degree of preciseness, and in many (though not all) instances, external courts and ad hoc tribunals are able to adjudicate upon them. *Peacekeeping POC* is [$_o$, p, $_d$]. The obligation of peacekeepers to provide decent protection, within their mandate and capacities, to civilians around them is not a legal obligation and there are no external courts empowered to adjudicate it. There is, however, sufficient preciseness to the duty that we may be confident in determining failures to perform it in at least some instances – for example, by some of the Belgian and Bangladeshi peacekeeping contingents in Rwanda in 1994. Complicatedly, however, some commentators have argued that the laws of occupation *inter alia* may apply to PKOs (Wills, 2009). If this proves to be the case, then *peacekeeping POC* must be ranked as [o, p, d]. *Security Council POC* is extremely soft law. With no legal obligations on the Council, little precision in dictating exactly what is required of them, and no judicial oversight, its ranking is [$_o$, $_p$, $_d$]. The same is true of *humanitarian POC*, whose duties are not legal and there is no delegation of authority. Still, while the duties imposed by *humanitarian POC* are currently quite amorphous, ongoing development of the concept may increase the preciseness of its duties, moving it towards [$_o$, p, $_d$].

The First Pillar of R2P is [O, p, d]. Every state has legal responsibilities to protect and not slaughter its citizens. Such responsibilities are reasonably precise and international courts such as the ICC and ad hoc tribunals can and do adjudicate them. Most of R2P's Second Pillar is very soft law: [$_o$, $_p$, $_d$]. States do not have international legal obligations to positively help other states build their First Pillar capacities, the duties in any case are not very precise, and there is no delegation to international courts to adjudicate breaches of those duties. There is a complexity, however: the 2007 judgment of the International Court of Justice in the Serbian Genocide Case showed that states do have legal duties to use their influence with regard to non-state forces that are under their influence and support, even when those forces are at work in other countries. In such cases, states are legally obliged to use their influence – in a manner resembling a "duty of care" – to prevent atrocity crimes being committed by those non-state forces.[3] As such, this specific part of R2P's Second Pillar may be ranked more robustly as [o, p, d]. Finally, R2P's Third Pillar is [$_o$, p, $_d$]. States in the international community and members of the Security Council do not have legal duties to respond to atrocity crimes in other countries, and there is no judicial oversight of their decisions in this regard. Still, R2P's duties are precise enough that it is possible to tell when failures occur – Darfur is one plausible example, and the position on Russia with respect to Syria in 2012 may be another.

Again, it bears repeating that all of these rankings may be questioned on a variety of grounds, and that further discrete elements within each principle may be ranked differently. The central point is merely to illustrate that each of the different principles' status in law must be approached as an individual matter. There is no simple answer as to whether R2P or POC has a stronger status in law.

3.4 Differentiating R2P and POC in the context of peacekeeping operations

The final mode of distinction this chapter will consider is in the context of PKOs. Several commentators have distinguished certain sorts of PKOs as "R2P missions", as opposed to those with more restricted capacities and mandates, which engage only in POC (Holt and Berkman, 2006; Holt and Smith, 2008). A similar distinction is provided by Wills (2009), who distinguishes between operations that have a *general* responsibility to protect, and those that have a more robust and systemic *mission* responsibility to protect. Wills' nomenclature has the advantage that it does not connote that R2P is only concerned with non-consensual military action. Other authorities have taken a different view. For instance, in interviews with this project team in 2010 a number of DPKO officials effectively divorced R2P cases from the POC concerns of peacekeepers. One argued that the DPKO "should not get into a position where we are meant to respond to R2P situations. We do not have the resources or the capacity." A second interviewee asserted that "To date personnel involved in peacekeeping missions are not trained to respond to genocide and there is no support for the idea that they should be."

In order to assess these views it is necessary to consider the several different factors that may be taken as indicia distinguishing R2P from POC missions. One possible indicium can be ruled out immediately. It might be thought that those missions where the Council explicitly affirms and refers to R2P would count as "R2P missions". However, references to R2P in this context are rare, and appear to bear little correlation to the R2P indicia that follow.[4]

A first indicium is the place that the protection of civilians holds in the overall mission mandate: is protection merely an adjunct and ad hoc objective for the peacekeepers to pay attention to as they go about their other tasks? For example, the *raison d'être* of the mission may be monitoring a ceasefire or a demilitarized zone, and the protection of civilians may be just an ancillary task that will be performed only if peacekeepers stumble upon isolated acts of violence. Alternatively, the protection of civilians might be the primary goal of the mission – the very reason it has been deployed. The second indicium is the consent granted by the host state for the mission, as POC peacekeeping missions (though perhaps not R2P missions) will always have host state consent. On a related note is the concern the peacekeeping operation will have for perceived neutrality by opposing forces on the ground. Again, the robust action called for by R2P may be thought to make perceptions of neutrality by all sides less of a priority. The third (potential – see below) indicium is the authorization given to the mission by the Security Council. Mandates given under Chapter VI of the UN Charter impose very substantial restraints on the use of robust force against belligerents, suggestive of at most a POC mission. Chapter VII mandates, however, allow for the robust use of force against belligerents (potentially even against state and state-sponsored belligerents) and are more suggestive of R2P's proactive stance. The Security Council can furthermore explicitly address the peacekeeping operation's use of robust military measures, emphasizing for example that peacekeepers may use "all necessary means" to secure protection. A fourth indicium is the type of threats to civilians that are anticipated. If the violence against civilians is expected to be deliberate and systematic, then the peacekeeping operation may well be faced with the need to prevent atrocity crimes, and an R2P appellation will be more appropriate. A fifth indicium is the force size and capacity that is mandated and subsequently deployed. Robust protection requires substantially more troops and military resources, and may involve a specific member state leading the operation, with the United Nations providing authorization but not operational leadership.

Categorizing peacekeeping missions would be a straightforward affair if either all or none of these indicia were present. In that case a peacekeeping mission pursuing protection only as an adjunct task, deployed with the consent of all parties to the conflict, under a Chapter VI mandate, expecting and resourced only to respond to isolated acts of violence against civilians, would be a POC mission. Contrariwise, a mission whose fundamental purpose was to protect civilians, deployed irrespective of state consent, under a Chapter VII mandate, expecting and resourced to respond to intended atrocity crimes against civilians, would be an R2P mission. Unfortunately, however, these factors rarely line up so neatly; for instance, almost all PKOs with civilian protection mandates now have Chapter VII authorization. Furthermore, there are often shades of grey within each factor. For example, depending on context it can be very hard to judge how much military power an operation needs in order to be able to defend civilians from determined attack from insurgents or state armed forces.

Because of this, any system of categorization will need to consider which factors it takes as being most significant. For example, both Wills

(2009) and Holt and Berkman (2006) focus attention on indicia one and three (whether protection is the central task, and whether robust means have been mandated). A different view is suggested in the DPKO interview comments above, which seem to focus purely on the fourth indicium (are atrocity crimes expected?) and to deny that peacekeepers have a role in such cases. This position looks difficult to sustain, however; contemporary PKOs may often be deployed, with (perhaps grudging) host state consent, into contexts where atrocity crimes are expected or indeed known to be occurring. It does not always require war-fighting and R2P Pillar Three for the international community to help protect against atrocity; ongoing missions in both Darfur and the DRC are plain examples of robust PKOs deployed to protect civilians from violence and atrocities.

With all this in mind, the following taxonomy develops three broad types of peacekeeping mission. First, there is a *traditional peacekeeping operation*. The primary objective of this type of operation is not to protect civilians, but rather to monitor ceasefire agreements, patrol demilitarized zones, prepare for democratic elections, or pursue other such force objectives. The threats of violence against civilians are anticipated as being neither widespread nor systematic. Reflecting these two factors, the Security Council mandate notes the protection of civilians as an ad hoc task, and the peacekeeping operation is deployed with only minimal resources for robustly protecting civilians. Consent by both sides of the conflict is vital for a traditional peacekeeping operation's initial deployment, and the continued perception by each side of the operation's ongoing neutrality is likewise essential. The mission is given a Chapter VI mandate, and will use robust force to protect civilians only in very rare instances, perhaps in response to an isolated act of wanton assault committed directly in front of peacekeeping troops. In general, the state (or each side of the armed conflict that controls territory) is held to be primarily responsible for civilian protection.

Second, there is a *POC mission* (or *mixed POC PKO*). In this case, protection activities are a key part of the mandate, but such objectives sit alongside other equally significant force priorities, such as ensuring the distribution of humanitarian aid, or the disarmament, demobilization and reintegration of militants. The expected threats to civilians are substantial, but are thought to arise as symptoms of the conflict, rather than as settled military strategies or war aims of either party. Robust military action to protect civilians is envisaged, but is assumed to be primarily responsive and reactive in nature. As such, robust force may be used against (usually non-state) actors when civilians are under imminent attack by such actors within the mission's area of operations. Means are provided to the POC mission commensurate with its undertaking such protective actions. In general, however, the state is considered primarily responsible for civilian security. Reflecting its need to use robust force in some circumstances the POC mission is given a Chapter VII mandate, but the initial and ongoing consent of the host state is crucial. Indeed, the mission will do its utmost to be perceived as neutral by both sides of the conflict, as it is not equipped to become a "third belligerent". Examples of such POC missions might include the early MONUC operation in the DRC and MINUSAH in Haiti.[5]

The third category is an R2P *Pillar Two mission* (or *primary POC PKO*). In this case there is a perceived risk of atrocity crimes. There are genuine concerns that local military forces have war aims that can be achieved through, for example, ethnic cleansing, terror, or mass rape. The Pillar Two mission has been deployed with the primary purpose of preventing such atrocities; all other tasks are ancillary. It is intended to undertake proactive, preventive action requiring systemic strategy and direct use (or credible threat) of robust force in order to prevent atrocities to civilians within the area of operations. Since determined resistance to the Pillar Two PKO's civilian protection activities is expected, the mission must be resourced accordingly – in some cases it may therefore not be UN-led. While the host state is understood to have primary responsibility for civilian security in an aspirational sense – such that the mission should not impede or replace the state's developing bona fide attempts at protection – the Pillar Two mission is nevertheless responsible for providing protection where it can. Such a mission will always be authorized with a Chapter VII mandate, but some level of (albeit grudging) host state consent is still necessary – if not politically then logistically – to get the force deployed and operational. A perception of neutrality among the different parties to the conflict will be important, but is not essential. Examples of R2P Pillar Two missions might include the mission status of MONUC in the DRC in 2008–2010 (note the MONUC POC Draft Protection Strategy described by Holt and Kelly (2009: 186–189) and of UNOCI in the Côte d'Ivoire, at least from 2010 (UNSC, 2010)).

All such PKOs need to be distinguished from a further type of operation: an *R2P Pillar Three mission*. In such a case there is envisaged to be a state that is actively committing atrocity crimes against its own citizens, or about to do so, and non-military measures have been tried and failed, or hold no prospects of success in the available timeframe. The mandated mission will be authorized under Chapter VII, and will almost certainly not be United Nations-led. The mission will be to engage in war-fighting in order to constrain or neutralize the regime's capacity to harm the vulnerable civilian population and perhaps in extreme cases to defeat the regime (see Chapter 1, section 1.7). The actions in Libya under UNSC Resolution 1973 (UNSC, 2011c) are a clear case of this type of mission.

Even with these three mission categories, however, there are still cases that fall between them, sitting somewhere between a traditional peace-keeping operation and a POC mission, or between a POC mission and a Pillar Two mission. Still, having this taxonomy allows clear articulation of the situation when there is a mismatch between the needs of a situa-tion and the operation deployed to it. For instance, the UN mission for Rwanda, UNAMIR, had a capacity and mandate of little more than a traditional peacekeeping operation, while what was needed was an R2P Pillar Two mission. UNPROFOR in Bosnia-Herzegovina had a capacity of little more than a traditional peacekeeping operation, and a mandate suggestive of a POC mission, while what was realistically necessary was a particularly robust R2P Pillar Two mission.

This system of categorization also reminds us that R2P is not all about non-consensual military intervention; R2P Pillar Two missions are an im-portant part of the international community's protective armoury. In-deed, as the stakes continue to rise for states that categorically reject the deployment of peacekeeping missions that might thwart their objectives, it is perhaps to be expected that formal consent to R2P Pillar Two mis-sions will increase in the future, with all the difficulty and ambiguity such missions involve.

3.5 Conclusion

This chapter has analysed the key distinctions drawn between R2P and POC. A consistent theme has been that it is vital to articulate which pil-lar of R2P or which POC concept we are considering when we make such comparisons. While accepting the view that R2P is narrower in scope than POC (applying only to the four atrocity crimes) and deeper in re-sponse (with a stronger and more determinate preventive agenda), the chapter has argued that several other alleged differences – the restriction of POC to "armed conflict", POC's status as a "humanitarian principle" and the different status in law of R2P and POC – are less significant than popularly thought. The chapter developed two key similarities between the principles – namely, their basis in human rights and the cross-cutting similarities between R2P Pillar One and *combatant POC* on the one hand and R2P Pillar Three and *Security Council POC* on the other. The final section advanced a range of indicia for distinguishing POC from R2P PKOs, and suggested that the concept of R2P Pillar Two missions was significant and liable to remain so in the future.

Notes

1. Bellamy (2009), though see Hehir (2010).
2. Abbott and Snidal use dashes "–" to indicate low levels.
3. See Arbour (2008), though compare Carvin (2010).
4. See, e.g., UNSC (2006) and compare UNSC (2011c).
5. See the account of POC aspects of UN-authorized missions in Holt and Berkman (2006: Annex).

REFERENCES

Abbott, Kenneth, and Duncan Snidal (2000) "Hard and Soft Law in International Governance", *International Organisation* 54(3): 421–456.

Arbour, Louise (2008) "The Responsibility to Protect as a Duty of Care in International Law and Practice", *Review of International Studies* 34(3): 445–458.

Bellamy, Alex (2009) *Responsibility to Protect: The Global Effort to End Mass Atrocities*. Cambridge: Polity.

Brahimi, Lakhdar (2000) *Report of the Panel on UN Peace Operations*, A/44/305-S/2000/809, 21 August 2000.

Buckle, Stephen (1991) *Natural Law and the Theory of Property: Grotius to Hume*. Oxford: Clarendon Press.

Carvin, Stephanie (2010) "A Responsibility to Reality: A Reply to Louise Arbour", *British International Studies Association* 36: 47–54.

Caverzasio, S. G. (2001) *Strengthening Protection in War: A Search for Professional Standards*. Geneva: International Committee of the Red Cross.

CESCR, Committee on Economic Social and Cultural Rights (1999) *Outline for Drafting General Comments on Specific Rights of the International Economic, Social and Cultural Rights*, E/2000/22, E/C.12/1999/11, Annex IX, 19 November 1999.

Deng, Francis (1993) *Protecting the Dispossessed: A Challenge for the International Community*. Washington, DC: Brookings Institution.

DPKO/DFS (2008) *United Nations Peacekeeping Operations: Principles and Guidelines*, 18 January 2008.

Durch, William J. (2010) "Cross-Cutting Issues in Protection of Civilians for UN Peace Operations", *Challenges of Protecting Civilians in Multidimensional Peace Operations*. Canberra: International Forum for the Challenges of Peace Operations. 27 April 2010.

Gasser, Hans-Peter (1988) "A Measure of Humanity in Internal Disturbances and Tensions: Proposal for a Code of Conduct", *International Review of the Red Cross* 262: 38–58.

GCR2P (2011) *Policy Brief: The Relationship between the Responsibility to Protect and the Protection of Civilians in Armed Conflict (Update)*, Global Centre for the Responsibility to Protect, 9 May 2011.

Hehir, Aidan (2010) "The Responsibility to Protect: 'Sound and Fury Signifying Nothing'?", *International Relations* 24(2): 218–239.

Henckaerts, Jean-Marie (2005) "Study on Customary International Humanitarian Law: A Contribution to the Understanding and Respect for the Rule of Law in Armed Conflict", *International Review of the Red Cross* 87(857): 175–212.

Holt, Victoria, and Tobias Berkman (2006) *The Impossible Mandate? Military Preparedness, the Responsibility to Protect and Modern Peace Operations.* Washington, DC: The Henry L. Stimson Center.

Holt, Victoria, and Joshua Smith (2008) *Halting Widespread or Systematic Attacks on Civilians: Military Strategies & Operational Concepts.* Washington, DC: Henry L. Stimson Center.

Holt, Victoria, Glyn Taylor and Max Kelly (2009) *Protecting Civilians in the Context of UN Peacekeeping Operations: Successes, Setbacks and Remaining Challenges.* New York: DPKO, UNOCHA.

IASC, Inter-Agency Standing Committee (2002) *Growing the Sheltering Tree: Protecting Rights through Humanitarian Action, Programmes and Practice Gathered from the Field.* Geneva: UNICEF.

ICISS, International Commission on Intervention and State Sovereignty (2001) *The Responsibility to Protect.* Ottawa: IDRC.

ICRC, International Committee of the Red Cross (2008) *Enhancing Protection for Civilians in Armed Conflict and Other Situations of Violence.* Geneva: ICRC.

IRRC (1988a) "ICRC Protection and Assistance Activities in Situations Not Covered by International Humanitarian Law", *International Review of the Red Cross* 262: 9–37.

IRRC (1988b) "Internal Disturbances and Tensions: A New Humanitarian Approach?", *International Review of the Red Cross* 262: 3–8.

Kolb, Robert, and Richard Hyde (2008) *An Introduction to the International Law of Armed Conflicts.* Oxford: Hart Publishing.

Lie, Jon H. S. (2008) *Protection of Civilians, the Responsibility to Protect and Peace Operations*, NUPI Report No. 4, 2008.

Locke, John (1947) *Two Treatises of Government.* New York: Hafner.

Mitsis, Phillip (2003) "Locke's Offices", in Brad Inwood and Jon Miller, *Hellenistic and Early Modern Philosophy.* New York: Cambridge University Press, 45–61.

OCHA (2010) *OCHA on Message: Protection*, Version 1, June 2010.

OCHA (2011) *Aide Memoire: For the Consideration of Issues Pertaining to the Protection of Civilians in Armed Conflict*, 4th ed. New York: United Nations.

Scheffer, David (2009) "Atrocity Crimes: Framing the Responsibility to Protect", in R. H. Cooper and J. V. Kohler, eds. *Responsibility to Protect: The Global Moral Compact for the 21st Century.* New York: Palgrave Macmillan, 77–98.

Shue, Henry (1980) *Basic Rights: Subsistence, Affluence and US Foreign Policy.* Princeton, NJ: Princeton University Press.

Slim, Hugo, and Andrew Bonwick (2005) *Protection: An ALNAP Guide for Humanitarian Agencies.* London: Overseas Development Institute.

Stahn, Carsten (2007) "Responsibility to Protect: Political Rhetoric or Emerging Legal Norm?", *American Journal of International Law* 101(1): 99–120.

Strauss, Ekkehard (2009) "A Bird in the Hand Is Worth Two in the Bush: On the Assumed Legal Nature of the Responsibility to Protect", *Global Responsibility to Protect* 1(3): 291–323.

UNGA (2005) *UN General Assembly Resolution 60/1: World Summit Outcome Document*, A/Res/60/1, 16 September 2005.

UNSC (1999) *UN Security Council Resolution 1265 (1999): On the Protection of Civilians in Armed Conflict*, S/RES/1265, 17 September 1999.

UNSC (2000) *UN Security Council Resolution 1296 (2000): Protection of Civilians in Armed Conflict*, S/RES/1296, 19 April 2000.

UNSC (2006) *UN Security Council Resolution 1706 (2006): Reports of the Secretary-General on the Sudan*, S/RES/1706, 31 August 2006.

UNSC (2010) *UN Security Council Resolution 1933 (2010): The Situation in Côte d'Ivoire*, S/RES/1933, 30 June 2010.

UNSC (2011a) *May 2011 Meeting: Protection of Civilians in Armed Conflict*, S/PV.6531, 10 May 2011.

UNSC (2011b) *November 2011 Meeting: Protection of Civilians in Armed Conflict*, S/PV.6650, 9 November 2011.

UNSC (2011c) *UN Security Council Resolution 1973 (2011): The Situation in Libya*, S/RES/1973, 17 March 2011.

UNSG (1999a) *Report of the Secretary General Pursuant to General Assembly Resolution 53/55: The Fall of Srebrenica*, A/54/549, 15 November 1999.

UNSG (1999b) *Report to the Security Council on the Protection of Civilians in Armed Conflict*, S/1999/957, 8 September 1999.

UNSG (2009) *Report of the Secretary-General: Implementing the Responsibility to Protect*, A/63/677, 12 January 2009.

UNSG (2010) *Report of the Secretary-General: Early Warning, Assessment and the Responsibility to Protect*, A/64/864, 14 July 2010.

Ward, Lee (2006) "Locke on the Moral Basis of International Relations", *American Journal of Political Science* 50(3): 691–705.

Wills, Siobhán (2009) *Protecting Civilians: The Obligations of Peacekeepers*. Oxford: Oxford University Press.

4

The responsibility to protect and the protection of civilians: A view from the United Nations

Angus Francis and Vesselin Popovski

This chapter is part of the study of the relationship between the responsibility to protect (R2P) and the protection of civilians (POC). The authors[1] undertook extensive theme-focused interviews at the relevant UN offices in New York and Geneva and the Australian mission in New York as part of the process of mapping the relationship between R2P and POC and their relevance to UN protection operations. The aim of this chapter is to present the opinions of UN officials as a way of understanding the practicalities and application of POC and R2P to the UN system, drawing links between the issues raised by respondents and the wider debate on POC and R2P. In this way, this chapter complements the project's overview of the literature on R2P and POC presented in the preceding chapter of this collection.

The chapter explores the relevance of POC and R2P to the UN system as viewed through the eyes of those working within the UN protection architecture or within other organizations collaborating closely with UN bodies in the protection field. Against this background, we present the views of the respondents to the following specific issues: the relationship between R2P and POC; the relevance of R2P and POC to field missions; existing gaps in POC or R2P agendas and how those gaps are being filled, e.g. through strategies, guidance and workshops; and future plans for the development of R2P and POC within the United Nations.

Norms of protection: Responsibility to protect, protection of civilians and their interaction,
Francis, Popovski and Sampford (eds),
United Nations University Press, 2012, ISBN 978-92-808-1218-3

4.1 Relevance of POC to the UN system

4.1.1 Growth of POC in the UN system

The protection of civilians is relevant to a wide range of UN activities, including peacekeeping operations, humanitarian assistance, protection of refugees, respect for international humanitarian law (IHL), safety and security of humanitarian personnel, and legal accountability of perpetrators of crimes against civilians. A series of Secretary-General reports S/1999/957, S/2001/331, S/2002/1300, S/2004/431, S/2005/740, S/2007/643, S/2009/277 and S/2010/579, Security Council resolutions 1265 (1999), 1296 (2000), 1674 and 1738 (2006), 1820 (2008), 1882, 1888, 1889 and 1894 (2009), and reports by the UN Department of Peacekeeping Operations (DPKO) and Department of Field Support (DFS)[2] point to the maturation and breadth of POC in the UN system.

The relevance of POC to the UN system is strong and undisputed.[3] A major driving force behind the rise of POC within the UN system, as suggested by DPKO respondents, is the inclusion of POC in peacekeeping mandates: Sierra Leone (UNAMSIL), Côte d'Ivoire (UNOCI), Darfur (UNAMID), Democratic Republic of Congo (MONUSCO), Central African Republic and Chad (MINURCAT), Haiti (MINUSTAH), Liberia (UNMIL) and Sudan (UNMIS). This has spurred on discussion of POC in the UN Special Committee on Peacekeeping Operations (C-34), which referred to POC in the reports at its 2009 and 2010 sessions (A/63/19 and A/64/19). Certain UN country missions have also actively promoted POC in the peacekeeping operational context, especially the Australian and Uruguayan Permanent Missions to the UN which held workshops on the topic in 2009 and 2010 as precursors to the C-34 meetings.

Respondents from UN humanitarian agencies agree that the emergence of POC in the peacekeeping operational context has brought new dimensions to protection, with peacekeeping operations becoming engaged in civilian protection. While UNHCR officials regard protection of civilians as something they have been doing for 60 years, they acknowledge that "at the level of processes and influencing standards of behaviour", the latest developments within the United Nations in relation to POC are significant, and the question is how can UNHCR's work benefit from these developments and how does the UNHCR engage with POC. According to one official, "UNHCR has become a specialist in adapting its language according to the concept used, i.e. POC, R2P, development aid, etc. Semantics do matter because they speak to different audiences who are potentially influential or important for our work."

4.1.2 The meaning and scope of POC

The increasing focus on POC in the UN system has presented definitional challenges. Breakey's analysis of POC in this book demonstrates that there are various conceptions of POC found in IHL, UN operational discussions and reports, Secretary-General reports, Security Council resolutions, and the guidelines and policy statements of protection actors such as the International Committee of the Red Cross (ICRC) and UNHCR. The independent report on POC commissioned by DPKO and the UN Office for the Coordination of Humanitarian Affairs (OCHA) (Holt and Taylor, 2009) also showed that there was not one conception of POC. Consistent with these analyses, a range of views were presented by respondents on the scope and meaning of POC.

Despite the diversity of definitional opinions, there appeared to be a general agreement that POC requires positive and concerted action. One respondent remarked that historically international humanitarian law has been about what *not* to do, whereas POC is about what *to* do – it demands positive action, rather than simply negative obligations of preventing violations. OCHA similarly shared a concept of POC that is much broader than just "don't shoot" or "don't rape". POC is also about rule of law, restitution of property, reconciliation and the return of internally displaced people. Some UN agencies were cautious and wished to constrain their traditional vision of POC to purely civilian life protection activities and the groups that they are mandated to protect, instead of expanding to protect all people at risk and from all sorts of threats to their interests.

DPKO acknowledged that, while POC has been a major part of their work for 10 years, it was not until 2009 that they started conceptualizing and developing POC strategies in peacekeeping operations. After a period of introspection DPKO is now looking at how other agencies see protection. One official observed:

> UNHCR and the humanitarian community have a broad view of POC, whereas historically DPKO's view has been based on the protection of civilians against physical harm.

DPKO's articulation of a conceptual framework for POC evidences a move toward a broader POC agenda, albeit one confined to the peacekeeping operational context. The DPKO/DFS *Operational Concept on the Protection of Civilians in UN Peacekeeping Operations* goes beyond DPKO's traditional view of protection as the prevention of physical harm and outlines three tiers of protection: (i) protection through the political process, e.g. supporting peace processes; (ii) protection against physical violence by preventing and responding to attacks on civilians; and (iii) building a protective environment through institution-building, legal protection and humanitarian activity.

Nonetheless, the *Operational Concept* does not yet represent a UN system-wide strategy or understanding of POC. It may be that a universal UN-wide definition of POC is not the way forward, given the multitude of operational contexts and mandates of protection actors. For example, POC in the peacekeeping context is only part of UNHCR's work in relation to the protection of refugees, internally displaced persons and other civilians (Deschamp, 2010: 8). UNHCR has stated that "the concept of POC in peacekeeping should specifically recognize the mandates and expertise of other protection actors. It should also be clear that peacekeeping missions do not supplant other specialized regimes and mandates" (ibid.: 20).

An important issue remains the agreement of protection actors on the meaning of POC and their respective roles. MONUSCO (the UN Organization Stabilization Mission in the Democratic Republic of Congo; DRC) is put forward as an example of effective inter-agency cooperation in the delivery of a robust and comprehensive POC mandate (UNSC Res. 1565/2004, 1794/2007, 1856/2008 and 1925/2010). Para. 12 of Resolution 1925 defines POC broadly to include: physical protection; supporting the government to ensure the protection of civilians from violations of IHL and human rights abuses; supporting efforts to bring perpetrators to justice; working with the government to protect children; implementing the UN system-wide protection strategy; supporting the government and international partners and neighbouring countries to create an environment conducive to the voluntary, safe and dignified return of IDPs and refugees, or voluntary local integration or resettlement; supporting the efforts of the government against armed groups in compliance with IHL, human rights and refugee law and the need to protect civilians. Coupled with its broad POC mandate, a "joint-protection" concept of operations was developed by MONUSCO's Civil Affairs Section and military and humanitarian partners.

Building on this approach, DPKO has developed a *Framework for Drafting Comprehensive POC Strategies in UN Peacekeeping Operations*. The Framework provides basic parameters and considerations for drafting comprehensive POC strategies that ensure coherence in approach, minimize gaps, avoid duplication and maximize the use of all mission resources (civilian, military, police and support elements). Using the broad and inclusive definition of POC in its *Operational Concept* as a reference point, the Framework includes an annotated template that assists senior mission leadership in articulating POC risks and identifying activities to be undertaken by the mission itself and by the mission in coordination with other protection actors to address those risks. The Framework recognizes the importance of engaging UN protection actors, the host government, non-state armed groups, independent humanitarian organizations, the Security Council, troop- and police-contributing countries and the local population. Thus, the Framework marks an important milestone in the development of a common understanding of POC in the UN system and more broadly.

4.2   Relevance of R2P to the UN system

4.2.1   The gradual rise of R2P in the UN system

Respondents agreed that R2P is gradually, though slowly, winning its place in the United Nations. This is recognized in key developments, including: the Report by the International Commission on Intervention and State Sovereignty (ICISS, 2001); the High-Level Panel on Threats, Challenges and Change's report, *A More Secure World: Our Shared Responsibility* (2004); the *World Summit Outcome Document* (2005); the Security Council's Resolution 1674 (2006) affirming Paras. 138 and 139; the Secretary-General's Report for implementing R2P (2009); and the General Assembly's debates on R2P (Luck, 2010: 355; UNGA, 2009). Respondents also acknowledged the role and importance of the Secretary-General's Special Representative on R2P, appointed in 2007 (UNSG, 2008). They also referred us to discussions on R2P in the Secretary-General's Policy Committee, including the discussions on Kenya (2008) and DRC (2009). R2P was also raised when the Security Council was briefed on Kyrgyzstan.

R2P became a central topic in the United Nations after a large number of civilian protesters in Libya were killed by the Gaddafi regime in February and March 2011. UN Secretary-General Ban Ki-moon urged Gaddafi to exercise restraint and impose a ceasefire. The UN High Commissioner for Human Rights, Navi Pillay, declared that the violence committed by Libyan authorities may amount to crimes against humanity. The UN Human Rights Council condemned the use of force against civilians and the UN General Assembly expelled Libya from its membership in the Human Rights Council. On 26 February 2011 the UNSC urgently considered the need for protection of the Libyan people from the atrocities of the Gaddafi regime. Resolution 1970, adopted with a unanimous 15–0 vote, condemned the use of force against civilians, deplored the gross systematic violations of human rights, and expressed deep concerns at the deaths of civilians and the incitement to hostility by the Libyan government. It considered that the widespread and systematic attacks

against the civilian population may amount to crimes against humanity –
triggering the applicability of R2P. In a separate paragraph, Resolution
1970 expressly recalled the Libya government's *responsibility to protect*
its population, imposed mandatory sanctions on Libya and referred the
situation to the International Criminal Court (ICC).

On 17 March 2011, the UNSC adopted a second resolution, 1973, which
urged the "parties to armed conflict" to "bear the primary responsibility
to take all feasible steps to ensure the protection of civilians". Resolution
1973 built on obligations under IHL and international criminal law, in
conjunction with the Security Council's authority under Chapter VII of
the UN Charter to restore international peace and security, to protect the
life of civilians at risk and to establish a no-fly zone. The decision of the
Security Council is considered a timely and important reaffirmation of
the R2P principle, including its Third Pillar (Thakur, 2011).

4.2.2 The meaning and scope of R2P

A close observer of the development of R2P in the United Nations remarked: "People have tended to hide their anxieties about R2P (and
POC) by exaggerating the definitional problems. But I think that they
are capable of definition. R2P covers mass atrocities against civilians –
genocide, war crimes, crimes against humanity. It is quite precise." By and
large, respondents accepted that R2P is clearly about preventing and
responding to the "four crimes" (war crimes, genocide, crimes against
humanity and ethnic cleansing). On the other hand, a number of respondents highlighted the lack of clarity that exists among states as to the
means for the implementation of R2P.

The respondents echoed a key issue in the broader R2P discourse:
R2P's normative quality (Barbour and Gorlick, 2008: 535; Stahn 2007:
110; Strauss, 2009: 292). Is it a legal norm or a political norm? OCHA and
ICRC respondents shared scepticism in using R2P because of its lack
of independent treaty status and the fact that it does not, of itself, create
legal obligations. Another view was that R2P was designed by ICISS to
respond to mass atrocities by adding political momentum to calls for action. R2P acts as a kind of "speech act": a catalyst for international action
(Bellamy, 2010: 159). According to one respondent,

> R2P was designed not as a new norm, but as a mobilizing factor for action
> when atrocities were committed. R2P does not add anything to the existing
> law; it is a normative [political], rather than a legal, obligation to act. R2P
> builds on existing laws, such as the 1948 Genocide Convention, the 1949
> Geneva Conventions and its Additional Protocols, the 1998 Rome Statute for
> ICC, etc. It is meant to overcome the reluctance to name genocide and other

crimes as a reason for non-intervention. It was thought too important to let fine legal technicalities decide the question of intervention in mass atrocities situations.

R2P, as a policy tool for coordinating and acting upon existing legal obligations, has therefore a strategic significance: if it is promoted, not as adding new obligations, but rather as a policy tool for coordinating existing laws and institutions, this will placate states that are worried that R2P imposes new legal obligations. This is the approach advocated by the Special Representative on R2P (Luck, 2010: 356) and arguably mirrored in the UN Secretary-General's 2009 Report on the implementation of R2P.

4.3 Relationship between POC and R2P

Opinions varied on the extent R2P and POC were related and as to which concept is broader. Some accept that the two concepts overlap and speak of the same needs. One respondent described R2P and POC as "cousins". Others argue that the relationship depends on how one views different needs in the field. R2P is narrowed by its applicability to mass atrocities (war crimes, ethnic cleansing, genocide and crimes against humanity). POC, on the other hand, as evident from the DPKO/DFS *Operational Concept on the Protection of Civilians in UN Peacekeeping Operations* and the *Framework for Drafting Comprehensive POC Strategies in UN Peacekeeping Operations,* supports a wide array of protection, including protection against physical violence and the promotion of human rights.

There was a view expressed that equating POC and R2P may create resistance from member states to the promotion of POC in the peacekeeping context. DPKO and other proponents of POC in peacekeeping operations raised concerns that the R2P/POC connection can be problematic because R2P is seen by certain states to be a "Trojan horse" for intervention. Peacekeeping operations are based on the fundamental principle of consent and impartiality, and risks might arise when countries start suspecting that there is an R2P agenda in the POC work of a UN agency. However, one could consider the same risks to arise anytime there is a UN mission with a POC mandate faced with host-state-sanctioned atrocities.

Workshops on POC in peacekeeping missions had been held by the Australian and Uruguayan Missions to the UN in New York, which were precursors to the introduction of POC into the deliberations of the C-34. Australia and Uruguay actively promoted POC in peacekeeping operations, while clearly distinguishing it from R2P. There is a general consensus among UN agencies and NGOs that a careful and cautious approach should be taken not to simplify and equate R2P with POC so as not to undermine UN agencies' work on the ground.

On the other hand, there is increasing recognition that peacekeeping plays an essential role in the preventive and rebuilding aspects of the implementation of R2P. The scope of R2P includes a responsibility to prevent atrocities and a responsibility to reintegrate and reconcile communities and rebuild life after atrocities. The UN peacekeeping and peacebuilding operations can play a central role in preventing a relapse to violence and assisting in post-conflict recovery. Also, the Second Pillar of R2P requires states and international organizations to assist states that lack capacities to exercise the responsibility to protect. DPKO officials recognized that UN peacekeeping has a role to play in this respect – something expressly incorporated into DPKO's *Framework for Drafting Comprehensive POC Strategies in UN Peacekeeping Operations.*

A respondent from a country mission to the United Nations, while maintaining that there should not be a conflation of R2P and POC when it comes to peacekeeping, was also adamant that a peacekeeping mission in country with the consent of the government should protect civilians against atrocities. Another respondent agreed that "logically any mandate that deals with POC must include most egregious crimes". He noted, in this respect, that the language used over the last 10 years in POC mandates was first used in 1994 for the stillborn UN force that was to go into Rwanda. Thus, language obviously intended to cover genocide has since been picked up by the Security Council and applied to POC.

R2P proponents also thought POC and R2P should not be conflated, but for different reasons. There was a tendency to view POC as specific to peacekeeping mandates in post-conflict situations (a view not necessarily consistent with the concept of POC as it has developed in international humanitarian law), whereas the tools for implementing R2P were viewed as applicable in a much broader context, including where no peacekeepers are in place, e.g. Kyrgyzstan. R2P proponents also point out that efforts have been made to overcome state resistance to R2P by distinguishing it from humanitarian intervention through focus on prevention and capacity-building.

4.4 Are POC and R2P relevant for field missions?

The relevance of POC for field missions is clear. There is consensus that, at the level of process and influencing standards of behaviour for field missions, talking about POC makes sense. DPKO highlighted the increasing relevance of POC to peacekeeping operations. A senior UNHCR official also noted that POC is relevant to UNHCR field missions because it is central to the protection cluster in the field, which closely engages OCHA and DPKO. In this regard, the emergence of POC has coincided with the reform of the UN humanitarian assistance system, initiated in 2005.

This process of reform identified protection of civilians as a gap in humanitarian efforts and instigated institutional mechanisms to ensure that protection of civilians is a core component of humanitarian responses. Principals of the Inter-Agency Standing Committee (IASC) established the "cluster approach" in 2005 whereby responsibilities are assigned to lead agencies in order to provide a more effective response to humanitarian emergencies, particularly those involving mass internal displacement. The Global Protection Cluster Working Group, chaired by the UNHCR, is the main forum at the global level for coordination of protection in humanitarian action (PCWG, 2007). The development of the protection cluster is recognition that refugee flows, internal displacement and humanitarian crises "often occur in complex emergencies characterized by a partial or even complete breakdown of State authority, including lack of capacity, and in some cases willingness, to ensure the protection of civilians" (ibid.). The response required is a "multi-dimensional approach – humanitarian, human rights, development, security, political" and must involve the combined efforts of an array of actors at national, regional and international levels (ibid.).

The IASC has been instrumental in redefining civil-military collaborations, which have increased in importance as the mandates of UN protection missions increasingly cover POC. The protection cluster approach and the principles and practices associated with POC are converging, as evident in the joint leadership of the protection cluster, granted to UNHCR and the UN's peacekeeping mission in the DRC (MONUSCO) (Murthy, 2007), which also involves the participation of other international protection actors such as UNICEF, OCHA, ICRC and international NGOs alongside civil-military actors (ibid.).

Overall, agencies such as OCHA, UNHCR and ICRC are keen for coordination with the UN peacekeeping missions to continue, but also for responsibilities to be clearly defined. They are happy to do their own specific protection work without heavily time-consuming coordination, as long as each agency understands POC in the same way. MONUSCO could be explored as a good example of humanitarian actors working together to formulate a common approach to POC. There was coordination of (otherwise overlapping) responsibilities between agencies through the "joint protection matrices" identifying priority focus areas. This was seen as succeeding partly due to officers on all sides being willing to work together, but also due to the local circumstances that demanded people work together. UNHCR also thought that MONUSCO showed how POC can be successfully done, if there is goodwill and determination to pro-actively interpret the mandate to include physical protection and robustly combat gender-based violence.

Respondents were more ambivalent about the relevance of R2P to field missions. DPKO believes there are practical limits to the relevance of R2P in peacekeeping and would avoid getting into a position where its missions are meant to respond to R2P situations. This is seen to be essen-tially a matter of limited resources and capacity to respond to mass atroc-ity crimes. To date, personnel involved in peacekeeping missions are not trained in how to respond to genocide. However, DPKO's *Framework for Drafting Comprehensive POC Strategies in UN Peacekeeping Operations* expressly recognizes that in instances where the government is unable or unwilling to fulfil its responsibility to protect civilians, Security Council mandates give missions the authority to act independently to protect ci-vilians. This may include the use of force against any party, including gov-ernment forces, where those elements are engaged in physical violence against civilians. In the extreme situations where peacekeepers are called upon to prevent or to respond to mass atrocities, the distinction between POC and R2P breaks down.

4.5 Existing gaps or omissions in POC or R2P agendas

Respondents agreed that more work needs to be done on the implemen-tation of POC on the ground. In the past, some peacekeeping operations have determined the POC agenda better than others. In addition to MONUSCO, the missions in East Timor, Chad and Haiti would be inter-esting to analyse in terms of how much POC and R2P do, or do not, in-fluence daily operational matters. In relation to R2P, respondents pointed to the need to clarify how existing UN agencies feed into the work of the Special Representative for R2P (Edward Luck) and the Special Adviser on the Prevention of Genocide (Francis Deng). According to a UNHCR official, the issue is how the various UN agencies can bring together in-formation-gathering and then build on analysis, which is weak at present. Another respondent observed that "what is missing is the political inter-face that manages early warning and response. The UN is too slow and does not have mechanisms to analyse intelligence dispassionately." "The UN has no emergency mode," said one official. While R2P is set out in official documents, it lacks an institutionalized framework that can urge early response.

Respondents also considered that more attention should be given to the relevance of POC and R2P to vulnerable populations. They noted that, while there are many reports concerning sexual abuse during conflict and exploitation of child soldiers and so on, there is still insufficient capacity and understanding on how to combat these abuses. Another commonly identified gap was in relation to the protection of refugees. It was thought that R2P could be used as a way of providing UNHCR with more traction in the UN system. But there is insufficient reference in the R2P literature to asylum as a tool for responding to humanitarian crisis. If atrocities are designated as R2P, then neighbouring countries can be called upon to open their borders to refugees; otherwise they would be breaching their obligations under international refugee law and international human rights law.

Another issue of concern remains the selective implementation of POC and R2P and their heavy dependence on political will. Some respondents considered that the North continues to manifest double standards in the implementation of POC and R2P – something that has antagonized the South and aggravated sensitivities over the scope and application of R2P particularly. A respondent from a UN agency told us that "the Palestinian case always comes up. Do we have 'unprotected populations' and 'protected populations'? The question of POC and R2P is always highly politicized." There remains the perception, despite the endorsement of R2P in the Outcome Document, that R2P is a somehow "Western" or "neo-imperialist" concept, imposed by the North on the South. But the R2P concept, one can argue, started in Africa with Francis Deng's writings in the early 1990s ("Sovereignty as Responsibility") and was first named in an official document by the African Union, establishing its Peace and Security Council in 1999 – long before the International Commission on Intervention and State Sovereignty (ICISS) used the phrase in its 2001 Report. One may add that even ICISS was not a "Northern" establishment – it was co-chaired by a Southerner (Mohamed Sahnoun) and had a broad geographical representation.

The countries most vocal in support of POC and R2P are, by and large, not the big troop contributors. This may have a dual explanation – they already accept POC and R2P and do not need to be too vocal. But a more problematic assumption would be that troop-contributing countries shy away from robust peacekeeping because of the inevitable controversies surrounding the use of force and intervention. It was noted that objections by several states to the use of R2P in humanitarian settings misrepresented the principle because they focused solely on intervention. But R2P has many options before it comes to military measures, and the last-resort measures are strictly under Chapter VII of the UN Charter.

Even the Third Pillar – timely and decisive action against states who are unwilling to protect – starts with peaceful settlement options, before moving to sanctions and the military option. One may argue that R2P is 99% about states able and willing to protect (First Pillar), states in need of assistance to protect (Second Pillar), and states that will prevent atrocities under diplomatic pressure or sanctions (Third Pillar options). Only in very limited, extreme circumstances will R2P move to the last option – military intervention. The only example so far of the use of this last-resort military option of R2P is Security Council Resolution 1973 on Libya.

4.6 How are gaps being filled?

Respondents consider the Secretary-General's appointment of a Special Representative for R2P in 2007 as a starting point for the introduction of R2P architecture within the UN system. Respondents also mentioned as important the move to create a joint office on prevention of genocide and the promotion of R2P – a key recommendation of the Secretary-General's 2009 Report on the implementation of R2P (UNSG, 2009: 33). A framework for identifying genocide risks has been developed by Francis Deng's office and training for UN staff has been prepared, based on OCHA work, overcoming some resistance from DPKO to training of mission personnel in identifying risks of genocide.

DPKO has recognized that strategies must be developed now that POC has entered peacekeeping mandates. The C-34, which gives directives to the UN Secretariat on the development of peacekeeping operations, including POC, called on the Secretariat to develop a POC strategy document that can be used for missions; training modules for protection personnel; and better indications by DPKO and DFS of the resources and capacities required by missions to perform the POC mandates. Following the C-34's report, DPKO has expanded POC training provided by troop-contributing countries "which tended in the past to focus narrowly on IHL, telling a peacekeeper what not to do, rather than what a peacekeeper should do". DPKO has also examined the existing capacity and resources for POC.

In 2010, DPKO conducted a workshop in Addis Ababa involving six missions and other agencies where it developed the template for implementation of POC mandates, noted above (*Framework for Drafting Comprehensive POC Strategies in UN Peacekeeping Operations*). The template is regarded as providing only general guidance and several officials spoke in favour of the need to develop a tailored strategy for each mission. DPKO's integrated training service has also drafted POC training modules and peacekeeping missions have been encouraged to utilize these and also to develop their own training exercises. DPKO is also working with the UN Entity for Gender Equality and the Empowerment of Women (UNIFEM) to develop a scenario addressing sexual violence. Work is also under way with national peacekeeping training centres.

UNHCR was involved in developing the template for implementation of POC mandates. It also noted that work was being done on enhanced reporting from peacekeeping missions, which may help to improve POC mandates. In addition, UNHCR noted that it works extensively with communities on how they can protect themselves. In this respect, it highlighted the work that UNHCR was doing in the field in terms of conducting participatory assessment whereby protection coordinators are able to identify the needs of refugees and internally displaced persons. DPKO agreed that we cannot just talk about "protection substitutes", but there is also a need to empower national *and* local institutions.

4.7 Future plans

There is wide belief that UN architecture should be established to sustain R2P by referencing existing UN operations. While the Security Council, General Assembly, regional organizations (African Union, NATO, EU), and countries such as Australia and New Zealand are involved in the promulgation of R2P, a political interface is needed that manages early warning. One NGO respondent proposed that the United Nations:

> should produce a watch desk that is capable of giving everyone the heads up, including the Secretary-General. This will help avoid surprises like the situation in Kyrgyzstan. The information is there, it has just not been assessed by people looking through the R2P lens.

Some also thought that UN peacekeeping operations have the capacity to monitor situations on the ground and provide information on early warning when civilians are at risk of R2P crimes. Peacekeeping therefore could be a tool for data collection for the early-warning interface as well as the UNDP Bureau for Crisis Prevention. However, it was noted that an early-warning office had failed to meet expectations in the past, and furthermore, even when good early warning was provided, a lack of political will can kill any potential response.

Even though there has not been much progress to date, proponents considered it important that a Joint Office be promoted to deal with R2P situations in the future. The intention would be to continue in an apolitical way, and thus not accept funds from country donors. The Secretary-General has proposed a process whereby the Special Advisers for R2P and on Prevention of Genocide can convene a meeting of key Under-

Secretaries-General to discuss an R2P situation. Options with pros and cons can then be put to the Secretary-General, who can then take the matter to the Security Council. One of the challenges will be not to call upon the Secretary-General too often, in order to maintain credibility. There is also an expectation that UN agencies will be required to report to the Secretary-General's Policy Committee on what they are doing to implement R2P.

In relation to building political support, many agree that states are fearful of being implicated in R2P, and the best way to advance R2P is from the "bottom up". This will avoid the need to reopen the debates and jeopardize the 2005 consensus on R2P. Incidentally this is similar to the strategy of the Australian and Uruguayan UN missions pursuing inclusion of POC language through informal workshops in New York rather than through UN negotiations. Promoting R2P can be also done at the level of practitioners, who can make a difference, particularly the military from both Western and non-Western troop-contributing countries. Training the military on what to do when facing warning signals or encountering mass atrocities, and building local capacity to prevent and respond to such atrocities, will be crucial if there is a decision to deploy a robust mission in an R2P situation.

4.8 Conclusion

The POC and R2P agendas have evolved separately in the United Nations over the last decade without sufficient cross-references and mutual learning of lessons. Naturally POC evolved rapidly through its strong legal basis in international humanitarian law and its resonance with the core mandates of various agencies – UNHCR, OCHA and ICRC. Furthermore, POC has gained momentum from the continuous attention to the issue in dozens of Security Council resolutions – both thematic and country-specific – and in the several substantive Secretary-General reports. The project, of which this book forms a part, is bringing together the two concepts and identifies overlaps, parallels, and also gaps in protection that need to be filled.

The respondents – UN and other agency officials – agreed that the two concepts are vital parts of the United Nations and they both need to be further strengthened. At the same time, they signalled possible tensions, particularly if promoting R2P as a militarist interventionist tool, and advised what tactics can be deployed so as not to jeopardize the enhancement of the two concepts. It will be vital to monitor the development of the two concepts in the context of the recent actions taken with regard to the protection of civilians in Libya and Syria. If in the context of Libya the rapid reaction by the Security Council, exercising its powers under Chapter VII to impose sanctions and "all necessary measures", is a triumph of R2P and POC, the slow and indecisive response to similarly grave violence, abuses and excessive use of lethal force by governmental agencies against civilian protesters in Syria may turn into a step back and diminish previous efforts, achievements and consensus.

Notes

1. Popovski and Francis undertook the interviews in New York, while the interviews in Geneva were undertaken by Popovski and Mark Notaras.
2. *A New Partnership Agenda: Charting a New Horizon for UN Peacekeeping; Lessons Learned Note on the Protection of Civilians in UN Peacekeeping Operations: Dilemmas, Emerging Practices and Lessons Learned; Operational Concept on the Protection of Civilians in UN Peacekeeping Operations;* and *Concept Note on Robust Peacekeeping, Protecting Civilians in the Context of UN Peacekeeping Operations.*
3. Unless otherwise indicated, interviews were conducted in New York and Geneva during June and July 2010.

REFERENCES

Barbour, Brian, and Brian Gorlick (2008) "Embracing the 'Responsibility to Protect': A Repertoire of Measures Including Asylum for Potential Victims", *International Journal of Refugee Law* 20(4): 533–566.

Bellamy, Alex J. (2010) "The Responsibility to Protect – Five Years On", *Ethics and International Affairs* 24(2): 143–169.

Deschamp, Brian (2010) *A Review of the Protection of Civilians Concept and its Relevance to UNHCR's Mandate*, UNHCR Policy Development and Evaluation Service, September, PDES/2010/11.

DPKO/DFS (2009) *An Agenda for Partnership: New Horizon for UN Peacekeeping.*

High-Level Panel on Threats, Challenges and Change (2004) Report of the Secretary-General's High-level Panel on Threats, Challenges and Change, *A More Secure World: Our Shared Responsibility*, United Nations.

ICISS, International Commission on Intervention and State Sovereignty (2001) *The Responsibility to Protect.* [Online] Available at: ⟨http://www.iciss.ca/report-en.asp⟩ (accessed 23 February 2011).

Holt, Victoria, and Glyn Taylor (2009) Independent study jointly commissioned by UN DPKO/OCHA, *Protecting Civilians in the Context of UN Peacekeeping Operations*, 17 November.

Luck, Edward C. (2010) "The Responsibility to Protect: Growing Pains or Early Promise?", *Ethics & International Affairs* 24(4): 349–365.

Murthy, Jaya (2007) "Mandating the Protection Cluster with the Responsibility to Protect: A Policy Recommendation Based on the Protection Cluster's Implementation in South Kivu, DRC", *Journal of Humanitarian Assistance*, 5 October. [Online] Available at ⟨http://sites.tufts.edu/jha/archives/55⟩.

PCWG, Protection Cluster Working Group (2007) *Mission Statement and Terms of Reference*, 21 March. [Online] Available at: ⟨http://www.unhcr.org/refworld/category,REFERENCE,IASC,4ae9acb71a3,0.html⟩.

Rothchild, Donald, Francis M. Deng, I. William Zartman, Sadikiel Kimaro and Terrence Lyons, eds. (1996) *Sovereignty as Responsibility: Conflict Management in Africa*. Washington, DC: Brookings Institution Press.

Stahn, Carsten (2007) "Responsibility to Protect: Political Rhetoric or Emerging Legal Norm?", *American Journal of International Law* 101(1): 99–120.

Strauss, Ekkehard (2009) "A Bird in the Hand is Worth Two in the Bush: On the Assumed Legal Nature of the Responsibility to Protect", *Global Responsibility to Protect* 1(3): 291–323.

Thakur, Ramesh (2011) "UN Breathes Life into 'Responsibility to Protect'," thestar.com, 21 March. [Online] Available at: ⟨http://www.thestar.com/opinion/editorialopinion/article/957664--un-breathes-life-into-responsibility-to-protect⟩ (accessed 21 March 2011).

UNGA (2005) *UN General Assembly Resolution 60/1: World Summit Outcome Document*, A/Res/60/1, 16 September 2005.

UNGA (2009) *Resolution Adopted by the General Assembly: The Responsibility to Protect*, A/RES/63/308, 14 September 2009.

UNSC (2006) *UN Security Council Resolution 1674 (2006): Protection of Civilians in Armed Conflict*, S/RES/1674, 28 April 2006.

UNSG (2008) "Secretary-General Appoints Edward C. Luck of United States Special Adviser, Secretary-General", SG/A/1120, BIO/3963, 21 February 2008.

UNSG (2009) *Report of the Secretary-General: Implementing the Responsibility to Protect*, A/63/677, 12 January 2009.

Willmot, Haidi (2010) 3rd International Forum for the Challenges of Peace Operations, Canberra, Australia, 27–29 April, *Challenges of Strengthening the Protection of Civilians in Multidimensional Peace Operations, Summary Report*, June 2010.

5

A tale of two norms

Charles Sampford

In late 2008, one of the authors of R2P accosted me in the quadrangle of Magdalen College, Oxford, during an alumni dinner. He was clearly displeased that some were suggesting that R2P was not a norm of international law but merely a "principle" or an "emerging norm".[1] He was not at all happy that the genuinely impressive normative work done by the International Commission on Intervention and State Sovereignty (ICISS) in general and himself and the other lead drafters might not yet have the status of a norm even after its unanimous adoption by the World Summit in 2005. I doubt that he was also reacting to the rising star of Protection of Civilians (POC) which was also being promoted by the Australian government, which many countries feel more comfortable in advocating and which the UN Security Council has used much more.

However, the development and use of these two norms covering similar ground does call for some clarity on what might be meant by saying that responsibility to protect (R2P) or POC is a norm in international affairs, the relationship between them, their origins and their exemplars. This distinction leads into the biggest concern – the concern at potential overreach and abuse and the ways in which the risk of such abuse may be limited. I will argue that they should not be seen as ideas from the West imposed on the rest. They are much more broadly grounded than that, finding support in (i) the empathy for others that is part of being human and which finds a variety of expressions in the religions and cultures of

Norms of protection: Responsibility to protect, protection of civilians and their interaction,
Francis, Popovski and Sampford (eds),
United Nations University Press, 2012, ISBN 978-92-808-1218-3

the world; (ii) the claims by all rulers to protect their followers; and (iii) the fact that many rulers have persecuted rather than protected their subjects.

Similarly, the reservations are at least as firmly grounded in Western tradition as in that of others. Indeed, it was the miseries inflicted by seventeenth-century interventions purportedly to protect co-religionists that led to the principles of non-intervention in the first place.

However, I will argue that the latter fear should not trump the feelings of empathy for unprotected civilians whose lives and livelihoods are threatened by conflict. The risk of abuse should be recognized and addressed by institutional means.

5.1 Norms in international affairs

When discussing the status of these, or any other, international laws, norms and principles, we must always recognize that the distinction between various kinds of international norms is much less clear than in sovereign jurisdictions. Sovereign states claim to be the only authority to determine what is law within their territories – providing clear "source rules"[2] for what is law and what is not. Laws are made by legislature and, to various degrees, the executive and courts. Courts provide authoritative determinations of what those laws mean in common law countries – a role shared with law professors in civil law systems.

In the domestic law of sovereign states, legal rules are reasonably precise statements that will be applied by courts in relevant cases until overruled by courts or modified by statute. There is a role for more general norms. Dworkin (1967: 35) famously called them "principles" which inform and influence the law and its development but are not sufficiently precise or authoritative to be seen as determining the result in individual cases. These may be found in *obiter dicta* of common law judgments and the views of civil law professors seeking to make sense of areas of law with a multiplicity of legal rules.

However, in international law, the distinction between international norms and international law is not so clear. The range of sources is more varied, they have less authority and not only is enforcement limited but the authoritative interpretation of norms by international courts is only possible if they are relevant to a dispute between parties who consent to jurisdiction. Furthermore, with few exceptions, international law only binds states that have agreed to it and, in many cases, it gains its effect when incorporated into domestic legislation which will be in a range of forms and languages and interpreted in a variety of ways.[3]

These difficulties in establishing, interpreting and enforcing legal rules in international law give to more general norms (such as R2P and POC) particularly important roles. They:

1 Provide guidance to those who are seeking to create international law via treaties or interpret it in international tribunals;
2 Influence views about what international law should be and, during the process of signing and ratification, about what it should do;
3 Provide guidance for international actors in the absence of law.

To some extent, it is useful to think of international norms that are debated, discussed and which influence actors. Such norms derive institutional support from a number of international actors who are attracted to them:

1 Influential actors – states and groups of states, and, increasingly, corporations and, in some cases, NGOs;[4]
2 Commissions and expert panels;
3 UN agencies that adopt such norms for their own guidance;
4 The General Assembly (UNGA);
5 The Security Council (UNSC);
6 International courts, especially the International Court of Justice (ICJ) and the International Criminal Court (ICC).

The relative rarity with which emerging norms secure support from the UNSC, the ICJ or through ratification in treaties suggests a different relationship between norms and laws in international law. In domestic law, competing norms and competing versions of those norms may affect debate in legislatures and courts but those debates are largely resolved by statute or precedent. In international law, different norms and various versions of them will tend to wax and wane, becoming more or less influential. This protracted and frequently indeterminate process leads to a number of important dynamics:

1 Related but different norms may be found that cover similar material (e.g. R2P and POC);
2 During this process, different parts or different aspects of a norm may be emphasized by particular institutions (e.g. in 2005, R2P was limited to the four major war crimes);
3 Governments and other actors may emphasize different aspects, or interpretations, of the relevant norms.

This last process may be self-serving but can serve a vital purpose. Although many international norms are seen as universal, they emerge in particular times, places, contexts and cultures. These should not be simply exported to other cultures. Those within different cultures and contexts should not "import" those norms but look for supportive traditions within their own culture and consider how they may contribute to the development and refinement of the emerging norm.[5] This process involves what

Amitara Acharya[6] refers to as "norm localization" and "norm universalization". Looking for supportive traditions within local cultures and linking them to R2P and POC provides an example of norm localization. Such localization provides a better foundation for the norm than a Western import and heads off norm spoilers.[7] For example, links have been noted between Islamic and Christian doctrines regarding rights and duties of military intervention for human protection purposes,[8] and the Jewish case for R2P has been explicitly made[9] with contributions from non-cosmopolitan writers.[10] However, by bringing in the insights of other cultures, such work also contributes to the global debate and content of R2P and POC, leading to norm universalization.

I can now summarize a more nuanced response to Gareth Evans. R2P is now clearly a norm that has not only been stated but used (in UNSC Res. 1973). But the key point is that norms such as R2P are not likely to be strong statements of international law. It is not necessarily a prediction of what international law will be like in the future. The future of the norm depends on normative input and institutional support.

Both norms are emerging – gathering support and changing as they are applied. They may well have different trajectories in which they merge, diverge, wax or wane. Local, regional and cultural engagement, refinement, adaptation and strengthening of norms are important parts of that process and affect the trajectories of these norms.[11]

5.2 Shared origins

It is widely said that R2P and POC share common origins in international humanitarian law and in human rights law (see Chapter 3). I will emphasize two such origins.

Both norms[12] emphasize the value of protecting members of other communities from violence (R2P and POC) and other severe deprivations (POC). All cultures celebrate the special ties we have with particular groups of fellow humans (kin, locality, ethnicity, religion and culture itself) (Gibbs, 2010: 76; Nichols, 2004: 48). While these values may be utilized to generate conflict, most or all cultures recognize, in one form or another, a common humanity, and a concern for others. The duties to avoid harming others and to go to the aid of those who are suffering are a prominent part of many religions. In the last century, it has been formalized in IHL, reinforced by the UN Charter, the UN Declaration on Human Rights and the Human Rights Conventions – while the immediacy of the visual media has made vivid the consequences of breach. While these are obligations to which all nations have committed, this does not mean that we should ignore the variety of supports found within the cultures and religions of the world. It means that we should emphasize these as part of "norm localization".

Both norms emphasize the primary responsibility of the relevant sovereign states – an idea that is grounded in the long-standing attempts by rulers to legitimize their regimes based on the claim that they protected their people. While there were other claims to legitimacy including the claim to be anointed by God (or simply to be a god), this is always, at least, a supplementary claim of those who justify the power they wield.

5.3 Protectors and persecutors: Leviathans and tyrants

Of course, with every grant of power comes the possibility of abuse. What happens if the ruler does not live up to their claims and their rule is not such a good deal for their subjects?[13] What if they cannot or will not protect their subjects? Worse still, what if they become a threat to the very people whose defence is the core of their *raison d'être*?[14] There is a special obloquy for those who are entrusted with power for the benefit of another and use it against them – doctors who murder patients, parents who abuse their children, teachers who brainwash rather than educate their pupils. It is common for the law to treat such abuse of power as an aggravating offence. Sovereigns turn out to be a greater threat to their peoples than the real or imagined enemies against whom they claim to protect their people, and are rarely punished at all. Even when they kill thousands, prison doors do not generally open for them. The doors that open for them are those of the palace at home, the embassy abroad and the private jet in between – as well as the doors to bankers who lend the tyrant money to buy the plane and the palace and to pay for the persecution of civilians. And after it is all over, the citizens will have the responsibility to repay this "sovereign debt".

Why is this tolerated? Why do other states not intervene to protect citizens from the tyrants who oppress them? The answer lies in the wars of religion culminating in the Thirty Years' War of 1618–1648 which involved frequent interventions to purportedly protect co-religionists from persecution. Such interventions were generally undertaken for other reasons and, therefore, the plight of those needing protection worsened and the intervening forces added to that plight. Indeed, the 1648 Treaty of Westphalia can be seen as based on the idea that the consequences of intervention were so bad that it was better to let the tyrant do what tyrants do, and so the principle of non-intervention was born. It was seen as better to have refugees streaming over the border out of the tyranny than to have troops going the other way to stop it. For this reason, I have called the Treaty of Westphalia "a tyrant's charter" – written of the ty-rants, by the tyrants, for the tyrants.[15]

Despite the claims of sovereigns to protect their peoples, the Westphalian concept of sovereignty and sovereign legitimacy is effectively predicated on its opposite. Sovereignty is based on control of territory. This concept had a number of different formulations, most notably Hans Kelsen's formulation that the regime had to be "by and large effective". The effectiveness is initially established by what I have dubbed the "prior successful use of force"[16] against a previous sovereign in order to gain effective control. It is maintained by a continued perceived willingness and capacity to use that force against anyone who would seek to similarly supplant them. The main threat was traditionally other tyrants or groups demanding religious or other freedoms. Members of such groups are not protected from attack but subject to it. If people did not like the sovereign or what was done in his or her name then it was necessary for the sovereign to impose his will and demonstrate his authority by massacring groups of subjects and gruesomely executing their leaders. Rather than giving way to the wishes of the people, sovereigns saw it as their duty to enforce their will and demonstrate their sovereignty. Their *raison d'être* was not the rights of citizens but the preservation of the dynasty and its authority.[17] Where the criterion of sovereignty was the prior successful use of force, human rights violations did not so much undermine sovereign legitimacy as prove it.

One may conclude that, despite the traditional claim of sovereigns to protect their people, the heart of Westphalian sovereignty undermined it. The authoritarian states that were emerging during the century of Westphalia and those that followed are not so much concerned with protection of civilians but protection *from* civilians and used their claimed monopoly of legitimate force[18] against them. If one were to formulate an R2P or POC principle for Westphalian states, they would be more likely to refer to a "Responsibility to Power" and power over citizens. For some of the more religiously minded, it might be seen as the "Responsibility to Persecute".

This idea has been embraced by tyrants the world over. This is not an "Eastern" or "Asian" value. It is a Western idea that has been picked up with obscene alacrity.

5.4 Sovereign legitimacy: Domestic and international

As we have seen, in 1648 legitimacy in both domestic and international law and theory was based on the effectiveness of the sovereign's rule. Within some European states, it was challenged almost immediately and within 30 years concepts of sovereignty in domestic and international law started to diverge. John Locke argued that sovereigns were entrusted with power. If they abused that trust and became a threat to their people, the latter had a right to revolt. That was a pretty inefficient form of regime change and the right to revolt against governments who did not protect their civilians became a right to choose the government that best reflected their interests and values. This shift was part of what I call the Enlightenment's great leap forward in which a variety of governance values (*liberté, égalité, fraternité*, democracy, human rights and the rule of law) were demanded and partly secured in the United States, the United Kingdom and a growing number of European countries. At its centre was a Feuerbachian reversal of the way rulers and ruled related to each other. (Feuerbach, a nineteenth-century German philosopher, pondered the relationship between God and humankind. Christians believe that God created humanity in his own image. Feuerbach suggested that it was at least as likely that humanity created God in his own image.)

Enlightenment *philosophes* suggested a similar inversion for sovereignty. Before the Enlightenment, "subjects" had to demonstrate their allegiance and loyalty to their "sovereign". The *philosophes* proclaimed that "governments" had to justify their existence to "citizens" who chose them. Once the reversal of the relationship was suggested, it was very hard to go back to the old way of looking at things.[19] Indeed, it became as broadly popular with civilians as Westphalian sovereignty was with some authoritarian states.

This approach led to the new basis of sovereign legitimacy in the domestic law and political theory in the increasingly large number of democracies – the acquiescence, then consent, then the active choice of the governed.

International law, however, has continued to recognize states and governments on the basis of who exercises effective political control over discrete territories. Even when a democratically elected government is overturned by a *coup d'état*, the ambassadors of the new regime are accredited by foreign powers[20] and are allowed to take that country's seat at the United Nations and other international forums. This glaring inconsistency caused considerable tension and great soul-searching within democratic states and led to the tentative and controversial claims that a norm of humanitarian intervention was emerging. This revival of pre-Westphalian ideas of intervention faced a lot of hostile reaction which cited not only Westphalian norms but also the sorry history of interventions which led to the treaty in the first place. One of the problems was that this was formulated as a right of states rather than of civilians. One of the great achievements of the ICISS was to effect a similar "Feuerbachian inversion" on the "Right to Intervene". The relevant rights belonged to human beings. States had responsibilities to protect them – with the primary responsibility being of the state in which people reside and contingent responsibility on other states. It is radical because it denies tyrants the right to do what tyrants have always done and for which international law rewarded them. Accordingly, I see R2P not as a Western attempt to interfere in other people's problems but a global attempt to deal with a Western problem at the heart of the Westphalian system.

5.5 POC and R2P: Differences in origins and exemplars

R2P and POC share similar normative origins and are both directed at the idea that states should live up to their claims to protect their civilians, should receive international support in doing so, and could be ultimately required to do so. The two principles came together in Libya. In UNSC Res. 1970, Colonel Gaddafi was referred to the ICC for doing what tyrants traditionally do to protect their power. In UNSC Res. 1970 and 1973, Colonel Gaddafi's domestic responsibility to protect civilians (R2P Pillar One) was explicitly recognized and the use of international uninvited force was authorized for the protection of civilians in Libya. It is notable that the UNSC used POC rather than R2P Pillar Three in this case.

Although the two merged in Libya, R2P and POC have been developing along different paths and can be illustrated by different exemplars which go a long way to explaining the varying level of international support.

Discussion of POC at the international level started with existing armed conflicts and sought to protect civilians in pre-existing conflicts according to well-accepted principles of international humanitarian law (IHL). Accordingly, POC was, from the beginning, about reducing the effects of conflict by an institution established to prevent conflict because of the disastrous effects of previous conflicts. As such, it has grown with less fanfare and much more consensus than R2P and does not appear to depart from that core business of the United Nations.

By contrast, R2P emerged as a proposed response to enormous challenges posed by Rwanda, Srebrenica and Kosovo where the consequences of internal conflict appeared so great that the creation of what would be effectively a new international conflict was seriously contemplated. Indeed, the US and UK considered the consequences so serious that they were prepared to start a war that appeared to be contrary to international law.[21]

In fact, both POC and R2P represent a continuum of responses. There are three "pillars" of R2P: (i) the responsibility of the state; (ii) the responsibility of the international community to help the state; and, only in rare circumstances, (iii) the above responsibility to act in spite of non-consent. POC can be seen to have a range of "pillars" or forms (see Chapter 2) with different versions of the norm for relevant actors (combatant POC, humanitarian POC, peacekeeping POC and Security Council POC).

R2P was contentious from the beginning because it was a response to an event that led to "Pillar Three" action without the legal authority that many (including this author) argued was necessary at the time and which ICISS later argued. POC was less controversial because it started with the accepted legal obligations of combatants.

5.6 From pillars to pyramids

While the architectural metaphor of a pillar is a common one, I am increasingly inclined to doubt its utility here.[22] Pillars are seen as separate and of similar size and height (without which they cannot hold up a lintel). But in R2P and POC, the various elements are only effective if they interact and none are, nor intended to be, of similar size and weight. In R2P, the primary emphasis is on the responsibilities of host governments and the responsibility of other states to assist them in that responsibility rather than to supplant them in this role. In POC, the primary obligation is on combatants and the state (if it is not one of the combatants) with international actors filling in gaps. This suggests a different architectural metaphor – a pyramid:

1 The less coercive versions of the norm will have the largest application – indicating the solid and broad base of the pyramid. The more interventionist and ultimate coercive measures are the higher and narrower steps on the pyramid.
2 Even if the norms covered by Pillar Two or Pillar Three are called on, the Pillar One responsibility of states remains in force and the state will be expected to contribute where it can. International assistance is still to assist, not to supplant that responsibility. Thus the various norms build on each other and are simultaneously present and in force. The same is true of POC where combatant POC is primary.
3 It gives the greatest role in protection to the sovereigns who claim to provide it as justification for their sovereign power.
4 In terms of protection actually given, most is provided by intra-state forces – though it is important to emphasize the critical role of non-state elements. The latter play a critical and not always recognized role in normal times when civilian security is supported not only by security forces such as army, police and fire brigades but by community groups,

the way people live and physical barriers such as locks on doors which together constitute what I call "civilian protection systems".[23] It is even more relevant in times of disorder when the security forces are ineffective, feral[24] or partially replaced by international civil-military forces. Effective international assistance with the agreement of the sovereign state (Pillar Two) or with UNSC mandate (Pillar Three) can only do so much; successful assistance needs the collaboration and support of community groups from the populations to be protected even more than from international NGOs.

5 One might go further and suggest that communities have been protecting themselves since prehistoric times and that this constitutes the real base of the pyramid on which the state (generally) provides another, smaller step and international action an even smaller one.

This approach reflects much thinking about norms and regulation such as Braithwaite's "enforcement pyramid" for corporate regulation.[25] Regulatory goals are not principally achieved by the threat, let alone the imposition, of sanctions. The availability of sanctions is useful and sometimes necessary to secure compliance from some and to provide extra reasons for compliance from others. But most compliance needs to be through norm-setting that taps into pre-existing norms – the lowest and broadest step. These should be publicized and justified with the engagement of relevant sanctions – one view of the next step. Minor and first breaches generate reminders (another step) which, if ignored, lead to minor or conditional sanctions (yet another). The imposition of significant sanctions is near the top and "corporate capital punishment" is the tiny but very useful peak. While capital punishment for individuals is unacceptable for most, using it for organizations may be a very sensible approach and should be considered more often. If a regime is no longer recognized by the international community as a whole and by key international institutions (such as the United Nations, the World Trade Organization or the Bank of International Settlements), its viability is, at the very least, limited.[26]

The pyramid metaphor might be useful in emphasizing the time and effort that must go into building them. The pyramid metaphor is also useful in understanding the greater difficulties in securing acceptance for R2P. While POC has been built up from its broad base – and the pointy end has only been attached this year through UNSC Res. 1973 – with R2P, the construction had to start from the pointy end because that was what addressed the Kosovo issue which was the *raison d'être* for its creation. While there is a great deal of mystery about the way that the pyramids were built, one does not have to be a stonemason or an engineer to know that this is not the recommended method of building pyramids. Given the construction brief, progress has been remarkable.

5.7 Potential overreach and abuse

The largest obstacle to securing broader support for R2P is, of course, the concern that it may be abused through its use to justify invasions mounted for other reasons. This is a concern that should be fully acknowledged and addressed. The thoroughly Western, Westphalian principle of non-intervention was generated by direct experience of the consequences of abuse. The ICISS report acknowledged the risk – a risk that materialized almost immediately when Commissioner Ignatieff used it to justify the invasion of Iraq.[27]

The potential of overreach is not confined to R2P. The Red Cross defines POC as "all activities aimed at obtaining full respect for the rights of the individual in accordance with the letter and spirit of the relevant bodies of law" – a formulation that seems to go beyond protection to promoting rights and better societies. I could imagine a member of the G8 seeing in those words the possibility that foreign forces might enter a country with UNSC and home state approval but would then set about pursuing "*all* activities aimed at obtaining full respect for the rights of the individual in accordance with the letter and spirit of the relevant bodies of law". Given the range of international human rights laws and their expansive and ambitious spirit, the foreign forces would be there forever. Indeed, none of the Western countries that contribute to peacekeeping forces provide full respect for individual rights set out in the UN Conventions that they have ratified. Of course, the Red Cross did not intend such outcomes. In international civil-military operations, foreign forces are fully extended trying to secure basic protection, securing food and medical supplies and support for the rule of law. The spirit of human rights is left to supportive NGOs and state officials. However, fine words penned with good intentions by those with the purest motives can be used for other purposes and it is well to address and limit those risks.

5.8 Limiting the risk of abuse

Four ways of limiting this risk occur to me – sticking to the Westphalian formula, narrowing the scope, utilizing two R2P "moves" and subjecting all action in pursuit of R2P and POC to the international rule of law. I will discuss these in turn.

5.8.1 Westphalian formula

Pillar Three of R2P and UNSC POC is an exception to the Westphalian principle of non-intervention. While it uses the medium of UNSC power and authority granted by the UN Charter and subject to the UNSC voting constraints, it could be argued that action to deal with internal conflict goes beyond the UNSC's powers under Article 39 to "maintain or restore international peace and security". The Westphalian approach would insist that there be no international protective actions within the borders of a state without that state's approval.

5.8.2 Narrower scope

The 2005 summit sought to limit the potential for abuse of R2P by restricting its application to four particularly heinous crimes: genocide, war crimes, ethnic cleansing and crimes against humanity. This makes it harder for states to hold out on signing and easier to override concerns about sovereignty and non-intervention if the occasion arises.

However, in restricting R2P to such crimes, it is narrowed to cases where there will be pressure to intervene earlier and more strongly – leading directly to Pillar Three and thereby undermining the strategy of emphasizing Pillars One and Two.

5.8.3 Emphasizing two ICISS "moves"

The ICISS made two very important moves in constructing R2P to make it less amenable to abuse. The first was to perform the "Feuerbachian inversion" on the claimed "right of humanitarian intervention" by insisting that the only rights were those of the civilian population – states had responsibility. The second was to emphasize that the primary responsibility was that of the state where the relevant civilians lived. Responsibilities of others was to assist that state with its agreement and only on the rarest of occasions, and even then only with full legal authority, without that agreement. This was formalized in the 2005 three pillars approach.

POC effectively operates under a similar regime – starting with, and defined by, individual human rights and with a strong emphasis on assisting states to fulfil their primary duty. I have suggested that similar moves might clarify POC and avoid any concerns at overreach under the Red Cross definition.[28] The number and scope of rights covered by POC stands: but the primary responsibility for their realization lies with the state where the civilians are located. Humanitarian actors and peace-keepers have a role in assisting – with the latter involved in more limited security roles set out in their mission. The UNSC has an overall responsibility for helping to marshal international support and, in very rare cases, insisting on it.

The pillars approach is not only a means for preventing abuse but enables clearer thinking and more effective action. A general norm is not self-implementing. Such implementation will usually require several actors to contribute consecutively, contemporaneously and sometimes in both ways. If they are to play their role in implementing the norm, it is important to ensure detailed normative guidance through customized norms and, where necessary, formal prescription through detailed laws. They also need appropriate institutional structures and operational procedures to fulfil that role. The R2P pillars can be seen as structured in this way. Pillar One addresses the role of the state. Pillar Two addresses the role of other states when consensually assisting a state. Pillar Three addresses the role of the UNSC and member states providing that assistance without the consent of the host state.

As indicated, POC could be similarly "pillarized" (if not pilloried). *Combatant POC* deals with the role of the combatants, *peacekeeping POC* with peacekeepers, *humanitarian POC* with other humanitarian actors and *Security Council POC* with the UNSC and the Office of the Secretary-General. We have sought to identify the relevant norms, institutions and operational procedures for each (though we do not attempt, in this project, to do so in the detail that military and police forces do).

This pillars approach might be seen as reflecting a more general pattern of normative, institutional and operational responses to horrific events (natural or human-made) that generate widespread revulsion and evoke empathy for their victims. The revulsion generates a public outcry demanding action. The revulsion will generally be informed by moral values[29] but will rarely take the form of detailed moral argument. This is where lawyers and ethicists will ask what the relevant norm is, to whom it applies and what action it demands. But those who feel the revulsion will demand action of those institutions which are seen as having either a duty or the capacity to act. While the public outcry might focus on governments or the United Nations, successful responses will generally require several actors. They will need to understand their roles in response to a particular event and think about their roles in any similar future crisis. For this to work effectively, they need to delineate a general norm, particular norms and legal rules, institutional structures and operational procedures.

5.8.4 Better procedures: Subjecting all R2P and POC action to the international rule of law

R2P and POC ultimately seek to give the UNSC (and those it authorizes) the authority to use their coercive powers within the sovereign territory of other states. In so doing, it extends the ways in which the UNSC's powers may operate.[30] There is natural concern that such a power might not be used for the noble purposes for which it is established but abused by being used to further other selfish ends at the expense of those in need of protection. The first way of addressing this danger avoids the problem by withholding the power – preventing the abuse but also precluding the benefit of protecting citizens from the worst atrocities. The second approach narrows the power to the most significant failures of protection. The third seeks to refine the relevant norms. The final approach seeks procedural safeguards to prevent the likelihood of abuse by judicial review of those who are exercising these extended powers.

Rather than reducing or eliminating these interpretively extended powers, it seeks to confine the use of the power to the purposes intended and renders the use of that power for improper purposes invalid.

When I first wrote about this in 1999 for the closing keynote of the World Congress of Legal and Social Philosophy (held mainly in the World Trade Center),[31] I advanced the following:

> [a] simple proposition is that no country may intervene unless it submits itself, at least for that particular intervention, to the jurisdiction of the International Court of Justice and the International Criminal Court (when established). No country should engage in any intervention without so subjecting itself, no country should support such intervention without this proviso and no international body should endorse or authorise such intervention without it.

The reasons were simple. Those who seek to enforce international law (for example, IHL) should be bound by international law. "The international community should consider it intolerable for anyone to claim to enforce international law without being bound by it." I suggested that, if we found the unlawful use of force by a police officer carrying a baton disturbing, how much more should we be concerned when "the self-appointed policeman is not just carrying a baton but an arsenal of cruise missiles"; it is, quite frankly, terrifying.

Within the current formulations of R2P and POC, this would mean that UNSC authorization of the use of force should be conditional on those so authorized accepting the jurisdiction of the ICJ and ICC to determine whether its use of its powers was in accord with the relevant UNSC resolution and whether the UNSC resolution was within the UNSC's power. This would give the decisions greater legitimacy and would also make the UNSC more likely to authorize the use of force because it would know that it could not be unilaterally extended by being given an expansive view of the mandate by a permanent member (as had happened with the First Gulf War).

Those who are concerned at potential abuses of R2P and POC have a right to demand this. The UNSC and those seeking to enforce IHL should cheerfully concede it.

Some might wonder whether member states would be willing to contribute forces to mandates subject to the rule of law. States committed to the international rule of law should have no problem with this requirement – unless their acceptance of the international rule of law is made in bad faith, a point that is difficult to plead. We should be as wary of states who will only act if they are not subject to law as we are of police officers who make the same demands. The dangers to emerging norms of using them to authorize action by those who may abuse them should be clear. To do so would endanger the legitimacy of the norm and of the UNSC itself.[32] It may well be that fewer missions can be mounted and evil will go unanswered. But evil has been going unanswered for millennia and continues when the UNSC cannot agree, where insufficient force can be secured or the mission goes wrong for lack of clarity, poor leadership, and so on. It is better to start with fewer missions that are effective and legitimate. They may be the more extreme and obvious cases with later extensions as the principles and practices are developed. Much effective institutional and legal reform proceeds on this basis. It may be the best we can hope for but in the long term it may be simply the best and only way to proceed.

5.9 Conclusion

This chapter commenced with the question of whether R2P is an international norm (legal or otherwise). It concluded by arguing that both R2P and POC would be more secure and more likely to be used if fully subject to international law. In between, we have considered some of the pertinent differences between domestic and international law and norms, focusing on the way that they may wax and wane, gather and lose support as well as the way that they may diverge, converge or merge and suggested that this was happening with R2P and POC. We also looked at the different origins and exemplars for R2P and POC which tended to make the R2P more controversial. We considered the importance of the "pillared" approach to R2P and its potential application to POC but considered pyramids the better metaphor because of the primary importance of the state's responsibility to protect. We then examined the genuine concerns that R2P (and POC) could be abused and considered the various ways of mitigating the likelihood of abuse – focusing on the rule of law.

Notes

1. While conversations during such breaks are rarely fully footnoted, I am reasonably sure that this reference was, *inter alia*, to Luck (2006).
2. See Raz (1979).
3. However, this does not mean that international law is not followed or is generally ineffective. Its most notable weakness is also one of its great strengths. The fact that it is generally only those states who have agreed to the law that are bound by it also means that all of those who are bound by law have almost always agreed to it. This indicates levels of support almost unknown in domestic jurisdictions. In a well-ordered democracy, laws only need support of parties carrying 50% of the voters. Gerrymanders, first-past-the-post systems and statistical aberrations may mean that voter support for government and opposition parties may be well under that figure – and on particular bills the majorities may be even less than that. And many countries are either not well-ordered or not democracies.
4. For example, the role of the Red Cross and, more recently, Médecins Sans Frontières on human rights and Transparency International in fighting corruption and pressing for relevant OECD conventions, and finally the UN Convention Against Corruption (UNCAC).
5. Our Institute ran a series of dialogues on governance values involving Islamic and Western academics and practitioners supported by the Open Society Institute – see Azra and Hudson (2008).
6. *International Studies Quarterly* March 2011.
7. Some of this work has been done on R2P and intervention by Durham (2008).
8. While Islamic nations have clear concerns about Western imperialism, their views on the need for intervention in Bosnia show that they are not averse to military intervention for human protection purposes in principle – quite the contrary. See Ramsbotham (1998: 95).
9. Dorfman and Messinger (2009).
10. Less cosmopolitan theorists are also able to uphold a cross-cultural "overlapping consensus" on norms against genocide. See Taylor (1999). Ramsbotham (1998) argues for an overlapping consensus on rights and duties of military intervention for human protection purposes. (In this regard, note also Dorfman and Messinger (2009) and Walsh (2007).) Consider, in this regard, Walzer's view that we praise military intervention for human protection purposes because it upholds: "the values of individual life and communal liberty *of which sovereignty itself is merely an expression*" [my emphasis] (2000: 108). Walzer's (1995) focus on people's self-determination is able to allow action in egregious cases because in such cases, as he says, the people "are not determining anything for themselves". That is, Walzer's normative concern is of political communities – rather than states or governments. Intervention can thus be justified in those extreme cases where the lack of fit between government and community is "radically apparent". See Walzer (1980: 124).
11. Chataway (2007: 210) traces R2P's development in terms of theories of norm evolution. Though see also Bellamy (2005: 32) and Welsh (2010: 426). The classic in norm development literature is Finnemore and Sikkink (1998).
12. I will not take a position as to whether the pillars (or pyramids) of R2P and POC are separate norms or elements of the same norms.
13. Of course, these claims may have been totally fraudulent, made without any sincerity. They may well have been liars as well as tyrants but they would not generally admit to being liars on this matter.

14. Locke's repudiation of Hobbes puts it quite nicely: "This is to think, that men are so foolish, that they take care to avoid what mischiefs may be done them by *pole-cats,* or *foxes;* but are content, nay, think it safety, to be devoured by *lions*" Locke (1947: II, 93).

15. With apologies to the United Dutch Provinces, the only signatory clearly not a tyranny, and to Abraham Lincoln and his Gettysburg address.

16. See Sampford (1999).

17. If they claimed higher purposes and external responsibilities, these were more likely to be to do with religion rather than human rights. Sovereigns might purport to be more concerned about the afterlife of their subjects than their present life – to the extent that some thoughtfully burned heretics.

18. Although Max Weber did not refer to the "monopoly of legitimate force" until 250 years later, the seventeenth-century rulers were very much concerned to establish such a monopoly against their "over-mighty subjects". See Weber (1922 [1979]).

19. This is what I have called the "great leap forward" of the Enlightenment – choosing those words because of the greater commitment of peoples to states that claimed to rule for their people and the killing and dying that leaders of such states could require.

20. I have tended to think that it will all depend on whether China becomes a democracy before it becomes the most powerful economy. If we have, by then, built a rules-based international system founded on respect for human rights, democracy and the rule of law, China will then take its place within that system. More recently, the rise of India and Brazil indicates a more multipolar world so that we will not have to wait for the United States to resume its former leadership role in developing that system.

21. This is not the place to discuss the legality of the Kosovo War. Suffice it to say that the early advice on both sides of the Atlantic was that it would be illegal and the belligerents struggled to avoid the issue being determined in the ICJ.

22. See discussion in Sampford, Smith and Brown (2005).

23. See Sampford (2010).

24. That is, acting against the civilians they are supposed to protect.

25. See Ayres and Braithwaite (1995). Similar ideas are found in normative theories of rights and backup duties – see Shue (1980, 1996) and successive waves of duties – see Waldron (2001).

26. I argued in "Sovereignty and Intervention" that, in a globalized world, recognition is necessary for effectiveness – and consequently the policy of recognizing effective regimes was either circular or an active endorsement of the regime. See Sampford (2001).

27. Ignatieff (2003: 38ff).

28. This approach addressed concerns raised by the Egyptian representative at an African Union Symposium on POC in Addis Ababa in March 2010.

29. We will not enter into debate whether such revulsions can be untouched by moral considerations and are purely visceral or natural. By the time that individuals are in a position to demand action, even their "gut" instincts are likely to be informed by moral training.

30. It might be argued that the UNSC already has the power under Chapter VII of the UN Charter because of the difficulty of reviewing its exercise of that power. However, the likelihood of the UNSC authorizing action beyond what most believe to be its powers is small and its legitimacy less. Accordingly, an accepted norm that authorizes an extended use of a power does extend the extent of the power.

31. Sampford (2001).

32. I have argued that the First Gulf War was a brilliant success in securing its stated goals very quickly. It was the failure to secure the unstated goal of removing Saddam Hussein that meant the American administration managed to pull defeat from the jaws of vic-

tory, to blatantly exceed the powers they had been given and to make it very difficult to secure authorization for future action. See Sampford (1999).

REFERENCES

Ayres, Ian, and John Braithwaite (1995) *Responsive Regulation: Transcending the Deregulation Debate*. Oxford, Oxford University Press.

Azra, Azyumardi, and Wayne Hudson, eds. (2008) *Islam Beyond Conflict: Indonesian Islam and Western Political Theory*. Aldershot, UK: Ashgate.

Bellamy, Alex (2005) "Responsibility to Protect or Trojan Horse? The Crisis in Darfur and Humanitarian Intervention after Iraq", *Ethics and International Affairs* 19: 31.

Chataway, Teresa (2007) "Towards Normative Consensus on Responsibility to Protect", *Griffith Law Review* 16: 193.

Dorfman, Aaron, and Ruth Messinger (2009) "Toward a Jewish Argument for the Responsibility to Protect", in Richard Cooper and Juliette Kohler, eds. *Responsibility to Protect: The Global Moral Compact for the 21st Century*. Basingstoke, UK: Palgrave Macmillan.

Durham, Helen (2008) "The Laws of War and Traditional Cultures: A Case Study of the Pacific Region", *Commonwealth Law Bulletin* 34: 833.

Dworkin, R. M. (1967) "The Model of Rules", *University of Chicago Law Review* 35: 14.

Finnemore, Martha, and Kathryn Sikkink (1998) "International Norm Dynamics and Political Change", *International Organisation* 52: 887.

Gibbs, John (2010) *Moral Development and Reality: Beyond the Theories of Kohlberg and Hoffman,* 2nd edn. London: Penguin Academics.

Ignatieff, M. (2003) "Why are we in Iraq?", *New York Times,* 7 September, 38ff.

Locke, John (1947) *Two Treatises of Government.* New York: Hafner.

Luck, Edward (2006) *UN Security Council: Practice and Promise.* London: Routledge.

Nichols, Shaun (2004) Sentimental Rules: On the Natural Foundations of Moral Judgment. Oxford: Oxford University Press.

Ramsbotham, Oliver P. (1998) "Islam, Christianity, and Forcible Humanitarian Intervention", *Ethics and International Affairs* 12: 81.

Raz, J. (1979) *Authority of Law*. Oxford: Oxford University Press.

Sampford, Charles (1999) *Challenges to the Concepts of "Sovereignty" and "Intervention"*, World Congress on Legal and Social Philosophy. New York, 29 June 1999.

Sampford, Charles (2001) "Sovereignty and Intervention", in T. Campbell and B. Leiser, eds. *Human Rights in Theory and Practice*. Aldershot, UK: Ashgate, 335.

Sampford, Charles (2010) *Protection of Civilians and the Rule of Law*. 3rd International Forum for the Challenges of Peace Operations, "Challenges of Protecting Civilians in Multidimensional Peace Operations". Asia Pacific Civil-Military Centre of Excellence, Australia, 27–29 April 2010.

Sampford, Charles, Rodney Smith and A. Brown (2005) "From Greek Temple to Bird's Nest: Towards a Theory of Coherence and Mutual Accountability for National Integrity Systems", *Australian Journal of Public Administration* 64: 96.

Shue, H. (1980, 1996) *Basic Rights: Subsistence, Affluence, and US Foreign Policy.* Princeton, NJ: Princeton University Press.

Taylor, Charles (1999) "Conditions of an Unforced Consensus on Human Rights", in J. Bauer and D. Bell, eds. *The East Asian Challenge for Human Rights.* Cambridge: Cambridge University Press, 124.

Waldron, Jeremy (2001) *Law and Disagreement.* Oxford: Oxford University Press.

Walsh, Caroline (2007) "Rawls and Walzer on Non-Domestic Justice", *Contemporary Political Theory* 6: 419.

Walzer, Michael (1980) "The Moral Standing of States: A Response to Four Critics", *Philosophy and Public Affairs* 9: 209.

Walzer, Michael (1995) "The Politics of Rescue", *Social Research* 1: 53.

Walzer, Michael (2000) *Just and Unjust Wars: A Moral Argument with Historical Illustrations*, 3rd edn. New York: Basic Books.

Weber, Max (1922 [1979]) *Economy and Society.* Berkeley, CA: University of California Press.

Welsh, Jennifer (2010) "Implementing the 'Responsibility to Protect': Where Expectations Meet Reality", *Ethics and International Affairs* 24: 415.

6

Peacekeeping, civilian protection mandates and the responsibility to protect

Hitoshi Nasu

The idea that the United Nations, acting through the Security Council, should intervene when civilian lives are threatened or being violated came about in the late 1990s as a result of independent inquiries into the failure to prevent mass atrocity crimes in Rwanda and Srebrenica.[1] This idea spawned a two-pronged response within the UN. First, the responsibility to protect (R2P) concept emerged in 2001 from the report of the International Commission on Intervention and State Sovereignty (ICISS, 2001). The concept has since then been variably embraced by UN documents (UN High-Level Panel, 2004: 66; UNSG, 2005: para. 135), and was contained in the 2005 *World Summit Outcome Document* (WSOD), in which world leaders, albeit restrictively, affirmed their commitment to the responsibility to protect populations from genocide, ethnic cleansing, crimes against humanity and war crimes (UNGA, 2005: paras. 138–139). Much of the discussion about the concept still remains largely as a policy agenda (UNGA, 2009b; Bellamy, 2010: 158, 166), posing challenges to the operationalization of the concept in practice.

Second, the Security Council has since 1999 developed the practice of mandating peacekeepers to protect civilians under imminent threat of physical violence within their capabilities and area of deployment. The civilian protection mandate was explicitly given to the UN mission in Sierra Leone (UNAMSIL) in 1999 for the first time (UNSC, 1999a: para. 14), and since then to the UN peace operations in the Democratic Republic of Congo, Liberia, Côte d'Ivoire, Burundi, Sudan (also in Darfur), and the Central African Republic and Chad in an almost identical

Norms of protection: Responsibility to protect, protection of civilians and their interaction,
Francis, Popovski and Sampford (eds),
United Nations University Press, 2012, ISBN 978-92-808-1218-3

formula (Holt and Berkman, 2007: 85–91). The Security Council's recognition of the importance of a civilian protection mandate is reflected in the reference to Chapter VII of the UN Charter explicitly, yet rather restrictively, authorizing the use of armed force to protect civilians (Breau, 2006: 445–452). Despite many positive developments and the recognition of its significance by the UN Security Council (UNSC, 2009a; UNSC, 2006a: para. 16), continued operational difficulties and failures in the field have raised concerns over the lack of operational guidelines in relation to civilian protection tasks (Holt and Taylor, 2009). In 2009, the Security Council member states recognized the seriousness of this issue and the need for comprehensive operational guidance on the tasks and responsibilities of peacekeepers in the implementation of civilian protection mandates (UNSC, 2009b: para. 22). The political consensus on what is required to implement civilian protection mandates is currently lacking, with some states criticizing civilian protection mandates for being unclear or impracticable (Holt and Taylor, 2009: 41–42, 75–77).

The R2P concept could be seen as essentially relating to the protection of civilians (POC) during an armed conflict in the sense that both are guided by deontological norms of humanity. However, the two are not synonymous as POC potentially involves a broad range of issues beyond the four mass atrocity crimes identified in the 2005 WSOD (Williams, 2010: 14). While some commentators attempt to find a link between the two concepts (Wills, 2009: ch. 5, 2004: 406–409), some states have been explicit in setting them apart (UNGA, 2009a: 5). The civilian protection activities of peacekeepers may well serve as an explicit interpretation of R2P in the long run (Johnstone, 2008: 99). However, currently the relationship between the Security Council's practice of mandating peacekeepers to protect civilians and the R2P concept remains unclear (Luck, 2010: 67).

This chapter examines the relationship between the two concepts in an attempt to consider whether and to what extent the civilian protection mandate may operationalize the R2P concept in practice. To that end, it will first review the development of the Security Council's practice to deploy peacekeeping missions with a civilian protection mandate for the purpose of clarifying the extent to which that development has been influenced by or otherwise linked to the R2P concept. The relationship between the two concepts will then be examined by reference to the classification of R2P into prevention, reaction and rebuilding in the 2001 ICISS Report (2001: 19–45), as well as the three pillars proposed in the Secretary-General's 2009 Report, *Implementing the Responsibility to Protect* (UNSG, 2009). It identifies three possible ways of visualizing the relationship between the two concepts: (i) civilian protection mandate as the implementation of Pillar Two strategy; (ii) civilian protection mandate as operationalizing the responsibility to prevent; and (iii) civilian protection mandate as operationalizing the responsibility to react (or Pillar Three strategy). It will be argued that, while there is a potential for merging the two concepts, such an attempt will entail different implications for the existing mode of peacekeeping operations depending on which policy option is pursued.

6.1 The development of civilian protection mandates

Peacekeepers have long been involved in operations with the mandate to enhance the security of civilians and support human rights (Månsson, 2005). Yet the idea that peacekeepers should intervene to protect civilians when they are under imminent threat of physical violence emerged in the aftermath of mass atrocities in Rwanda and Srebrenica, which the international community failed to prevent despite the presence of UN peacekeepers in the field. Thus, the 1999 *Report of the Independent Inquiry on Rwanda* concluded that the UN "must be prepared to respond to the perception and the expectation created by its very presence" (UN, 1999: 51). In 2000, the Brahimi Report went so far as to propose that peacekeepers "who witness violence against civilians should be *presumed* to be authorized to stop it, within their means" (emphasis added) (Brahimi, 2000: para. 62; van Baarda and van Iersel, 2002: 33–44).

The idea was put into practice when the Security Council established UN peacekeeping missions in Sierra Leone (UNAMSIL) and the Democratic Republic of Congo (MONUC) with an explicit civilian protection mandate (UNSC, 1999a: para. 14; UNSC, 2000c: para. 8). When the UN Secretary-General proposed the deployment of a peacekeeping force in Sierra Leone, it was envisaged to be a traditional peacekeeping operation mandated to assist the Sierra Leone government in creating "the conditions of confidence and stability required for the smooth implementation of the peace process" (UNSG, 1999b: para. 41). The inclusion of this mandate was pressed by the Canadian delegation, reflecting upon and being heavily influenced by the failure to protect civilians from mass atrocities in Rwanda (UNSC, 1999c: 10; UNSC, 2000b: 9–12). Canada's advocacy for a clear mandate to prevent and respond to physical violence against civilians was reportedly grounded in the concept of human security (UNSC, 1999b: 17; UNSC, 2000b: 10–11; UNSC, 2000d: 7; Golberg and Hubert, 2001: 223), given that Canada, along with Japan, had been the leading advocate of the concept since its official appearance in the UNDP *Human Development Report* (UNDP, 1994: 22). Although human security provides one of the rationales behind the R2P concept, the mandate was not discussed in terms of the language of responsibility.

Other states appear to have been more cautious towards the introduction of this new mandate of civilian protection. The United Kingdom delegate cautiously welcomed the mandate, stating that the mission "should be prepared to act to defend civilians when and where it is able to do so" and emphasizing that "ultimately ECOMOG and the Government of Sierra Leone have responsibility for security under the Peace Agreement" (UNSC, 1999b: 9). The Netherlands stressed that "robust rules of engagement are indeed essential if UNAMSIL is to fulfil its mandate and protect itself and civilians under threat" (ibid.: 13). Argentina regarded POC under Chapter VII as "a pertinent development in the context of the mandate of a peacekeeping operation" and "significant in that it introduces a new, fundamental political, legal and moral dimension" (ibid.: 16). However, it then observed that "the objective to be fulfilled must be consonant with the means provided", emphasizing the geographical limit (area of deployment) and functional limit (meaning that it does not overlap the specific security responsibilities entrusted to ECOMOG) attached to the mandate (ibid.: 16).

Similarly, Canada was the driving force behind the adoption of Resolution 1291 authorizing the UN Organization Mission in the Congo (MONUC) to protect civilians. Canada, along with Namibia (UNSC, 2000d: 3), Rwanda (UNSC 2000a: 21–23) and Uganda (UNSC, 2000a: 20), urged that the mission's mandate "should include clear and unequivocal provision for the protection of civilians under Chapter VII of the Charter" (UNSC, 2000b: 11). However, other states provided no particular comment on the civilian protection mandate. Since then, the practice has developed to include the civilian protection mandate under Chapter VII in peacekeeping missions without much deliberation, as was the case in establishing the UN operation in Côte d'Ivoire and the UN mission in Sudan (Holt and Taylor, 2009: 293, 319–321).

After the 2005 WSOD was adopted, there were two occasions where the R2P concept was referred to in relation to civilian protection.[2] The first reference was made in a general context of adopting Resolution 1674 (UNSC, 2006a) on civilian protection in armed conflict by reaffirming "the provisions of paragraphs 138 and 139 of the 2005 World Summit Outcome Document regarding the responsibility to protect populations from genocide, war crimes, ethnic cleansing and crimes against humanity" (UNSC, 2006a: para. 4). There is no discussion record that would have indicated the intention of the Security Council members as to what the reference to the R2P concept in the context of civilian protection in armed conflict meant for the civilian protection mandate given to peacekeepers (UNSC, 2006b). However, the Security Council reaffirmed, without reference to R2P, "its practice of ensuring that the mandates of United Nations peacekeeping, ... include, *where appropriate and on a case-by-case basis*, provisions regarding (i) the protection of civilians, particularly those under imminent threat of physical danger within their zones of operation" (emphasis added) (UNSC, 2006a: para. 16). Although at the same time it expressed its intention that POC should be given priority in decisions about the use of available capacity and resources in the implementation of the mandates (ibid.: para. 16; UNSC, 2009a: 5), the wording appears to indicate a reserved position not dissimilar to the Security Council's preparedness to take collective action to fulfil the international community's R2P as expressed by world leaders in the 2005 WSOD (UNGA, 2005: para. 139).

The second is Resolution 1706, which was adopted in relation to the situation in Darfur, Sudan. As pointed out by the UK delegation, this became the first resolution to deploy a peacekeeping operation with a civilian protection mandate that made an explicit reference to R2P (UNSC, 2006d: 4). Yet again, the reference to R2P was of a general nature in the preamble (UNSC, 2006c: pream. para. 2), and was not explicitly linked to the mandate that authorized peacekeepers to use all necessary means to protect civilians under threat of physical violence (UNSC, 2006c: para. 12(a)). Although some states explicitly referred to the Security Council's responsibility to protect in adopting the resolution (UNSC, 2006d: 3–4, 7, 9, 10), none of the remarks clarified how the civilian protection mandate for this peacekeeping mission will be related to the international community's R2P.

The Security Council's mandate of civilian protection has been crafted with a clear intention to avoid creating unrealistic expectations both internationally and in host states about the extent to which peacekeepers are able to provide protection, as evidenced in the key caveats that serve to restrict the scope of the mandate (Holt and Taylor, 2009: 39–41). The scope of R2P has also been narrowly defined since the adoption of the 2005 WSOD by reference only to four mass atrocity crimes – genocide, war crimes, ethnic cleansing and crimes against humanity. Those limitations to the scope of each concept, however, appear to be based on different rationales in that the former is the result of taking into account when peacekeepers *can* act, whereas the latter is the minimum consensus that states were able to reach as to when the international community *ought to* act.

6.2 Operationalizing R2P through a civilian protection mandate

As examined above, the development of a civilian protection mandate has had only a tenuous link to the overall policy debates on R2P. While the R2P concept has been a subject of controversy at the policy level, civilian protection as a new mandate of peacekeepers has been criticized as sustaining a doctrinal deficit because of the ambiguity of its scope at the operational level. It would be too optimistic to expect that a combination of the two concepts will solve all the conceptual and practical issues at both ends. However, one may consider that the application of R2P as the basic principle may assist in clarifying the scope of civilian protection activities by peacekeepers, and in turn contribute to operationalizing R2P in practice.

Based on the classification of R2P into prevention, reaction and rebuilding in the 2001 ICISS Report, as well as the three pillars envisaged in the Secretary-General's 2009 Report, the following section identifies three possible ways of conceptualizing the relationship between R2P and POC: (i) civilian protection mandate as the implementation of Pillar Two strategy; (ii) civilian protection mandate as operationalizing the responsibility to prevent; and (iii) civilian protection mandate as operationalizing the responsibility to react (or Pillar Three strategy). Those three possibilities overlap to the extent that an element of the responsibility to prevent can be found in Pillar Two and even in Pillar Three in the form of operational prevention. However, the idea of examining the responsibility to prevent separately helps identify a different type of civilian protection operation by peacekeepers, which does not fit the characteristics of peacekeeping as envisaged in the three pillars.

6.2.1 Civilian protection as the implementation of Pillar Two strategy

The idea of operationalizing R2P was turned into a set of policy proposals when the UN Secretary-General, Ban Ki-moon, issued the Secretary-General's 2009 Report, *Implementing the Responsibility to Protect*. Based on the R2P concept as enunciated in the 2005 WSOD, the Secretary-General suggested three pillars for advancing the agenda: the protection responsibilities of the state (Pillar One); international assistance and capacity-building (Pillar Two); and timely and decisive response by the international community (Pillar Three). The deployment of peacekeeping forces with a civilian protection mandate can be conceptualized as the measure to implement the Pillar Two strategy. In fact the Secretary-General notes in his report that "pillar two could also encompass military assistance to help beleaguered States deal with armed non-state actors threatening both the State and its population" (UNSG, 2009: para. 29).

The military assistance envisaged in his Pillar Two strategy involves peacekeeping operations based on the host government's consent. Armed force can be employed "to save lives and bring a measure of stability" in support of the state to meet its obligations relating to the responsibility to protect (ibid.: para. 40). Such intention can be found in the caveat attached to some of the civilian protection mandates: "without prejudice to the responsibility of the host state".

The consent-based deployment of a peacekeeping mission with the mandate to protect civilians without prejudice to the responsibility of the host state must face an inevitable limit to the operationalization of R2P when the national authorities are manifestly failing to protect civilians. This fundamental principle of consent-based peacekeeping operation poses a particular difficulty in implementing the civilian protection mandate when the state authorities, troops and police force themselves are committing violence against the civilian population. UN peacekeepers operating in the Democratic Republic of Congo (MONUC) and Haiti (MINUSTAH) to assist the government in maintaining peace and security, while being tasked to protect civilians, for example, have been heavily criticized on this ground (Sloan, 2011: 203–206, 249).

As a consent-based operation, peacekeepers are to be guided by the principle of impartiality during the course of their operation. This requirement of impartiality poses another challenge to peacekeepers in the field when it requires peacekeepers to take a side to protect civilians even at the risk of tarnishing the perception of impartiality in the eyes of a warring party.

Impartiality can be conceived of in two different ways. First, it requires peacekeepers to deal with all the warring parties even-handedly (subjective impartiality). Second, it means a commitment to objectively observe and respect their mandates and the principles of the UN Charter (objective impartiality). Although the focus of impartiality has recently been shifted to the latter meaning (Brahimi, 2000: para. 50; DPKO/DFS, 2008: 33–35, also known as the Capstone doctrine), it does not mean that peacekeepers are no longer required to be *seen* as even-handed by the parties involved in a conflict (Nasu, 2009a: 154–158). Maintaining subjective impartiality is fundamental to peacekeepers' involvement in and facilitation of the peace process even if one of the warring parties has an unsatisfactory human rights record. It is conceivable that peacekeepers are forced to compromise this position in favour of objective impartiality should they observe that the peace process is being undermined by a warring party acting in contravention of its obligations under relevant Security Council resolutions. Whether this same approach can be maintained to save civilian lives, when the action of peacekeepers itself may result in undermining the peace process, is an altogether different issue.

The Italian delegate warned against the excessive use of force in enforcing the civilian protection mandate, observing that it will, under circumstances in which certain parties are not participating in the ceasefire agreement or peace accord, risk changing the current practices of peacekeeping operations and plunging the troops into very complicated situations, in which they may be required to engage in combat as if they were parties to the conflict. (UNSC, 2003: 34)

Indeed, a robust operation to protect civilians within the framework of traditional peacekeeping may increase the risk of peacekeepers becoming a target of irregular forces attempting to terrorize civilians as a means of pursuing political or partisan objectives. Illustrative is the coercive approach taken by MONUC under the renewed civilian protection mandate,[3] which met a backlash from armed groups who killed nine Bangladeshi soldiers and more local civilians (Marks, 2007: 77). All these considerations point to the difficulties that confront peacekeeping missions with a civilian protection mandate in restraining their operation to fit within the Pillar Two strategy.

6.2.2 Civilian protection as operationalizing the responsibility to prevent

When the R2P concept was born in 2001, it was envisaged to include the responsibility to prevent, to react and to rebuild. Despite the recognition that "prevention is the single most important dimension of the responsibility to protect" (ICISS Report, 2001: xi; Evans, 2008: 79), prevention has been the most neglected aspect in the discourse of R2P (Rosenberg, 2009: 443). This is particularly so in terms of what the international community is expected to do to fulfil the responsibility to prevent.

The practical measures envisaged for the international community in fulfilling the responsibility to prevent basically mirror those that have been developed for conflict prevention in general including, notably, early warning and confidence-building (ICISS Report, 2001: 19–27). The commitment made by states to their responsibility to prevent was diluted by qualified expressions such as "should, *as appropriate*, encourage and help States to exercise this responsibility", and "*intend to* commit ourselves, *as necessary and appropriate*, to helping States build capacity to protect their populations" (emphasis added) (UNGA, 2005: paras. 138–139). The responsibility to prevent has thus been framed too broadly to have any distinguishing meaning as a juridical principle (Molier, 2006: 48).

In cases where a peacekeeping mission is already deployed with a civilian protection mandate, however, the international community's responsibility to prevent can be operationalized with a greater focus. Under the civilian protection mandate, peacekeepers will be able to collect intelligence, signal early warnings and foster confidence-building between warring parties and among civilians (Holt and Taylor, 2009). In fact, the 2009 aide memoire on the protection of civilians in armed conflict issued by the President of the Security Council suggested that the protection of civilians be prioritized in decisions about the use of information and intelligence resources (UNSC, 2009a: 5). Often acting under Chapter VII of the Charter, they are also authorized to use armed force to protect civilians before violence escalates into a mass atrocity. While the concept of "robust peacekeeping" has been variably understood (Parker, 2009; Tardy, 2011), peacekeeping missions that are authorized to use armed force in order to protect civilians can be characterized as "robust peacekeeping" in the sense that it indicates the readiness to use force at the tactical level.

Thus, by emphasizing the robust nature of peacekeeping missions deployed under Chapter VII of the Charter, peacekeepers may well find it justifiable to depart from the traditional notion of impartiality when national authorities are manifestly failing to protect their own civilians. The consensus reached in the 2005 World Summit may support this position if it is interpreted as implying that peacekeepers acting on behalf of the international community would be prepared to intervene when the local authorities are manifestly failing to protect civilians from mass atrocity crimes, even if as a result the peace process may be put at risk.

At the operational level, however, significant challenges are posed to field commanders in understanding exactly when and under what circumstances peacekeepers are required to act to prevent mass atrocities. A conservative decision may hinder field commanders from taking prompt and decisive action required to suppress violence from escalating to mass atrocities. On the other hand, a liberal approach could be criticized as interfering with the responsibilities of the host state. Peacekeepers operating on the fault line between prevention and reaction inevitably face dilemmas arising from competing mandates, standards of action and ethical considerations (Nasu, 2009b: 230–238). Those considerations cast doubt on how effectively peacekeepers can fulfil their obligation to protect civilians if they simply focus on responding to actual or potential mass atrocities with the use of armed force.

This approach may well be seen as too narrowly focused, leaving civilian populations vulnerable to violence until field commanders decide that the situation escalates into mass atrocities. However, this vacuum in terms of protection should rather be assumed by the international community as part of the responsibility to prevent by creating specialized military police and associated multisectoral contingents specifically trained and dedicated to implementing the civilian protection mandate (ibid.: 240–241).

In the operational prevention phase, the obligation to protect civilians can be better implemented by proactively engaging in various measures to facilitate the creation of a secure environment where peacekeepers can maximize their capabilities in information-gathering, analysis and operational manoeuvre. The establishment of protected zones, for example, can be seen as an effective measure to operationalize the responsibility to prevent mass atrocities (UNSC, 2000e: para. 15).[4] One may consider that in light of the failure in Srebrenica (UNSG, 1999c), protected zones are ineffective as a measure for the protection of civilians, in the absence of sufficient political will and military capabilities. However, lessons need to be learned from the past failure to defend protected zones for the purpose of maximizing the potential of safety and protected zones as a way of implementing the positive obligation to protect civilians from the effects of attacks, operationalizing the responsibility to prevent mass atrocities.

6.2.3 Civilian protection as operationalizing the responsibility to react (Pillar Three strategy)

The 2001 ICISS Report envisages the responsibility to react as a variety of enforcement measures, including both military and non-military actions, available to the United Nations (ICISS, 2001: 29–31). The Secretary-General's 2009 Report notes that Pillar Three encompasses a wide range of non-coercive measures and non-violent response measures as well as more robust steps (UNSG, 2009: para. 51). It is widely recognized that much of the discussion concerning the responsibility to react has been made by traditional reference to humanitarian intervention (Joyner, 2007; Payandeh, 2010; Zahar, 2005). However, the relatively wide conception of the responsibility to react or Pillar Three strategy may allow scope for conceptualizing the implementation of a civilian protection mandate by peacekeepers in this phase.

The scope of civilian protection mandates has been left undefined despite the fact that numerous UN documents have been produced in relation to this topic (Holt and Taylor, 2009: 57; Martinelli, 2008: 9–11). Due to the lack of operational definition or guidance, civilian protection assigned for peacekeepers could range from physical protection to providing political and institutional stability, securing humanitarian assistance, and deterring and addressing human rights abuses, which may require the arrest of war criminals (UNSG, 1999a: para. 57). In this respect, three key caveats attached to civilian protection mandates – "imminent threat of physical violence", "area of deployment" and "capabilities" – play an important role in delimiting, albeit ambiguously, the reach of such mandates and in balancing civilian protection activities against other, more traditional, peacekeeping duties. Peacekeepers will be able to mitigate, if not resolve, the dilemmas experienced in implementing a civilian protection mandate within the traditional framework of peacekeeping by conceiving of their civilian protection role as a last-resort option.

The "responsibility to react" concept may inform a restrictive interpretation of civilian protection mandates in light of those caveats. Although different ideas had earlier been expressed about the scope of the responsibility to protect concept,[5] the consensus among world leaders in the 2005 World Summit was that the responsibility to protect would apply only in relation to four types of mass atrocities, namely genocide, ethnic cleansing, crimes against humanity and war crimes (UNGA, 2005: para. 138). Focusing on identifying and responding to the possible outbreak of those mass atrocity crimes might provide peacekeepers with a clear standard of action in that they are only required to take military action to prevent and react to the rise of mass atrocity crimes. Thus, rather than envisaging their involvement in every single case of violence, peacekeepers can reserve their military capabilities for robust military response to mass atrocity crimes, while in the preventive phase leading up to the escalation of violence to mass atrocities, playing supporting roles in information-gathering, logistical support and precautionary planning to minimize the risk of violence against civilians which may lead to mass atrocity crimes (Cottey and Bikin-Kita, 2006: 22).

Recognizing that national militaries are not traditionally trained for proactive operations to protect civilians, the UN Department of Peacekeeping Operations (DPKO) in *A New Partnership Agenda* identifies the need for the United Nations to take a lead in consultation with troop-contributing states in developing practical guidance on options and factors for planners and commanders to consider when implementing the civilian protection mandate (DPKO/DFS, 2009: 20). The history of peacekeeping shows that peacekeeping troops tend to be under-resourced and may well be ill-suited to civilian protection tasks (White, 2009: 331, 352–355). The limited resources of the military are arguably better utilized by reserving their civilian protection tasks for the case of mass atrocity crimes, leaving non-military contingents such as military police and civilian police with the role to fill the gap in protecting civilians from violence during an initial phase.

This approach is clearly distinguished from an idea of robust peacekeeping in that it does not call for a proactive use of armed force at an early phase of violence or an increased number of troops and military resources available to peacekeepers. It rather recognizes that the military-focused civilian protection activities by peacekeepers may grow less robust in terms of their strategic effects due to the ultimately limited peacekeeping resources (Gowan and Tortolani, 2009; Johnston, 2006).

Increased numbers of troops and resources made available to them in a particular mission may well give an impression that peacekeepers are able to undertake more robust and effective civilian protection activities, which in turn stretches the capabilities of the mission.

There can be no denying that the implementation of a civilian protection mandate by peacekeepers is subject to restraint on the basis of their troop capabilities. The need for such self-restraint is also echoed in the 2001 ICISS version of R2P, which sets a reasonable prospect of success as one of the precautionary criteria for military intervention (ICISS, 2001: 37; Pattison, 2008: 265). It is difficult to find justification for the sacrifice of soldiers' lives for the sake of normative coherence when there is no reasonable prospect of success in protecting civilians or even themselves from mass atrocities (Wainer and Aolain, 1996: 353). However, a reasonable prospect of success is not a fixed factor but is influenced by making efforts to maximize the potential capabilities of peacekeeping troops to prevent and respond to the rise of mass atrocities. It is important to ensure that what peacekeepers *can* do under a civilian protection mandate matches what the peacekeepers *ought to* do to implement R2P by maximizing the prospect of success of civilian protection operations with well-planned and coordinated allocation of resources.

6.3 Conclusion

The origin and development of civilian protection mandates given to UN peacekeepers indicate that the primary motivation behind the move was to prevent the kinds of atrocities witnessed in Rwanda and Srebrenica during UN deployments. The normative basis of the concept is thus shared by the R2P concept. However, the relationship between the two concepts has so far not been explicitly set out, leaving the question unanswered as to whether and how civilian protection operations by peacekeepers contribute to the operationalization of the R2P concept or vice versa.

This chapter explored three different ways of conceptualizing civilian protection mandates in relation to R2P. First, military assistance for the host government as part of Pillar Two strategy provides a nice fit for conceptualizing the role of peacekeepers in implementing their civilian protection mandate, yet causes frictions with the principle of impartiality. Second, the responsibility to prevent, understood more widely than Pillar Two strategy, provides a scope for accommodating the robust operation involving the use of armed force to protect civilians as authorized under Chapter VII of the Charter, yet poses dilemmas arising from competing mandates, standards of action and ethical considerations. Third, civilian protection operations by peacekeepers can be conceived of as a way of implementing the responsibility to react or Pillar Three strategy by focusing on identifying and responding to the possible outbreak of mass atrocity crimes relevant to R2P as agreed in the 2005 World Summit. The third option would require a considerable amount of investment in resources and training to build capacity of non-military contingents such as military police and civilian police to act as an initial response to protect civilians from physical violence.

These three possibilities suggest three different ways of conceptualizing the relationship between R2P and POC. Each option has different implications for the existing mode of peacekeeping operations. The question of which option is worth pursuing ultimately comes down to a policy decision. However, a conceptually coherent decision must take into account the rationales and policy implications as discussed in this chapter. A conceptually incoherent decision, for example, to deploy a traditional peacekeeping mission as part of Pillar Two strategy with the expectation that armed force is robustly used to fulfil the international community's responsibility to protect, would only lead to confusion among peacekeepers deployed in the field.

Notes

1. UN Department of Peacekeeping Operations (DPKO) was prior to this development sceptical about peacekeepers' role in civilian protection. See DPKO (1995: paras. 29, 38).
2. Cf. UNSC Res. 1975 (2011: para. 6), which recalled the Security Council's pre-existing authorization for UNOCI to use all necessary means to carry out its mandate to protect civilians under imminent threat of physical violence, and does not make an explicit reference to the responsibility to protect.
3. UNSC Res. 1565 (2004: para. 6), authorizing MONUC to "use all necessary means"; UNSC Res. 1592 (2005: para. 7), clarifying that all necessary means include "cordon and search tactics to prevent attacks on civilians and disrupt the military capability of illegal armed groups that continue to use violence".
4. Protected zones as part of UN peacekeeping operations are distinguished from various types of safety zones in international humanitarian law in that protected zones need not be based on the consent of the parties to the conflict, and that they are not required to have an exclusively civilian character. See Landgren (1995: 436–458).
5. For example, the UN High-Level Panel (2004: para. 201) Report encompasses mass murder and rape, deliberate starvation and exposure to disease as well.

REFERENCES

Bellamy, A. J. (2010) "The Responsibility to Protect – Five Years On", *Ethics & International Affairs* 24(2): 143–169.
Brahimi, Lakhdar (2000) *Report of the Panel on United Nations Peace Operations* (Brahimi Report), A/55/305-S/2000/809 (21 August 2000).

Breau, S. C. (2006) "The Impact of the Responsibility to Protect on Peacekeeping", *Journal of Conflict & Security Law* 11: 429–464.

Cottey, A., and T. Bikin-Kita (2006) "The Military and Humanitarianism: Emerging Patterns of Intervention and Engagement", in Victoria Wheeler and Adele Harmer, eds. *Resetting the Rules of Engagement: Trends and Issues in Military-Humanitarian Relations*. Humanitarian Policy Group Research Report 21, London: Overseas Development Institute, 21–38.

DPKO, Department of Peacekeeping Operations (1995) *General Guidelines for Peacekeeping Operations*. [Online] Available at: ⟨http://www.reliefweb.int/rw/lib.nsf/db900sid/LGEL-5SYHEK/$file/un-peacekeeping-1995.pdf?openelement⟩.

DPKO/DFS (2008) *United Nations Peacekeeping Operations: Principles and Guidelines*.

DPKO/DFS (2009) *A New Partnership Agenda*. [Online] Available at: ⟨http://www.un.org/en/peacekeeping/documents/newhorizon.pdf⟩.

Evans, G. (2008) *The Responsibility to Protect: Ending Mass Atrocity Crimes Once and For All*. Washington, DC: Brookings Institution Press.

Golberg, E., and D. Hubert (2001) "The Security Council and the Protection of Civilians", in Rob McRae and Don Hubert, eds. *Human Security and the New Diplomacy: Protecting People, Promoting Peace*. Montreal: McGill-Queen's University Press, 223–230.

Gowan, R., and B. Tortolani (2009) "Robust Peacekeeping and Its Limitations", in *Robust Peacekeeping: The Politics of Force*. New York: NYU Center on International Cooperation, 49–54.

Holt, V. K., and T. C. Berkman (2007) *The Impossible Mandate? Military Preparedness, the Responsibility to Protect and Modern Peace Operations*. Washington, DC: The Henry L. Stimson Centre.

Holt, V., and G. Taylor (2009) "Protecting Civilians in the Context of UN Peacekeeping Operations: Successes, Setbacks and Remaining Challenges", Independent Study Jointly Commissioned by the Department of Peacekeeping Operations and the Office for the Coordination of Humanitarian Affairs.

ICISS, International Commission on Intervention and State Sovereignty (2001) *The Responsibility to Protect*. Ottawa: International Development Research Centre.

Johnstone, I. (2006) "Dilemmas of Robust Peace Operations", in *Annual Review of Global Peace Operations 2006*. Boulder, CO: Lynne Rienner, 1–14.

Johnstone, I. (2008) "Law-Making through the Operational Activities of International Organizations", *George Washington International Law Review* 40: 87–122.

Joyner, C. C. (2007) "'The Responsibility to Protect': Humanitarian Concern and the Lawfulness of Armed Intervention", *Virginia Journal of International Law* 47: 693–723.

Landgren, K. (1995) "Safety Zones and International Protection: A Dark Grey Area", *International Journal of Refugee Law* 7: 436–458.

Luck, E. C. (2010) "Taking Stock and Looking Ahead – Implementing the Responsibility to Protect", in Hans Winkler, Terje Rød-Larsen and Christoph Mikulaschek, eds. *The UN Security Council and the Responsibility to Protect:*

Policy, Process, and Practice. Favorita Paper 01/2010, Diplomatic Academy of Vienna.

Månsson, K. (2005) "The Forgotten Agenda: Human Rights Protection and Promotion in Cold War Peacekeeping", *Journal of Conflict & Security Law* 10: 379–403.

Marks, J. (2007) "The Pitfalls of Action and Inaction: Civilian Protection in MONUC's Peacekeeping Operations", *African Security Review* 16(3): 67–80.

Martinelli, M. (2008) "The Protection of Civilians During Peacekeeping Operations", European Parliament, June 2008. [Online] Available at: ⟨http://www.isis-europe.org/pdf/2008_artrel_183_08-06-epstudy-protection-of-civilians.pdf⟩.

Molier, G. (2006) "Humanitarian Intervention and the Responsibility to Protect After 9/11", *Netherlands International Law Review* 53: 37–62.

Nasu, H. (2009a) *International Law on Peacekeeping: A Study of Article 40 of the UN Charter.* Leiden: Martinus Nijhoff.

Nasu, H. (2009b) "Operationalizing the 'Responsibility to Protect' and Conflict Prevention: Dilemmas of Civilian Protection in Armed Conflict", *Journal of Conflict & Security Law* 14: 209–241.

Parker, J. N. (2009) "Robust Peacekeeping: The Politics of Force", in *Robust Peacekeeping: The Politics of Force.* New York: NYU Center on International Cooperation, 2–6.

Pattison, J. (2008) "Whose Responsibility to Protect? The Duties of Humanitarian Intervention", *Journal of Military Ethics* 7: 262–283.

Payandeh, M. (2010) "With Great Power Comes Great Responsibility? The Concept of the Responsibility to Protect within the Processes of International Lawmaking", *Yale Journal of International Law* 35: 469–516.

Rosenberg, S. P. (2009) "Responsibility to Protect: A Framework for Prevention", *Global Responsibility to Protect* 1: 442–477.

Sloan, J. (2011) *The Militarisation of Peacekeeping in the Twenty-First Century.* Oxford and Portland, OR: Hart Publishing.

Tardy, T. (2011) "A Critique of Robust Peacekeeping in Contemporary Peace Operations", *International Peacekeeping* 18(2): 152–167.

UN (1999) *Report of the Independent Inquiry into the Actions of the United Nations During the 1994 Genocide in Rwanda,* S/1999/1257/Annex, 16 December 1999.

UNDP, UN Development Programme (1994) *Human Development Report 1994.*

UNGA (2005) *UN General Assembly Resolution 60/1: World Summit Outcome Document,* A/Res/60/1, 16 September 2005.

UNGA (2009a) UN General Assembly 63rd session, 98th plenary meeting, A/63/PV.98, 24 July 2009.

UNGA (2009b) *UN General Assembly Resolution 63/308 on the Responsibility to Protect,* A/RES/63/308, 14 September 2009.

UN High-Level Panel on Threats, Challenges and Change (2004) *A More Secure World: Our Shared Responsibility.* New York: UN Department of Public Information.

UNSC (1999a) *UN Security Council Resolution 1270 (1999): On the Situation in Sierra Leone,* S/RES/1270, 22 October 1999.

UNSC (1999b) Security Council Verbatim Records, 4054th meeting, S/PV.4054, 22 October 1999.

UNSC (1999c) Security Council Verbatim Records, 4083rd meeting, S/PV.4083, 16 December 1999.

UNSC (2000a) Security Council Verbatim Records, 4092nd meeting, S/PV.4092, 24 January 2000.

UNSC (2000b) Security Council Verbatim Records, 4092nd meeting S/PV.4092 (Resumption 1), 24 January 2000.

UNSC (2000c) *UN Security Council Resolution 1291 (2000): On the Situation concerning the Democratic Republic of the Congo*, S/RES/1291, 24 February 2000.

UNSC (2000d) Security Council Verbatim Records, 4104th meeting, S/PV.4104, 24 February 2000.

UNSC (2000e) *UN Security Council Resolution 1296 (2000): Protection of Civilians in Armed Conflict*, S/RES/1296, 19 April 2000.

UNSC (2003) Security Council Verbatim Records, 4790th meeting, S/PV.4790, 18 July 2003.

UNSC (2004) *UN Security Council Resolution 1565 (2004): Concerning the Democratic Republic of the Congo*, S/RES/1565, 1 October 2004.

UNSC (2005) *UN Security Council Resolution 1592 (2005): The Situation concerning the Democratic Republic of the Congo*, S/RES/1592, 30 March 2005.

UNSC (2006a) *UN Security Council Resolution 1674 (2006): Protection of Civilians in Armed Conflict*, S/RES/1674, 28 April 2006.

UNSC (2006b) Security Council Verbatim Records, 5430th meeting, S/PV.5430, 28 April 2006.

UNSC (2006c) *UN Security Council Resolution 1706 (2006): Reports of the Secretary-General on the Sudan*, S/RES/1706, 31 August 2006.

UNSC (2006d) Security Council Verbatim Records, 5519th meeting, S/PV.5519, 31 August 2006.

UNSC (2009a) "Statement by the President of the Security Council: Aide-Memoire for the Consideration of Issues pertaining to the Protection of Civilians in Armed Conflict", S/PRST/2009/1, 14 January 2009.

UNSC (2009b) *UN Security Council Resolution 1894 (2009): Protection of Civilians in Armed Conflict*, S/RES/1894, 11 November 2009.

UNSC (2011) *UN Security Council Resolution 1975 (2011): The Situation in Côte d'Ivoire*, S/RES/1975, 30 March 2011.

UNSG (1999a) *Report of the Secretary-General to the Security Council on the Protection of Civilians in Armed Conflict*, S/1999/957, 8 September 1999.

UNSG (1999b) *Eighth Report of the Secretary-General on the United Nations Observer Mission in Sierra Leone*, S/1999/1003, 28 September 1999.

UNSG (1999c) *Report of the Secretary-General pursuant to General Assembly Resolution 53/35: The Fall of Srebrenica*, A/54/549, 15 November 1999.

UNSG (2005) *In Larger Freedom: Towards Development, Security and Human Rights for All*, A/59/2005, 21 March 2005.

UNSG (2009) *Implementing the Responsibility to Protect: Report of the Secretary-General*, A/63/677, 12 January 2009.

van Baarda, T., and F. van Iersel, (2002) "The Uneasy Relationship between Conscience and Military Law: The Brahimi Report's Unresolved Dilemma", *International Peacekeeping* 9(3): 25–50.

Wainer, R. O., and F. N. Aolain (1996) "Beyond the Laws of War: Peacekeeping in Search of a Legal Framework", *Columbia Human Rights Law Review* 27: 293–354.

White, N. D. (2009) "Empowering Peace Operations to Protect Civilians: Form Over Substance?", *Journal of International Peacekeeping* 13: 327–355.

Williams, P. D. (2010) "Enhancing Civilian Protection in Peace Operations: Insights from Africa", The Africa Center for Strategic Studies Research Paper No. 1. [Online] Available at: ⟨http://africacenter.org/wp-content/uploads/2010/09/ACSS-Research-Paper-1.pdf⟩.

Wills, S. (2004) "Military Interventions on behalf of Vulnerable Populations: The Legal Responsibilities of States and International Organizations Engaged in Peace Support Operations", *Journal of Conflict & Security Law* 9: 387–418.

Wills, S. (2009) *Protecting Civilians*. Oxford: Oxford University Press.

Zahar, M. J. (2005) "Intervention, Prevention, and the 'Responsibility to Protect': Considerations for Canadian Foreign Policy", *International Journal* 60: 723–734.

7

Enhancing protection of civilians through "responsibility to protect" preventive action

Andrew Garwood-Gowers

In the context of conflict and complex emergencies ... the UN serves as a fire-fighter. We are now trying to change this, by trying to prevent the fire in the first place.

UN Secretary-General Ban Ki-moon (2011)

The responsibility to protect (R2P) and the protection of civilians in armed conflict (POC) are closely related but distinct concepts that have gained prominence within the United Nations (UN) system in recent years. In general terms, R2P seeks to prevent, and respond to, genocide and other mass atrocity crimes by recognizing duties held by individual states and the international community. POC, on the other hand, is a broader framework covering the protection of civilians from the effects of armed conflict, often implemented through peacekeeping operations mandated to protect civilian populations. While R2P and POC share the same normative basis – namely, protection of civilians from violence – there are differing interpretations of the precise nature and scope of each concept, as well as the relationship between the two agendas (Lie, 2008). Although there is growing international acceptance of R2P, a minority of states remain suspicious of the concept, particularly because its association with non-consensual military action for humanitarian purposes presents challenges to traditional notions of state sovereignty and non-intervention in domestic affairs.[1] Those concerns are exacerbated by a perception that R2P is, or could be, applied selectively and inconsistently as a tool of powerful Western states.[2] Given this controversy there are fears among some states and actors in the POC field that linking R2P to

Norms of protection: Responsibility to protect, protection of civilians and their interaction,
Francis, Popovski and Sampford (eds),
United Nations University Press, 2012, ISBN 978-92-808-1218-3

the POC agenda may undermine consensus on civilian protection measures (Welsh, 2010).

Despite those political concerns, on a practical level there is potential for R2P and POC to operate as mutually reinforcing principles in the international community's efforts to protect civilian populations from violence. This is particularly the case in relation to the less controversial area of preventive action to protect civilians, which is the focus of this chapter. Although most academic attention and political debate on R2P has centred on the military intervention aspect of the concept, it is the preventive dimension which offers the greatest potential to enhance civilian protection. As UN Secretary-General Ban Ki-moon (2011) has stressed:

> The best form of protection is prevention. Prevention saves lives as well as resources.

While few would disagree with this view, in practice preventive action has remained an under-utilized part of the civilian protection toolkit (Breau, 2007). Decisive international action to protect civilians has usually been taken only *after* full-scale conflict or mass violence has erupted (ibid.). However, R2P offers the promise of more effective international engagement to assist states under stress or at risk of imminent crisis. This potential stems from R2P's dual functions as a "speech act" to catalyse political will for earlier action, and as a specific "policy agenda" for preventing mass atrocity violence (Bellamy, 2009: 160). Although commentators typically emphasize one function over the other – for example, Evans (2008) concentrates on the former, whereas Bellamy (2010) adopts the latter as his preferred characterization of R2P – this chapter argues that *both* the "speech act" and "policy agenda" functions may contribute to improved civilian protection. In this regard, the international community's success in halting post-election violence in Kenya in 2008 provides a recent example of how R2P preventive strategies can be utilized to de-escalate tensions and protect civilians from violence (GCR2P, 2010b).

This chapter considers ways in which R2P and POC could complement each other and thereby enhance the overall effectiveness of civilian protection. As indicated, the focus is on consensual preventive action, rather than non-consensual responses to full-scale mass atrocity violence where a state is "manifestly failing" to protect its population (UNGA, 2005: para. 139).[3] Section 7.1 briefly outlines the conceptual boundaries of R2P and POC, and considers the relationship between the two. It argues that in contrast to POC, which in practice is primarily reactive, R2P contains greater explicit emphasis on prevention. This focus on preventive action

– contained in the First and Second Pillars of R2P – offers a policy frame-work for earlier action to protect civilians, thereby expanding the tempo-ral scope of civilian protection. Section 7.2 then examines possible ways in which R2P and POC could add value to each other in practice. It con-siders circumstances of imminent crisis in which a state is willing but un-able to prevent or bring an end to violence that threatens its population, and is therefore prepared to consent to international assistance. In such situations R2P's Second Pillar envisages the international community employing a range of non-coercive and coercive operational prevention measures prior to, or in the early stages of, an outbreak of violence.[4] In addition to preventive diplomacy and fact-finding missions, more robust action such as the deployment of peace operations with a POC mandate might be required. This type of "preventive deployment" would represent a shift in current peacekeeping (or peace enforcement) practice, which typically involves deployment either *after* full-scale armed conflict has broken out or once a peace agreement has been reached. R2P's potential to mobilize preventive peace operations represents an opportunity to re-alize long-standing UN recommendations (UNSG, 1992: para. 28) to im-plement "preventive deployment" in peacekeeping practice.[5]

In order to take timely preventive action the development of an effec-tive early-warning and assessment system within the R2P framework is crucial. Recent UN initiatives establishing a joint office on Genocide Pre-vention and the Responsibility to Protect have the potential to fill a gap in the current POC architecture, which lacks an early-warning system. POC actors could also contribute to R2P's early warning system via input from peace operations and other monitoring missions that are already on the ground. With appropriate training, such missions could provide a valuable tool for monitoring and reporting on signs of renewed violence or imminent conflict which place civilians at risk of mass atrocity crimes. In this way it becomes possible to view R2P and POC as interdependent or mutually reinforcing principles.

7.1 The concepts of R2P and POC

7.1.1 The responsibility to protect (R2P)

The concept of R2P evolved out of dismay at the international commu-nity's failure to prevent mass atrocity crimes in Rwanda and elsewhere in the 1990s. It represents a re-conceptualization of the relationship be-tween state sovereignty and human rights, in which sovereignty is viewed "not as an absolute term of authority but as a kind of responsibility" (Thakur, 2006: 251). In its current form, as distinct from its earlier 2001 conception (ICISS, 2001), R2P consists of three mutually reinforcing pillars laid out in the UN Secretary-General's 2009 Report, *Implementing the Responsibility to Protect* (UNSG, 2009). The First Pillar is that states have an obligation to protect their populations from mass atrocity crimes (genocide, war crimes, ethnic cleansing and crimes against humanity).[6] The Second Pillar stipulates that the international community should assist states in fulfilling their Pillar One obligations. Where states are "manifestly failing" to protect their populations the Third Pillar provides that the international community has a responsibility to respond in a "timely and decisive manner" (UNGA, 2005: para. 139). Action under the Third Pillar can include non-coercive means such as diplomacy and humanitarian assistance and, as a last resort, coercive measures involving the use of force.

There is general acceptance that R2P is based on existing principles of international law and does not add anything new in the way of *legal* duties (Bellamy and Reike, 2010; Rosenberg, 2009; Stahn, 2007). R2P can be seen primarily as a political or moral commitment to implementing established (Pillar One and Two) duties created in treaty law and customary international law.[7] Coercive action under R2P's Third Pillar is envisaged only in accordance with existing UN Charter Chapter VII procedures governing the Security Council's authorization of the use of force. As such, it can be seen as a course of action that is *available* to the Security Council in circumstances where states are "manifestly failing" to protect their populations.[8] The Third Pillar is yet to reach the status of a legal duty *requiring* positive action to protect civilians against mass atrocity crimes, although with the evolution of state practice in the future it may crystallize into such a duty (Bellamy and Reike, 2010). At present, however, the international community's "responsibility" to respond to such circumstances exists only on a political or moral level.

7.1.2 Protection of civilians (POC)

As Lie (2008: 25) notes, there is "no unified understanding of POC, although all actors subscribe to the overarching idea of the concept", namely, the protection of individuals in times of armed conflict. Different segments within the POC sphere – military, development and humanitarian – tend to interpret POC from slightly different perspectives. For instance, peacekeepers see the primary focus of POC as the physical protection of civilians under their mandate, whereas representatives from the development field place emphasis on an extended protection concept that includes provision of food, shelter and education (ibid.).

This chapter adopts the definition of POC used by the Global Centre for the Responsibility to Protect (GCR2P, 2009: 1): "measures that can be taken to protect the safety, dignity and integrity of all human beings in times of war which are rooted in obligations under international humanitarian law (IHL), refugee law, and human rights law". The POC agenda involves a range of actors, including states, organized armed groups, UN bodies, peacekeeping operations and non-governmental organizations (NGOs). It encompasses IHL's primarily negative duties requiring parties to an armed conflict to avoid harming civilians, as well as role-based duties adopted under peacekeeping mandates to "protect civilians under imminent threat of physical violence".[9]

7.1.3 The relationship between R2P and POC

The precise nature of the relationship between R2P and POC is a source of ongoing academic consideration (Breakey, 2012; Holt and Berkman, 2006; Hunt, 2009; Strauss, 2009). It is generally recognized that the two concepts "overlap but each extends beyond the other" in certain respects (GCR2P, 2009: 3). A number of key differences should be noted. First, R2P has a narrower application than POC, as it covers only the four mass atrocity crimes, whereas POC applies to a broader range of crimes against civilians. Second, R2P encompasses mass atrocity crimes occurring both within armed conflict and outside conflict situations (UNSG, 2010a). POC, on the other hand, appears at first glance to be narrower, in that it has traditionally been seen as applicable only in the context of armed conflict. However, contemporary interpretations of IHL view the concept broadly enough to apply to circumstances of violence falling short of armed conflict, such as in Darfur and Rwanda (Brahimi, 2000). Hence, POC is applicable not only in situations of armed conflict narrowly construed but also in cases of generalized violence against civilians. Thus, in this regard there is significant overlap between R2P and POC.

A third key difference – and the one of most significance for this chapter – is that in comparison with POC, R2P contains a stronger explicit emphasis on prevention. This important point of distinction has not been widely noted in the academic literature to date. One exception is Hunt (2009: 8) who recognizes that "aspects of the preventive components of R2P extend beyond POC". R2P's emphasis on prevention is evident in a number of key texts. First, the *World Summit Outcome Document* (WSOD) expressly refers to the international community's commitment to assist states that are "under stress *before crises and conflicts break out*" (emphasis added) (UNGA, 2005: para. 139). Second, the preventive dimension of R2P is reinforced strongly in the 2009 report, *Implementing the Responsibility to Protect* (UNSG, 2009). There, the Secretary-General laid out plans for a range of institutional measures, including a centralized early-warning system and a joint office on R2P and the Prevention of Genocide – intended to bolster the UN's capacity for prevention. While the Secretary-General's apparent prioritization of prevention (Pillars One and Two) over reaction (Pillar Three) has been criticized for "sacrific[ing] substance for the sake of building consensus" on R2P, for the purposes of this chapter the emphasis on preventive measures is significant as it offers an important point of contrast to POC, which is primarily reactive in practice (Sharma, 2010: 131).

This is not to say that POC ignores preventive measures altogether: several important documents do indicate that prevention is envisaged as part of the POC agenda. For example, as far back as 1992 *An Agenda for Peace* (UNSG, 1992) identified the potential benefits of preventive deployment of peacekeeping operations. In addition, the UN Secretary-General's reports on POC make reference to preventive strategies such as arms embargoes and action to counter hate media (UNSG, 1999, 2010b). International humanitarian law – as part of the POC sphere – also includes some provisions of a preventive nature: one example being the obligation to "avoid locating military objectives within or near densely populated areas" (Protocol I, 1977: Art. 58(b)). Overall, however, the focus on prevention is less explicit and less emphatic within POC sources than it is in R2P texts.

Furthermore, as Breau (2007: 463) notes, in *practice* "prevention is a rarely utilised part of the [POC] tool kit". This is evident in the current POC architecture at the UN level, which lacks a formal early-warning system for identifying potential crises or flashpoints.[10] Additionally, and most significantly, the major vehicle for implementing POC – namely, peace operations – continues to be utilized primarily in post-conflict situations where violence against civilians has *already* occurred. In this sense, POC can be characterized as principally reactive. With its greater emphasis on prevention, R2P is more attractive in this regard. As will be discussed in section 7.2, the preventive dimension of R2P offers potential for catalysing *earlier* action to protect civilians and may, therefore, add value to the POC agenda by expanding the temporal scope of protection.

7.2 R2P and POC: Adding value to each other

This section considers potential ways in which R2P and POC could add value to each other in practice. Two preliminary points should be noted in relation to the context. First, as outlined above, the focus is on R2P's scope for preventive action carried out with the consent of a state (Pillar Two), rather than the more controversial aspect of non-consensual intervention (Pillar Three). As a result, the following discussion applies to circumstances where a state is *willing but unable* to prevent or put an end to violence which is being perpetrated primarily by non-state actors. Uganda's consent to international assistance in the fight against the Lord's Resistance Army (LRA) is a current example of such a scenario (International Crisis Group, 2011). Conversely, situations in which violence against civilians is being carried out, or directed, *by the state itself* will generally mean that the state is unwilling to accept assistance from the international community, thereby leading to any international involvement being non-consensual under R2P's Third Pillar.

Second, the discussion in this section is limited to operational preventive measures, which are "measures applicable in the face of immediate crisis" (Carnegie Commission, 1997: xix). It does not extend to the equally important but far broader notion of structural prevention, which refers to longer-term strategies that address the root causes of conflict and violence (ibid.). This distinction between the two forms of prevention is not maintained in the Secretary-General's approach to R2P.[11] As a result, there has been criticism that conflating R2P's preventive dimension with structural prevention leads to R2P being stretched too broadly, resulting in the concept losing both its independent identity and political clout (Nasu, 2009; Sharma, 2010; Stamnes, 2008). To avoid such criticism, this chapter focuses only on operational prevention in the context of addressing early signs of violence or an imminent crisis that threatens civilians.

7.2.1 R2P's potential to expand the temporal scope of POC

R2P's major contribution to advancing the POC agenda lies with its scope for mobilizing political support for operational preventive action in circumstances where a state is willing but unable to fulfil its obligations under the First Pillar. Where there are initial signs of violence that threatens civilians, R2P may act as the catalyst for the international community to offer timely assistance to a state to stabilize a volatile situation before it escalates to the point of mass atrocity crimes. In such circumstances, international involvement occurs with the consent of the state. The international community's engagement in Kenya's post-election unrest in 2008, discussed below, is a successful case in point.

Operational preventive measures under R2P's Second Pillar can involve both non-coercive and coercive means carried out with the consent of the state in question. Non-coercive action includes a range of diplomatic and humanitarian efforts, including fact-finding or human rights monitoring missions. When non-coercive tools are ineffective, coercive measures such as the preventive deployment of peace operations with a POC mandate could be utilized to protect civilians on the ground.

7.2.2 Non-coercive measures

Article 34 of the UN Charter gives the Security Council the power to "investigate any dispute, or any situation that might lead to international friction or give rise to a dispute, in order to determine whether the continuation of the dispute or situation is likely to endanger the maintenance of international peace and security". While this investigative function remains under-utilized, Secretary-General Ban Ki-moon (UNSG, 2011) recently referred to Article 34 as a basis for a range of non-coercive preventive measures in the face of impending crises. Two of the tools mentioned by the Secretary-General are briefly considered in this section.

The first is the use of preventive diplomacy and mediation to de-escalate situations where mass atrocity crimes are looming. Once again, Kenya is the most commonly cited example of the successful employment of such preventive tools in an R2P context. In that case, early action by African Union mediators, with the support of the United Nations and civil society actors, is credited with contributing to a cessation of post-election violence. One of the African Union mediators, Kofi Annan, has explained that he:

> saw the crisis in the R2P prism with a Kenyan government unable to contain the situation or protect its people. I knew that if the international community did not intervene, things would go hopelessly wrong. The problem is when we say "intervention", people think military, when in fact that's a last resort. Kenya is a successful example of R2P at work. (Cohen, 2008: 48)

A similarly positive assessment is offered by the Global Centre for the Responsibility to Protect (GCR2P, 2010b: 2), which has described international engagement in the Kenyan crisis as a model of "how non-coercive tools, such as mediation, can help halt atrocities when employed early with sufficient resources and international support". Although others such as Bellamy (2010) have suggested that the African Union's involvement, rather than R2P, was the major catalyst for international engagement with Kenya, it is clear that R2P language played a central role in framing the international community's diplomatic response. Secretary-General Ban Ki-moon, Special Adviser on the Prevention of Genocide, Francis Deng, and a Security Council presidential statement all made reference to R2P in discussion of the Kenyan issue (Bellamy, 2010). While Kenya might be regarded as a relatively unusual situation, in that non-coercive tools were effective in diffusing mounting violence, it nevertheless remains an important example of R2P preventive strategies in action.

A second type of non-coercive preventive action that may be utilized in the face of mounting violence is the deployment of fact-finding missions or human rights monitors. Such missions have the potential to contribute to civilian protection in at least two ways. First, an international presence on the ground may help to de-escalate a volatile situation and contribute to a decrease in violence. In this regard, Gareth Evans (2010) cites the example of the 2005 establishment of a UN human rights monitoring field operation in Nepal as contributing to a "dramatic reduction in violations, with summary executions and disappearances nearly eliminated". Although human rights violations in Nepal's civil war did not reach the levels seen in many conflicts in sub-Saharan Africa, the United Nations' initiatives in Nepal nevertheless provide an important example of successful de-escalation of tensions (Weinstein, 2007). Second, even if the presence of a UN mission is not sufficient to prevent violence from increasing, such field operations may still be able to operate as a valuable source of information-gathering and reporting for R2P early-warning systems. By sounding the alarm bells on possible mass atrocity crimes, they could contribute to the mobilization of political support for more robust international assistance involving coercive measures.

7.2.3 Coercive measures

In addition to non-coercive preventive measures, R2P's Second Pillar envisages the possibility of preventive deployment of military forces to assist a state that is under stress. The Secretary-General's 2009 Report expressly states that "pillar two could also encompass military assistance to help beleaguered States deal with armed non-state actors threatening both the State and its population" (UNSG, 2009: para. 29). In this regard, R2P is entirely consistent with, and seeks to build on, earlier UN reports (DPKO, 1995; UNSG, 1992; Brahimi, 2000) that have identified preventive deployment of peace operations in the early stages of unrest as an important component of the Security Council's tools for preventing conflict and maintaining international peace and security. As mentioned, the 1992 document, An Agenda for Peace (UNSG, 1992: para. 28), recognized that while "United Nations operations in areas of crisis have generally been established after conflict has occurred, . . . the time has come to plan for circumstances warranting preventive deployment". In the context of internal crises, the report referred to deployment "when the Government requests or all parties consent" (ibid.). Reference is also made to the potential for preventive deployment to contribute to "maintaining security" and that it "could save lives" (ibid.).

Despite this long-standing UN recommendation to utilize preventive deployment, there has been little progress towards implementing such a vision. To date the only major instance of preventive deployment remains the Macedonian example, where the UN Preventive Deployment Force (UNPREDEP) operated between 1992 and 1999. Aside from this single occasion, the Security Council's approach to peace operations has continued to be reactive in nature, intervening only after societies have disintegrated and full-scale conflict has broken out (Breau, 2007).

R2P's explicit emphasis on preventive action to assist states under stress could provide an opportunity to finally realize the potential of preventive deployment. While UNPREDEP's original mandate was limited to monitoring border areas with Albania and the Federal Republic of Yugoslavia, and did not include a specific directive to protect civilians, a variation of this type of preventive deployment – with a robust POC mandate – could be utilized in crises involving the threat of mass atrocities. Stamnes (2008: 19) suggests that in this context preventive deployment should consist of "multi-faceted" operations with at least "three constitutive pillars" – military, political and socioeconomic. In addition, given that every R2P situation will be based on its own set of historical, political and cultural circumstances, each preventive deployment should be specifically tailored to those conditions on a case-by-case basis (ibid.).

Recent initiatives in Central Africa to combat the threat posed by the Lord's Resistance Army (LRA) suggest a growing willingness to consider forms of preventive deployment of peace operations for civilian protection purposes. Renewed efforts in 2011 by the African Union and UNSC to coordinate international assistance have seen existing UN peace missions – such as the UN Organization Stabilization Mission in the Democratic Republic of Congo (MONUSCO) and UN Mission to the Republic of South Sudan (UNMISS) – redeployed to other locations at risk of LRA violence (UNSG, 2011). These developments differ from the UNPREDEP template in that they involve redeployment of existing forces rather than the creation of new preventive missions. The objectives of this form of preventive deployment are to "help deter attacks against civilians and facilitate humanitarian operations" (ibid.: para. 71). While these are positive steps, the UN Secretary-General acknowledges that current UN missions in Central Africa are "constrained by limited resources, competing mandated priorities, and operating areas that are confined by national borders" (ibid.).

When a state requests, or consents to, preventive deployment, and there is the necessary political will to approve such a deployment, two key issues arise. The first is the capacity to deploy quickly in order to provide protection to civilians where there is an imminent threat of mass atrocities. Current UN peace operations require approximately 90 days before a mandated force arrives on the ground (CSCAP, 2010). Such time lags may mean that a situation will have evolved since the time of the original mandate, with serious violence against civilians having already occurred (ibid.). Given the current logistical difficulties, there is a clear need for other, more specialized rapid response forces to be available for deployment. The UN Emergency Peace Service (UNEPS) model proposed by a coalition of non-governmental actors is one template for a UN-level standing force of peacekeepers that could be deployed at short notice.[12] At a regional level, the African Standby Force (ASF) is currently being established by the African Union with a view to deployment in crisis situations in Africa.[13] Similar rapid response capabilities should be developed at other regional or sub-regional levels in order to provide more deployment of preventive peace operations.

The second critical issue concerns the capacity of such missions, once on the ground, to uphold a robust POC mandate in circumstances of potential mass atrocity crimes. Existing UN peace forces are not trained to identify the risks of, or respond to, genocide and other mass atrocity crimes. At present, within the UN Department of Peacekeeping Operations (DPKO) there is some resistance to the idea that they should be trained to carry out such tasks.[14] This reluctance appears to be due to political and strategic concerns about losing consensus over POC if the concept is linked too closely with R2P. However, as R2P gains traction as a principle and becomes entrenched within the UN system, this resistance is likely to become less of a barrier. It is crucial that this change occurs, as the provision of adequate training and resources to peace operations will be a vital step in ensuring that those mandated to protect civilians from mass atrocities are able to do so effectively.

7.2.4 R2P early-warning systems

One of the key mechanisms for mobilizing effective preventive action in crisis situations is efficient early-warning and assessment systems. In circumstances where mass atrocity crimes occur they are generally preceded by deteriorating human rights conditions or incitement to commit acts of violence (UNSG, 2010a). As a result, there are usually warning signs that mass atrocity crimes are imminent. Early awareness and assessment of such conditions on the ground is a necessary (though not always sufficient) condition for generating the political will to take effective preventive action to protect civilians and deter mass atrocity crimes.

The need for an early-warning capability within the R2P framework was recognized in the 2005 WSOD (UNGA, 2005). The challenge since then has been determining the best way to implement such a system. The Secretary-General's July 2010 report on early-warning capability recognizes that, while information-gathering has improved in recent years, there remain gaps in the way such information is shared and assessed (UNSG, 2010a). In particular, it was noted that "the existing mechanisms for gathering and analysing information for the purpose of early warning do not view that information through the lens of the responsibility to protect" (ibid.: para. 10).

Since 2010 two important initiatives in this area have strengthened the United Nations' institutional capacity to assess the risk of mass atrocity violence and facilitate timely, preventive action. The first was the development of an analysis framework (OSAPG, 2009) identifying risks of genocide. This contains a list of eight factors which cumulatively increase the potential for genocidal violence. While the current framework is specific to the crime of genocide, similar frameworks are being developed to assess the risk of crimes against humanity, war crimes and ethnic cleansing (UNSG, 2010a). The second key development was the establishment in 2011 of a joint office on Genocide Prevention and the Responsibility to Protect, which formalized collaboration between the OSAPG and the Special Adviser on R2P (ibid.). The joint office has an early warning mechanism, through which it can notify the Secretary-General of situations of concern, and provide advice on a range of policy options for dealing with those situations (ibid.). In appropriate circumstances this advice could result in the matter being put before the Security Council to consider possible action.

As well as developing early-warning systems at the UN level, the Secretary-General has recognized that regional and sub-regional organizations have a role to play in preventing and halting mass atrocity crimes (ibid.). The African Union has already developed a Continental Early Warning System (CEWS) and a number of other bodies have taken steps in this direction (Wulf and Debiel, 2009). However, the Asia-Pacific zone currently lacks a formal early-warning system and thus lags behind other regions in this regard.[15] The continuing need to improve regional and sub-regional arrangements was highlighted in the July 2011 General Assembly dialogue on R2P (UNGA, 2011).

While most UN member states support the development of early-warning systems, some R2P sceptics have raised questions about their operation. Pakistan, for example, has pointed to the dangers of "false alarms" being raised in relation to possible mass atrocity situations, and warned of the resulting stigma that might be attached to states wrongly accused of failing to protect their populations (GCR2P, 2010a: 4). In this regard, care will be needed to ensure thorough assessment of relevant information before reports are made to the Secretary-General. One of the challenges will be not to call upon the Secretary-General too often, in order to maintain credibility in light of the Secretary-General's caution in bringing issues before the Security Council.

7.2.5 POC's potential to contribute to R2P early-warning systems

So far section 7.2 has concentrated on ways in which R2P might be utilized to enhance the scope of the POC agenda. However, it should be noted that there is also potential for POC to contribute to key mechanisms within the R2P framework. In this way, it becomes possible to view the two concepts as mutually reinforcing principles for advancing the goal of civilian protection.

POC's most valuable contribution to the operationalization of R2P is likely to be in relation to R2P's early-warning system. As discussed above, the implementation of effective early-warning capability will play a crucial role in the ability of the international community to prevent and respond to potential mass atrocity crimes. POC actors already on the ground – such as fact-finding missions and post-conflict peacekeeping operations – could be useful vehicles for gathering information for R2P's early-warning systems. These actors could sound the alarm bells to the two Special Advisers on R2P and Genocide on signs of renewed tensions and vulnerability to mass atrocity crimes. In doing so, the POC field would be contributing to the preventive aspect of the R2P framework. As noted above, in order for POC actors to make credible and accurate reports to the early-warning system, such personnel would require special training on identifying risk factors associated with mass atrocity crimes.

There remains a need for further work on how best to implement effective early-warning capabilities both within the UN system and within regional and sub-regional organizations. This will be a vital step towards developing an institutional framework for advancing the R2P and POC agendas and providing a better overall civilian protection regime. Recognizing the potential for the two concepts to operate as mutually reinforcing principles may assist in building this architecture.

7.3 Conclusion

Despite the 2011 Libyan intervention raising concerns among some states over R2P's Third Pillar, the principle retains broad support within the international community, particularly in relation to the preventive dimension. Although closely related to the concept of POC, R2P places additional emphasis on, and offers greater scope for, preventive measures to protect civilians. In this respect, R2P has the potential to expand the temporal scope of civilian protection by acting both as a catalyst for earlier action to de-escalate crisis situations and as a policy agenda for preventing mass atrocity crimes. Where a state under stress is prepared to consent to international assistance, non-coercive measures such as preventive diplomacy and fact-finding missions, or coercive means involving the preventive deployment of peace operations, may be utilized to protect civilians *before* full-scale conflict breaks out or mass atrocities are committed. An important feature of the R2P architecture will be the institutionalization of effective early-warning and assessment systems which can identify situations in which civilians are at risk of mass atrocities. The POC agenda could also contribute to the realization of R2P through actors such as UN fact-finding missions and peace operations transmitting information to these early-warning and assessment mechanisms.

It is hoped that lingering controversy over the military intervention aspect of R2P's Third Pillar does not overshadow the crucial contribution that preventive action under R2P's First and Second Pillars can make to the advancement of civilian protection. As Bellamy (2009: 4) has noted, the real promise of R2P lies in providing a framework for earlier, preventive action that reduces "the frequency with which governments are forced to choose between standing aside and going to war for humanitarian purposes". Viewing R2P and POC as mutually reinforcing concepts may assist in realizing this potential.

Notes

1. An August 2010 survey of states' positions on R2P found 81% supported the concept while 19% opposed it (GCR2P, 2010b).
2. Boreham (2011) notes the recent selectivity in applying R2P to Libya but not to Bahrain, Syria or other Arab states where similar violence against civilians has occurred.
3. While the line between prevention and response is not always easy to draw, this chapter considers that measures taken to de-escalate an imminent crisis fall within the category of preventive action. A similar approach is taken by UN Secretary-General Ban Ki-moon (UNSG, 2009) and Edward Luck (2010).
4. Operational preventive measures are specific "measures applicable in the face of immediate crisis". They are distinguished from "structural prevention", which is a broader concept that includes "measures to ensure that crises do not arise in the first place or, if they do, that they do not recur" (Carnegie Commission, 1997: xix).
5. See the discussion of preventive deployment in Macedonia in section 7.2 of this chapter.
6. For discussion of the legal definitions of the four crimes see Scheffer (2009).
7. For example, the *Genocide Convention* has been interpreted by the International Court of Justice as imposing a legal duty on a state to take peaceful measures to prevent genocide in circumstances where that state has relevant information and capacity to take such steps. See *Genocide Case* (2007: [430]); Arbour (2008).
8. Recent military action against Libya is the first case in which coercive action has been taken against a state that is "manifesting failing" to protect its population. On 17 March 2011 the UN Security Council authorized the use of "all necessary means ... to protect civilians and civilian populated areas under threat of attack". See UN Doc. S/RES/1973 (2010).

9. This is the standard wording in UN mandates for robust peacekeeping operations. See for example, UNMIL (Liberia) UN S/RES/1509 (2003); UNOCI (Ivory Coast) UN S/RES/1528 (2004); UNMIS (Sudan: North-South) UN S/RES/1590 (2005); UNAMID (Sudan: Darfur) UN S/RES/1769 (2007); MONUC (DRC) UN S/RES/1856 (2008).
10. Existing UN early-warning systems such as Humanitarian Early Warning Service (HEWS) and ReliefWeb focus on monitoring natural hazards such as floods and storms.
11. See, for example, references to improving human rights, education and strengthening institutions in *Implementing the Responsibility to Protect* (UNSG, 2009).
12. See Johansen (2006) and Chapter 8 by Herro and Suthanthiraraj in this collection.
13. On the African Standby Force see *Policy Framework for the Establishment of the African Standby Force and the Military Staff Committee* (2003).
14. Statements from confidential interviews, on file with author.
15. The absence of such a system is due primarily to most Asia-Pacific states retaining a strong view of state sovereignty which rejects intervention in domestic affairs. See CSCAP (2010).

REFERENCES

Application of the Convention on the Prevention and Punishment of the Crime of Genocide (Bosnia and Herzegovina v *Serbia and Montenegro) Judgment*, ICJ Rep. 2007.

Arbour, L. (2008) "The Responsibility to Protect as a Duty of Care in International Law and Practice", *Review of International Studies* 34: 445–458.

Ban, Ki-moon (2011) "Human Protection and the 21st Century United Nations" [Online] Available at: ⟨http://www.un.org/apps/news/infocus/sgspeeches/search_full.asp?statID=1064⟩.

Bellamy, A. (2009) *Responsibility to Protect: The Global Effort to End Mass Atrocities.* Cambridge: Polity Press.

Bellamy, A. (2010) "The Responsibility to Protect – Five Years On", *Ethics & International Affairs* 24(2): 143–169.

Bellamy, A. and R. Reike (2010) "The Responsibility to Protect and International Law", *Global Responsibility to Protect* 2: 267–286.

Boreham, K. (2011) "Libya and R2P: The limits of responsibility". *East Asian Forum* (31 March), [Online] Available at: ⟨http://www.eastasiaforum.org/2011/03/31/libya-and-r2p-the-limits-of-responsibility/⟩.

Brahimi, Lakhdar (2000) *Report of the Panel on United Nations Peace Operations* (Brahimi Report), A/55/305-S/2000/809, 21 August 2000.

Breakey, H. (2012) "Protection Norms and Human Rights: A Rights-Based Analysis of the Responsibility to Protect and the Protection of Civilians in Armed Conflict", *Global Responsibility to Protect* 4(3): 309–333.

Breau, S. (2007) "The Impact of the Responsibility to Protect on Peacekeeping", *Journal of Conflict and Security Law* 11: 429–464.

Carnegie Commission on Preventing Deadly Conflict (1997) *Preventing Deadly Conflict: Final Report.* New York: Carnegie Corporation of New York.

Cohen, R. (2008) "How Kofi Annan Rescued Kenya", *New York Review of Books* 55(13): 48–49.

Council for Security Cooperation in the Asia Pacific (CSCAP) Study Group on the Responsibility to Protect (2010) *Second Meeting Full Report*. [Online] Available at: ⟨http://www.cscap.org/uploads/docs/RtoP/2RtoPSGMtgRpt%20Sep%202010.pdf⟩.

DPKO, UN Department of Peacekeeping Operations (1995) *General Guidelines for Peacekeeping Operations*. [Online] Available at: ⟨http://www.reliefweb.int/rw/lib.nsf/db900sid/LGEL-5SYHEK/$file/un-peacekeeping-1995.pdf?openelement⟩.

Evans, G. (2008) *The Responsibility to Protect: Ending Mass Atrocity Crimes Once and for All*. Washington, DC: Brookings Institution Press.

Evans, G. (2010) "Making the Responsibility to Protect Work in the Asia-Pacific", Presentation to ASEAN-ISIS 24th Asia-Pacific Roundtable, Kuala Lumpur (8 June 2010). [Online] Available at: ⟨http://www.gevans.org/speeches/speech413.html⟩.

GCR2P (Global Centre for the Responsibility to Protect) (2009) "The Relationship between the Responsibility to Protect and the Protection of Civilians in Armed Conflict". (January 2009). [Online] Available at: ⟨http://www.globalr2p.org/media/pdf/GCR2PPolicyBrief-ProtectCivConflict.pdf⟩.

GCR2P (Global Centre for the Responsibility to Protect) (2010a) "'Early Warning, Assessment, and the Responsibility to Protect': Informal Interactive Dialogue of the General Assembly held on 9 August 2010". (September 2010). [Online] Available at: ⟨http://globalr2p.org/media/pdf/GCR2P_Report_Informal_Interactive_Dailogue_2010.pdf⟩.

GCR2P (Global Centre for the Responsibility to Protect) (2010b) "The Responsibility to Protect and Kenya: Past Successes and Current Challenges". (13 August 2010). [Online] Available at: ⟨http://globalr2p.org/media/pdf/The_Responsibility_to_Protect_and_Kenya_Past_Successes_and_Current_Challenges.pdf⟩.

GCR2P (Global Centre for the Responsibility to Protect) (2011) "The Lord's Resistance Army and the Responsibility to Protect". (9 November 2011). [Online] Available at: http://www.globalr2p.org/media/pdf/LRA_and_R2P.pdf.

Holt, V. and T. Berkman (2006) *The Impossible Mandate? Military Preparedness, the Responsibility to Protect and Modern Peace Operations*. Washington, DC: The Henry L. Stimson Center.

Hunt, C. (2009) "Protection of Civilians and the Responsibility to Protect: Perspectives and Precedents in the Asia-Pacific", *Working Paper No. 2, Program on the Protection of Civilians*. Brisbane: Asia-Pacific Centre for the Responsibility to Protect.

International Commission on Intervention and State Sovereignty (ICISS) (2001) *The Responsibility to Protect*. Ottawa: International Development Research Centre.

International Crisis Group (2011) "The Lord's Resistance Army: End Game?" *Crisis Group Africa Report No. 182*. Nairobi/Brussels: International Crisis Group.

Johansen, R., ed. (2006) *A United Nations Emergency Peace Service: to prevent genocide and crimes against humanity*. New York: Global Action to Prevent War, Nuclear Age Peace Foundation and World Federalist Movement.

Lie, J. H. S. (2008) "Protection of Civilians, the Responsibility to Protect and Peace Operations", *NUPI Report* No. 4: 1–32. [Online] Available at: ⟨http://www.globalr2p.org/pdf/R2P-4-Sande%20Lie.pdf⟩.

Luck, E. (2010) "The Responsibility to Protect: Growing Pains or Early Promise?", *Ethics and International Affairs* 24(4): 349–365.

Nasu, H. (2009) "Operationalising the 'Responsibility to Protect' and Conflict Prevention: Dilemmas of Civilian Protection in Armed Conflict", *Journal of Conflict and Security Law* 14: 209–241.

OSAPG, Office of the Special Adviser on the Prevention of Genocide (2009) *OSAPG Analysis Framework*. [Online] Available at: ⟨http://www.un.org/en/preventgenocide/adviser/pdf/osapg_analysis_framework.pdf⟩.

Policy Framework for the Establishment of the African Standby Force and the Military Staff Committee (2003) Document adopted by the Third Meeting of African Chiefs of Defense Staff, 15–16 May 2003, Addis Ababa.

Protocol Additional to the Geneva Conventions of 12 August 1949, and Relating to Victims of International Armed Conflict (Protocol I) 1125 UNTS 3.

Rosenberg, S. (2009) "Responsibility to Protect: A Framework for Prevention", *Global Responsibility to Protect* 1: 442–477.

Scheffer, D. (2009) "Atrocity Crimes Framing the Responsibility to Protect", *Case Western Journal of International Law* 40: 111–135.

Sharma, S. (2010) "Toward a Global Responsibility to Protect: Setbacks on the Path to Implementation", *Global Governance* 16: 121–138.

Stahn, C. (2007) "Responsibility to Protect: Political Rhetoric or Emerging Legal Norm?", *American Journal of International Law* 101: 99–120.

Stamnes, E. (2008) "Operationalising the Preventive Aspects of the Responsibility to Protect". *NUPI Report* No. 1: 1–27. [Online] Available at: ⟨http://www.globalr2p.org/pdf/R2P-1-Stamnes.pdf⟩.

Strauss, E. (2009) "A Bird in the Hand is Worth Two in the Bush: On the Assumed Legal Nature of the Responsibility to Protect", *Global Responsibility to Protect* 1: 291–323.

Thakur, R. (2006) *The United Nations, Peace and Security*. Cambridge: Cambridge University Press.

UNGA (2005) *UN General Assembly Resolution 60/1: World Summit Outcome Document*, A/RES/60/1, 24 October 2005.

UNGA (2011) *Sixty-Fifth General Assembly Informal Thematic Debate*, GA/11112, 12 July 2011.

UNSC (1992) *UN Security Council Resolution 795*. S/RES/795, 11 December 1992.

UNSC (1993) *UN Security Council Resolution 842*. S/RES/842, 18 June 1993.

UNSC (1995) *UN Security Council Resolution 983*. S/RES/983, 31 March 1995.

UNSC (1996a) *UN Security Council Resolution 1046*. S/RES/1046, 13 February 1996.

UNSC (1996b) *UN Security Council Resolution 1082*. S/RES/1082, 27 November 1996.

UNSC (1998a) *UN Security Council Resolution 1160*. S/RES/1160, 31 March 1998.

UNSC (1998b) *UN Security Council Resolution 1186*. S/RES/1186, 21 July 1998.

UNSC (2003) *UN Security Council Resolution 1509*. S/RES/1509, 19 September 2003.

UNSC (2004) *UN Security Council Resolution 1528*. S/RES/1528, 27 February 2004.

UNSC (2005) *UN Security Council Resolution 1590*. S/RES/1590, 24 March 2005.

UNSC (2007) *UN Security Council Resolution 1769*. S/RES/1769, 31 July 2007.

UNSC (2008) *UN Security Council Resolution 1856*. S/RES/1856, 22 December 2008.

UNSC (2011) *UN Security Council Resolution 1973*. S/RES/1973, 17 March 2011.

UNSG (1992) *An Agenda for Peace*, A/47/277-S/24111, 17 June 1992.

UNSG (1999) *Report of the Secretary-General to the Security Council on the Protection of Civilians in Armed Conflict*, S/1999/957, 8 September 1999.

UNSG (2009) *Report of the Secretary-General: Implementing the Responsibility to Protect*, A/63/677, 12 January 2009.

UNSG (2010a) *Report of the Secretary-General: Early Warning, Assessment and the Responsibility to Protect*, A/64/864, 14 July 2010.

UNSG (2010b) *Report of the Secretary-General to the Security Council on the Protection of Civilians in Armed Conflict*, S/2010/579, 11 November 2010.

UNSG (2011) *Report of the Secretary-General on the Lord's Resistance Army-affected areas pursuant to Security Council press statement*, S/2011/693, 4 November 2011.

Weinstein, J. (2007) *Inside Rebellion: The Politics of Insurgent Violence*. Cambridge: Cambridge University Press.

Welsh, J. (2010) "Implementing the 'Responsibility to Protect': Where Expectations Meet Reality", *Ethics and International Affairs* 24(14): 415–430.

Wulf, H. and T. Debiel (2009) "Conflict Early Warning and Response Mechanisms: Tools for Enhancing the Effectiveness of Regional Organisations?" *Crisis States Research Centre Working Paper No. 49*, London: London School of Economics and Political Science.

8

Framing a protection service

Annie Herro and Kavitha Suthanthiraraj

The United Nations has recognized that the plight of civilians is fundamental to its mandate (UNSG, 1999: paras. 67, 68). While protecting civilians has been an aim of UN peacekeeping operations for over a decade,
the organization has not always succeeded in achieving this goal. Civilians
are still under threat in places such as the Democratic Republic of Congo
(DRC) where UN peacekeeping operations are currently deployed (UNSC,
2010). While governments honoured their responsibility to protect civilians in Libya and Côte d'Ivoire, calls for the international community to
stop mass atrocity crimes in Sri Lanka (Egeland et al., 2009), Syria (Stack
and MacFarquhar, 2012) and elsewhere have fallen on deaf ears.

The UN Emergency Peace Service (UNEPS) is an ambitious reform
proposal for a standing peacekeeping service that would provide the
United Nations with the capability to respond rapidly and effectively to
acts of extreme violence against civilians. The proposed UNEPS would
comprise well-trained and well-equipped troops, police and civilians who
would be able to deploy at short notice "to prevent genocide and crimes
against humanity" (Johansen, 2006). The UNEPS proposal, like most
policy prescriptions, is inspired by two ideas: one normative, the other
problem-solving (Cooper and English, 2005: 7). It is punctuated by the
interrelated norms of the responsibility to protect (R2P)[1] and the protection of civilians (POC) in conflict. UNEPS also responds to practical and
political obstacles faced by the United Nations which often result in UN
peacekeeping operations deploying "too little, too late" and failing in
their duty to protect (Herro, Lambourne and Penklis, 2009).

Norms of protection: Responsibility to protect, protection of civilians and their interaction,
Francis, Popovski and Sampford (eds),
United Nations University Press, 2012, ISBN 978-92-808-1218-3

We are interested in ways to increase support for the UNEPS proposal. But ideas do not achieve political prominence on their merits alone. Theorists have argued that such ideas must be carried by transnational agents – individual "moral entrepreneurs" (Nadelmann, 1990), specialized "epistemic communities" (Haas, 1992) or social movements (Khagram, Riker and Sikkink, 2002). According to Finnemore and Sikkink (1998: 897), these agents call attention to issues by "naming, interpreting and dramatizing them", otherwise known as "framing", in an effort to persuade people to change the way they think or act.[2] Guided by this scholarship and based on interviews with over 80 respondents, we explore whether an R2P or POC frame would be the most effective means to persuade decision-makers across diverse professions and global regions to support the UNEPS proposal. Specifically, we examine the perceived legitimacy of both frames from normative and problem-solving perspectives and consider how this influences respondents' support for UNEPS.

We argue that POC carries greater currency among decision-makers than R2P and should be used not just to frame the UNEPS proposal but also to influence its attributes, how it is advocated and by which entrepreneurs. We use Acharya's (2004) theory on norm localization as a heuristic tool to help us apply the lessons from our framing analysis to suggest ways of increasing support for the UNEPS proposal. Localization occurs when "norm-takers" (local agents who must be persuaded to adopt an external norm) are able to build congruence between an external (or transnational) norm and their local beliefs and practices. We explore how our respondents seek to harmonize the UNEPS proposal with their political and normative priorities. We use the findings from our analysis to consider how to persuade decision-makers to support UNEPS by identifying opportunities for localization.[3]

In this paper, we first outline some of the shortcomings of the current peacekeeping system in protecting civilians in conflict. Next we explore the origins of the UNEPS proposal and suggest how it might address some of these shortcomings. After briefly outlining the methods employed to conduct our interviews, we discuss respondents' perceptions on R2P and POC and how this appears to influence their support for UNEPS. We conclude with a discussion on how the UNEPS proposal might be localized and the implications this could have for its design and advocacy.

8.1 R2P, POC and peacekeeping: Connecting the dots

Despite the history of attempts to protect civilians against physical violence, peacekeeping operations have continually fallen short. Throughout most of the 1990s, peacekeeping operations were not given mandates to protect civilians. In cases where such authorization was provided, the missions were ill-equipped and under-resourced, which limited their ability to protect. For example, the mandate for UNPROFOR in Bosnia was initially to provide humanitarian assistance but later expanded to "protect the civilian populations of the designated safe areas against armed attacks and other hostile acts" (UNSG, 1994: 5). Protection was more symbolic than militarily feasible as there was minimal troop deployment and a narrow interpretation of the mandate. In Rwanda, the peacekeepers tasked with implementing the 1993 Arusha Peace Accords[4] were not authorized to protect civilians, which proved tragic as genocide unfolded the following year. Thus, in stark contrast to the high expectations of those needing protection, peacekeeping operations are often modestly resourced due to member states' lack of capacity or political interest in protecting large numbers of civilians in conflicts. Consequently, tools to operationalize R2P and POC in peacekeeping operations have often been ad hoc and weak.

Breakey presents a helpful taxonomy that identifies different types of peace operations relating to R2P and POC. We summarize four types of mission within this taxonomy as an introduction to the ensuing discussion on the difficulties faced by such operations as well as respondents' perceptions of UNEPS, R2P and POC. First, a POC mission refers to peacekeepers who are tasked with protecting civilians as one of many potential roles within a Chapter VII mission. The threats to civilians are viewed as symptoms of the conflict rather than military strategies or the aim of the warring parties. Robust military action to protect civilians is anticipated, but is generally reactive in nature. Consent of the state is crucial and the mission is committed to being perceived as neutral by conflicting parties (see Chapter 3 by Hugh Breakey).[5] Second, a humanitarian POC mission refers to non-military action undertaken by humanitarian actors, such as Oxfam and the International Committee of the Red Cross, to protect civilians in instances of large-scale violence. This can be applied to situations broader than armed conflict including post-conflict and civil unrest.

Third, an R2P Pillar Two mission is deployed when there is a risk of atrocity crimes breaking out. It has the primary aim of proactively *preventing* such atrocities utilizing a systematic strategy and the robust use of force under Chapter VII. Because resistance to such an operation is anticipated, the mission must be sufficiently resourced and thus, in some cases, not led by the United Nations. Host state consent is necessary for logistical and political reasons. The perception of the mission's neutrality is helpful though not essential.[6] Finally, an R2P Pillar Three mission refers to an operation that is deployed when a state is actively committing atrocity crimes against its own population or is preparing to do so. Non-military measures have been deemed ineffective in the available timeframe. The mission will have a Chapter VII mandate and will not be led by the United Nations. It will engage in war-fighting and take all necessary measures to protect the civilian populations (Breakey, Chapter 3).[7]

8.2 Peacekeeping challenges

Despite these missions' focus on protecting civilians, peacekeepers face several challenges relating to resource availability, training and skills shortages.[8] The first challenge that the United Nations faces in its efforts to protect civilians from violence in conflict zones is the sluggish pace at which peacekeepers deploy (Roessler and Prendergast, 2006; Suthanthiraraj, 2008: 2). There is no set sequence of events and each operation must be formed "from scratch" (DPKO/DFS, 2008: 63; Suthanthiraraj and Quinn, 2009: 47).

In 1993 the UN Standby Arrangements System was created to improve the UN's access to readily available deployment capabilities. A few years later, the Multinational Standby High Readiness Brigade (SHIRBRIG) was established with comparable goals in mind, but has since ceased operations. These mechanisms, however, resulted in similar deployment delays and shortages of personnel and equipment to those faced by the UN's Department of Peacekeeping Operations (DPKO) (Langille, 2002: 40; 2009: 294). There are also regional arrangements including the European Union Battlegroup and the North Atlantic Treaty Organization; however, these groups still depend on national political will and the provision of national standby personnel which frequently stymie rapid response to crises (Langille, 2009: 299–300).

Second, governments might be unable or unwilling to contribute personnel, advanced weaponry, "enabling units" and "strategic airlift" to peacekeeping operations (Holt and Berkman, 2006: 6). Specifically, such operations may lack the necessary number of troops, police, civilians, engineering and communications systems, logistics, intelligence or long-distance transport (Durch, 2006: 72–73, 583; 2010: 15). This may be because the country to which the operation is deployed carries little political, strategic or economic interest. It may also be because member states either do not have these resources or cannot afford to hand them over to a peacekeeping operation (Durch, 1993: 50). Consequently, missions such as UNAMID in the Sudan continue to be under-staffed and under-resourced, with civilians bearing the brunt of this capacity gap (Herro, Lambourne and Penklis, 2009).

Third, while the UNSC has regularly referenced the protection of civilians "under imminent threat of physical violence" in mandates for UN-led peacekeeping operations authorized under Chapter VII of the UN Charter (Holt and Berkman, 2006: 5), peacekeepers (troops and police) are under the authority of their government, which sometimes prevents them from taking the necessary risks to protect civilians (Bellamy, Williams and Griffin, 2010: 57). Furthermore, peacekeepers can lack the requisite skills and training as well as the operational guidance and conceptual clarity needed to effectively protect civilians (Holt and Berkman, 2006: 8; Holt, Taylor and Kelly, 2009: 99–100, 121). Only recently has DPKO (with the Department of Field Support, DFS) provided strategic direction to troop- and police-contributing nations on what the "protection of civilians under imminent threat of physical violence" actually means, but is yet to commence any scenario-based or detailed task-driven training (APCMCOE, 2010: 8).

Fourth, while many of the world's peacekeepers come from the global South, virtually all missions that are deployed rapidly are led by a pivotal state(s) or regional organization, with the resources – troops, armoured equipment and supplies – from the West.[9] This has sometimes led to claims of neo-colonial interference (Anderson, 2006: 74; Ahmed, Keating and Solinas, 2007: 6) and a subsequent backlash against peacekeepers. This was recently illustrated when additional French forces were deployed to strengthen the UN peacekeeping mission in the Côte d'Ivoire (UNOCI).[10] Accusations by former leader, Laurent Gbagbo, that his country was a victim of a "global conspiracy led by France and the United Nations" culminated in attacks on UN peacekeepers (Reuters, 2011; UNSC, 2010: para. 17).

These challenges have impacted both peacekeepers' "ability to protect" as well as the legitimacy and effectiveness of UN peace operations (Holt, Taylor and Kelly, 2009: 3–4). This raises the question: how can peacekeeping be strengthened to aid in the protection of civilians?

8.3   UNEPS: Overcoming history

In an effort to address these shortcomings in the peacekeeping system and to improve the United Nations' efforts to prevent and respond rapidly to genocide and other crimes against humanity, UNEPS was conceived. UNEPS, however, is not the first attempt to create a standing UN peacekeeping capacity. From 1948 to 1994, more than a dozen proposals were presented ranging from former UN Secretary-General Trygve Lie's appeal for a UN Guard Force to Ronald Reagan's call at the end of his presidency for a "standing UN force – an army of conscience" (Urquhart,

2006). The motivation behind some of these proposals was to improve the United Nations' response to mass killings, known today as R2P crimes (Roberts, 2008: 99). UNEPS' most recent predecessor was the proposal by Brian Urquhart (1993) for a UN Volunteer Military Force which was designed to provide early, robust intervention to buttress preventive diplomacy. Commentators, however, argued that practical, political and conceptual factors would hinder the realization of Urquhart's idea (Hamilton et al., 1993). But the problems that prompted those like Urquhart to present such a proposal – deployment delays, inadequate numbers of well-trained and equipped peacekeepers who were ill-prepared to protect civilians – did not disappear.

In 2003, activists, academics, former UN officials, government representatives and peacekeepers from around the world came together to design the UNEPS proposal (Johansen, 2006: 16). They met in Santa Barbara, California, and have met almost every year since through the coordination of the New York-based NGO, Global Action to Prevent War (GAPW), to increase awareness of the need for UN-based rapid reaction capabilities.[11] UNEPS is proposed to overcome some of the obstacles peace operations face in protecting civilians in a number of ways.[12] First, UNEPS would be a permanent service comprising citizens of member nations acting in their individual capacity. It would have the ability to respond rapidly to crises, operating with a "first-in, first-out" deployment philosophy, with a maximum deployment of six months. It would thus close the gap between the approved UNSC resolution and action. Having UNEPS readily available might also assist in obtaining UNSC authorization for the use of force and reduce unilateral interventions.

Second, since UNEPS would be self-contained with readily available personnel (around 15,000–18,000 civilians, police and military), equipment and supplies at the disposal of the United Nations, it could overcome governments' unwillingness to expose their citizens and resources to security threats in countries perceived to be of little geopolitical significance.[13] For example, UNEPS could have buttressed the African Union mission in Sudan and UN support packages in Darfur (2006–2008) by providing self-sufficient and combat-ready special services with adequate deployable military elements. This might have been able to provide reassurances to governments contributing to the UN support packages that their equipment and personnel would be protected (Herro, Lambourne and Penklis, 2009: 59).

Third, because UNEPS personnel would be trained as "protection specialists", the service would possess an operational expertise in protecting "civilians under imminent threat of physical violence", including R2P crimes. UNEPS personnel would be capable of undertaking a full range of measures to provide protection, to ensure security and to support actions that eliminate the ability of perpetrators, or potential perpetrators, to threaten the population. For example, while the UN mission in the DRC (MONUC, now MONUSCO) has a protection mandate (UNSC, 2008: para. 2), attacks on civilians continue unabated (Reynaert, 2011). Despite the release of the *Practical Protection Handbook for Peacekeepers* in 2009, peacekeepers in the DRC lack clarity on whether POC functions should be "reactive" or "defensive" as well as the training to complement the guidelines (Working Group on the Protection of Civilians, 2009). UNEPS could supplement the poorly resourced Joint Protection Teams in repelling forces threatening civilians, monitoring and intelligence-gathering to identify at-risk communities, protecting those delivering humanitarian aid and formulating longer-term protection strategies.

Fourth, the proposed UNEPS would comprise personnel from diverse cultural, religious, social and geographical backgrounds and be based at UN-designated sites, including field headquarters. This diversity is intended to both facilitate better interaction with host communities and to remove some of the neo-colonial stigma that is often associated with interventions. Personnel would also be trained in cultural and religious sensitivities pertaining to their operational environments (Suthanthiraraj and Quinn, 2009: 16). In the case of Darfur, since UNEPS personnel would have had an international composition, its presence could have helped to avert regional accusations of neo-colonialism and the political quagmire of sending American (or Western) troops into a Muslim country after the Iraq and Afghanistan interventions (Herro, Lambourne and Penklis 2009: 58).

UNEPS thus could be used for R2P or POC-type interventions. According to its promoters, it would never, however, be the sole provider of protection. Not only would it rapidly bring its skills to places where other protection actors are present, including the host governments, UN protection agencies and NGOs, it would need to be replaced by a more robust, longer-term peacekeeping operation competent in protecting civilians against physical violence and other threats. UNEPS could not completely remove the critical issue of political will and entrenched concerns over intervention, but it might remove important obstacles and provide a valuable instrument of policy (Mendez, 2009).

8.4 Research methods

Between 2008 and 2010, we conducted semi-structured interviews and workshops on the UNEPS proposal with over 80 respondents from different professional, political and cultural backgrounds, to gain some idea

about how the proposal might be received.[14] These included political analysts, senior military officers as well as current and former representatives
of UN departments and government bureaucracies, in particular the departments of defence and foreign affairs. Respondents were selected as
being influential stakeholders in international and public affairs. Most
offered valuable insights into the practical and normative feasibility and
legitimacy of the UNEPS proposal and the conditions under which it
could be supported. Those who worked (at the time of the interview or
previously) within the machinery of government were able to share first-
hand experiences working within national or multilateral institutions on
issues relating to peacekeeping and other types of intervention. In particular, government officials serving in UN country missions provided insights into processes through which (emerging) transnational norms such
as POC and R2P are diffused into states and the UN system. Furthermore, the attitudes of knowledgeable observers, such as political analysts,
offered valuable insights into their respective governments' (or regions')
responses to the proposed UNEPS. Since these analysts remain influential actors in their respective domestic and regional political arenas, they
also provided important perspectives on the UNEPS proposal in their
own right. The following section discusses the impact of R2P and POC
frames on respondents' levels of support for a proposed UNEPS.

8.5 The "responsibility to protect" frame

8.5.1 "[Don't] shy away from Third Pillar conversations"

A small group of respondents, mainly Australian academics and government officials, and representatives of UN agencies, argued that R2P
should be used to frame the proposed UNEPS. Their support for R2P led
them to urge UNEPS advocates to pursue an R2P frame and "not shy
away from Third Pillar conversations". Rather, they advised that R2P
must be tackled "head-on" through solid legal arguments, clarifying that
force would be used by UNEPS only as a last resort in relation to a narrow class of issues (i.e. R2P crimes) and under the close scrutiny of the
UNSC. This small group, which included representatives from the UN
Office for Special Adviser on Genocide Prevention and the UN Office
for the High Commissioner for Human Rights (OHCHR), and a member
of the Australian government,[15] believed that highlighting the safeguards
built into R2P would go some way towards overcoming mistrust of the
doctrine and, by association, the UNEPS proposal.

   The bulk of respondents, however, stated or implied that R2P –
conceived of as R2P Pillar Three missions – was an unhelpful frame for

UNEPS advocates to use as a means to generating support for the proposal. Some respondents held this position because they were suspicious of R2P. Others advised against using R2P as a frame because, while supporting the doctrine themselves, they were mindful of its hostile reception in certain political and cultural circles. There were two principal reasons for their cautious approach: the perceptions that R2P is a tool of powerful states and that R2P is synonymous with the use of force.

8.5.2 R2P as a Western ploy

Despite receiving almost universal support at the World Summit in 2005, many respondents believed that R2P is championed by the most powerful states, especially those in the West, which, in turn, reduced their support for UNEPS. A prominent Indonesian political analyst was among those concerned that R2P is a Western doctrine. He said: "R2P is problematic because it's so selective. I'd never imagine that the UN would be able to intervene into China, or Chechnya even, if there were genocide ... The perception is that R2P has double standards."[16] A former Secretary-General of ASEAN suggested that if R2P Pillar Three missions became commonplace, they would be used to advance the foreign policy of certain powerful states,[17] while a former South African government official viewed R2P as Western-centric and vulnerable to realpolitik within the Security Council. He claimed that "It's a tool being developed for meddling in our affairs ..."[18] These respondents worried that R2P licenses the most powerful states to impose their values on the rest of the world.[19] Their caution implies a lack of ownership and understanding of the doctrine. The latter respondent also noted: "I strongly agree that states should protect their citizens, but we don't need others telling us how to do this." It is the perceived paternalistic and neo-imperialist character of R2P that is contributing to their hostility.

Comparable sentiments spilled over into respondents' reactions to UNEPS. Several interviewees were concerned that UNEPS would be politicized in a similar way to R2P. For example, a Ugandan diplomat expressed concern that smaller states might be fearful that UNEPS could be used to interfere in their affairs.[20] Highlighting the dangers of UNEPS being associated with the West, a Japanese parliamentarian who has supported and incorporated UNEPS into his policy platform said: "The face of UNEPS is critical ... to sell it I need a non-Western face."[21] Indeed, the perception that Western states were driving earlier initiatives to establish a standing or rapidly deployable peacekeeping service deterred potential supporters and contributed to the demise of these proposals. Ahmad Kamal, the Pakistani Ambassador to the United Nations, responded to the group "Friends of Rapid Reaction" (a collection of nations that championed previous UN peacekeeping reform proposals) that he "supported the concept of a rapid deployment headquarters team but was concerned at the action of a self-appointed group ... operating without legitimacy, and having half-baked ideas developed without broad consultations with the countries most concerned" (Langille, 2000: 226). Similar attitudes led other states to be uncooperative and to question the legitimacy of alleged Western-centric arrangements, such as SHIRBRIG, which was based in Denmark and comprised mainly Western troops (ibid.: 230). In sum, the perception that UNEPS and R2P Pillar Three missions are Western initiatives is unhelpful in advocating UNEPS due to fears that R2P licenses Western states to interfere in the affairs of weaker states.

8.5.3 R2P and the use of force

Another interpretation of R2P that hindered support for the UNEPS proposal was the perception that the former was synonymous with military intervention. Many respondents ignored or failed to understand that prevention is at the heart of the doctrine. Despite efforts to divorce R2P from its cousin, humanitarian intervention (Evans, 2008: 31–76; Thakur, 2006: 266–267) the association stubbornly remains. For example, a former Indonesian Ambassador who is an outspoken proponent of ASEAN reform announced that "R2P means a developed country intervening in a developing country. It has no credibility because of Mr. Bush. What we see is the UN using force to introduce democracy."[22] Further reinforcing the perception of R2P as a "Trojan horse" used by the more powerful nations to legitimize meddling in the affairs of smaller, weaker ones, Hilary Charlesworth, Professor of International Law and Human Rights at the Australian National University, argued that R2P is legally flawed as it is based on the doctrine of humanitarian intervention which has always been controversial and open to abuse. The idea of conditional sovereignty at the heart of R2P – "abuse it and lose it" – is ineffective in preventing potential abuses, she maintained. She believes that, as a principled legal framework for intervention that saves lives, such a reformulation is likely to be used by powerful states against less powerful ones, running the risks of self-serving conflict assessments masquerading as humanitarian (CPACS, 2008: 3).

Such suspicions exacerbated respondents' mistrust of UNEPS. Fears that UNEPS would be an "international army" were particularly unhelpful in finding support for the proposal. An Indonesian political analyst who had previously served under former Indonesian President B. J. Habibie expressed the classic concern about external interventions violating state sovereignty. "That's why the idea isn't going to fly," she said, "because it is against the sovereignty of the state. While everyone agrees that we don't want Rwanda to happen, but what happens to you [i.e. intervention] can happen to us!"[23] It was challenging in these interviews to discuss the non-military components of UNEPS and opportunities to provide a range of tasks that the service would offer to protect civilians from violence. Further highlighting the sensitivities surrounding the language used to discuss interventions, a representative of the Uruguayan mission to the United Nations claimed that "even 'robust' peacekeeping has become toxic. Legitimacy will always be important and there's always the elephant in the room – sovereignty!"[24] These same concerns plagued an earlier proposal for a standing UN capacity to deal with peace and security issues. Trygve Lie's original plan to create a "UN Guard Force" was truncated partly because it encroached too closely on a military theme (Roberts, 2008: 102). He was compelled to remove the word "force" from the title and repackaged the proposal as a "UN Guard" (Cordier and Foote, 1969: 131).[25]

8.6 The "protection of civilians" frame

8.6.1 A POC mission: Addressing a problem

Would a POC mission frame be more effective in generating support for UNEPS? Despite the similarities between a POC mission and an R2P Pillar Two mission in practice, many respondents suggest, yes. A representative of the Permanent Mission of Uruguay to the United Nations illustrates the different reaction each frame invokes:

> There is still much friction being caused by the confusion between POC and R2P. These concepts overlap but one is more toxic than the other. This is why it's important to focus on pragmatic components like timing of deployment and training – this stops Member States from focusing on words and to take action![26]

On a similar note, other respondents cited the difficulties peacekeepers acting under a Chapter VII mandate face in protecting civilians from conflict as cause for concern. They complained about the absence of uniform training among peacekeepers, their lack of understanding about how to protect civilians on the ground as well as the minimal resources available to them.[27] In sum, framing UNEPS as a tool to support *existing* peacekeeping operations, acting under Chapter VII, in their efforts to protect civilians appeared to increase respondents' interest in the initiative.

8.6.2 A POC mission: Less threatening than R2P

Some respondents directly and indirectly mounted a case for using POC to frame UNEPS based on the argument that POC commands greater legitimacy within and outside the United Nations. According to a representative of the Permanent Mission of Australia to the United Nations, in contrast to R2P, POC (implying POC missions) is winning more acceptance in the UNGA partly because it is seen as less threatening.[28] While the recent UNSC resolution on Libya (2011a) referenced the First Pillar of R2P by stating that crimes against humanity were taking place and that it was the responsibility of the Libyan authorities to protect its population, the resolution principally employed POC language. POC was stated three times and received a separate heading that introduced the provisions of the resolution that authorized member states to take action (UNSC, 2011a: para. 4). When asked why R2P was not used explicitly in the resolution, former Canadian Minister of Foreign Affairs and early champion of R2P, Lloyd Axworthy, replied that "there may be some political reasons for not putting that label on it, in case it fires up opposition to the label itself or the branding itself" (Smith, 2011). The POC mission norm has also proved to be a helpful frame when hosting regional events on UNEPS. A central component of UNEPS advocacy is the development of a series of workshops/roundtables in regional centres such as Indonesia, Brazil and Cameroon to generate further interest in and support for the proposal (GAPW, 2009a, 2009b). Those involved in organizing these events discovered that using POC as "drawcard" attracted more participation and provided a useful, familiar and safe framework in which discussions on UNEPS could be pursued.

8.6.3 Breadth of POC attractive

Further supporting the case to use the POC mission norm to frame UNEPS, some respondents argued that R2P crimes, which would trigger a UNEPS deployment, are too rare to justify the creation of such a service. Indeed, peace operations with a POC mandate are far more common than those responding to R2P crimes. A former Australian politician, who had previously served as a director in the UN Secretariat, argued that it is an inefficient use of resources to create a service to prevent R2P crimes when "one sixth of the world is dying of hunger and one of the major impediments to addressing this is war".[29] Similarly, a Malaysian policy analyst suggested that R2P crimes are too infrequent to justify the resources and political will required for developing a UNEPS.[30] Such a shift in frame would of course have implications for UNEPS' proposed mandate. Its *raison d'être* would no longer be to prevent R2P crimes but rather to protect civilians from violence in armed conflict.

The scope of civilian protection is also broad enough to encompass populations displaced or at risk as a result of natural disasters (O'Callaghan and Pantuliano, 2007: 1). This version of protection is a combination of two POC norms identified by Breakey – a POC mission and humanitarian POC. The latter emphasizes neutrality (Breakey, Chapter 3), while the former responds to threats to human rights resulting from, *inter alia*, natural disasters (Breakey, Chapter 2).[31] Respondents agreed that interventions that respond to natural disasters are an area in which respect for state sovereignty is of less importance – "It's about human beings against nature" as one prominent Indonesian journalist put it[32] – suggesting such interventions could be an important gateway to broader international cooperation in response to more sensitive crises such as R2P crimes. Specifically, some respondents argued that, for political reasons, a UNEPS proposal that focused on natural disasters would be an effective entry point to start a conversation about UNEPS. For example, sensitivities about discussing human rights violations in the region, such as in Mindanao and Myanmar, convinced a Bangladeshi diplomat that UNEPS could be a means of responding to large-scale natural disasters and other "less politicized" tasks.[33] Others, including a senior Australian Defence Force (ADF) figure and a prominent Indonesian political and defence analyst, argued that creating a regional mechanism in the Asia-Pacific region capable of responding to natural disasters might build the necessary trust between states to create a service with an accepted mandate to also prevent mass human rights abuses.[34] Thus, natural disasters were a "hook" on which many respondents hung their desire to better protect civilians and enhance international cooperation.[35]

From a practical perspective, recent natural catastrophes such as the 2004 tsunami and Cyclone Nargis in Myanmar suggest that the international community needs a mechanism that addresses such disasters (Caballero-Anthony and Chng, 2009: 147).[36] Perhaps in part to generate normative support for the creation of such a mechanism, Southeast Asian commentators, Mely Cabarello-Anthony and Belinda Chng (ibid.), suggest creating a variation of R2P called "R2P-plus", tailored to a Southeast Asian context. R2P-plus would be devoid of coercive measures and could help to advance the application of R2P by concentrating on natural catastrophes and conflict situations that are on a lighter scale in terms of widespread and deliberate physical violence. Consequently, R2P-plus would "blunt the arguments of those who accuse R2P of being a neo-imperialist instrument" (ibid.: 145). While we support this attempt to localize R2P, given the hostility to R2P emerging from our interviews on UNEPS, we suggest using POC (possibly the humanitarian POC norm or some variant on it) to frame discussions on timely and decisive responses to natural disasters and, in turn, applying this to UNEPS.

8.7 "Localizing" UNEPS: Lessons from R2P and POC

What implications do these observations have for those trying to generate support for UNEPS? As prefaced in the chapter introduction, in answering this question we apply Acharya's theory of localization. First, Acharya (2004: 251) argues that a condition for the extraction of new instruments, such as UNEPS, out of a transnational norm, such as POC, is that some aspects of the existing (regional) normative order will already be discredited from within or found inadequate to meet with new and unforeseen challenges. Our respondents expressed concern about the inadequacy of current POC missions. This shortcoming piqued their interest in UNEPS, which suggests that pitching UNEPS as a service that would buttress existing peacekeeping operations' POC activities might attract more support for the proposal. This would necessitate modifications of the UNEPS proposal from the original conception of a "first in, first out" service to one that would strengthen POC missions that have already been deployed and provide protection specialist functions to these operations. Indeed, the notorious cases of genocide and crimes against humanity in Rwanda, Srebrenica, Darfur and the DRC occurred under the watch of UN peacekeepers who were unable to halt such acts. To counter perceptions that UNEPS would violate state sovereignty, another proposal modification could be that UNEPS would only be deployed with host country consent, especially since this is integral to POC missions. This reflects the present circumstances in international relations because, with the exception of Libya, full-scale military interventions to protect civilians have only been undertaken with host country consent or when there is no functioning government to consult, such as in Somalia and Rwanda (Bellamy, 2011).

Second, the key agents in the localization process are what Acharya (2004: 251) calls "insider proponents" because, ultimately, "the initiative to seek change normally belongs to the local agent". Indeed, Chong and Druckman (2007: 112) argue that frames that are invoked by credible sources are more likely to have a strong impact. Is UNEPS seen to be promoted by local proponents, or at least proponents that respondents trust? And does the way UNEPS is framed influence respondents' views on this issue? R2P is seen to be advanced by powerful states, especially those in the West, which has a negative bearing on generating support for UNEPS. This suggests that building trust among potential UNEPS supporters could include decentralizing and localizing UNEPS-related activities from GAPW in New York and into regional centres where some UNEPS proponents are currently based.[37] This could mean supporting such initiatives with necessary resources, identifying "non-Western" faces to champion the proposal as well as gaining support from states from the Non-Aligned Movement and medium-sized countries to placate fears that UNEPS is a Western initiative. For example, an influential Malaysian social and political commentator argued that the only way the Malaysian government, or any Southeast Asian government for that matter, would take the UNEPS proposal seriously is if it was presented to them by a few committed, medium-sized governments.[38]

Third, Acharya (2004: 244, 250) argues that localization occurs when the external norm is "pruned" and "grafted" by linking it to existing local norms and practices.[39] Given that many respondents viewed UNEPS as synonymous with humanitarian intervention – which was reinforced by perceptions of R2P as a Trojan horse – other variations of the proposal might need to be explored. Our framing analysis suggests that localizing the UNEPS proposal to ensure that it is congruent with the POC mission norm would extend beyond piggy-backing on POC-related initiatives towards using POC to shape UNEPS attributes. This might include reworking the UNEPS proposal as a mechanism to respond to natural disasters, which remains within the scope of civilian protection.[40]

8.8 Conclusion

We have shown that not only might R2P be an unhelpful frame in advocating UNEPS but that UNEPS might be an unhelpful frame in advocating R2P. While some respondents recommended that UNEPS entrepreneurs use R2P to frame the proposal, the vast majority expressed concerns that the norm is a tool of powerful states, especially those in the West, and that it is indistinguishable from the use of force. This was unhelpful for UNEPS advocates who are already confronting (mis)beliefs that UNEPS would be manipulated by the West and that it would be an army to intervene coercively in weaker states. The POC mission norm, on the other hand, enjoyed a much warmer reception among respondents. It draws attention to the logistical and operational challenges UN peacekeeping operations face in protecting civilians from violence in conflict and appears potentially less controversial than R2P Pillar Two and Pillar Three missions. The POC norm is also attractive because it encompasses a range of situations beyond the four R2P crimes where civilians might be at risk, including natural disasters.

Given the disparity between how our respondents reacted to R2P and POC, we argue that POC might be of greater value in generating interest in, and support for, the UNEPS proposal. Applying Acharya's (2004: 251) theory on norm localization helps us to suggest ways in which the findings from our framing analysis might be used to more effectively design and advocate a proposed UNEPS. We argue that presenting UNEPS as a mechanism to support POC missions might garner greater support for the proposal. Another proposal modification we offer is that UNEPS could only be deployed with host country consent, which is consistent with POC missions. We also suggest that localizing UNEPS-related activities into regional centres and encouraging members of the Non-Aligned Movement and medium-sized states to support the proposal might also increase its perceived legitimacy. We conclude that repackaging the UNEPS proposal as a mechanism to respond to natural disasters, perhaps using a new concept that combines properties of the POC mission and humanitarian POC norms, might result in incremental reform that could eventually build the momentum to create a service with a mandate to prevent R2P crimes. To conclude, the Canadian government (1995) conducted a comprehensive study on the feasibility of a rapid reaction capability that favoured incremental reform within the UN Secretariat as opposed to developing a UN standing army (Government of Canada, 1995, cited in Langille, 2000, 6–7). Such an approach was seen to involve fewer risks and obligations and was preferred over the creation of a supranational peacekeeping force because it would give states greater control over international peace and security issues. Sixteen years later, the situation looks more promising though the wisdom of incremental reform still resonates today.

Notes

1. A norm can be described statistically as a widely prevalent pattern of behaviour – what "is". It can also be ethical or prescriptive in nature, referring to a standard of behaviour that should be followed in accordance with a particular value system – what "ought" to be. Thakur (2011: 5) argues that there is no agreement on who can legitimately pinpoint "global norms". He also points out that norms can be held by an individual, shared by a group or shared universally (ibid.). We do not claim that R2P is a global norm in the statistical sense, or even in the ethical sense. We argue that R2P, as a normative idea constituting the UNEPS proposal, refers to values which influence the goals of a group of people – that is, UNEPS architects and promoters as well as others with similar identities and interests.

2. Keck and Sikkink (1998: 201, 204) point out that framing an idea transnationally is particularly challenging because, unlike in a domestic situation, the frame must reflect belief systems, stories and myths in many different countries and cultures.

3. Even though framing is one component of localization – along with discourse, grafting and cultural selection (Acharya, 2004: 241) – we are using the POC and R2P frames to understand how the localization of the UNEPS proposal might take place. In other words, we treat framing as an aspect of localization, as Acharya intended, as well as a guide to altering the attributes of the proposal and how it is advocated to increase interest in, and support for, UNEPS. Furthermore, Acharya's (2004: 240) theory is built

upon a regional analysis of two transnational norms in Southeast Asia. While our interviews comprise respondents who are from Southeast Asia, they also include those from other regions as we detail further in the section on research methods. This means that we are applying localization transnationally rather than regionally.

4. The Arusha Peace Agreement (or the Arusha Peace Accords) was the peace agreement between the Rwandan Patriotic Front and the Government of Rwanda. It consisted of five protocols (accords) which ended the civil war in Rwanda and began a peace process signed on 4 August 1993 (Dallaire, 2005: 524).

5. The UN peace operation in Liberia (UNMIL) is an example of a POC mission as the mandate of civilian protection is coupled with other tasks including monitoring the ceasefire, disarmament, security reform and more (UNSC, 2003).

6. The UN peace operation in the Côte d'Ivoire (UNOCI) is an example of such a mission, especially since the adoption of UNSC Resolution 1975. It charges UNOCI and the French forces, which were leading the security component of the mission, with primarily POC tasks (UNSC, 2011b).

7. While UNSC Resolution 1973 authorizes member states "to protect civilians and civilian populated areas under threat of attack" in Libya (UNSC, 2011a), it does not explicitly reference Pillar Three of R2P. However, governments supporting the intervention publicly used R2P language to justify it (Cotler and Genser, 2011; *Washington Times*, 2011). Furthermore, some commentators argued that using R2P to justify the operation in Libya was a cover for regime change (Boreham, 2011).

8. While there are many factors contributing to the challenge UN peace operations face in protecting civilians (Holt, Taylor and Kelly, 2009: 7), this chapter addresses only those factors which UNEPS might address.

9. For example, the UNSC-endorsed rapid interventions in Somalia (UNITAF), East Timor (INTERFET) and the DRC (Artemis), to name a few, would not have been possible without the lead support from the United States, Australia and France, respectively. The most recent case of this was the Chapter VII operation in Libya which was executed just two days after the UNSC resolution was adopted. This would not have been possible without resources from the US, UK and France.

10. While French forces (Operation Licorne) have been in Côte d'Ivoire since 2004 to support UNOCI and to ensure the security of French and foreign nationals, the troop numbers were strengthened to 1,700 as of 2011 (UNSC, 2011b).

11. Those who have attended conferences on UNEPS include: former Canadian Foreign Minister, Lloyd Axworthy; Richard Falk, Professor Emeritus of International Law, Princeton University; former Commander of the UN forces in the former Yugoslavia, Lt. Gen. (retired) Satish Nambiar, Indian Army. The momentum for UNEPS culminated in 2006 with the launch of the publication *A United Nations Emergency Peace Service: To prevent genocide and crimes against humanity* (Johansen).

12. Peter Langille (2000, 2009) has written extensively on the logistical and operational aspects of the proposed UNEPS, such as basing arrangements and command structure. Our purpose is to show that UNEPS could potentially address some of the shortcomings in the UN peacekeeping system discussed above rather than show exactly how this could be done.

13. The proposed size of UNEPS has been criticized by some commentators as being too small and incapable of responding to multiple crises concurrently. While it is true that UNEPS would not be able to respond to every case of atrocity crimes, in the words of the International Commission on Intervention and State Sovereignty, "can the fact that effective international action is not always possible in every instance of major humanitarian catastrophe ever be an excuse for inaction where effective responses are possible?" (ICISS, 2001: 6).

14. These interviews and workshops were undertaken under the auspices of Global Action to Prevent War and the Centre for Peace and Conflict Studies at the University of Sydney, often in collaboration with local universities or think-tanks. For more information on these workshops see Global Action to Prevent War's (n.d.) website.
15. Interview by Suthanthiraraj with representative from the Office of the Special Adviser on Genocide Prevention, 10 June 2010, New York; interview by Suthanthiraraj with representative from the OHCHR, 23 November 2010, New York; interview by Herro and Stuart Rees with member of the Australian Government, 27 June 2008, Sydney.
16. Interview by Herro, 7 May 2008, Jakarta.
17. Interview by Herro, 16 June 2009, Singapore.
18. Phone interview by Suthanthiraraj, 1 September 2008.
19. These concerns are not new and have been expressed by numerous academics who, for ideological reasons, believe that any form of external intervention would be driven, at least in part, by neo-colonialists pursuits (de Waal, 2008; Mamdani, 2007).
20. Interview by Suthanthiraraj, 21 December 2010, New York.
21. Phone interview by Suthanthiraraj, 1 July 2008.
22. Interview by Herro, 7 May 2008, Jakarta.
23. Interview by Herro, 8 May 2008, Jakarta.
24. Interview by Suthanthiraraj, 21 December 2010, New York.
25. In 1948, the first Secretary-General, Trygve Lie, made a speech at Harvard University proposing the establishment of a UN Guard Force consisting of 1,000–5,000 men at the disposal of the Security Council. He later renamed it a UN Guard and reduced the proposed strength to 300 troops (Cordier and Foote, 1969: 131).
26. Interview by Suthanthiraraj, 21 December 2010, New York.
27. Interview by Suthanthiraraj with the Australian Mission to the UN, 20 June 2010, New York; interview by Suthanthiraraj with representative from the OHCHR, 23 November 2010, New York.
28. Interview by Suthanthiraraj, 20 June 2010, New York.
29. Interview by Herro, Melbourne, 28 August 2008.
30. Interview by Herro, 1 May 2008, Kuala Lumpur.
31. Breakey argues that humanitarian POC is directed at "humanitarian actors" such as the Red Cross and Oxfam, thus excluding the work of peacekeepers (Breakey, Chapter 2). Similarly, POC missions, like all peace operations, do not respond to natural disasters but rather to conflict.
32. Interview by Herro, 30 April 2008, Jakarta.
33. Interview by Suthanthiraraj, 18 June 2010, New York.
34. Interview by Herro, 13 December 2008, Canberra; interview by Herro, 7 May 2008, Jakarta. For example, the respondent from the ADF, who was impressed with the skills of certain Southeast Asian neighbours in responding to recent tsunamis and earthquakes, argued in relation to the establishment of a UNEPS that "If you start with genocide, you probably won't do it; but if you start with humanitarian aid, it could go a long way towards establishing the trust that could flow into the other ... it's not about security, it's not about who's superior ... [it is] a recognition that working together is a smart thing to do that doesn't cause ... the loss of face" (interview by Herro, 13 December 2008, Canberra).
35. A member of the UNEPS working group, Dr Alejandro Soto Romero, of Health Alliance International, suggested that if the true goal of UNEPS is to save lives, the proposal should not focus solely on military capabilities in response to threats of genocide but also on providing humanitarian relief during complex emergencies, especially after natural disasters (GAPW, 2007: 8).

36. A number of services are provided by UN agencies and coordinated by the Office for the Coordination of Humanitarian Affairs (OCHA) in response to natural disasters and emergencies. These include a permanent standby Disaster Assessment and Coordination Team, On-Site Operations Coordination Centre and the coordination of civil-military assets and the management of a Central Emergency Response Fund. Despite these services, ECOSOC (2005: para. 10) adopted a resolution in response to the 2004 tsunami advising that more must be done to develop and improve mechanisms for the use of emergency standby capacities. Furthermore, in a report by the NGO, Forced Migration, it has been argued that "A standing global response mechanism under the auspices of the UN, with immediate authority to launch the initial response and build on available local and regional capacities, would lead to prompter dispatch of relief teams and supplies" (Couldrey and Morris, 2005: 7). Finally, in response to the March 2011 deadly earthquake and tsunami in Japan, the UN reiterated calls for the world to respond quickly to current worldwide disasters and streamline efforts to tackle their inevitable impacts (Musthofid, 2011).

37. GAPW is a strong proponent of the localization strategy and, over the past few years, has incorporated the findings from this research into its UNEPS advocacy programme.

38. Interview by Herro, 1 May 2008, Kuala Lumpur.

39. While Acharya (2004: 251) also says that local beliefs and practices might be adjusted in accordance with the external norm, this was very difficult to ascertain because we only carried out one interview with each respondent.

40. While the principles and strategies of POC seem to attract greater support for UNEPS, it is important to note that R2P is gaining traction. This can be seen through its recent association with Libya and Côte d'Ivoire (although specific language was not used in either resolutions), the advocacy of Special Adviser on the Responsibility to Protect, Ed Luck, and Special Adviser on the Prevention of Genocide, Francis Deng, and the establishment of global and regional centres on R2P.

REFERENCES

Acharya, A. (2004) "How Ideas Spread: Whose Norms Matter? Norm Localization and Institutional Change in Asian Regionalism", *International Organization* 58 (Spring): 239–275.

Ahmed, S., P. Keating, and U. Solinas (2007) "Shaping the Future of UN Peace Operations: Is There a Doctrine in the House?", *Cambridge Review of International Affairs* 20(1): 11–28.

Anderson, T. (2006) "Timor-Leste: The Second Australian Intervention", *Journal of Australian Political Economy* 58: 62–93.

Arbour, L. (2011) "Open letter to the UN Security Council on the situation in Côte d'Ivoire", *International Crisis Group*, 25 March. [Online] Available at: ⟨http://www.crisisgroup.org/en/publication-type/media-releases/2011/open-letter-unsc-cote-divoire.aspx⟩ (accessed 21 February 2012).

Asia Pacific Civil-Military Centre of Excellence (APCMCOE) (2010) *Challenges of Strengthening the Protection of Civilians in Multidimensional Peace Operations.* Canberra, 27–29 April. [Online] Available at: ⟨http://www.challengesforum.org/cms/images/pdf/Challenges_Forum_2010_SummaryReport.pdf⟩ (accessed 30 March 2011).

Bellamy, A. (2011) "We can't dodge the hard part stabilising Libya", *The Australian*, 21 March.

Bellamy, A., P. Williams, and S. Griffin (2010) *Understanding Peacekeeping*, 2nd edn. Cambridge: Polity.

Boreham, K. (2011) "Libya and R2P: The Limits of Responsibility", East Asian Forum, 31 March. [Online] Available at: ⟨http://www.eastasiaforum.org/2011/03/31/libya-and-r2p-the-limits-of-responsibility/⟩ (accessed 1 April 2011).

Caballero-Anthony, M., and B. Chng (2009) "Cyclones and Humanitarian Crises: Pushing the Limits of R2P in Southeast Asia", *Global Responsibility to Protect* 1(2): 135–155.

CPACS, Centre for Peace and Conflict Studies (2008) *Right to Protection: Whose Responsibility and How?* 4 September. [Online] Available at: ⟨http://sydney.edu.au/arts/peace_conflict/research/AH_Conference%20report%202.pdf⟩ (accessed 15 October 2011).

Chong, D., and J. N. Druckman (2007) "Framing Theory", *Political Science* 10 (1): 103–126.

Cooper, A. F., and J. English (2005) "International Commissions and the Mind of Global Governance", in R. C. Thakur, A. F. Cooper and J. English, eds. *International Commissions and the Power of Ideas*. Tokyo: United Nations University Press, 1–26.

Cordier, A. W., and W. Foote (1969) *Public Papers of the Secretaries General of the United Nations Volume 1: Trygve Lie*. New York: Columbia University Press.

Cotler, I., and J. Genser (2011) "Libya and the Responsibility to Protect", *New York Times*, 28 February.

Couldrey, M., and T. Morris (2005) "Tsunami: Learning from the Humanitarian Response", *Forced Migration Review Special Issue*, July. [Online] Available at: ⟨http://www.fmreview.org/FMRpdfs/Tsunami/full.pdf⟩ (accessed 14 November 2011).

Dallaire, R. (2005) *Shake Hands with the Devil: The Failure of Humanity in Rwanda*. Canada: Random House.

de Waal, A. (2008) "Why Darfur intervention is a mistake", *BBC*, 21 May.

DPKO/DFS (2008) *United Nations Peacekeeping Operations: Principles and Guidelines*. New York: United Nations. [Online] Available at: ⟨http://pbpu.unlb.org/pbps/Library/Capstone_Doctrine_ENG.pdf⟩ (accessed 20 February 2012).

Durch, W. J. (1993) *The Evolution of UN Peacekeeping*. New York: St. Martin's Press.

Durch, W. J. (2006) *Twenty-First-Century Peace Operations*. Washington, DC: United States Institute of Peace Press.

Durch, W. J. (2010) "United Nations Police Evolution, Present Capacity and Future Tasks". GRIPS Policy Research Centre. Prepared for the GRIPS State-Building workshop 2010: Organizing police forces in post-conflict peace-support operations, 27–28 January. [Online] Available at: ⟨http://www3.grips.ac.jp/~pinc/data/10-03.pdf⟩ (accessed 31 March 2011).

ECOSOC (2005) *ECOSOC Resolution 2004/5: Strengthening of the coordination of emergency humanitarian assistance of the United Nations*. 15 July.

Egeland, J., G. Evans, J. Mendez, M. Sahnoun, M. Serrano and R. Thakur (2009) "Open letter to the Security Council on the situation in Sri Lanka", *Global Centre for the Responsibility to Protect*, 15 April. [Online] Available at: ⟨http://globalr2p.org/media/pdf/OpenLetterSriLanka.pdf⟩ (accessed 30 March 2011).

Evans, G. (2008) *The Responsibility to Protect: Ending Mass Atrocity Crimes once and for all.* Washington, DC: Brookings Institution Press.

Finnemore, M., and K. Sikkink (1998) "International Norm Dynamics and Political Change", *International Organization* 52(4): 887–917.

GAPW, Global Action to Prevent War (2007) *To Prevent Genocide and Crimes Against Humanity: Diverse perspectives on a standing, rapid-reaction UN Emergency Peace Service.* [Online] Available at: ⟨http://www.globalactionpw.org/wp/wp-content/uploads/rutgers_uneps_conference_report_2007.pdf⟩ (accessed 30 April 2011).

GAPW, Global Action to Prevent War (2009a) *Report on Peacekeeping and Civilian Protection: Perspective from Latin America.* [Online] Available at: ⟨http://www.globalactionpw.org/wp/wp-content/uploads/brazil-outcome-report.pdf⟩ (accessed 30 March 2011).

GAPW, Global Action to Prevent War (2009b) *Report on Peacekeeping and Civilian Protection: Perspective from Latin America: Asia-Pacific Perspectives.* [Online] Available at: ⟨http://www.globalactionpw.org/wp/wp-content/uploads/jakarta-full-reportv6.pdf⟩ (accessed 30 March 2011).

GAPW, Global Action to Prevent War (n.d.) *Conference Reports.* [Online] Available at: ⟨http://www.globalactionpw.org/?page_id=79⟩ (accessed 9 May 2011).

Haas, P. M. (1992) "Introduction: Epistemic Communities and International Policy Coordination", *International Organization* 46 (01): 1–35.

Hamilton, L., G. Evans, S. Hoffmann, and B. Urquhart (1993) "A UN Volunteer Military Force: Four views", *New York Review of Books,* 24 June.

Herro, A., W. Lambourne and D. Penklis (2009) "Peacekeeping and Peace Enforcement in Africa: The Potential Contribution of a UN Emergency Peace Service", *African Security Review* 18(1): 49–62.

Holt, V. K., and T. C. Berkman (2006) *The Impossible Mandate? Military Preparedness, the Responsibility to Protect and Modern Peace Operations.* Washington, DC: The Henry L. Stimson Center.

Holt, V. K., G. Taylor and M. Kelly (2009) *Protecting Civilians in the Context of UN Peacekeeping Operations: Successes, Setbacks and Remaining Challenges.* Department of Peacekeeping Operations and the Office for the Coordination of Humanitarian Affairs. New York: United Nations.

Human Rights Watch (1995) "The Fall of Srebrenica and the Failure of UN Peacekeeping", *Human Rights Watch,* 7(13).

ICISS, International Commission on Intervention and State Sovereignty (2001) *The Responsibility to Protect.* Ottawa: International Development Research Centre.

Johansen, R. C., ed. (2006) *A United Nations Emergency Peace Service: To prevent genocide and crimes against humanity.* New York: Global Action to Prevent War, Nuclear Age Peace Foundation and World Federalist Movement.

Keck, M. E., and K. Sikkink (1998) *Activists Beyond Borders: Advocacy Networks in International Politics.* Ithaca, NY: Cornell University Press.

Khagram, S., J. V. Riker, and K. Sikkink (2002) *Restructuring World Politics: Transnational Social Movements, Networks, and Norms*. Minneapolis, MN: University of Minnesota Press.

Kinloch, S. P. (1996) "Utopian or Pragmatic? A UN Permanent Military Volunteer Force", *International Peacekeeping* 3(4): 166–190.

Langille, P. H. (2000) "Conflict Prevention: Options for Rapid Deployment and UN Standing Forces", *International Peacekeeping*, 7(1): 219–253.

Langille, P. H. (2002) *Bridging the Commitment-Capacity Gap: A Review of Existing Arrangements and Options for Enhancing UN Rapid Deployment*, Center for UN Reform Education.

Langille, P. H. (2009) "Preventing Genocide", in A. Grzyb, ed. *The World and Darfur: International Response to Crimes against Humanity in Western Sudan*. Montreal: McGill Queens University Press, 281–327.

Mamdani, M. (2007) "The Politics of Naming: Genocide, Civil War, Insurgency", *London Review of Books* 29(5): 5–8.

Mendez, J. (2009) *The Prevention of Genocide and Its Challenges*. [Online] Available at: ⟨http://www.globalactionpw.org/wp/wp-content/uploads/standing-for-change-final-may-09.pdf⟩ (accessed 29 March 2011).

Musthofid (2011) "UN calls for quicker responses to reduce impacts of disasters, *Jakarta Post*, 11 May.

Nadelmann, E. A. (1990) "Global prohibition regimes: The evolution of norms in international society", *International Organization* 44(4): 479–526.

O'Callaghan, S., and S. Pantuliano (2007) *Protective Action: Incorporating Civilian Protection into Humanitarian Response*. London: Overseas Development Institute.

Reuters (2011) "Propaganda war rages as violence escalates in Abidjan", 13 March. [Online] Available at: ⟨http://www.france24.com/en/20110313-propaganda-war-rages-violence-escalates-abidjan-civil-war-press-newspapers⟩ (accessed 30 April 2011).

Reynaert, J. (2011) "MONUC/MONUSCO and civilian protection in the Kivus", *International Peace Information Service*. [Online] Available at: ⟨http://reliefweb.int/rw/RWFiles2011.nsf/FilesByRWDocUnidFilename/SMDL-8EKJ8N-full_report.pdf/$File/full_report.pdf⟩ (accessed 21 February 2012).

Roberts, A. (2008) "Proposals for UN Standing Forces: A Critical History", in V. Lowe, A. Roberts, J. Welsh and D. Zaum, eds. *The United Nations Security Council and War: The Evolution of Thought and Practice since 1945*. New York: Oxford University Press, 99–132.

Roessler, P., and J. Prendergast (2006) "Democratic Republic of the Congo" in W. J. Durch, ed. *Twenty-First-Century Peace Operations*. Washington, DC: United States Institute of Peace.

Smith, G. (2011) "Explainer: What is Libya's 'responsibility to protect' its citizens?" *The Globe and Mail Update*, 18 March. [Online] Available at: ⟨http://www.responsibilitytoprotect.org/index.php/crises/190-crisis-in-libya/3283-lloyd-axworthy-and-graeme-smith-globe-and-mail-explainer-what-is-libyas-responsibility-to-protect-its-citizens⟩ (accessed 8 May 2011).

Stack, Liam, and N. MacFarquhar (2012) "Arab League Steps Up Pressure on Syria and Calls for U.N. Help", *New York Times*, 12 February.

Suthanthiraraj, K. (2008) *United Nations Peacekeeping Missions: Enhancing Capacity for Rapid and Effective Troop Deployment*. New York: Global Action To Prevent War.

Suthanthiraraj, K., and M. Quinn (2009) *Standing for Change in Peacekeeping Operations: Project for a United Nations Emergency Peace Service (UNEPS)*. New York: Global Action to Prevent War.

Thakur, R. (2006) *The United Nations, Peace and Security: From Collective Security to the Responsibility to Protect*. Cambridge: Cambridge University Press.

Thakur, R. (2011) *The Responsibility to Protect: Norms, Laws and the Use of Force in International Politics*. London: Routledge.

UNSC (2003) *UN Security Council Resolution 1509 (2003): The Situation in Liberia*, S/RES/1509, 19 September 2003.

UNSC (2008) *UN Security Council Resolution 1856 (2008): The Situation concerning the Democratic Republic of the Congo*, S/RES/1856, 22 December 2008.

UNSC (2010) *UN Security Council Resolution 1962 (2010): The Situation in Côte d'Ivoire*, S/RES/1962, 20 December 2010.

UNSC (2011a) *UN Security Council Resolution 1973 (2011): The Situation in Libya*, S/RES/1973, 17 March 2011.

UNSC (2011b) *UN Security Council Resolution 1975 (2011): The Situation in Côte d'Ivoire*, S/RES/1975, 30 March 2011.

UNSG (1994) *Report of the Secretary-General Pursuant to Resolution 844*, S/1994/555, 9 May 1994.

UNSG (1999) *Report of the Secretary-General to the Security Council on the protection of civilians in armed conflict*, S/1999/957, 8 September 1999.

UNSG (2009) *Report of the Secretary-General on implementing the responsibility to protect*, A/63/677, 12 January 2009.

Urquhart, B. (1993) "For a U.N. Volunteer Military Force", *New York Review of Books*, 10 June, 3–4.

Urquhart, B. (2006) "Preface", in R. Johansen, ed. *United Nations Emergency Peace Service: To prevent Genocide and Crimes against Humanity*. New York: Global Action to Prevent War, Nuclear Age Peace Foundation and World Federalist Movement. [Online] Available at: ⟨http://www.globalactionpw.org/wp/wp-content/uploads/uneps_publication.pdf⟩ (accessed 29 March 2011).

Washington Times (2011) "Team Obama, world police", 29 March.

Working Group on the Protection of Civilians (2009) *Protection in Practice: Practical Handbook for Peacekeepers: MONUC Protection Cluster*. Protection Cluster. Chaired by MONUC and UNHCR. [Online] Available at: ⟨http://www.internal-displacement.org/8025708F004CE90B/(httpDocuments)/F3421CEBE549BEBDC125760F004BEBEB/$file/0209+Protection+in+Practice+-+MONUC.pdf⟩ (accessed 30 March 2011).

9

The relationship between international humanitarian law and responsibility to protect: From Solferino to Srebrenica

Helen Durham and Phoebe Wynn-Pope

Since the earliest times people and communities have set rules intended to minimize the suffering caused by war.[1] Limitations on the way conflict is fought can be found in every culture, and traditionally these rules were often agreed upon by the specific parties involved. The founder of the International Red Cross and Red Crescent Movement, Henry Dunant, started the modern codification of the laws of war, after experiencing the horrors of a battlefield and urging the international community to create binding treaties in the area. This call for humanity during war resulted in the first Geneva Convention of 1864 and the development of international humanitarian law (IHL). Today the four Geneva Conventions of 1949 are universally ratified and have been added to by many other treaties, protocols and developments in customary international law.[2]

In contrast, the idea promoted by the international principle of a responsibility to protect (R2P) is relatively new. Since the Peace of Westphalia and the establishment of the modern state there has been an accepted international norm of non-interference in the domestic affairs of states. This principle is upheld in Article 2(7) of the Charter of the United Nations. However, the end of the Cold War, and the paralysis of the international community in the face of the genocides in Rwanda and Srebrenica, combined with the unilateral action of NATO in Kosovo, led to a recognition that non-interference in the face of atrocity crimes was no longer acceptable (UNSG, 1999). It is from these experiences that the R2P principle emerged.

Norms of protection: Responsibility to protect, protection of civilians and their interaction,
Francis, Popovski and Sampford (eds),
United Nations University Press, 2012, ISBN 978-92-808-1218-3

When comparing the relationship between IHL and R2P it is important to note two things. First, R2P is not, itself, a legal concept. It derives its authority from existing bodies of international law such as the *Convention for the Prevention and Punishment of Genocide* ("Genocide Convention"), the *Rome Statute of the International Criminal Court* ("Rome Statute") and, of course, from IHL. Second, R2P only focuses on the protection of vulnerable populations from the four crimes of genocide, ethnic cleansing, war crimes and crimes against humanity.[3] It is by nature narrow in scope, and should not be seen to be a replacement for the vast array of protections offered by IHL and other bodies of international law.

There are areas of commonality and points of difference between IHL and R2P. Both have a role to play in the protection of vulnerable populations, and understanding their relationship to one another may enhance our capacity to serve those at risk. This chapter will explore the parallels and distinctions between IHL and R2P with a particular focus on how R2P, having gained significant political momentum in recent years, can be used to strengthen and enhance IHL, not weaken it as some IHL commentators fear.

The chapter will begin with a discussion on the origins of IHL and R2P and how they both emerged from direct experience of outrages of the treatment of soldiers (IHL) and civilians (R2P) during times of armed conflict and extreme violence. It will then look at how IHL has developed since the early days in the nineteenth century to provide a framework for the conduct of hostilities. In contrast, the principle of R2P emerged only ten years ago, but has developed into a principle which has become widely accepted as a political concept.[4] In conclusion, the chapter will draw IHL and R2P together by looking at their points of similarity and difference, and where each regime is able to support and lend strength to the other.

9.1 Points of origin

9.1.1 International humanitarian law

As noted previously, the concept of limiting the conduct of hostilities is not new and can be found historically in some form or other in every society. From the Middle Ages (Keen, 1965), to ancient practices in the Pacific Islands (Durham, 2008), communities everywhere have always demonstrated the understanding and need to lay down rules when engaged in armed conflict.

In relation to legal codification of such agreements, reference to basic rules during war can be found in early treaties such as the 1785 Treaty of

Amity and Commerce between the United States and Prussia, which affirmed immunity for children, women and merchants if war were to occur (Roberts and Guelff, 2005: 4). The majority of such instruments were bilateral in nature in that they were usually negotiated between two or just a few parties and did not widely apply to other states. The 1856 Paris Declaration on maritime war can be seen as one of the first multilateral treaties which attempted to more broadly provide a legal framework and this was followed by the Geneva Convention of 1864. It was this Convention which paved the way for the current IHL framework.

The genesis of modern-day IHL arose out of the Battle of Solferino in 1859. The battle, fought by the Austro-Hungarian Empire and the Kingdom of Sardinia against France, was witnessed by Jean-Henri Dunant, a Swiss businessman. Dunant was particularly moved by the suffering of the wounded (Dunant, 1986) and he campaigned for an international agreement on the treatment of the sick and wounded in conflict as well as neutral relief societies to care for the wounded in wartime. This ultimately led to the Geneva Convention of 1864 and the establishment of the International Committee of the Red Cross, the founding element of the International Red Cross and Red Crescent Movement.

Since that time IHL has continued to develop and today includes a raft of treaties protecting certain categories of people as well as regulating the methods and means of warfare (ICRC, 2005). IHL also encompasses a range of customary norms,[5] and developing jurisprudence from international enforcement mechanisms such as tribunals and courts can be seen to add to the interpretations and understandings of this area of international law. A key difference between IHL and other areas of international law, such as those involving the use of force, is that IHL does not aim to regulate decisions on when and where armed force can be deployed. Rather IHL only applies once an armed conflict has commenced and regulates conduct during the hostilities. This distinction between the right to *go to* war (*jus ad bellum*) and the rights *during* war (*jus in bello*) is important to acknowledge and provides a key difference from R2P, which specifically allows for the use of force in certain circumstances.

Central to the IHL normative framework are the four Geneva Conventions of 1949 and their two Additional Protocols of 1977. The Geneva Conventions are mainly concerned with the protection of categories of "victims" of armed conflict including non-combatants (such as civilians) and those not or no longer engaged in hostilities (such as medical members of the military, wounded combatants or prisoners of war). Excluding Common Article 3, the Geneva Conventions also predominately regulate international armed conflict. Just as Dunant's horror at the conditions of wounded soldiers on the battlefield resulted in the first Geneva Convention, it was the world's shock at the treatment of civilians in the Second

World War which led to the codification of Geneva Convention IV and an update of the previous Conventions in 1949.

In the 1970s the international community responded to the increased attacks on civilians and the shifting of warfare from between states to within states, by adding the two protocols in 1977. These deal with limitations and prohibitions on methods and means of warfare (Protocol I) and expand Common Article 3 in the protection afforded during internal armed conflict (Protocol II).

In more recent times, as technological capacities for warfare advanced, developments in IHL treaty law have focused upon the regulation of specific weapons – from anti-personnel landmines to cluster munitions to blinding laser weapons. There are also specific IHL treaties and protocols relating to the protection of cultural property. All in all, the IHL legal regime contains over 90 treaties.[6]

Furthermore, the last decade has witnessed a proliferation of international and hybrid mechanisms to enforce obligations found in both IHL and the wider international criminal law regime such as crimes against humanity and genocide. For example, the creation of the ad hoc tribunals for the former Yugoslavia[7] and Rwanda,[8] as well as the permanent International Criminal Court (ICC), demonstrate the international community's commitment to ending the impunity of those accused of atrocities.

9.1.2 Responsibility to protect

In contrast, the principle of R2P emerged in 2001 as a response by an international community increasingly concerned by the dilemma presented by gross human rights violations on the one hand, and respect for sovereign integrity and the principle of non-interference on the other. Historically, this dilemma has been represented in debates in international law concerning the existence of a right to humanitarian intervention. This "right" has been used to justify military intervention by strong states in the affairs of weaker states, supposedly for "humanitarian purposes"; however, whether the right exists or not has been debated since the beginning of modern international law.

Grotius, commonly acknowledged as the father of modern international law, recognized that "if a tyrant practices atrocities towards his subjects, which no just man can approve, the right of human social connexion [sic] is not cut off" (Grotius, 1853: 438). He acknowledged the nature of sovereignty while placing limits upon it. For Grotius, a common humanity could, in some circumstances, override the sanctity of state sovereignty and that the "human connexion" should not be forgotten in the face of tyranny. On the other hand, there were commentators such as Vattel and Pradier-Fodéré who determined that no matter how a sovereign treated his or her subjects, if it did not affect another state, then there was no right to intervene. Their defence of state sovereignty was absolute: "If he [the sovereign] buries his subjects under taxes, if he treats them harshly, it is the Nation's business; no one else is called upon to admonish him" (Vattel, 1863: 55).[9]

The other side of the debate was also strongly presented and worked to place limits on the sovereignty of states (Fonteyne, 1974). However, the strength of both sides of the debate meant that there was no real agreement regarding the right to interfere in the domestic affairs of states on humanitarian grounds before the United Nations was created, and in 1945, the new Charter added strength to arguments in favour of non-intervention.

The Charter codified the long-held principle of non-interference at Article 2(7). This principle was repeatedly endorsed by UN General Assembly Resolutions and appeared sacrosanct.[10] In addition, and importantly for the anti-interventionists, the Charter, for the first time, codified the prohibition on the use of force in international affairs (Article 2(4)). This prohibition applied at all times except where force was used in self-defence (Article 55) or under the enforcement powers and with the authorization of the UN Security Council (UNSC) at Chapter VII.

The emergence of the Cold War so soon after the establishment of the United Nations meant that, in addition to these legal barriers to humanitarian intervention, for over 40 years the UNSC was effectively frozen. The veto power held by the permanent five members meant that there was little chance of a UN intervention on humanitarian grounds. In fact, there was so little support for the idea that even international actions that might have been presented as humanitarian intervention – India's intervention in East Pakistan (1971), Tanzania's intervention in Idi Amin's Uganda (1979) or the Vietnamese invasion of Kampuchea (1979) – were justified by the responsible states under the self-defence provision of the Charter. There was no suggestion by India, Tanzania or Vietnam that they were either undertaking, or had a right to undertake in law, humanitarian intervention.

Since the end of the Cold War "humanitarian intervention" has again been seen as a potential justification for forceful intervention in the affairs of another state, and the idea of it was used to great effect in Somalia in 1992. The onset of the famine and the political vacuum that existed led the UNSC to recognize that human suffering on the scale of that in Somalia was a threat to international peace and security. In so doing, the Council invoked Chapter VII of the Charter and authorized a military intervention for humanitarian relief.[11] For a time, the activism of the post-Cold War Security Council led to a sense of hope and expectation that human suffering on the scale of that in Somalia would no longer be tolerated by the international community. The perceived failure of the UN intervention in Somalia, and the retreat of United States forces less than 12 months after their arrival, brought an abrupt halt to Security Council activism.

As a result, the 1990s bore witness to a series of international disasters. Months after the retreat from Mogadishu, the fastest genocide in history occurred 1,000 miles away in Rwanda where, in 1994, 800,000 people were massacred in just 100 days while UN peacekeepers looked on. It took six weeks before the international community would call the killing of Tutsis in Rwanda by its real name – genocide – and later, US President Bill Clinton would call the lack of global response to the killing one of his administration's greatest failures. Another year passed and, in 1995, the United Nations was again impotent in the face of genocide – peacekeepers in Srebrenica had neither the means nor the mandate to prevent the massacre of 8,000 Bosnian men and boys. When it looked as though another genocide was about to occur in Kosovo, the UNSC was divided and still unable to make a decision for intervention. Fearing another genocide while the international community looked on, NATO violated the UN prohibition on the use of force, and some would argue it acted against its own Charter (Boggs, 2001), to intervene on humanitarian grounds in order to protect the people of Kosovo from Milošević's Serbian forces.

Of these three important international events in the development of the question of the right to humanitarian intervention, it was NATO's involvement in Kosovo that caused a crescendo in the debate – what was the role of the international community when faced with atrocity crimes? NATO's use of force in Kosovo, without authorization from the UNSC, was widely regarded as illegal under international law and the Charter. However, some began to suggest that while it may have been illegal, the intervention, seen as necessary for the protection of the civilian population from atrocity crimes, was legitimate and therefore justifiable (Simma, 1999). Such arguments led Kofi Annan to ask the General Assembly:

> To those for whom the greatest threat to the future of international order is the use of force in the absence of a Security Council mandate, one might ask – not in the context of Kosovo – but in the context of Rwanda: If, in those dark days and hours leading up to the genocide, a coalition of States had been prepared to act in defence of the Tutsi population, but did not receive prompt Council authorization, should such a coalition have stood aside and allowed the horror to unfold? (UNSG, 1999)

He went on to ask:

To those for whom the Kosovo action heralded a new era when States and groups of States can take military action outside the established mechanisms for enforcing international law, one might ask: Is there not a danger of such interventions undermining the imperfect, yet resilient, security system created after the Second World War, and of setting dangerous precedents for future interventions without a clear criterion to decide who might invoke these precedents, and in what circumstances? (ibid.)

This became a continuing theme for Secretary-General Annan – the dilemma between not acting, and acting against international law; between the norm of non-interference and the prohibition on the use of force on the one hand, and intervention on the other.

The moral outrage that emerged from the failure of the international community to respond in a timely or adequate manner in Rwanda, Srebrenica and Kosovo required an answer to this vexed question. As noted in Chapter 1 by Hugh Breakey in this volume, the establishment of the International Commission on Intervention and State Sovereignty followed this appeal, as did the development and emergence of the idea of a responsibility to protect (see Chapter 1 for a history of the development of R2P).

Since the World Summit in 2005 there has been further development of the R2P principle, and further definition of its key messages and purpose. The primary source for this development is Secretary-General Ban Ki-moon's report to the General Assembly in 2009 on the implementation of R2P. In it he described R2P as a principle both narrow and deep, and with three equal and enduring pillars that represent three underlying principles (UNSG, 2009).

The First Pillar is represented by the recognition that it is the enduring responsibility of all states to protect populations in their jurisdiction from the crimes of genocide, crimes against humanity, war crimes and ethnic cleansing. This responsibility is derived from pre-existing obligations of states and the underlying nature of state sovereignty.

The Second Pillar is represented by the commitment made by the international community to assist states to fulfil their responsibility to protect their own populations. This is possibly the most useful in terms of developing policy and successfully preventing R2P crimes as it allows for a wide array of activities and programmes aimed at the prevention of atrocity crimes.

In order to provide protection to vulnerable populations the Third Pillar of R2P allows for member states to respond collectively and in a timely manner when a state is "manifestly failing" to provide protection. The Secretary-General argues that this pillar is often understood too narrowly, particularly in the context of military intervention and, in an historic sense, it is often equated with the notion of "humanitarian intervention". Ban notes, however, that successful bilateral, regional and global efforts that are not of a military nature can also be R2P actions under Pillar Three, and he suggests that Kofi Annan's intervention in Kenya following elections there was a good example of R2P in action (UNSG, 2009).

Pillar Three is often equated with humanitarian intervention as it does allow for the Security Council to authorize the collective use of force for the protection of those suffering from, or at risk of suffering from, any of the four R2P crimes. However, it is noteworthy that the 2005 *World Summit Outcome Document* (WSOD) states that "we are *prepared to* take collective action, in a timely and decisive manner, through the Security Council, in accordance with the Charter, including Chapter VII, on a case-by-case basis" (UNGA, 2005: 31) and that there is no agreed binding obligation to do so. Many of the less coercive "actions" that can be taken by the United Nations can be done by the Secretary-General or through regional or sub-regional arrangements without authorization of the Security Council. Ban reiterates that coercive measures should only be adopted if two conditions are met: (i) "should peaceful means be inadequate"[12] and (ii) "national authorities are manifestly failing to protect their populations" from the four specified crimes and violations (UNSG, 2009: 22). These conditions would not allow for a NATO-type Kosovo intervention.

The Secretary-General was at pains to point out that the three pillars are concurrent and not consecutive. There is no room in the three-pillar formulation of R2P for defined "triggers" for action; however, he suggests that the duty of the United Nations is to focus on saving lives, not on "following arbitrary, sequential or graduated policy ladders that prize procedure over substance and process over results" (UNSG, 2009: 23).

Within this widely accepted three-pillar framework, there are three further elements that Ban Ki-moon emphasized. The first is that R2P should be seen as an "ally of sovereignty, not an adversary" (UNSG, 2009: 7). It is important that R2P is seen not as humanitarian intervention in sheep's clothing but rather a concept that supports and encourages states to fulfil their responsibility to protect, and by doing so they strengthen their own sovereign status. The second element is that the scope of R2P is narrow. It focuses only on protection from the crimes of genocide, crimes against humanity, war crimes and ethnic cleansing. The third, and important, element is that the responses, the implementation of R2P, should be deep. The way in which states protect their own citizens, and the international community assists states, may include a multitude of activities including, for example, establishing effective early-warning mechanisms, training and education in rule of law and human rights, effective

policing, military and legal infrastructure and training, establishment of
good governance and economic development. At the point where it may
appear that R2P crimes are imminent then diplomatic means, public and
private suasion, sanctions and the threat of the use of force may be required. These responses are deep and wide-ranging, and provide a framework for development that can assist in the prevention of the most
heinous international crimes.

As with the development of IHL, moral outrage promoted the development of R2P. If it were not for the humanitarian disasters of the 1990s,
and the apparent impotence of the international community when faced
with humanitarian versus legal dilemmas, R2P might not have been conceived. If Dunant had not seen the horrors of Solferino, the development of IHL might also have been quite different. While their origins are
arguably similar, R2P and IHL have developed in quite different ways.
Dunant worked towards a meeting of heads of state with the intention to
draw up a set of international rules and laws that would bind states' conduct in situations of armed conflict. R2P, on the other hand, has no laws
of its own, but rather draws from existing international law. R2P has no
rules or guidelines for the conduct of states fulfilling their responsibility
to protect vulnerable populations and yet IHL is full of rules providing
guidance to states on how to fulfil their responsibilities.

In the next section of this chapter we will explore this major point of
difference between R2P and IHL and see how R2P is a formulation reli-
ant for its legal credentials on existing international law and how IHL is
a fundamental contributor to R2P.

9.2 Points of difference

9.2.1 Legal status of IHL and R2P

This section of the chapter will review the status of the obligations on
states under IHL and with respect to the groups of crimes identified by
R2P. IHL has developed and expanded its scope through a range of legally binding instruments which require implementation at a domestic
level. The breadth of requirements upon states and the range of subject
matter covered by IHL demonstrate some significant points of difference
between the status of IHL and R2P in international law.

9.2.2 Legal status of IHL

The IHL legal regime contains numerous obligations on states to put in
place legislation, frameworks and training during times of peace. As a

legal framework it relies heavily on domestic implementation to ensure that the obligations are in existence well before an armed conflict occurs. IHL is often referred to as *lex specialis* in international law, meaning that it can only apply in certain situations, that is, during armed conflict, despite the obligation on states to ensure that implementation regimes are in place before the onset of hostilities.

The requirements for IHL to be codified into national practice and policy are broad.

For example, the Geneva Conventions and the Additional Protocols require states: to enact domestic enforcement legislation for those accused of grave breaches; to ensure that military sites and targets are not located near civilian populations or civilian infrastructure; to ensure that military codes, doctrines and training reflect IHL; to ensure that weapons acquired or adopted are consistent with IHL principles; to ensure that IHL is disseminated widely to the general public; to identify potential hospital and safety zones; to identify installations containing dangerous forces (such as nuclear plants) and ensure they are not placed close to military objectives, to highlight a few.

We examine one example in more detail, the obligation to disseminate IHL which is found in each of the Geneva Conventions and in both Additional Protocols. Article 47 of Geneva Convention I states:

> The High Contracting Parties undertake, in time of peace as in time of war, to disseminate the text of the present Convention as widely as possible in their respective countries, and, in particular, to include the study thereof in their programmes of military and, if possible, civil instruction, so that the principles thereof may become known to the entire population, in particular to the armed fighting forces, the medical personnel and the chaplains.

This requirement is found in Geneva Convention II (Article 48), Geneva Convention III (Article 127) and Geneva Convention IV (Article 144). A similar requirement is found in Additional Protocol I in Article 83 and indeed more details can be found in the obligations of Article 87(2) and the requirement pursuant to Article 82 to have legal officers available to advise military commanders on the Conventions and Protocols.

The obligation is clear in that it is "in time of peace as in time of war" that education and training must be undertaken. In this sense the requirements could be characterized in terms of being a "preventive" measure before conflict and violence occurs. However, the use of a legal officer to advise during the military operations obviously relates directly to the conflict while relying on pre-conflict implementation of IHL education and training. In many of the obligations mentioned above, such as the

principle of distinction (Article 48 Additional Protocol I) requiring attacks exclusively against military targets and not civilians or civilian infrastructure, there is a need for a range of professions to be involved – from
town planners to teachers – to ensure that pre-conflict the legal obligations in IHL are met. In the area of the protection of cultural property,
both Additional Protocol I (Article 53) and the 1954 Hague Convention
on this topic require special protections to be granted to such property
and actions such as identification pre-conflict and marking of these items
during conflict itself.

From both a practical and legal examination, the raft of IHL-related
treaties are deeply concerned with states implementing the elements into
domestic legislation and local policy. R2P is not a legal construct but acknowledges, and is derived from, the legal responsibility of states to protect populations from genocide, crimes against humanity and war crimes.
However, the responsibilities of states with regard to each of these crimes
are significantly varied. For example, there are mandatory obligations on
states with regard to the crime of genocide but few treaty obligations on
states to respond to crimes against humanity. Ethnic cleansing, for the
purposes of this section, will be considered as a crime against humanity
as defined in the Rome Statute at Article 7(d) – *Deportation or Forcible
Transfer of Population*, as ethnic cleansing does not exist as a separate
crime by that particular name in international law. While ethnic cleansing
can constitute genocide, it does not necessarily do so. This discussion will
explore each of the three groups of crimes – genocide, crimes against
humanity and war crimes – and the obligations on states towards each in
order to clarify the significantly different status of R2P and IHL in this
area.

9.2.3 Legal status of R2P

9.2.3.1 Obligations on states under the Genocide Convention

Existing legal obligations on states with regard to the crime of genocide
can be found in the Genocide Convention which, at Article 1, requires
states to "undertake to prevent and punish" the crime of genocide
"whether committed in time of peace or in time of war".[13] Genocide
Convention obligations were explored at length in the *Case Concerning
the Application of the Convention on the Prevention and Punishment of
the Crime of Genocide (Bosnia Herzegovina* v. *Yugoslavia)* (Genocide
Case; ICJ, 1996). The case examined the test for the international responsibility of states for breach of the Convention, the territorial limits of
the Convention obligations, and the obligation on states "to prevent" the
commission of genocide. This last obligation will be discussed at some

length as it directly relates to the R2P obligation to protect populations from genocide.

In Article 1 of the Genocide Convention, the contracting parties "undertake" to prevent and punish the crime of genocide. The Court noted that the term "undertake" is "to give formal promise, to bind or engage oneself, to give a pledge or promise, to agree to accept an obligation" (ICJ, 1996: 162). The Court noted that genocide can be committed in time of peace or in war. The obligation on states parties to the Genocide Convention to prevent genocide provides a strong foundation for R2P, as the best form of protection for populations is prevention of the crime in the first instance. The Court acknowledged, however, that the obligation to prevent genocide is clearly "one of conduct and not of result, in the sense that a State cannot be under an obligation to succeed ... Rather to employ all means reasonably available to them, so as to prevent genocide as far as possible" (ICJ, 1996: 429).

This is significant in the context of R2P as the Court went on to note that, given the significant disparity in capacity to prevent genocide, the action required by states to fulfil their obligation to prevent genocide under the Convention would necessarily be different depending on national capacity "to influence effectively the action of persons likely to commit, or already committing genocide" (ICJ, 1996: 430). So, in acknowledging that there is a disparity of action required in order to fulfil responsibilities under the Convention, the Court also acknowledged that a state would be failing in its obligations if it failed to do anything at all.

The Court addressed possible territorial limits of the obligation to prevent the commission of genocide, and while it noted that the obligation is "not territorially limited by the Convention" it also went on to say that the matter of the territorial scope for each particular obligation a rising under the Convention remains imprecise because the issue has not been ruled upon *res judicata* (ICJ, 1996: 154). This lack of clarity regarding the territorial limits of the Genocide Convention, combined with the R2P commitment to protect vulnerable communities from the crime of genocide, leads to some confusion regarding legal obligations relative to genocide under R2P. It could be argued that R2P suggests that all states have a responsibility at all times to protect communities from the crime of genocide; however, the ICJ did not necessarily find this to be the case under the Genocide Convention, and it is important that R2P does not have an independent legal status that imposes on states new or additional legal obligations to those that already exist in international law.

9.2.3.2 *Crimes against humanity and the role of states*

Crimes against humanity provide the weakest legal link in the R2P framework. While crimes against humanity have been defined at length in the Rome Statute (Article 7), there are no treaty obligations pertaining to states' obligations relative to crimes against humanity as a distinct category of international crime. There are conventions relating to specific crimes that are also crimes against humanity such as torture and slavery, and the obligations imposed on states parties under those conventions can arguably serve to strengthen the legal position of R2P.

The *Convention against Torture and Other Cruel, Inhuman or Degrading Treatment or Punishment* (Torture Convention) has provisions not only to extradite or prosecute those accused of torture, but also obligations to protect people from torture. Article 2 requires that "Each State Party shall take effective legislative, administrative, judicial or other measures to prevent acts of torture in any territory under its jurisdiction." These are significant legal obligations requiring states to act and could provide a basis for some codification of crimes against humanity in the future; however, notable in the context of R2P is that there is no obligation to intervene in another state to protect or prevent the commission of torture there.

Slavery is a crime against humanity defined at Article 7 of the Rome Statute. The Slavery Convention of 1926 is another mechanism imposing obligations on states parties to prevent slavery within their own jurisdiction. However, while there is an obligation to "give to one another every assistance with the object of securing the abolition of slavery and the slave trade" (Article 4) this is permissive in nature, giving states the opportunity to assist without compelling them to do so. The Convention has no extra-territorial scope and is therefore limited as a model for R2P obligations relative to crimes against humanity, even though the potential to assist states has parallels with Pillar Two of the Secretary-General's three-pillar formulation of R2P.

9.2.3.3 States' obligations with regard to war crimes

Finally, and most importantly for the purpose of this chapter exploring the relationship between IHL and R2P, the third subset of crimes that form the basis of R2P are war crimes. The principal source of binding treaty obligations in relation to war crimes are the four Geneva Conventions of 1949 and their two Additional Protocols of 1977. Clearly, this is where there is significant overlap in obligations, for these Conventions provide the legal framework for the conduct of hostilities in the context of armed conflict, form a considerable part of IHL, and provide a substantial legal foundation for the R2P principle – relating to the responsibility to protect populations from war crimes.

The Geneva Conventions are clear in that they contain specific provisions relating to the obligation on states to not only create domestic legislation to prosecute those accused of grave breaches but to also:

search for persons alleged to have committed, or to have ordered to be committed, such grave breaches, and shall bring such persons, regardless of their nationality, before its own courts. (Article 49, Geneva Convention I)

All four Conventions contain this Article and also list the crimes considered "grave breaches" (Article 50, Geneva Convention I). Grave breaches include:
- wilful killing;
- torture or inhuman treatment including biological experiments;
- wilfully causing great suffering or serious injury to body or health;
- extensive destruction and appropriation of property not justified by military necessity and carried out unlawfully and wantonly.

With the development of the 1977 Additional Protocols, a much wider list of war crimes can be seen to be developed beyond the "grave breaches" found in the Conventions. Additional Protocol I includes a more extensive list of crimes. For example, Article 85 of Additional Protocol I makes it a war crime to:
- make the civilian population the object of attack;
- launch indiscriminate attacks;
- perfidiously use the Red Cross or Red Crescent emblem;
- practise apartheid and other inhuman and degrading practices;
- deprive a protected person the rights of a fair and regular trial.

Over time the development of enforcement mechanisms, such as the ad hoc tribunals for the Former Yugoslavia and Rwanda and the ICC, have moved war crimes beyond crimes committed in international armed conflict to include such acts during non-international conflict. The long list of crimes found in Article 8 of the Rome Statute demonstrates that today war crimes have moved beyond just "grave breaches" committed in international conflict and also include a range of serious violations committed in armed conflict not of an international character. These developments add significantly to the IHL regimes and the result is a much wider definition of war crimes than that understood even a decade ago.

As previously noted, obligations under IHL are extremely broad and include many elements that have no direct relationship to the narrow scope of the three crimes in R2P. For example, IHL ensures the protection of objects such as cultural property and hospitals, requires training and education as a legal obligation and contains a full framework on the regulation of the conduct of hostilities including limitations on the use of specific weapons. The linkage between IHL and R2P demonstrates the need for the two areas to strengthen and reinforce understanding about the need to prosecute those accused of war crimes.

9.3 Points of similarity

9.3.1 Implementation of IHL and R2P

As discussed above, the main point of intersection between IHL and R2P can be found in the area of war crimes. While genocide and crimes against humanity can be committed in time of war, those crimes do not necessarily require a threshold of armed conflict to be committed and in such instances would fall outside the purview of IHL. War crimes, however, do require the threshold of armed conflict necessary for the application of IHL and therefore a direct relationship to R2P emerges.

Unlike the legal regime guiding states' obligations for the implementation of IHL, the question of how to implement R2P is far from resolved. There are no rules or guidelines, and no direct legal obligations with regard to R2P itself but only, as this chapter explored in the previous section, obligations that states currently hold with regard to the crimes of genocide, crimes against humanity and war crimes. Through exploring states' obligations under IHL it is possible to see some parallels with the three-pillar conceptual framework that Secretary-General Ban outlined for R2P (UNSG, 2009), and the legal framework established under the Geneva Conventions. There are two articles of particular relevance that will be explored in this chapter. The first relates to the capacity to prevent the commission of war crimes, and draws parallels between Common Article 1 of the Geneva Conventions and Ban Ki-moon's Pillars One and Two of the three-pillar framework he established relating to R2P. The second is the capacity for collective response to the commission of war crimes that can be found in Pillar Three of Ban's formulation, and at Article 89 of the Additional Protocol I to the Geneva Conventions.

9.3.2 Common Article 1 and Pillars One and Two of R2P

Common Article 1 of the four Geneva Conventions and Additional Protocol I reads: "The High Contracting Parties undertake to respect and to ensure respect for the present Convention in all circumstances." This is one of the key obligations under IHL. First, states parties "undertake" to "respect and to ensure respect". Undertake, in this context and similarly to the undertaking of states in the Genocide Convention discussed above, is "to give formal promise, to bind or engage oneself, to give a pledge or promise, to agree to accept an obligation" (ICJ, 1996: 162). This obligation is a positive one – promising to engage and accept an obligation and, in the case of Common Article 1, it is an obligation to "respect and to ensure respect for" the Geneva Conventions and Additional Protocol I.

According to the ICRC Commentaries (Pictet, 1952) on the Geneva Conventions this is significant because it would not be enough "for a State to give orders or directives to the military authorities ... The State must supervise their execution." In addition, it is not enough for a state to respect the law itself, but it has an obligation, under the Conventions, to "ensure" that respect for IHL is universally applied.

Despite the ICRC's Commentaries, interpretation of Common Article 1, particularly with regard to "respect" and "ensure respect", has been divided into two differing approaches. The first is a restrictive "individual compliance" approach that suggests that Article 1 only imposes an obligation on contracting parties to take all necessary measures to ensure that the Conventions are respected within their own jurisdictions and by their own organs and private individuals (Focarelli, 2010). By relating this interpretation of Article 1 to R2P there is a direct parallel with the First Pillar of R2P being the responsibility of all states to protect communities and populations within their own jurisdictions from the R2P crimes – including war crimes.

The second approach to Common Article 1 is an extensive "state-compliance" approach which means that states must "ensure respect" for the Geneva Conventions by their own organs and individuals, and that they have also undertaken to "ensure respect" for the Conventions by all other contracting states (Focarelli, 2010). This is a much more widely accepted interpretation of Article 1, is consistent with the ICRC Commentaries, and relates much more directly to the principle of R2P.

It is possible to draw direct parallels between the state-compliance interpretation of Common Article 1 and the first two pillars of R2P. In the first instance, R2P Pillar One suggests a state has responsibility to protect populations within its jurisdiction from war crimes. If a state is fulfilling its obligation under Common Article 1 and respecting IHL in the manner in which it conducts hostilities, then war crimes should not be committed. With respect to the Second Pillar of R2P, a state has the responsibility to assist other states to fulfil their responsibilities to protect populations in their jurisdiction from war crimes. It is possible to suggest that by "ensuring respect" for IHL in a "state-compliance" sense, in other words not only within their own jurisdiction but beyond, then states will also be fulfilling their responsibility to protect against war crimes.

It is reasonable to wonder, therefore, whether R2P brings anything new or beneficial to the protection of victims of war crimes. If states' obligations under the Geneva Conventions are such as to ensure that war crimes are not committed, then what is the additional purpose of R2P with respect to war crimes? Is it possible that the most significant element of R2P with respect to war crimes is paragraph 139 in the WSOD, that allows for the collective use of force under UNSC authority, for the prevention of R2P crimes?

The next section will explore the parallels between IHL and Pillar Three of R2P which includes the capacity for the international community to take collective action up to and including the use of force, under the authority of the UNSC, for protection purposes.

9.3.3 Article 89 and Pillar Three of R2P

Additional Protocol I of the Geneva Conventions was designed to address some of the gaps that were identified in the protection of civilians in international armed conflict. As noted above, the purpose of IHL is to offer rules for the conduct of hostilities and protection of civilians and military personnel who are *hors de combat*.

Article 89 of Additional Protocol I is particularly interesting in the comparison between IHL and R2P as it allows for collective action by the international community when there are serious violations of the Geneva Conventions and the two Protocols. Article 89 specifies:

> In situations of serious violations of the Conventions or of this Protocol, the High Contracting Parties undertake to act jointly or individually, in co-operation with the United Nations and in conformity with the United Nations Charter.

The wording of Article 89 follows that of Article 56 of the Charter, which is aimed at cooperation for the universal respect for, and observance of, human rights and fundamental freedoms (Pictet, 1952: 3595). This is also consistent with Common Article 1 obligations. As noted above, "undertake" in international law is a firm commitment to fulfil an obligation. Consistent with the aims of the Conventions in the protection of victims of armed conflict, in Article 89, the high contracting parties *undertake* to act, either "jointly or individually", in situations of serious violations (either acts or omissions contrary to the Conventions or the Protocol) (ibid.: 3589). While such an undertaking may be somewhat limited in the same way as the undertaking to prevent and punish the crime of genocide is limited (for example, by capacity or geography), the undertaking is a significantly strong obligation and should be seen as such.

The words *in situations of serious violations* were not elucidated in the drafting conference (Pictet, 1952: 3588); however, the terms "violation" and "breach" may be considered synonymous (ibid.: 3590). The ICRC Commentaries note that Article 89 relates to situations where there are grave breaches, or other serious violations, but is not concerned with situations where the wrongful conduct is rare or isolated.

The Commentaries conclude that UN actions to which Article 89 refers may include setting up inquiries of compliance, appeals to respect IHL, or even coercive action under Chapter VII which may include the use of armed force. Such coercive action can only be undertaken where the UNSC decides that such situations of serious violations constitute a threat to international peace and security and therefore acts under Chapter VII. Article 89 itself does not allow for the use of force, but rather confers an obligation on states parties to cooperate with the United Nations in conformity with the Charter.

It is significant that these activities are similar to some of those envisioned by Ban Ki-moon under the Third Pillar of his three-pillar formulation of R2P which suggests that, in order to protect vulnerable populations from the R2P crimes, the United Nations can undertake fact-finding missions, pursue public or private suasion, impose diplomatic or other sanctions and, as a last resort where peaceful means have failed, employ the collective use of force, once again through UNSC authorization.

The parallel between Article 89 and Pillar Three of R2P is significant. As noted above, R2P draws its legal authority from existing international law and, with regard to war crimes, from the wide array of IHL that has been developed over the last 150 years. In this legal context IHL goes further than R2P. States parties to the Conventions "undertake to act". Article 89 allows for either individual or joint action in cooperation with the United Nations to instigate the collective use of force under Chapter VII of the Charter in response to serious violations of the Geneva Conventions. R2P, on the other hand, notes that the international community is "prepared to take collective action" which *may* include use of force under Chapter VII of the Charter.

Pillar Three of the R2P formulation outlined by Ban Ki-moon is the most contentious. Commentators and states have argued that Pillar Three is the same as humanitarian intervention and, of all the elements of R2P, it is this pillar that has the most difficulty in international forums, because of the possibility of the use of force. However, with respect to war crimes, the R2P commitment to be "prepared to take action" in paragraph 139 of the WSOD is supported by, but is significantly less powerful than, the as yet unfulfilled legal obligation to "undertake" to take action under Article 89 of Additional Protocol I.

9.4 Conclusion

The long history of the development of IHL is in direct contrast to the stellar rise of the emergent principle of R2P into the international arena.

The suffering of soldiers and of civilians that led to the development of both IHL and R2P reflect the standards of their time. The fact that IHL has grown through legal development, both bilateral and multilateral conventions and treaties as well as through jurisprudence, is significant because it ultimately provides the legal underpinning for the new principle of R2P with respect to war crimes.

Common Article 1 of the Geneva Conventions gives R2P significant legal support. The obligations on states to work to "respect and to ensure respect" for IHL ultimately serve to prevent breaches of IHL. This in turn prevents the commission of war crimes and therefore satisfies not only the states' legal obligations under IHL, but also the responsibility to protect with respect to war crimes, which was agreed to in the R2P principle. The toolbox used by states to "ensure respect for" IHL includes many of the tools and methods recommended by Ban Ki-moon for the successful implementation of Pillars One and Two of R2P (UNSG, 2009).

Similarly, Article 89 of Additional Protocol I provides legal support for collective action through the United Nations (up to and including the use of force) to address serious violations of the Geneva Conventions and Protocols. This provides the legal underpinning for the Third Pillar of the R2P formulation, which includes the possibility of the use of force under Chapter VII of the Charter.

An important question is raised by these findings. If R2P activities for the prevention of war crimes are existing legal obligations held by states through IHL, then does R2P have any additional legal protection to offer potential victims of war crimes? Does R2P actually contribute to the legal protection of people from war crimes, or rather, does it serve a different purpose?

First, it is significant that R2P is not only about war crimes but also about crimes against humanity and genocide. Both these crimes can be committed outside the context of armed conflict, and in such a situation IHL provides no protection for victims of those crimes. However, within the context of armed conflict IHL provides protection against the commission of war crimes, and a multitude of other protections that would not fall within the scope of R2P.

In this sense it appears that R2P is an extremely useful political and policy tool, drawing on elements of existing IHL and international criminal law, but providing a "rallying call" for a range of actions focused on the protection of civilians. As has been demonstrated in this chapter, IHL is wider and relies on implementation before, after and during conflict. The well-developed international criminal regime, from genocide to crimes against humanity, is another important element to stand side by side with R2P and IHL. Academics and practitioners in this area need to have a detailed understanding of the historical narrative on which IHL and R2P are founded, and the distinct and similar elements they contain, and then to work hard across disciplines to ensure that IHL and R2P support and lend strength to each other in the pursuit of protecting civilians.

Notes

1. For information on the various ancient laws of war see McCormack (1997: 33) and Durham (2007).
2. See, for example, the list of conventions at ICRC (2005).
3. It should be noted that ethnic cleansing is an anomaly here as it does not exist as a crime on its own in international law. Ethnic cleansing, however, is an element of a crime against humanity or a war crime.
4. R2P was included at paragraphs 138–140 of the *World Summit Outcome Document* from the UN General Assembly, 60th Session, Agenda items 46 and 120, UN Doc. A/Res.60/1 (2005). This assembly included the largest ever gathering of heads of state and government. Since that time R2P has been cited in Security Council resolutions (S/RES/1674 (2006), S/RES/1706 (2006) and S/RES/1820 (2008)), and debated and accepted in the UN General Assembly (A/RES/63/306).
5. For ICRC customary IHL database see ICRC (2012).
6. Above note 5; specifically the page at: ⟨http://www.icrc.org/ihl.nsf/TOPICS?OpenView⟩.
7. International Tribunal for the Prosecution of Persons Responsible for Serious Violations of International Humanitarian Law Committed in the Territory of the Former Yugoslavia since 1991.
8. International Criminal Tribunal for Rwanda (1994).
9. See also Wynn-Pope, P. (2008) for a discussion on the doctrine of humanitarian intervention before and after the UN Charter.
10. See, for example, the 1965 *Declaration on the Inadmissibility of Intervention in the Domestic Affairs of States and the Protection of Their Independence and Sovereignty*: GA/Res/2131, UNGAOR, 20th Session, Supp. No. 14, 12, UN Doc. A/6014 (1965), GA Res 2625, UN GAOR, 25th Session, Supp. No. 28 Annex 337, UN Doc. A/8028 (1970), and *Declaration on the Inadmissibility of Intervention and Interference in the Internal Affairs of States*, GA Res 36/103, 36th Session, 91st plenary meeting, UN Doc. A/RES/36/103 (1981).
11. S/RES/872 (1992) was the first ever humanitarian intervention undertaken under Chapter VII of the UN Charter.
12. This is the opening wording of Article 42, Chapter VII of the UN Charter.
13. See *Case Concerning the Application of the Convention on the Prevention and Punishment of the Crime of Genocide (Bosnia and Herzegovina v. Serbia and Montenegro) (Judgment) [2007]* ICJ for a discussion by the Court on the nature of ethnic cleansing and when it may constitute genocide.

REFERENCES

Boggs, C. (2001) *The End of Politics: Corporate Power and the Decline of the Public Sphere.* New York: Guilford Press.

Convention against Torture and Other Cruel, Inhuman or Degrading Treatment or Punishment (1984), 1465 UNTS 85 (entered into force 26 June 1987).

Convention for the Amelioration of the Condition of the Wounded in Armies in the Field (1864) Geneva, 22 August 1864.

Convention for the Protection of Cultural Property in the Event of Armed Conflict (1954), 249 UNTS 40 (entered into force 7 August 1956).

Convention on Cluster Munitions (2008), CCM/77 (entered into force 1 August 2010).

Convention on the Prevention and Punishment of the Crime of Genocide (1948), 78 UNTS 277 (entered into force 12 January 1951).

Convention on the Prohibition of the Use, Stockpiling, Production and Transfer of Anti-Personnel Mines and on their Destruction (1997), 2056 UNTS 211 (entered into force 1 March 1999).

Convention to Suppress the Slave Trade and Slavery (1926), 60 LNTS 253 (entered into force 9 March 1927).

Dunant, H. (1986 [1862]) *A Memory of Solferino*. Geneva: International Committee of the Red Cross.

Durham, H. (2007) "IHL and the Gods of War: The Story of Athena versus Ares", *Melbourne University Journal of International Law* 8(2): 148–158.

Durham, H. (2008) "The Laws of War and Traditional Cultures: A Case Study of the Pacific Region", *Commonwealth Law Bulletin* 34(4): 833.

Focarelli, C. (2010) "Common Article 1 of the 1949 Geneva Conventions: A Soap Bubble?", *European Journal of International Law* 21(1): 125–171.

Fonteyne, J. (1974) "The Customary International Law Doctrine of Humanitarian Intervention: Its Current Validity under the UN Charter", *California Western International Law Journal* 4(2): 203–270.

Geneva Convention for the amelioration of the condition of the wounded and sick in armed forces in the field (1949), 75 UNTS 31 (entered into force: 21 October 1950).

Geneva Convention for the amelioration of the condition of the wounded, sick and shipwrecked members of the armed forces at sea (1949), 75 UNTS 85 (entered into force: 21 October 1950).

Geneva Convention relative to the protection of civilian persons in time of war (1949), 75 UNTS 287 (entered into force: 21 October 1950).

Geneva Convention relative to the treatment of prisoners of war (1949), 75 UNTS 135 (entered into force 21 October 1950).

Grotius, H. (1853 [1625]) *On the Law of War and Peace*. Cambridge: John W. Parker.

ICJ, International Court of Justice (1996) *Case Concerning the Application of the Convention on the Prevention and Punishment of the Crime of Genocide (Bosnia Herzegovina v. Yugoslavia)*. ICJ, 11 July 1996.

ICRC, International Committee of the Red Cross (2005) *International Humanitarian Law: Treaties & Documents*. [Online] Available at: ⟨http://www.icrc.org/ihl⟩ (accessed 23 February 2012).

ICRC, International Committee of the Red Cross (2012) *Customary IHL*. [Online] Available at: ⟨http://www.icrc.org/customary-ihl/eng/docs/home⟩ (accessed 23 February 2012).

Keen, M. (1965) *The Laws of War in the Late Middle Ages*. London: Routledge & Kegan Paul.

McCormack, T. (1997) "From Sun Tzu to the Sixth Committee: The Evolution of the International Criminal Law Regime", in T. McCormack and G. Simpson, eds. *The Law of War Crimes*. The Hague: Kluwer Law International.

Pictet, J. (1952) *Geneva Convention for the Amelioration of the Condition of the Wounded and Sick in Armed Forces in the Field: Commentary*. Geneva: International Committee of the Red Cross.

Protocol Additional to the Geneva Conventions of 12 August 1949, and relating to the Protection of Victims of International Armed Conflicts (1977), 1125 UNTS 3 (entered into force 7 December 1978).

Protocol Additional to the Geneva Conventions of 12 August 1949, and relating to the Protection of Victims of Non-International Armed Conflicts (1977), 1125 UNTS 609 (entered into force 7 December 1978).

Roberts, A., and R. Guelff (2005) *Documents on the Laws of War*. New York: Oxford University Press.

Rome Statute of the International Criminal Court (1998), 2187 UNTS 3 (entered into force 1 July 2002).

Simma, B. (1999) "NATO, the UN and the Use of Force: Legal Aspects", *European Journal of International Law* 10(1): 1–22.

UNGA (2005) *UN General Assembly Resolution 60/1: World Summit Outcome Document*, A/Res/60/1, 16 September 2005. [Online] Available at: 〈http://unpan1.un.org/intradoc/groups/public/documents/un/unpan021752.pdf〉.

UNSG (1999) *Preventing War and Disaster: A Growing Global Challenge. Annual report on the work of the Organization*, A/54/1, 31 August 1999.

UNSG (2009) *Report of the Secretary-General: Implementing the Responsibility to Protect*, A/63/677, 12 January 2009.

Vattel, E. (1863) *The Law of Nations*. Philadelphia: T. & J. W. Johnson.

Wynn-Pope, P. (2008) *A Responsibility to Protect against Crimes Against Humanity and Genocide: Effective Operationalization of the Principle* (PhD thesis). Copy available in Law Library, Melbourne Law School, Australia.

10

The responsibility to protect civilians from political violence: Locating necessity between the rule and its exception

Edwin Bikundo

This chapter inquires into the expansion of the rule of law in international law as it relates to the use of force. The promise of international law to promote and protect human welfare is limited by the means at the disposal of the international community where, normatively speaking, peace is the rule and armed conflict the exception. The consequential but regrettable necessity of a forcible response to real or threatened mass atrocities underscores this fundamental undesirability of violence versus its inevitability. The compromise forged is that force, although inevitable, should be used sparingly and only where necessary: specifically in emergencies and especially to protect civilians from mass atrocities. There are two, on the face of it contradictory, approaches clear in the debate on the role of force or violence in international law. The first relates to the fundamental undesirability of violence generally. The second relates to the inevitability of violence and consequential regrettable *necessity* of a forcible response in defence. The role of law in this debate is to navigate between these two coasts of undesirability and inevitability on the ship of necessity. This meandering approach is crystallized in the rules relating to the use of force, which try to restrict force only to extreme circumstances. The compromise reached is that force, although inevitable, should only be used sparingly.

Norms of protection: Responsibility to protect, protection of civilians and their interaction,
Francis, Popovski and Sampford (eds),
United Nations University Press, 2012, ISBN 978-92-808-1218-3

10.1 Managing the necessity to use force

The principled management of necessity therefore increasingly governs how the responsibility to protect civilians is achieved in international affairs. As Durham and Wynne-Pope point out in Chapter 9, the responsibility to protect (R2P) is not of itself a legal concept. It is better viewed as a meta-legal concept from which a number of legal rules and principles can be derived. These include the rules and principles regarding the protection of civilians (POC). Force is made available to protect human life and violence is outlawed precisely because it is targeted against human life. In order to counter illegal violence, R2P may be viewed as reconciling the undesirability of violence to the inevitability of lawful force. Force is in this way legitimated as a means by which the ends of POC are to be achieved.

Linking force and the sanctity of human life through a means–ends relationship, where force is the means by which the sanctity of human life is protected, reconciles otherwise intractable contradictions. This approach can be seen in the UN Charter's preamble when reciting the background to the United Nations, its aims and the means to achieve those aims. The foundational principles of the United Nations are to save humanity from war, reaffirm human rights, establish the conditions for achieving justice and the international rule of law and to promote social progress and better living standards in enlarging freedom. These principles of course are accompanied with the sovereign equality of states, the self-determination of peoples and non-intervention in essentially domestic issues. The ends of the United Nations are to be achieved by practising tolerance and peaceful coexistence and uniting in strength to maintain international peace and security. Most crucially for this discussion, armed force shall not be used except in the common interest, and the international machinery shall be employed for the promotion of the economic and social advancement of all peoples. As a rule the use of force is generally prohibited. The traditionally accepted exceptions to this rule are legitimate self-defence and action taken under the UN Charter for the restoration and maintenance of international peace and security. Peace is the rule and war (armed conflict) the exception. In fact, armed force is only justifiable for facilitating the return to peace. This is why it is notable, for example, that even UNSC resolutions authorizing the use of force do not do so explicitly but instead use wording referring to *all necessary* means or measures to achieve their object. Such wording is deemed sufficient to permit the use of force without specifically recommending it (Freudenschuß, 1994: 492; Baker and DeFrank, 1995: 304–305.). That in principle is what the member states of the United Nations have signed up to, to pool their collective capacities for the maintenance of peace and security within a legal framework. This legalization of the legitimate use of force by progressively outlawing political violence is supposed to promote and provide the rule of law in international affairs. This rule of law discourages war/armed conflict and instead promotes peace principally through differentiating of the legal regimes that are applicable during war and peace. Consequently this chapter's thesis is that a rule and exception scheme where peace is the norm and violence the exception generates an outlawing and criminalization of political violence.

The recent return to United Nations Security Council (UNSC) resolutions to authorize the use of force under Chapter VII of the UN Charter in the Libyan Arab Jamahiriya and Côte d'Ivoire appear to continue the long-term trend towards bringing violence within the ambit of legality. This relationship brought about between law and violence has at least two facets. The first involves criminalizing political violence. The second increasingly invokes legality to justify or excuse the use of force against political violence. The occurrences of political violence in Libya and Côte d'Ivoire that are now under consideration by the International Criminal Court (ICC) can be used as examples (of political violence, not of criminal aggression). The broad question of the illegal use of violence brings together international humanitarian law/the law of armed conflict, public international law and both international and domestic criminal law. The legitimacy and legality of the use of force has two senses: not only a negative prohibition on deliberately targeting civilians but a positive obligation that any use of armed force is to protect civilians. Or at the very least that civilians must not be deliberately targeted (even when states use force to ensure self-determination or to protect against secession or insurgencies). As is to be demonstrated below, the responsibility to protect (R2P) can be conceived of as a subset of the protection of civilians (POC).

10.2 Reconciling sovereignty and intervention

In conceptualizing R2P the International Commission on Intervention and State Sovereignty (ICISS) managed to reconcile the ostensibly incompatible principles of sovereignty and humanitarian intervention (Knight, 2011: 34). Indeed one contributing factor animating the ICISS was to avoid any terminology that espoused military force as either the primary or the sole way to respond to actual or impending mass atrocities (ICISS, 2001: 40). Apart from the use of force as a last resort, other criteria for using force during R2P intervention are the right authority, a just cause, the right intentions, a proportionate response and a reasonable likelihood of success (ibid.: 47). These are substantially a reiteration of *jus ad bellum* principles enjoying a long pedigree (Aquinas, 1981; Augustine, 2003; Walzer, 1977).

R2P principles hold that each state has the responsibility to protect its populations from genocide, war crimes, ethnic cleansing and crimes against humanity (UNGA, 2005: paras. 138 and 139). The international community should encourage and help states to exercise this responsibility. There is a view that the United Nations through then Secretary-General Kofi Annan's reform agenda established the responsibility to protect as a new norm legalizing humanitarian intervention (Stedman, 2007: 938). The Security Council likewise has a responsibility to protect populations by using appropriate collective action via diplomatic, humanitarian and other peaceful means under Chapters VI and VIII of the UN Charter. Should peaceful means be inadequate and national authorities fail to protect their populations as required, then resort may be had to Chapter VII of the UN Charter, which authorizes the use of necessary measures including armed force. UN Secretary-General Ban Ki-moon (UNSG, 2009) refers to these as three equal and mutually reinforcing pillars. A contrary take on this is that the 2005 World Summit agreement and the affirmation of this agreement in Security Council and the General Assembly resolutions in themselves did not constitute new legal norms about the responsibilities of the international community to protect populations from genocide, ethnic cleansing, war crimes and crimes against humanity. They merely contributed to interpret and clarify existing international legal responsibilities in customary international law (Rosenberg, 2009: 445–446).

The Obama administration's National Security Strategy appears to reaffirm America's commitment to pursue its interests through an international system in which all nations have both rights and responsibilities. These include preventing genocide and mass atrocities under the UN auspices via R2P (US National Security Strategy, 2010: 48). This recognizes that, although the primary responsibility for preventing genocide and mass atrocity rests with sovereign governments, this responsibility passes on to the broader international community either when it is sovereign governments themselves who commit genocide or mass atrocities, or when they prove unable or unwilling to take necessary action to prevent or respond to such crimes inside their borders (ibid.). This is a departure by Obama in relation to R2P from the Bush era doctrine of pre-emptive and if necessary unilateral use of force (Reinold, 2011). R2P, including its potential for collective action, is increasingly supported by globally shared understandings (Brunnée and Toope, 2010: 211). It is, however, considered a threat to national sovereignty (Eckhard, 2011: 90); moreover, there is a predominant view that it is yet to become a binding norm of international law (Matthews, 2008; Stahn, 2007: 102).

10.2.1 Concepts of sovereignty

The European Treaty of Westphalia in 1648 marked the first phase in the development of modern notions of sovereignty, which established a system of modern nation-states in which the sovereign reigned supreme domestically as well as in the state's international relations (Deng, 2010: 356). As early as 1651 Thomas Hobbes wrote that the end for which sovereigns were entrusted with authority was the protection of the safety of the people (Hobbes, 1996: 222). Even in international law "the raison d'être of the State is the protection of its citizens" (Brownlie, 1963: 289). R2P has conceptualized sovereignty as responsibility rather than only authority (Thakur, 2006: 255). This means that current understandings hold that the international community is obligated by humanitarian and human rights norms to protect populations from mass deprivation and death, all of which make humanitarian intervention imperative (Deng, 2010: 354).

The second phase in conceptualizing sovereignty is traceable to the end of the Second World War in 1945 in which sovereign power was challenged by the domestic development of democratic values and institutions and by accountability to an international community that sought adherence to human rights and humanitarian standards (Deng, 2010: 356). The third phase was brought about during the 1990s through the end of the Cold War, which rendered state sovereignty vulnerable to international scrutiny (ibid.). The fourth phase of this phenomenon is the contemporary pragmatic attempt to reconcile state sovereignty over domestic affairs with responsibility for the welfare of its citizens (ibid.). To sum up, the current normative status of sovereignty is derived from humanity, as the legal principle that human rights, interests, needs and security must be respected and promoted, and this is also the *telos* or final purpose of the international legal system (Peters, 2009: 514).

10.3 The law on the use of force

Ramesh Thakur (2010: 10) recently observed that "repeated US assaults on UN-centred law governing the international use of force have undermined the norm of a world of laws, international law's efficacy and the UN's legitimacy as the authoritative validator of international behaviour". According to Thakur, because international law is intended to align political power to legal justice, when the powerful subvert the law to make it serve their agenda for keeping others in line, many will resist such perversion of justice (ibid.: 24). Taking a cue from Thakur's admonition regarding aligning political power to legal justice, this chapter argues that civilians are increasingly protected by both the regimes of law relating to the law on the use of force, *jus ad bellum,* and the law relating to the resort to force, *jus in bello.* The chapter does this principally by examining recent UNSC practice evidencing the coordination and convergence of the Protection of Civilians (POC), the Responsibility to Protect (R2P) and referrals to the International Criminal Court (ICC) for political violence. In light of recent practice an argument can be made that the international community bears a moral, legal and political responsibility to protect (Glanville, 2010).

POC moreover seems to be emerging as more than mere political rhetoric and more of a *jus cogens* norm in the following ways. First, it is impermissible for states themselves to use violence against their own citizens in a way that would cause atrocity crimes to happen (Stahn, 2007). Second and following on from the first, it is at the very least permissible for the international community to intervene under the Third Pillar of R2P to protect civilians from political violence leading to atrocity crimes. In other words, high-level and sustained armed force may not be used deliberately contrary to the welfare of civilians and, if it is nevertheless consciously used against them to the level of committing mass atrocities contrary to this stipulation, then that would be criminal under international law *and* a justification for armed force against the responsible government.

In public international law, the central provision relevant to R2P and now POC is the United Nations Charter's Article 39:

> The Security Council shall determine the existence of any threat to the peace, breach of the peace, or act of aggression and shall make recommendations, or decide what measures shall be taken in accordance with Articles 41 and 42, to maintain or restore international peace and security.

Historically, the origin of the Article as reflected in the framer's intent was to give as unrestricted a hand as possible to the UNSC for freedom of action (Frowein and Krisch, 2002: 718–719). With reference to international criminal law, it and related articles were expansively construed in the Tadić case discussed below (*Prosecutor* v. *Tadić* 1995). More recently, it was considered by the ICC state parties to be closely related to the ICC Statute's (Rome Statute) Article 15 (UN Diplomatic Conference, 1998), which was drafted in contemplation of the UN Charter. Prior to the states parties agreeing to a definition, the connection between the identical word "aggression" in public international law and international criminal law was by no means co-extensive. The same word in the same language and discipline could nevertheless have different semantic effect, let alone tenor and import; for instance, aggression under the UN Charter and aggression in the Nuremberg Charter, Judgment and Principles. The former relates to law on the use of force by states under public international law, and the latter to individual criminal responsibility under international criminal law by natural persons. Now the Rome Statute has blurred the boundary between the two meanings to a certain extent. Additionally R2P is specifically tied to four core international crimes: genocide, war crimes, ethnic cleansing and crimes against humanity (Orford, 2009: 1006). R2P was therefore boosted by the establishment of the ICC (Sarkin, 2010). Even the International Court of Justice (ICJ) has ruled that states are obliged to take all reasonable measures within existing international law to prevent genocide and punish the perpetrators (*Bosnia* v. *Serbia* [2007] para. 425). R2P's First Pillar is therefore a *jus cogens* or peremptory norm of customary international law, imposing on states the legal responsibility to protect their populations from genocide, war crimes, ethnic cleansing and crimes against humanity (Bellamy and Reike, 2010: 285–286). Côte d'Ivoire and Libya before the UNSC serve as locations where R2P, POC and international criminal responsibility are utilized in tandem to address international peace and security challenges.

10.3.1 The example of Côte d'Ivoire

Following disputed presidential elections and civil armed conflict in Côte d'Ivoire, the UNSC authorized the UN Operation in Côte d'Ivoire (UNOCI) to use "all necessary means" under Chapter VII of the UN Charter to carry out its mandate of protecting civilians under threat of imminent physical violence (UNSC, 2004: para. 8; UNSC, 2007: para. 5). The UNSC also authorized French forces stationed in Côte d'Ivoire to use "all necessary means" in order to help protect civilians (UNSC, 2004: para. 16; UNSC, 2010: para. 17). Furthermore, the UNSC urged Laurent Gbagbo, the previous incumbent president, to hand over power to Alessane Ouattara, the internationally recognized winner of the elections, in accordance with the voting result. The ICC prosecutor on his part stated that widespread or systematic killings in Côte d'Ivoire might trigger an investigation (ICC, 2011). Alessane Ouattara, the incoming president, promised legal action against Laurent Gbagbo for atrocities committed during the post-election violence (Kaka, 2011).

10.3.2 The example of Libya

Regarding Libya, on 26 February 2011 the UNSC unanimously adopted Resolution 1970 (2011) under Chapter VII, Article 41 (measures not involving the use of armed force) of the UN Charter (UNSC, 2011a). This was in consideration of "widespread and systematic attacks" taking place in Libya against the civilian population, possibly amounting to crimes against humanity. Invoking the Libyan authorities' responsibility to protect its population, the UNSC decided to refer that situation dating from 15 February 2011 to the ICC Prosecutor. Speaking in favour of the resolution, Nigeria's representative was convinced not only would it address the ongoing violence, but it would also provide for the protection of civilians as well as enhance respect for international humanitarian and human rights law. The Brazilian representative agreed that the measures adopted were meant to halt the violence, ensure the protection of civilians and promote respect for international law (except for the exemption from jurisdiction of nationals of those countries not parties to the Rome Statute). In fact the Prosecutor was reported as being confident of charges ultimately being brought against Muammar Gaddafi, the now deceased Libyan leader (Richey, 2011). On 17 March 2011 the UNSC adopted Resolution 1973 (UNSC, 2011b) by a vote of ten in favour to none against (Brazil, China, Germany, India and the Russian Federation all abstained). In it, while reiterating the primary responsibility of the Libyan authorities to protect the Libyan population, the Council authorized member states, acting nationally or through regional organizations or arrangements, to take *all necessary measures* to protect civilians under threat of attack in the country, outside of deploying ground troops (ibid.).

The representatives of the United Kingdom, Lebanon and Colombia stated that the Libyan authorities had lost all their legitimacy and therefore the UNSC resolution was aimed at protecting Libyan civilians. Lebanon's representative hoped that the resolution would have a deterrent role and end the Libyan authorities' use of force against its civilians. Germany's representative, for their part, said the UNSC's intention was to stop the violence in Libya. The United States agreed, saying the Council had responded to the Libyan people's cry for help and the purpose was to protect Libyan civilians. Bosnia and Herzegovina's representative was of the view that the Libyan people desperately needed humanitarian assistance, and the unimpeded access of that relief was an absolute *necessity*. He therefore called on the Libyan authorities to end their violence against the Libyan people and believed that the resolution was an answer to their legitimate call.

Colombia's representative said his delegation was convinced that the purpose of the new resolution was essentially humanitarian and was conducive to bringing about conditions that would lead to the protection of civilians. In their view the Council had acted because the Libyan government, through its actions, had shown that it was not up to protecting and promoting the rights of its people. The Russian Federation abstained, while making clear their opposition to violence against civilians. Portugal's representative said his country had voted in favour of the text because the attacks against civilians had continued after the passage of the last Council resolution, and affirmed that today's resolution addressed his country's priorities, including protecting civilians and the facilitation of unimpeded humanitarian aid.

Nigeria's representative said the resolution had been *necessitated* by the persistently grave and dire situation in Libya. This created the need to ensure the protection of civilians and the delivery of humanitarian assistance to those most in need, adding that when the fate of innocent civilians was in question, the international community must be ready to respond. The League of Arab States and the African Union had spoken with one voice in condemnation of the situation in Libya. South Africa agreed the Council had acted responsibly to answer the call of Libyan people. It would also speed humanitarian assistance to those that needed it most. China said that the continuing deterioration of the situation in Libya was of great concern. However, the UN Charter must be respected and the crisis ended through peaceful means, not the use of force, until peaceful means were exhausted. It did not, however, veto the resolution because it attached great importance to the requests of the Arab League and the African Union. Brazil, on their part, were not convinced that the use of force as provided for in the resolution would lead to the realization of the immediate end to violence and the protection of civilians. These, according to the Brazilian representative, demanded a political process.

There was therefore a broad consensus discernible that the Libyan government had used force on its citizens contrary to human rights and R2P norms which led to the regime losing its legitimacy in the eyes of the international community that necessitated both the referral to the ICC and the taking of all necessary means or measures including the use of armed force to protect Libyan citizens. According to Alex Bellamy (2011: 263) the adoption of Resolution 1973 "reflected a change in the Security Council's attitude toward the use of force for human protection purposes". In spite of identifying this means–ends relationship where force is used to protect human beings, Bellamy (ibid.: 265–266) considers R2P in relation to Libya as being more the exception than the rule. He identifies three factors that lead to this conclusion. First was the clear threat of mass atrocity, second was an extremely short timeframe for an appropriate response, and third was the support of regional organizations, especially the Arab League. According to Simon Chesterman (2011: 280–281) the intervention in Libya, while interesting, was not exactly groundbreaking. But, as he points out, there was no need to employ phraseology referencing "unique" and/or "exceptional" circumstances that were used earlier in order to avoid vetos by some Security Council Permanent Members. This in my view is the real difference offered by Resolution 1973: it referred to no unique or exceptional circumstances but only "necessity" because it was a *normative* development. It was normative in the sense that it relied on necessity as the justification for the use of force while not relying on unique or exceptional circumstances to justify the use of force. This was the distinction between the Libyan intervention and all previous interventions.

10.3.3 The example of Yugoslavia

The clear capacity of the UNSC's power to generate law and indeed even create judicial institutions was affirmed by the jurisprudence of the International Criminal Tribunal for the former Yugoslavia (ICTY). That court's decision also had a clear influence on the drafting of the Rome Statute for the ICC. Article 13 of the Rome Statute provides the trigger mechanism for the ICC's jurisdiction. The article codifies three separate modes for exercising jurisdiction. The first is the traditional basis of the consent of states. The second (already used in the case of Libya) is through a referral of the UNSC by a resolution under Chapter VII of the UN Charter. The third provides for the independent prosecutorial power to refer a case. The first and the third are directly derived from state consent and also flow from specific articles of the Rome Statute, namely Articles 14 and 15, respectively. The second, however, is conceptually a very different proposition in that the power therein flows from UNSC action. This UNSC power received judicial affirmation in the Tadić case (*Prosecutor* v. *Tadić* 1995: paras. 26–28). According to Jose E. Alvarez (1996: 245) the Tadić decision was foundational because among other things it indirectly reinvigorated the rule of law. It was also political, given that its intention was to help restore peace. Alvarez (ibid.: 263) argues that the appellate judges in that case turned to "necessity" as the ultimate justification to dismiss Tadić's arguments. That court said, with reference to UNSC Resolution 808 setting up the tribunal, that "neither the text nor the spirit of the [United Nations] Charter conceives of the UNSC as *legibus solutus* (unbound by law)". Mia Swart (2011: 986) on her part is of the view that, whether or not the ICTY initially had a defect in its legitimacy, this could subsequently be remedied by its moral power and the fairness of its proceedings. Yet, the court essentially recognized a power of UNSC that did not proceed from anything more than the acts of the UNSC itself. However, as the court pointed out, because that power was not limitless or subject to no review, the power had to comply with the conditions of its exercise, which in this case were the restoration and maintenance of international peace and security. The inherent jurisdiction of the court to decide was described as inversely proportional to the textual discretion of the UNSC to act. In other words, the UNSC could act to give jurisdiction to the ICTY only insofar as doing so was consistent with the Council's mandate. Further, the court clarified that the Charter conceived of the Council as having specific powers (not absolute fiat), which could not exceed those of the United Nations itself: it was instead limited by the jurisdiction of and the internal division of power within the United Nations. The power of the UNSC to invoke Chapter VII powers to initiate or indeed stop an investigation by the ICC in Article 15 of the Rome Statute historically originated from UNSC Resolution 808 of 1993 as affirmed by the ICTY. The essential connectedness between the UNSC's power to regulate international violence and the ability to set up criminal tribunals was first confirmed in the Tadić case explicating *legibus solutus* and only then did it subsequently find its way to Article 13 of the Rome Statute.

10.4 The United Nations as bound by law

What can a concept drawn from twelfth- and thirteenth-century canon and civil law teach us about the contemporary regulation of violence in international law? Well, a lot more than would be considered obvious, if recent developments in the application of R2P and POC are anything to go by. It is mildly interesting that when the ICTY needed to explain and justify the then novel idea that the UNSC could create an international tribunal, it reached for a rather arcane expression in order to state what the Security Council *is*, i.e. a creature of law, in comparison to what it is *not*, i.e. a lawless entity. Thanos Zartaloudis (2010: 102) painstakingly traces how the Latin maxim was transferred from the Roman Empire to medieval ecclesiastical authorities and onward to the notion of "the people" as a politically legitimizing entity. Kenneth Pennington (1993: 90–91) in turn provides four different but related meanings for *legibus solutus*:

1 The prince's authority to change, derogate, or dispense from positive law (shared with all governmental legislative bodies);
2 The prince's immunity from prosecution;
3 The prince's authority to transgress or dispense from the normal rules governing the legal system;
4 The prince's power to transgress the rights of the subject.

Pennington's classification above seems to indicate that the ICTY in Tadić only applied the third meaning encompassing the authority to transgress or dispense from the normal rules governing the legal system. So the ICTY was saying the UNSC was not *legibus solutus* in the sense that it did not have the authority to transgress the system's normal legal rules. According to Christian Tomuschat (2006: 830) the Nuremberg trials following the Second World War (coupled with the UN Charter) brought forth the international community as a legal concept that placed the leaders of all human communities under the rule of international law. Therefore, a state (actually a government) should never be above the law. The principle elevating the king above the law, *rex legibus solutus*, and its equivalent raising the republic above the law, *res publica legibus solute,* were resoundingly rejected.

In a recent case, the British House of Lords found a clash between the power and duty to detain exercisable on the express authority of the UNSC and fundamental human rights (*R* v. *Secretary of State for Defence* 2007). It held, however, that the United Kingdom could lawfully, where *necessary* for imperative security reasons, exercise this power to intern so as to minimize human rights infringements. The reason for holding the proscription on internment to be qualified or displaced was that Article 25 of the UN Charter requires member states to accept and carry out UNSC decisions, while Article 103 provides that, in the event of a conflict between that obligation and the member state's obligations under any other international agreement, the Charter prevails. This would mean that the UNSC is *legibus solutus* in Pennington's third sense.

The point is that this does not mean that the UNSC is absolved of legal obligations (*Prosecutor* v. *Tadić* 1995: para. 35; Gill, 1995: 48). This is the only legally defensible position because a legal system is the weaving of legal rules to legally regulated institutions, leaving no power in the state or in society that is *de legibus solutus* (O'Donnell, 2001). That is, all powers are subject to the legal authority of other powers and nobody is supposed to be above or beyond the rules. However, given the centrality of necessity to our inquiry, what about the well-known maxim that "necessity knows no law"? The ICJ (which was evenly split with seven votes to seven, only resolved by the presiding judge's casting vote) had this to say on the legality of the threat or use of nuclear weapons in the Legality of the Threat or Use of Nuclear Weapons case (ICJ, 1996: para. 105):

> It follows from the above-mentioned requirements that the threat or use of nuclear weapons would generally be contrary to the rules of international law applicable in armed conflict, and in particular the principles and rules of humanitarian law.
>
> However, in view of the current state of international law, and of the elements of fact at its disposal, the Court cannot conclude definitively whether the threat or use of nuclear weapons would be lawful or unlawful in an extreme circumstance of self-defence, in which the very survival of a State would be at stake.

This case is extraordinary in that the ICJ essentially ruled that it was unable to answer a question before it: it was unable to distinguish between the lawful and the unlawful even after accepting jurisdiction. It was clearly a reaffirmation of the principle "necessity knows no law", which renders definition and decision impossible in that indistinct boundary between law and politics. This *non-liquet* or identification of a gap in the law that the law cannot answer illustrates a "state of exception" contemplated by the law (Agamben, 2005). Actions taken by the Security Council in addressing aggression and breaches of the peace are paradoxically unbound by law but sanctioned by the law (Noll, 2008: 578–579). Indeed, the UNSC's Chapter VII powers, especially as read with Article 25 (which binds all members to UNSC decisions) and Article 103, raise obligations to the Charter above all other legal obligations (*Lockerbie* [1992] paras. 39–46).[1] In my view, this in principle shows the rejection of incorporating violence into law by law. This rejection of violence (and assimilation of force) by law means that the law is permanently at work defining and limiting the exception and in that way, *manages* it as a matter of necessity. To sum up: the UNSC is not *legibus solutus* because its legally mandated ends bind it – and the protection of civilians is coming to assume a central place in those ends, by force if necessary.

10.5 States' use of force

The legal formulation by *all necessary* means or measures is a familiar one in the law on the use of force. However, linking it explicitly to POC and to R2P of both the nation-state and the international community, coupled with a referral to the ICC, annexes the regulation of violence to a means–ends economy. Economy, in this instance, is an assembly of means and methods for the ad hoc realization of abstract principles (justice or the welfare of humanity) linking contingent means (including armed force) for realizing permanent humanitarian ends. In *Politics as a Vocation*, Max Weber (2004: 77–78) set out to sociologically define a "state". According to him, the state could not be defined in terms of its *ends,* because there was scarcely any task that the state has not taken in hand, and there was no task that one could say has always been exclusive and peculiar to it. Ultimately, the modern state can only be defined sociologically in terms of the specific *means* peculiar to it (including presumably, the international community), i.e. the use of physical force. Intriguingly enough, Weber linked this force to violence without specifying their difference (if any) and indeed further links this to the law itself, arguing that anarchy follows lack of violence. He was of the view that every state was founded on force and that, if no social institutions existed which knew the use of violence, then the concept of "state" would be eliminated, and anarchy in its specific sense would emerge.

Weber concedes that force is neither normal nor the exclusive means open to the state. He nevertheless holds that the relationship is an intimate one because it is the means specific to the state. However, Weber distinguishes the use of force as normal before the modern state and then goes on to give his famous and influential definition of the state as "a human community that (successfully) claims the monopoly of the legitimate use of physical force within a given territory". Weber noted that the right to use physical force is ascribed to other institutions or to individuals only to the extent to which a state permitted it. This was because the state is considered the sole source of the "right" to use violence. Weber here appears to refer to a normative rule-generative *claim* as opposed to descriptive fact-based assertion.

Whatever else that may be said about this definition, its sole referent is a state in control of territory. This in itself tends to sound a bit dated to current readers. With globalization, the state is increasingly marginalized and the monopoly on the use *of* force is becoming a monopoly on the use *for* force. That is, humanitarian and security concerns increasingly underpin resort to force. Claims to sovereignty in justifying resorts to force are no longer legitimate as such. Weber's approach is strikingly similar to Walter Benjamin's (1986: 277) own take. Benjamin sets out his own purpose as explicating the relationships between violence, law and justice. He said that "it is clear that the most elementary relationship within any legal system is that of ends to means, and, further, that violence can first be sought only in the realm of means, not of ends". This teleological approach taken to violence meant that his criterion for judgement was the intention of the violence. Therefore, violence without any intention other than to be violent did not fall under his critique. However, from the legal perspective a crime is either an unlawful act or a lawful act done by unlawful means. Therefore legitimate self-defence is excluded from the prohibition of the use of force, just as is the action of the UNSC under Chapter VII of the UN Charter. Weber, therefore, is now superseded. Were he alive to see contemporary developments he would be compelled to revise his definition of the state and its supposed monopoly on the legitimate use of force. Nowadays the state is defined in terms of both its end of civilian welfare and protection, which are the only justification for its means, and its means, which *ultimately include* the use of force. In sum, we are entering a situation in law where the state can no longer be defined in terms of its (Weberian) monopoly on forceful means, but rather must be defined in terms of the ends that it pursues without excluding the use of force.

10.6 Conclusion

What therefore legitimates and legalizes the international community's use of force in R2P contexts is precisely because it is used to protect civilians despite their own state having the primary responsibility to protect them. This is why POC is at the centre of both legality and legitimacy in both international and domestic law and practice. This means that both means and ends are liable to criminalization. In terms of means and ends, POC is covered under both legal regimes of resort to force and the use of force. This is despite there being no defence of humanitarian intervention being made explicitly available for criminal aggression as defined under the Rome Statute. Does this mean that the time-honoured public international law distinction between the law of war and the law of peace has now been replaced by an emerging normative monopoly on the legitimate use of force? If such a monopoly has arisen it can only be a normative claim as opposed to a descriptive statement of the status quo. POC nevertheless now governs both how and why force is used globally and, as such, protection of human life is now elevated to front and centre in the legal regime. This legal regime is such that force is not the sole or even the primary means for the protection of civilians but is nevertheless the ultimate means of protection. In other words, the relationship between the responsibility to protect and the protection of civilians is one of means and ends. The use of armed force is the means by which civilians are protected and civilian protection is the end of any legitimate use of force.

Note

1. The effect of paras. 39–46 is that a Security Council decision under Chapter VII of the UN Charter prevails over any other treaty-based right that is found inconsistent with it.

REFERENCES

Agamben, G. (2005) *State of Exception*. Chicago: University of Chicago Press.

Alvarez, J. E. (1996) "Nuremberg Revisited: The Tadic Case", *European Journal of International Law* 7(2): 245–264.

Aquinas, T. and Dominicans (1981) *Summa Theologica. Complete English Edition*. Allen: Christian Classics.

Augustine (2003) *Concerning the City of God against the Pagans*. London: Penguin Classics.

Baker, J. A., and T. M. DeFrank (1995) *The Politics of Diplomacy: Revolution, War, and Peace, 1989–1992*. New York: Putnam.

Bellamy, A. J. (2011) "Libya and the Responsibility to Protect: The Exception and the Norm", *Ethics & International Affairs* 25(3): 263–269.

Bellamy, A. J., and R. Reike (2010) "The Responsibility to Protect and International Law". *Global Responsibility to Protect* 2: 267–286.

Benjamin, W. (1986) *Critique of Violence, Reflections: Essays, Aphorisms, Autobiographical Writings*. New York: Schocken.

Brownlie, I. (1963) *International Law and the Use of Force by States*. Oxford: Clarendon Press.

Brunnée, J. and S. J. Toope (2010) "The Responsibility to Protect and the Use of Force: Building Legality?", *Global Responsibility to Protect* 2: 191–212.

Chesterman, S. (2011) "'Leading from Behind', The Responsibility to Protect, the Obama Doctrine, and Humanitarian Intervention after Libya", *Ethics & International Affairs* 25(3): 279–285.

Deng, F. M. (2010) "From 'Sovereignty as Responsibility' to the 'Responsibility to Protect'", *Global Responsibility to Protect* 2: 353–370.

Eckhard, F. (2011) "Whose Responsibility to Protect?", *Global Responsibility to Protect* 3: 89–101.

Freudenschuß, H. (1994) "Between Unilateralism and Collective Security: Authorizations of the Use of Force by the UN Security Council", *European Journal of International Law* 5(4): 492. [Online] Available at: ⟨http://207.57.19.226/journal/Vol5/No4/art2-02.html⟩.

Frowein, J., and N. Krisch (2002) "Chapter VII: Action With Respect to Threats to the Peace, Breaches of the Peace, and Acts of Aggression", in Bruno Simma, ed. *The Charter of the United Nations: A Commentary*. Oxford: Oxford University Press, 701–737.

Gill, T. D. (1995) "Legal and Some Political Limitations on the Power of the UN Security Council to Exercise its Enforcement Powers Under Chapter VII of the Charter", *Netherlands Year Book of International Law* 26: 33–138.

Glanville, L. (2010) "The International Community's Responsibility to Protect". *Global Responsibility to Protect* 2: 287–306.

Hobbes, T. (1996) *Leviathan*. Cambridge: Cambridge University Press.

ICC, Statement (2011) *Widespread or systematic killings in Cote d'Ivoire may trigger OTP investigation*, 6 April. [Online] Available at: ⟨http://www.icc-cpi.int/menus/icc/structure%20of%20the%20court/office%20of%20the%20prosecutor/reports%20and%20Statements/Statement/otpStatement060411⟩.

ICISS, International Commission on Intervention and State Sovereignty (2001) *The Responsibility to Protect*. Ottawa: International Development Research Centre.

ICJ, *Libyan Arab Jamahirya* v. *United Kingdom* (Lockerbie case) [1992] ICJ Rep 3.

ICJ, *Questions of Interpretation and Application of the 1971 Montreal Convention arising from the Aerial Incident at Lockerbie (Libyan Arab Jamahiriya* v. *United Kingdom)* [1992] ICJ Reports.

ICJ, *The Application of the Convention on the Prevention and Punishment of the Crime of* Genocide *(Bosnia and Herzegovina* v. *Serbia and Montenegro)* [2007] Judgment, ICJ.

ICJ, *The Legality of the Threat or Use of Nuclear Weapons*, International Court of Justice (Advisory Opinion of 8 July 1996) General List no. 95.

ICTY, International Criminal Tribunal for the former Yugoslavia, *Prosecutor* v. *Dusko Tadić*, Decision on the Defence Motion for Interlocutory Appeal on Jurisdiction, ICTY, case No IT-94-1-AR72, Appeals Chamber of 2 October 1995.

International Law Committee (1996) *Draft Code of Crimes against the Peace and Security of Mankind 1996.* [Online] Available at: ⟨http://untreaty.un.org/ilc/texts/instruments/english/draft%20articles/7_4_1996.pdf⟩.

Kaka, A. (2011) "Ivory Coast leader Ouattara promises legal action against Gbagbo", *Jurist,* 12 April. [Online] Available at: ⟨http://jurist.org/paperchase/2011/04/ivory-coast-leader-ouattara-promises-legal-action-against-gbagbo.php⟩.

Knight, W. Andy (2011) "The Development of the Responsibility to Protect: From Evolving Norm to Practice", *Global Responsibility to Protect* 3(1): 3–36.

Matthews, M. W. (2008) "Tracking the Emergence of a New International Norm: The Responsibility to Protect and the Crisis in Darfur", *BostonCollege International & Comparative Law Review* 31: 137–152.

Noll, G. (2008) "The Miracle of Generative Violence: René Girard and the Use of Force in International Law", *Leiden Journal of International Law* 21: 563–580.

O'Donnell, G. A. (2001) "Democratic Theory and Comparative Politics", *Studies in Comparative International Development* 1(36): 45. [Online] Available at: ⟨http://democracy.stanford.edu/Seminar/O'Donnell.pdf⟩ (accessed 6 March 2012).

Orford, A. (2009) "Jurisdiction without Territory: From the Holy Roman Empire to the Responsibility to Protect", *Michigan Journal of International Law* 30(3): 981–1015.

Pennington, K. (1993) *The Prince and the Law 1200–1600: Sovereignty and Rights in the Western Legal Tradition.* Los Angeles: University of California Press.

Peters, A. (2009) "Humanity as the A and Ω of Sovereignty", *European Journal of International Law* 20(3): 513–544.

Reinold, T. (2011) "The United States and the Responsibility to Protect: Impediment, Bystander, or Norm Leader?", *Global Responsibility to Protect* 3: 61–87.

Richey, D. (2011) "ICC prosecutor certain of Gaddafi war crimes charges", *Jurist,* 25 March. [Online] Available at: ⟨http://jurist.org/paperchase/2011/03/icc-prosecutor-certain-of-gaddafi-war-crimes-charges.php?utm_source=feedburner&utm_medium=feed&utm_campaign=Feed%3A+pitt%2FvLdl+%28JURIST+-+Paper+Chase+%5Bfull%5D%29⟩.

Rosenberg, S. P. (2009) "Responsibility to Protect: A Framework for Prevention", *Global Responsibility to Protect* 1: 442–477.

Sarkin, J. (2010) "The Responsibility to Protect and Humanitarian Intervention in Africa", *Global Responsibility to Protect* 2: 371–387.

Stahn, Carsten (2007) "Responsibility to Protect: Political Rhetoric or Emerging Legal Norm?", *American Journal of International Law* 101: 99–120.

Stedman, S. J. (2007) "UN Transformation in an Era of Soft Balancing", *International Affairs* 83(5): 933–944.

Swart, M. (2011) "Tadic Revisited: Some Critical Comments on the Legacy and the Legitimacy of the ICTY", *Goettingen Journal of International Law* 3(30): 985–1009.

Thakur, R. (2006) *The United Nations, Peace and Security.* Cambridge: Cambridge University Press.

Thakur, R. (2010) "Law, Legitimacy and United Nations", *Melbourne Journal of International Law* 11(1): 1–26.

Tomuschat, C. (2006) "The Legacy of Nuremberg", *International Criminal Justice* 4(4): 830.

UK House of Lords, *R (on the application of Al-Jedda) (FC) (Appellant)* v. *Secretary of State for Defence (Respondent)* [2007]. The UK House of Lords per Lord Bingham of Cornhill.

UN Department of Public Information (2011a) Security Council 6491st Meeting* (PM). *In Swift, Decisive Action, Security Council Imposes Tough Measures On Libyan Regime, Adopting Resolution 1970 In Wake Of Crackdown On Protesters*, 26 February 2011. [Online] Available at: ⟨http://www.un.org/News/Press/docs/2011/sc10187.doc.htm⟩.

UN Department of Public Information (2011b) Security Council 6498th Meeting (Night). *Security Council Approves 'No-Fly Zone' Over Libya, Authorizing 'All Necessary Measures' To Protect Civilians, By Vote Of 10 In Favour With 5 Abstentions*, 17 March 2011. [Online] Available at: ⟨http://www.un.org/News/Press/docs/2011/sc10200.doc.htm⟩.

UN Diplomatic Conference of Plenipotentiaries on the Establishment of an International Criminal Court. Rome, 15 June–17 July 1998. *Official Records Volume II Summary records of the Plenary Meetings and of the Meetings of the Committee of the Whole*, A/CONF.183/13 (Vol. II).

UNGA (2005) *UN General Assembly Resolution 60/1: World Summit Outcome Document*, A/Res/60/1, 16 September 2005.

UNSC (1993) *UN Security Council Resolution 808 (1993): On the International Criminal Tribunal for the Former Yugoslavia (ICTY)*, S/RES/808, 22 February 1993.

UNSC (2004) *UN Security Council Resolution 1528 (2004): The Situation in Côte d'Ivoire*, S/RES/1528, 27 February 2004.

UNSC (2007) *UN Security Council Resolution 1739 (2007): The Situation in Côte d'Ivoire*, S/RES/1739, 10 January 2007.

UNSC (2010) *UN Security Council Resolution 1933 (2010): The Situation in Côte d'Ivoire*, S/RES/1933, 30 June 2010.

UNSC (2011a) *UN Security Council Resolution 1970 (2011): Peace and Security in Africa*, S/RES/1970, 26 February 2011.

UNSC (2011b) *UN Security Council Resolution 1973 (2011): The Situation in Libya*, S/RES/1973, 17 March 2011.

UNSG (2009) *Report of the Secretary General: Implementing the Responsibility to Protect*, UN A/63/677, 12 January 2009. [Online] Available at: ⟨http://www.responsibilitytoprotect.org/index.php?module=uploads&func=download&fileId=655⟩.

US National Security Strategy (May 2010). [Online] Available at: ⟨http://www.whitehouse.gov/sites/default/files/rss_viewer/national_security_strategy.pdf⟩.

Walzer, M. (1977) *Just and Unjust Wars*. New York: Basic Books.

Weber, M. (2004) *The Vocation Lectures*. Edited and introduced by David S. Owen, Tracy B. Strong, translated by Rodney Livingstone. Indianapolis: Hackett Publishing Company.

Zartaloudis, T. (2010) *Giorgio Agamben: Power, Law and the Uses of Criticism* (Nomikoi, critical legal thinkers). New York: Routledge.

11

The responsibility to protect and the international refugee regime

Angus Francis

A series of humanitarian tragedies in the 1990s (Somalia, Rwanda, Srebrenica, Kosovo and East Timor) highlighted the failure of the international community to prevent mass atrocities. Since that time "a newly energized international conscience" (Thakur, 2009) has seen the international community's response to mass atrocities undergo a significant rethink. Arguably the most important development has been the conceptualization and promotion of the responsibility to protect (R2P) principle. The R2P principle, as endorsed by states, recognizes that states acting individually, and collectively through the United Nations, have a responsibility to protect persons within their jurisdiction from mass atrocities.[1]

A criticism of the R2P principle is that it is "old wine in new bottles" (Molier, 2006: 48). Critics point to long-standing notions of "sovereignty as responsibility" (Stahn, 2007: 111–112) and argue that the R2P principle simply repackages well-established international laws dealing with mass atrocities.[2] The Secretary-General's "three pillars" have similarly drawn criticism on the ground that they have little new to offer (Molier, 2006: 52; Strauss, 2009: 319). But others argue that the R2P principle registers and facilitates a norm shift toward responsible sovereignty, as well as acting as an "umbrella concept" that strengthens existing legal instruments by filling gaps and encouraging their adoption and implementation (Thakur and Weiss, 2009: 26).

Leading R2P proponents further argue that the principle is a norm in progress and, like other norms, requires agents to promote and shepherd it through the "maze of UN politics" (Thakur and Weiss, 2009: 33). In

Norms of protection: Responsibility to protect, protection of civilians and their interaction,
Francis, Popovski and Sampford (eds),
United Nations University Press, 2012, ISBN 978-92-808-1218-3

this respect, they can point to growing evidence of the entrenchment of R2P in the UN system through the appointment of a Special Adviser on R2P in 2007 (UNSG, 2008) and steps towards the creation of a joint office on the prevention of genocide and the promotion of the R2P principle that formalizes existing collaboration between the Secretary-General's Special Adviser on the Prevention of Genocide and his Special Adviser responsible for R2P (Luck, 2010: 351; UNSG, 2009: 33; 2010: para. 17).

The Special Adviser on R2P acknowledges that the R2P principle adds little to the international law on the prevention of genocide, war crimes and crimes against humanity, or to the legal bases for action under the UN Charter (Chapters VI, VII and VIII); but rather, "the affirmation and recommitment embodied in the [Outcome Document] add a universal and high-level political dimension" to the struggle against mass atrocities (Luck, 2010: 356). The R2P principle is in essence a strategy for identifying the intersection of threats and the norms and institutions responsible for responding to the same. In a similar way to the human security framework (Edwards, 2008–09: 783), the R2P principle is not intended to usurp existing legal frameworks, but to ensure their better coordination and utilization. Thus, it should be judged on how well it is able to achieve this goal.

How the R2P principle builds on existing legal norms (Arbour, 2008: 447–448; Barbour and Gorlick, 2008: 541–548; ICISS, 2001a: 16; Luck, 2010: 356) requires study and elaboration. How the R2P principle might work in tandem with these norms to prevent and respond to mass atrocities, and in the context of diverse domestic, regional and international institutions, is the key challenge facing the successful operationalization of the R2P principle. This chapter asks what the R2P principle could contribute to the protection of refugees, who as a class are especially vulnerable to the commission of such crimes. Section 11.1 examines some of the key challenges and gaps confronting the international protection regime for refugees. Section 11.2 will then consider what benefits the R2P principle might have for refugees in light of these issues.

11.1 Protection challenges confronting the refugee regime

11.1.1 Increasing use of forced displacement as an objective of conflict

The 1990s saw forced displacement increasingly become a strategy in asserting control over territory (Loescher, 2008: 50). Forced displacements emerged at the centre of crises in the Great Lakes region of Africa, West

Africa, the Balkans and East Timor (Human Rights Watch, 1999: C1107; Loescher, 2008: 52). The increasing use of forced displacement as an objective of conflict, rather than a consequence of conflict, reflects that intra-state conflict has replaced inter-state conflict as the dominant form of conflict worldwide (Orchard, 2010: 38). The aim of these "new wars" is to control population and territory by killing or expelling those of a different ethnic, religious or political identity (Kaldor, 1999: 100; Orchard, 2010: 39).

This poses major challenges to the international community. First, "facts of displacement frequently become acts of mass atrocity" (Orchard, 2010: 39). Second, the grant of asylum to the victims of such atrocities is increasingly not available, leading to greater numbers of internally displaced persons (IDPs) (Loescher, 2008: 50; Orchard, 2010: 41). Third, the decline of asylum has gone hand in hand with a shift from the protection offered by states (via the grant of asylum) to the less effective in-country aid and assistance offered by humanitarian organizations (Orchard, 2010: 41). It is worthwhile considering each of these challenges in more detail.

11.1.2 The nexus between forced displacement and mass atrocities

The commission of international crimes as a means of forced displacement is a disturbing feature of modern warfare, involving the use of torture, murder, arbitrary arrest and detention, extrajudicial executions, rape and sexual assaults, deliberate military attacks or threats of attacks on civilian areas, and wanton destruction of property (UNSC Commission of Experts, 1994: paras. 129, 130). As a matter of international law, forced displacement/forcible transfer/deportation can itself amount to: a breach of international humanitarian law (*Geneva Convention Relative to the Protection of Civilian Persons in Time of War*, 1949: Art 49); a crime against humanity (*Rome Statute* Art. 7(1)(d); UNGA Res. 58/177, 2003, Preamble, para. 9); a war crime (*Rome Statute* Art. 8(2)(a)(vii); UNGA Res. 58/177, 2003, Preamble, para. 9); and genocide if intended to destroy the group (ICJ, *Application of the Convention on the Prevention and Punishment of the Crime of Genocide*, para. 190).[3]

11.1.3 The decline of protection and failing international solidarity and burden-sharing

At the same time as forced displacement as an objective of conflict has increased (Orchard, 2010: 38), the protection available to refugees has declined. The *Convention Relating to the Status of Refugees*, 1951 (Refugee Convention), encapsulates a kind of "collectivized surrogacy" that has its origins in earlier international efforts to protect national minorities and aliens (Hathaway, 2005: 75–83). The Convention's "decentralized implementation structure" means "governments themselves . . . ultimately remain responsible to ensure that refugees are treated as the Convention requires" (ibid.: 992–993). The protection of refugees in situations of mass influx, which calls for a collective response, is ultimately dependent on international solidarity and the ability of the UNHCR to broker temporary protection or resettlement packages on a case-by-case basis (such as Kosovo).

This regime has come under increasing pressure. Developed countries have deliberately reduced access to their territory for asylum-seekers through tighter immigration controls (Francis, 2009). These policies seek to keep refugee situations at "arm's length" (Loescher, 2008: 47). Yet at the same time as developed countries have restricted the entry of asylum-seekers, they have not offered a commensurate expansion of burden-sharing arrangements to assist developing countries faced with large refugee flows in the regions of origin (Chimni, 2000: 250–251). This has contributed to protracted refugee situations in developing countries least able to afford large refugee populations (Adelman, 2008; Loescher, 2008: 31). Developing countries in Africa and elsewhere are responding by adopting similarly restrictive asylum policies, which they justify in part by reference to the precedents established in the developed world, but which result in a greater number of IDPs unable to access protection outside their country of origin (Crisp, 2010: 5). These developments further highlight the gaps in the oversight and compliance provisions of the Refugee Convention (Kalin, 2003: 613).

11.1.4 In-country protection replacing external protection

Developed states have also championed policies that have the effect of containing refugees in their countries or regions of origin by averting refugee flows, ensuring speedy repatriation, assisting IDPs, and providing emergency aid in-country (Loescher, 2000: 53). The United Nations deployed an array of humanitarian tools that coincided with this trend (the grant of temporary protection rather than permanent asylum; the creation of safe areas to reduce the likelihood of refugee flows or to encourage return; the authorization of military interventions in conflicts producing mass refugee flows; and cross-border delivery of assistance, sometimes with the use of the military, to at-risk populations) (Loescher, 2000: 54; Roberts, 1998: 375–376). UNHCR, in particular, took the lead in providing humanitarian assistance in countries of refugee origin, often in the middle of intra-state conflicts (Loescher, 2000: 47, 80), and began to heavily promote policies focused on "preventive protection", "the right to remain" (Barutciski, 1996: 60, 96) and the early return (repatriation) of refugees to their country of origin (Loescher, 2000: 49).

Two key factors underpinned these developments. First, policies aimed at preventing refugee flows coincided with the increasingly stringent non-entrée policies of developed states noted above (Chimni, 1998). Second, there was greater willingness on the part of the international community to intervene in the internal affairs of sovereign states on humanitarian grounds, including where internal conflicts caused refugee flows. In what represented a significant extension of the international refugee regime beyond UNHCR, the Security Council in the post-Cold War period was prepared to be more assertive in characterizing refugee flows as a threat to regional and international security and thus a justification for action under Chapter VII of the UN Charter (Loescher, 2000: 54; Roberts, 1998: 383). During this time the Security Council emerged as a key proponent of addressing crises leading to displacement "at or near the source" (Roberts, 1998: 382–383).

The practice of "in-country protection" (for want of a better term) has found favour among commentators who see it as a comprehensive and more sustainable approach in the long term to refugee situations (Coles, 1990: 392). Roberts, although sceptical about the overall effectiveness of the Security Council's attempts to tackle crises leading to displacement in the 1990s (Northern Iraq, the former Yugoslavia, Somalia, Rwanda and Haiti), argues that international efforts helped limit refugee flows by establishing conditions for Kurds to return to northern Iraq, feeding besieged cities in Bosnia and the starving in Somalia, and restoring an elected government in Haiti (Roberts, 1998: 388).

Others are more critical. Loescher (2000: 54–56) observes that it quickly became evident by the mid 1990s that new in-country protection practices were ad hoc, reactive, self-interested, ineffective, and failed to tackle the root causes of conflict. He suggests that in many instances governments used humanitarian relief "as a substitute for political action to address the root causes of mass displacement" (ibid.: 49). The UNHCR is also alleged to have compromised its protection function by being a willing tool for the containment policies of its major donors (developed states), thus undermining the palliative role of refugee protection (Barutciski, 1996; Barutciski and Suhrke, 2001; Cuncliffe and Pugh, 1997, 1999; Frelick, 1992, 1993; Goodwin-Gill, 1999; Hathaway, 1995).

Today, the debate has shifted to IDPs. The rise of intra-state conflict and the non-entrée policies of states have led to greater numbers of IDPs (Lewis, 1992: 699; UNGA Res. 558/1995). In contrast to refugees, who by definition have crossed an international frontier and can theoretically seek protection in another country, IDPs are often dependent on receiving protection or assistance from their own government, which may be unable or unwilling to offer protection, especially where government policy is the cause of their displacement (Carey, 1999: 246). Some argue that it would be impracticable and immoral for UNHCR to distinguish between refugees and IDPs when distributing aid because of the complex and regional nature of modern armed conflicts, which have produced greater numbers of IDPs as forced displacement has been used as a deliberate tactic of war and where refugees and IDPs from different countries often intermix (Lanz, 2008: 205; Mooney, 1999: 201).

Viewed in a positive light, UNHCR's expanding mandate over IDPs may be evidence of international law's ever growing reach over the internal affairs of states, and IDPs in particular (Crisp, 2010: 22). "It is now widely recognized," Crisp (ibid.) observes, "that people in need of aid and protection in their own countries have claims on the international community when their Governments do not fulfil their responsibilities, or where there is a disintegration of the nation-state." From this perspective, UNHCR is extending, not undermining, international protection through its involvement with IDPs. After all, the reason international protection, as enshrined in the Refugee Convention, was confined to persons who had crossed an international frontier was because of practical considerations of limited resources and respect for sovereignty – what Shacknove (1985: 277) referred to as a function of the "art of the possible".[4] It could be argued that as displaced persons within states have become more accessible to the international community, the territorial limitation in the Refugee Convention has decreased in importance as a tool for defining the scope of international protection to displaced persons.

An opposing view is that the recent conflation between the assistance offered to refugees and IDPs is diminishing the international community's commitment to recognizing and addressing the specificity of the refugee's circumstances and options (Hathaway, 2007: 363). The debate may be academic. Roberts (1998: 391), for one, views the new approaches to handling refugees as an inevitable result of the reluctance of Western states to accept large numbers of refugees after they lost their strategic value with the end of the Cold War – a fact of international life, which cannot be ignored (or remedied).

And yet the international community's adoption of the Refugee Convention represents a commitment to address the humanitarian needs of refugees that existed before the Cold War, and should continue long after (Jackson, 2008: 39). The UNHCR argues that the interests of states continue to be best served through a collective commitment to dealing with refugee flows in a humane and orderly way, which entails greater (not less) respect for international refugee law (and regional variants) (Crisp, 2010: 8–9). At the same time, the fact remains that "not all people *can* leave their countries" (Cohen, 2007: 372). States *should* be encouraged to respect their obligations towards IDPs alongside other victims of human rights abuses (Crisp, 2010: 8–9). The challenge is to pursue this objective while at the same time preserving and fostering greater respect for the distinctive rights of refugees, including access to protection.

Having identified some of the key challenges confronting the international regime for the protection of refugees – the nexus between forced displacement and mass atrocity, the general decline in access to protection for refugees and burden-sharing, and the provision of in-country assistance in lieu of asylum – the next part of this chapter looks at whether the R2P principle may assist in meeting these challenges in a way that is beneficial to refugee protection.

11.2 R2P and protecting refugees

11.2.1 Do refugees fall within the scope of the R2P principle?

A threshold issue is whether refugees, as defined in the Refugee Convention, fall within the scope of the R2P principle in light of its narrow focus on mass atrocities. The short answer is yes. A common misconception is that the definition of refugee found in the Refugee Convention is limited to persons subject to individualized persecution (Durieux and McAdam, 2004: 9). If this were the case, then the R2P principle as encapsulated in the *World Summit Outcome Document* (WSOD) would be of little relevance as it deals predominantly with gross systematic violence against groups. However, the definition of refugee in the Refugee Convention is not limited to cases of individualized persecution (UNHCR, 2011c: 17). The definition extends to persons fleeing attacks on a racial, political, religious, ethnic or other group in the context of internal war,[5] including victims of ethnic cleansing[6] or inter-clan struggles in unstable or failed states.[7] In Africa, regional refugee law goes further and encompasses all persons fleeing from "aggression, occupation, foreign domination or events seriously disturbing public order".[8] Thus refugees, as a defined class in international law, stand to benefit from any tangible impacts that the R2P principle might have in preventing and responding to mass atrocities inflicted on groups, whatever the nature of the conflict involved.

11.2.2 Severing the nexus between forced displacement and mass atrocities

Recalling the nexus between forced displacement and mass atrocities, noted in section 11.1.2 above, one of the strengths of the R2P principle is that it emphasizes *prevention* of mass atrocities. Preventing mass atrocities will prevent displacement and preventing displacement will lessen the risk of mass atrocities (Harris, 2010: 13). R2P's preventive component has the potential to make a significant contribution to addressing the "root causes" of refugee flows. Early studies identified a number of factors leading to mass exodus that resonate with the factors leading to mass atrocity crimes: human rights abuses; wars and insurrections; the absence of rule of law; oppression and anarchy; underlying ethnic strife associated with the formation of nation-states; minority regimes holding power through violence; persecution; and the denial of social and economic development opportunities.[9]

Measures aimed at addressing the root causes of refugee flows and mass atrocities can usefully be conceptualized and applied in tandem. For example, in terms of targeting widespread human rights abuse, Pillar One of the R2P principle as expressed in the Secretary-General's 2009 Report (paras. 13, 15, 16, 20, 21, 27) affirms that the primary responsibility for preventing mass atrocity crimes lies with the state, including fostering respect for human rights and diversity, tolerance, and building legal, political and civil society institutions that ensure greater protection. But Pillar Two of the R2P principle recognizes the role of the international community in preventing mass atrocities through exerting pressure on states to comply with their international obligations and by assisting states to build capacity via, for example, a UN or regional presence or development assistance (UNSG, 2009: paras. 28, 35–48). Early warning and assessment are also an important part of the preventive strategy advocated by the Secretary-General (UNSG, 2010).

At the same time, the preventive and response measures in the R2P toolkit should be informed by the lessons learned from the application of preventive tools to situations of mass displacement. This is especially important, given that ethnic cleansing is one of the four atrocity crimes. Most importantly, the use of force to prevent refugee flows is a high-risk strategy (Loescher, 2008: 56). NATO characterized the military operation in Kosovo as a humanitarian intervention aimed at stopping Serbia's ethnic cleansing of Albanians from Kosovo (Solana, 1999). But the NATO intervention "triggered rather than deterred" Serbia's forced deportation of the Albanians (Snyder, 2011: 34). Snyder regards NATO's regional security concerns as a motivating factor in the Kosovo intervention, with the result that "humanitarian concerns took a back seat to the desire to keep the interveners' casualties low" (ibid.). The resulting bombing campaign was a "perverse" form of protection (Roberts, 2011: 228). However, the assumption that forced displacement could be prevented by the presence of foreign troops was contradicted by experiences in Kosovo post-June 1999 when ethnic cleansing (this time of minorities) continued even with a huge international military and civilian presence (Barutciski, 2002: 369).

How does R2P propose to grapple with these issues? Resolution 1973 makes clear that the plight of refugees forced to flee the violence was a factor leading to the Security Council's decision to authorize collective coercive action against Libya under Chapter VII of the Charter of the United Nations (UNSC Res. 1973: 2). Yet international intervention has not stopped refugee flows from Libya. The jury is also still out on whether intervention in Libya will lessen the likelihood of prolonged displacement – an endemic feature of many refugee situations where the international community has failed to intervene (Crisp, 2010: 13). Northern Iraq, Bosnia, Kosovo and East Timor are said to be four conflicts which produced an eventual decisive response from the international community that enabled large-scale repatriations to take place (ibid.: 13).

Whether international intervention will have the same effect in Libya remains to be seen. Evidence of escalating tribal conflict following the overthrow of the old regime, coupled with the fact that many of the refugees who fled were sub-Saharan refugees who face possible detention and forced repatriation if they are returned to Libya, means that repatriation for many refugees from the conflict may not be possible – at least in the short to medium term. In fact, in the case of sub-Saharan refugees, resettlement may be the only viable long-term option. But this will depend on the willingness of countries in Europe and elsewhere to resettle sub-Saharan refugees in larger numbers. This brings us to the next challenge – international solidarity and burden-sharing.

11.2.3 Bolstering protection and international solidarity and burden-sharing

Turning to the second challenge facing the international refugee regime noted in section 11.1.3 above – the declining solidarity of states to address refugee flows – a key strength of the R2P principle is its potential to contribute "a universal and high-level political dimension" to responses to mass atrocity. The case of Libya would suggest that the R2P principle is becoming part of the "diplomat language of humanitarian emergencies, used by governments, international organizations, NGOs, and independent commissions to justify behaviour, cajole compliance, and demand international action" (Bellamy, 2010: 145). Can the principle be utilized in order to bolster flagging state commitment to offering protection to victims of mass atrocities? UNHCR's governing Executive Committee (ExCom), currently consisting of 85 member states, has repeatedly called on states parties to respect their obligations under the Refugee Convention.[10] Can R2P add anything to these calls?

Early signs were not promising. The ICISS report focused on the destabilizing effects of refugee flows on neighbouring countries and how this possibility can be exploited to mobilize the political will (domestically, regionally and internationally) to intervene in civil conflicts (ICISS, 2001a: paras. 1.20, 4.35, 4.36, 6.31, 8.15). The Refugee Convention does not rate a mention. This was despite roundtable discussions between the Commission and UNHCR (ICISS, 2001b: 354). Later, the High-Level Panel's report spends much time on threats to states of "eroded borders" (UNHLP, 2004: 14, 16, 54, 55). This early focus of R2P is regrettable because it parrots a view of refugees as threats to national borders and security and, collectively, as threats to international peace and security, rather than as persons deserving of protection (Chimni, 2000: 252; Edwards, 2008–2009: 775; Hammerstad, 2011: 245–247, 252–253).

The WSOD also missed the opportunity of spelling out the application of the R2P principle to refugees. It could be argued that the word "populations" in paragraphs 138 and 139 should be read in light of paragraph 133, whereby states commit themselves to safeguard "the principle of refugee protection" and "to upholding [their] responsibility in resolving the plight of refugees". This reading is supported by Security Council Resolution 1674 (2006), which reaffirms paragraphs 138 and 139 of the WSOD, and also recalls "the particular impact which armed conflict has on women and children, including as refugees and internally displaced persons, as well as on other civilians who may have specific vulnerabilities, and stress[es] the protection and assistance needs of *all* affected civilian populations" (emphasis added) (UNSC Res. 1674: para. 4 and Preamble). Yet it would have been much preferable for paragraphs 138 and 139 to make this link explicit, rather than use the word "populations" that is capable of being inclusive (all persons) or exclusive (citizens only).

It was not until the Secretary-General's 2009 Report on the implementation of the R2P principle that the plight of refugees was finally addressed. This can largely be attributed to behind-the-scenes work of the UNHCR, which pushed for greater acknowledgement of refugee protection in R2P discourse. The 2009 Report recognizes that the grant of protection to refugees has historically been a key tool by which the international community has protected potential victims of mass atrocities (UNSG, 2009: para. 35). Mainstreaming of the R2P principle is stated to include the protection of refugees and the internally displaced in the policies, activities and field operations of UN agencies, funds and programmes (whether in the areas of human rights, humanitarian affairs, peacekeeping, peacebuilding, political affairs or development). Moreover, the report encourages ratification and domestic implementation of treaties on human rights and refugee law (as well as international humanitarian law and international criminal law) (UNSG, 2009: para. 17).

The Secretary-General's report also acknowledges the work of the UNHCR "in obtaining grants of asylum and protecting refugees", thereby serving "numerous potential victims of crimes and violations relating to the responsibility to protect" (UNSG, 2009: para. 35). The UNHCR has shown a willingness to engage with the R2P doctrine on the basis that it offers a way forward in addressing "asylum fatigue" by shifting the characterization of refugees away from "broader concerns about international security, transnational crime and terrorism" (Feller, 2006). This reflects a "desecuritization" of UNHCR's own discourse on refugees, which has seen UNHCR wind back its security approach of the 1990s in favour of one that stresses the humanitarian nature of refugee protection (Hammerstad, 2011: 255).

The added attention given to refugees in R2P discourse may have fed back into the work of the Security Council. The Security Council's first resolution authorizing collective coercive action to protect civilians in Libya (Res. 1973/2011) takes a distinctly humanitarian perspective on the plight of refugees fleeing the violence. Rather than portray the refugees as a threat to the security of neighbouring countries, the Council appealed to the international community to support efforts by host countries to address the needs of the refugees. Arguably, this language and intent is closer to the humanitarian aims of the Refugee Convention *and* the R2P principle. Use of the R2P principle in this context may have the effect of elevating the call for assistance and focusing action on redressing the plight of the individual victims (Stamnes, 2009: 77). However, the litmus test for the R2P principle will be the response of European and other developed and developing countries to refugees fleeing the mass atrocities being committed in places such as Libya, Sri Lanka and Afghanistan.

11.2.4 In-country protection while sustaining the institution of asylum

While preventive action along the lines of early warning, preventive diplomacy, conflict resolution, human rights protection, and the presence of UN military units and humanitarian agencies, can help calm internal tensions that could easily boil over into mass atrocities, such efforts should not be at the expense of contingency plans for the protection of refugees (Barutciski, 1996: 61). The UN preventive deployment in Macedonia is seen as a good example of where effective preventive protection went hand in hand with contingency plans worked out by UNHCR and the United Nations Protection Force (UNPROFOR) in the event that mass displacement of Albanians from Kosovo destabilized the region. Contingency planning for mass refugee exoduses is now a priority of the UNHCR, as demonstrated by the recent crises in Libya (UNHCR, 2011a) and Côte d'Ivoire (UNHCR, 2011b).

Traditional in-country protection devices, such as safe areas, may be necessary to protect persons unable to flee. However, they need to be linked to a clear political plan that addresses the root causes of the conflict (Barutciski, 1996: 103). The use of safe areas as a means of combating ethnic cleansing is fraught with danger (Weiner, 1998: 449). The Security Council's endorsement of this policy in Bosnia-Herzegovina ended in tragedy (ibid.: 449). A better approach evident in more recent UNHCR practice (UNHCR, 2011a, 2011b) is to prepare for – and inform relevant international actors of the likelihood of – displacement and to look for feasible protection options *outside* the country of refugee origin (Barutciski, 2002: 369, 379–380).

The Assistant UN High Commissioner for Refugees makes the case that the R2P principle has the potential to provide a valuable framework for addressing protection gaps or deficits in relation to IDPs (Feller, 2006). The *Guiding Principles on Internal Displacement* (UN Commission on Human Rights, 1998) reflect the R2P principle by recognizing the primary responsibility of the state of origin to protect IDPs (ibid.: Principle 3.1). But the Guidelines do not seek to impose responsibility on states to accept international assistance. Instead, the Guidelines merely provide that when international assistance is offered it should be considered in good faith by the country of origin (ibid.: Principles 25, 30).

Better protection of IDPs should help prevent atrocities. This fact is acknowledged by the African Union *Convention for the Protection and Assistance of Internally Displaced Persons in Africa* (the Kampala Convention), which outlaws the use of displacement as an intentional method of warfare (Art. 4(4)(c)) and requires states parties to "declare as offences punishable by law acts of arbitrary displacement that amount to genocide, war crimes or crimes against humanity" (Art. 4(6)). Prevention of atrocities should also lessen the likelihood of internal displacement. It is recognized that prevention of violations of international humanitarian law can reduce armed conflict-induced IDPs (Ojeda, 2010: 60). Thus, the Kampala Convention provides that states shall "respect and ensure respect for their obligations under ... humanitarian law, so as to prevent and avoid conditions that might lead to the arbitrary displacement of persons" (Art. 4(1)). But the protection of IDPs and other civilians in-country should not be at the expense of the right to seek and enjoy asylum (UN Commission on Human Rights, 1998: Principle 2.2).

11.3 Conclusion

In conclusion, R2P has the potential to better address root causes of forced displacement where displacement is a consequence or objective of conflict. At the same time, the implementation of the R2P principle needs to take heed of past lessons and controversies in refugee protection. In particular, it must be recognized that prevention and intervention cannot always address the root causes of displacement and conflict. While preventive strategies which genuinely seek to tackle the root causes of conflict should be pursued, asylum must be preserved as a form of protection for persons fleeing mass atrocities. This requires a realistic appraisal on a case-by-case basis of the likelihood of refugee flows and appropriate preparation and planning to be done by UNHCR and the international community.

Notes

1. The R2P principle, as endorsed by states, is expressed in paragraphs 138 and 139 of the 2005 *World Summit Outcome Document*. The principle is first conceptualized in the ICISS report (2001a).
2. See the discussion of this criticism in Barbour and Gorlick (2008: 554).
3. Traditional justifications under international humanitarian law for forced displacement, e.g. the removal of civilians from besieged or encircled areas or evacuation of civilian populations if the security of the population or imperative military reasons demand (*Geneva Convention Relative to the Protection of Civilian Persons in Time of War*, 1949: Arts. 17, 49), are subject to tight humanitarian restrictions and will not hold in cases of mass atrocity (ICJ, *Application of the Convention on the Prevention and Punishment of the Crime of Genocide*, paras. 333, 334).
4. See the discussion in Hathaway (1991: 31–32, 2007: 353).
5. See, e.g., *Salibian* v. *Canada* [1990] FCJ 454 (Canada, Federal Court of Appeal); *Knezevic* v. *Ashcroft*, 367 F.3d 1206; 2004 U.S. App. LEXIS 10162 (US Court of Appeals for the 9th Circuit).
6. *Knezevic* v. *Ashcroft*, 367 F.3d 1206; 2004 U.S. App. LEXIS 10162 (US Court of Appeals for the 9th Circuit); *S* v. *Federal Ministry of the Interior*, Austrian Administrative Court, 26 January 1994, 93/01/0034.
7. Hagi-Mohammed v. Minister for Immigration and Multicultural Affairs [2001] FCA 1156.
8. Convention governing the specific aspects of refugee problems in Africa, Art. I(2).
9. Aga Khan (1981: 2–3). See also UN Commission on Human Rights, Res. 30, 11 March 1980; GA Res. 35/124, 11 December 1980; GA Res. 35/196, 15 December 1980; Report of the Secretary-General, (E/CN.4/1440), 27 January 1981; UN Commission on Human Rights, Res. 29, 11 March 1981; *Report of the Group of Governmental Experts on International Co-operation to Avert New Flows of Refugees* (A/41/324, annex); *Human Rights and Massive Exoduses, Note*, Secretary-General, E/CN.4/1983/33, 10 January 1983; *Human Rights and Mass Exoduses: Report of the Secretary-General*, A/44/622, 17 October 1989; GA Res. 44/164 of 15 December 1989; UN Commission on Human Rights, *Human Rights and Mass Exoduses*, 6 March 1990, (E/CN.4/RES/1990/52). *See also*, Aga Khan 1983. GA Res. 46/127, 17 December 1991; *Human Rights and Mass Exoduses: Report of the Secretary-General*, A/47/552, 21 October 1992; GA Res., *Human Rights and Mass Exoduses*, A/RES/48/139, 4 March 1994; *Human Rights and Mass Exoduses: Report of the Secretary-General*, E/CN.4/1995/49, 28 December 1994; *Human Rights and Mass Exoduses: Report of the High Commissioner for Human Rights Submitted Pursuant to*

Commission on Human Rights Resolution 1998/49, E/CN.4/2000/81, 6 December 1999; GA Res., *Human Rights and Mass Exoduses*, A/RES/54/180, 24 February 2000; *Human Rights and Mass Exoduses: Report of the Secretary-General*, A/56/334, 10 September 2001; GA Res., *Human Rights and Mass Exoduses*, A/RES/56/166, 26 February 2002; *Human Rights and Mass Exoduses: Report of the High Commissioner for Human Rights, Submitted Pursuant to Commission on Human Rights Resolution 2000/55*, E/CN.4/2003/84, 17 January 2003; *Human Rights and Mass Exoduses: Report of the Secretary-General*, A/58/186, 25 July 2003; GA Res., *Human Rights and Mass Exoduses*, A/RES/58/169, 15 September 2003; Commission on Human Rights, Res. 2005/48; *Report of the High Commissioner for Human Rights on Human Rights and Mass Exoduses*, E/CN.4/2005/80, 25 January 2005; *Report of the High Commissioner for Human Rights on Human Rights and Mass Exoduses*, A/HRC/4/105, 14 March 2007.
10. ExCom Conclusion No. 11 (adopted in 1978); ExCom Conclusion No. 82 (adopted in 1997); ExCom Conclusion No. 85 (adopted in 1998).

REFERENCES

Adelman, H. (2008) "Protracted Displacement," in H. Adelman, ed. *Protracted Displacement in Asia: No Place to Call Home*. Farnham, UK: Ashgate.

African Union Convention for the Protection and Assistance of Internally Displaced Persons in Africa (Kampala Convention), adopted by the Special Summit of the African Union held in Kampala, Uganda, 22 October 2009.

Aga Khan, S. (1981) *Study on Human Rights and Massive Exoduses*, Special Rapporteur to UN Commission on Human Rights (E/CN.4/1503).

Aga Khan, S. (1983) *Address by Sadruddin Aga Khan to the British Refugee Council*, 9 February 1983. [Online] Available at: ⟨http://www.forcedmigration.org/⟩.

Application of the Convention on the Prevention and Punishment of the Crime of Genocide (Bosnia and Herzegovina v. Serbia) [2007] ICJ Rep 43.

Arbour, L. (2008) "The Responsibility to Protect as a Duty of Care in International Law and Practice", *Review of International Studies* 34 (3): 445–458.

Barbour, B., and B. Gorlick (2008) "Embracing the 'Responsibility to Protect': A Repertoire of Measures Including Asylum for Potential Victims", *International Journal of Refugee Law* 20(4): 533–566.

Barutciski, M. (1996) "The Reinforcement of Non-Admission Policies and the Subversion of UNHCR: Displacement and Internal Assistance in Bosnia-Herzegovina (1992–94)", *International Journal of Refugee Law* 8(1/2): 49–110.

Barutciski, M., and A. Suhrke (2001) "Lessons from the Kosovo Refugee Crisis: Innovations in Protection and Burden-Sharing", *Journal of Refugee Studies* 14(2): 95.

Barutciski, M. (2002) "A Critical View on UNHCR's Mandate Dilemmas", *International Journal of Refugee Law* 14(2–3): 365–381.

Bellamy, A. (2010) "The Responsibility to Protect – Five Years On", *Ethics & International Affairs* 24(2): 144.

Carey, C. (1999) "Internal Displacement: Is Prevention Through Accountability Possible? A Kosovo Case Study", *American University Law Review* 49: 244–286.

Chimni, B. (1998) "The Geopolitics of Refugee Studies: A View from the South", *Journal of Refugee Studies* 11(4): 350–374.

Chimni, B. (2000) "Globalization, Humanitarianism and the Erosion of Refugee Protection", *Journal of Refugee Studies* 13(3): 243–263.

Cohen, R. (2007) "Response to Hathaway", *Journal of Refugee Studies* 20(3): 370–376.

Coles, G. (1990) "Approaching the Refugee Problem Today", in G. Loescher and L. Monahan, eds. *Refugees and International Relations*. Oxford: Clarendon Press, 373–410.

Convention Governing the Specific Aspects of Refugee Problems in Africa, 1001 UNTS 45 (entered into force 20 June 1974).

Crisp, J. (2010) "Forced Displacement in Africa: Dimensions, Difficulties, and Policy Directions", *Refugee Survey Quarterly* 29(3): 2–27.

Cunliff, S., and M. Pugh (1997) "The Politicization of the UNHCR in the Former Yugoslavia", *Journal of Refugee Studies* 10(2): 134–153.

Cunliff, S., and M. Pugh (1999) "UNHCR as Leader in Humanitarian Assistance: A Triumph of Politics over Law?", in F. Nicholson and P. Twomey, eds. *Refugee Rights and Realities: Evolving Concepts and Regimes*. Cambridge: Cambridge University Press, 175–199.

Durieux, J., and J. McAdam (2004) "Non-Refoulement through Time: The Case for a Derogation Clause to the Refugee Convention in Mass Influx Emergencies", *International Journal of Refugee Law* 16(1): 4–24.

Edwards, A. (2008–2009) "Human Security and the Rights of Refugees: Transcending Territorial and Disciplinary Boundaries", *Michigan Journal of International Law* 30: 763–807.

ExCom Conclusion No. 11 (adopted in 1978).

ExCom Conclusion No. 82 (adopted in 1997).

ExCom Conclusion No. 85 (adopted in 1998).

Convention Relating to the Status of Refugees, 28 July 1951, 189 UNTS 134, 150 (entered into force 22 April 1954).

Feller, E. (2006) "Towards a Culture of Protection", *8th Annual Forum on Human Rights, Dublin, Ireland: Global Human Rights Protection – the way forward,* 30 June.

Francis, A. (2009) "Removing Barriers to Protection at the Exported Border: Visas, Carrier Sanctions and International Obligation", in J. Farrall and K. Rubenstein, eds. *Sanctions, Accountability and Governance in a Globalised World*. Cambridge: Cambridge University Press, 378–406.

Frelick, B. (1992) "Preventive Protection and the Right to Seek Asylum: A Preliminary Look at Bosnia and Croatia", *International Journal of Refugee Law* 4: 439.

Frelick, B. (1993) "Preventing Refugee Flows: Protection or Peril?" *US Committee for Refugees World Refugee Survey 2000*. Washington, DC: USCRI.

Geneva Convention Relative to the Protection of Civilian Persons in Time of War, 12 August 1949, 75 UNTS 287 (entered into force 21 October 1950).

Goodwin-Gill, G. (1999) "Refugee Identity and Protection's Fading Prospect", in F. Nicholson and P. Twomey, eds. *Refugee Rights and Realities: Evolving Concepts and Regimes*. Cambridge: Cambridge University Press, 220–249.

Hagi-Mohammed v. *Minister for Immigration and Multicultural* Affairs [2001] FCA 1156.

Hammerstad, A. (2011) "UNHCR and the Securitization of Forced Migration", in A. Betts and G. Loescher, eds. *Refugees in International Relations*. Oxford: Oxford University Press, 237–260.

Hathaway, J. (1991) *The Law of Refugee Status*. Toronto: Butterworths.

Hathaway, J. (1995) "New Directions to Avoid Hard Problems: The Distortion of the Palliative Role of Refugee Protection", *Journal of Refugee Studies* 8: 288.

Hathaway, J. (2005) *The Rights of Refugees Under International Law*. Cambridge: Cambridge University Press.

Hathaway, J. (2007) "Forced Migration Studies: Could We Agree Just to Date?", *Journal of Refugee Studies* 20(3): 349–369.

Harris Rimmer, S. (2010) "Refugees, Internally Displaced Persons and the 'Responsibility to Protect'," Research Paper No 185, *New Issues in Refugee Research*.

Human Rights Watch (1999) *East Timor: Forced Expulsions to West Timor and the Refugee Crisis*. 1 December 1999, C1107. Available at: ⟨http://www.unhcr.org/refworld/docid/45cc24ac2.html⟩.

ICISS, International Commission on Intervention and State Sovereignty (2001a) *The Responsibility to Protect*. Ottawa: International Development Research Centre.

ICISS, International Commission on Intervention and State Sovereignty (2001b) *The Responsibility to Protect: Research, Bibliography, Background: Supplementary Volume to the Report of the International Commission on Intervention and State Sovereignty,* Ottawa: International Development Research Centre, December 2001. Available at: ⟨http://www.bits.de/NRANEU/docs/ICISS1201supplement.pdf⟩.

Jackson, I. (2008) "Some International Protection Issues Arising During the 1970s and 1980s With Particular Reference to the Role of the UNHCR Executive Committee", *Refugee Survey Quarterly* 27(1): 30–39.

Kaldor, M. (1999) *New and Old Wars: Organized Violence in a Global Era*. Stanford, CA: Stanford University Press.

Kalin, W. (2003) "Supervising the 1951 Convention Relating to the Status of Refugees: Article 35 and Beyond", in E. Feller, V. Turk and F. Nicholson, eds. *Refugee Protection in International Law: UNHCR's Global Consultations on International Protection*. Cambridge: Cambridge University Press.

Knezevic v. *Ashcroft*, 367 F.3d 1206; 2004 U.S. App. LEXIS 10162 (US Court of Appeals for the 9th Circuit).

Lanz, D. (2008) "Subversion or Reinvention? Dilemmas and Debates in the Context of UNHCR's Increasing Involvement with IDPs", *Journal of Refugee Studies* 21(2): 192–209.

Lewis, C. (1992) "Dealing with the Problem of Internally Displaced Persons", *Georgetown Immigration Law Journal* 6: 693.

Loescher, G. (2000) "UNHCR and the Erosion of Refugee Protection", *Forced Migration Review* 10: 28–30.

Loescher, G. (2008) *The United Nations High Commissioner for Refugees (UN-HCR): The Politics and Practice of Refugee Protection in the 21st Century*. Hoboken, NJ: Taylor & Francis.

Luck, E. (2010) "The Responsibility to Protect: Growing Pains or Early Promise?", *Ethics & International Affairs* 24(4): 349–365.

Molier, G. (2006) "Humanitarian Intervention and the Responsibility to Protect After 9/11", *Netherlands International Law Review* 53: 37–62.

Mooney, E. (1999) "In-Country Protection: Out of Bounds for UNHCR?", in F. Nicholson and P. Twomey, eds. *Refugee Rights and Realities: Evolving Concepts and Regimes*. Cambridge: Cambridge University Press, 200–219.

Ojeda, S. (2010) "Kampala Convention on Internally Displaced Persons: Some International Humanitarian Law Aspects", *Refugee Survey Quarterly* 29(3): 58–66.

Orchard, P. (2010) "The Perils of Humanitarianism: Refugee and IDP Protection in Situations of Regime-Induced Displacement", *Refugee Survey Quarterly* 29(1): 38–60.

Roberts, A. (1998) "More Refugees, Less Asylum: A Regime in Transformation", *Journal of Refugee Studies* 11(4): 375–395.

Roberts, A. (2011) "Refugees and Military Intervention", in A. Betts and G. Loescher, eds. *Refugees in International Relations*. Oxford: Oxford University Press, 213–235.

Rome Statute of the International Criminal Court, 17 July 1998, 2187 UNTS 3 (entered into force 1 July 2002).

Shacknove, A. (1985) "Who is a Refugee?", *Ethics* 95: 274.

Salibian v. *Canada* [1990] FCJ 454 (Canada, Federal Court of Appeal, 1990).

S v. *Federal Ministry of the Interior*, Austrian Administrative Court, 26 January 1994, 93/01/0034.

Solana, J. (1999) Secretary General of NATO, Press Conference, Wesley Clark, Supreme Allied Commander Europe of NATO (25 March 1999). [Online] Available at ⟨http://www.nato.int/kosovo/press/p990325a.htm⟩ (accessed 11 March 2011).

Snyder, J. (2011) "Realism, Refugees, and Strategies of Humanitarianism", in A. Betts and G. Loescher, eds. *Refugees in International Relations*. Oxford: Oxford University Press, 29–52.

Stahn, C. (2007) "Responsibility to Protect: Political Rhetoric or Emerging Legal Norm?", *American Journal of International Law* 101(1): 99–120.

Stamnes, E. (2009) "'Speaking R2P' and the Prevention of Mass Atrocities", *Global Responsibility to Protect* 1: 70–89.

Strauss, Ekkehard (2009) "A Bird in the Hand Is Worth Two in the Bush: On the Assumed Legal Nature of the Responsibility to Protect", *Global Responsibility to Protect* 1(3): 291–323.

Thakur, R. (2002) "Intervention, Sovereignty and the Responsibility to Protect: Experiences from ICISS", *Security Dialogue* 33(3): 324.

Thakur, R. (2009) "Next word on intervention", *The Japan Times*, 31 July.

Thakur, R., and T. Weiss (2009) "R2P: From Idea to Norm – and Action?", *Global Responsibility to Protect* 1: 22–53.

UN Commission on Human Rights, Resolution 30, 11 March 1980.

UN Commission on Human Rights, Resolution 29, 11 March 1981.

UN Commission on Human Rights, *Human Rights and Mass Exoduses*, 6 March 1990, (E/CN.4/RES/1990/52).

UN Commission on Human Rights, Resolution 2005/48.

UN Commission on Human Rights, *The Guiding Principles on Internal Displacement,* UN Doc. E/CN.4/1998/53/Add.2 (1998).

UNGA Resolution 35/124, 11 December 1980.

UNGA Resolution 35/196, 15 December 1980.

UNGA Resolution 44/164, 15 December 1989.

UNGA Resolution 46/127, 17 December 1991.

UNGA Resolution, *Human Rights and Mass Exoduses*, A/RES/48/139, 4 March 1994.

UNGA Resolution 558, U.N. GAOR, 50th Sess., Agenda Item 112(c), P6, UN Doc. A/50/558 (1995).

UNGA Resolution, *Human Rights and Mass Exoduses*, A/RES/54/180, 24 February 2000.

UNGA Resolution, *Human Rights and Mass Exoduses*, A/RES/56/166, 26 February 2002.

UNGA Resolution 58/177 (22 December 2003).

UNGA Resolution, *Human Rights and Mass Exoduses*, A/RES/58/169, 15 September 2003.

UNGA Resolution 60/1 (24 October 2005).

UN High Commissioner for Human Rights, *Human Rights and Mass Exoduses: Report of the High Commissioner for Human Rights Submitted Pursuant to Commission on Human Rights Resolution 1998/49,* E/CN.4/2000/81, 6 December 1999.

UN High Commissioner for Human Rights, *Human Rights and Mass Exoduses: Report of the High Commissioner for Human Rights, Submitted Pursuant to Commission on Human Rights Resolution 2000/55,* E/CN.4/2003/84, 17 January 2003.

UN High Commissioner for Human Rights, *Report of the High Commissioner for Human Rights on Human Rights and Mass Exoduses,* E/CN.4/2005/80, 25 January 2005.

UN High Commissioner for Human Rights, *Report of the High Commissioner for Human Rights on Human Rights and Mass Exoduses,* A/HRC/4/105, 14 March 2007.

UN High Commissioner for Refugees, ExCom Conclusion, No. 77 (adopted in 1995).

UN High Commissioner for Refugees, ExCom Conclusion, No. 87 (adopted in 1999).

UN High Commissioner for Refugees (2011a) *UNHCR warns of increased risk of mass displacement in Libya*, 18 March. [Online] Available at: ⟨http://www.unhcr.org/refworld/docid/4d834b502.html⟩ (accessed 25 March 2011).

UN High Commissioner for Refugees (2011b) *Côte d'Ivoire Situation*, 4 March. [Online] Available at: ⟨http://www.unhcr.org/refworld/docid/4d749c33c.html⟩ (accessed 25 March 2011).

UN High Commissioner for Refugees (2011c) "Safe At Last: Law and Practice in Selected EU Member States with Respect to Asylum-Seekers fleeing Indiscriminate Violence," 1 July.

UNHLP, High-Level Panel on Threats, Challenges and Change (2004) *A More Secure World: Our Shared Responsibility*. New York: United Nations.

UNSC (1994) Commission of Experts, *Final Report of the Commission of Experts Established Pursuant to Security Council Resolution 780 (1992)*, UN Doc S/1994/674, 27 May 1994.

UNSC (2006) *UN Security Council Resolution 1674 (2006): Protection of Civilians in Armed Conflict*, S/RES/1674, 28 April 2006.

UNSC (2011a) *UN Security Council Resolution 1970 (2011): Peace and Security in Africa*, S/RES/1970, 26 February 2011.

UNSC (2011b) *UN Security Council Resolution 1973 (2011): The Situation in Libya*, S/RES/1973, 17 March 2011.

UNSG (1981) *Report of the Secretary-General*, E/CN.4/1440, 27 January 1981.

UNSG (1983) *Human Rights and Massive Exoduses, Note*, Secretary-General, E/CN.4/1983/33, 10 January 1983.

UNSG (1989) *Report of the Secretary-General: Human Rights and Mass Exoduses*, A/44/622, 17 October 1989.

UNSG (1992) *Report of the Secretary-General: Human Rights and Mass Exoduses*, A/47/552, 21 October 1992.

UNSG (1994) *Report of the Secretary-General: Human Rights and Mass Exoduses*, E/CN.4/1995/49, 28 December 1994.

UNSG (2001) *Report of the Secretary-General: Human Rights and Mass Exoduses*, A/56/334, 10 September 2001.

UNSG (2003) *Report of the Secretary-General: Human Rights and Mass Exoduses*, A/58/186, 25 July 2003.

UNSG (2008) "Secretary-General Appoints Edward C. Luck of United States Special Adviser, Secretary-General", SG/A/1120, BIO/3963, 21 February 2008.

UNSG (2009) *Report of the Secretary-General: Implementing the Responsibility to Protect*, A/63/677, 12 January 2009.

UNSG (2010) *Report of the Secretary-General: Early warning, assessment and the responsibility to protect*, A/64/864, 14 July 2010.

Weiner, M. (1998) "The Clash of Norms: Dilemmas in Refugee Policies", *Journal of Refugee Studies* 11(4): 433.

12

Enhancing the capacities of state and regional institutions in transforming responsibility to protect from words to deeds: The case of Indonesia and ASEAN

Lina A. Alexandra

As a principle, Responsibility to Protect (R2P) has gained relatively wide acceptance at a rapid pace since it was first formally introduced through the release of the report of the International Commission on Intervention and State Sovereignty (ICISS) back in 2001. Within five years, the earlier reluctance to embrace R2P had shifted into a global step to endorse the principle as part of an effort to maintain international peace and security, particularly against mass atrocities anywhere in the world. At the UN World Summit in 2005, more than 150 countries gave their support to the R2P principle, which was then followed by the adoption of UN Security Council Resolution 1674 which affirmed the principle in 2006. This shows that the idea to reframe the global concern over such atrocities from emphasizing "intervention justified by humanitarian concern" into calling for "responsibility to protect", which lies primarily in the hands of the sovereign government, has become much more palatable.

However, the implementation of the R2P principle during the past few years has been far from the expectation. Cases, such as in Sudan, Côte d'Ivoire, and the latest, the "Arab Spring", where authoritarian governments used their strong military arm to suppress the people's calls for change, indicate that R2P has not yet become an accepted global norm. Furthermore, the UN Security Council resolution including critical reference to the R2P principle in the humanitarian crisis in Libya has sparked controversy over the decision to intervene in Libya (Cotler and Genser, 2011; Rieff, 2011). Meanwhile, in other regions such as Southeast Asia,

Norms of protection: Responsibility to protect, protection of civilians and their interaction,
Francis, Popovski and Sampford (eds),
United Nations University Press, 2012, ISBN 978-92-808-1218-3

where such potential is not imminent, the lack of action possibly arises from confusion over what needs to be done which can be considered as engaging R2P.

This chapter argues that in the context of Indonesia and Southeast Asia in general, the focus should be centred around efforts to build or strengthen the capacities of states and regional institutions in order to prevent the occurrence of serious human rights violations committed either by state authority or by other groups within the state. The fact that the four crimes covered by the R2P principle, i.e. genocide, war crimes, ethnic cleansing and crimes against humanity, are not considered as taking place in any country in Southeast Asia does not mean that countries will be immune to such threats in the future. Therefore, it is important to mainstream[1] the R2P principle first before actually moving on to capacity-building.

The chapter is divided into three parts. Section 12.1 elaborates on how the R2P principle has been understood so far by countries in the region, in particular, Indonesia. It also highlights the general views from civil society in Indonesia which are part of the result of the ongoing project of Mainstreaming R2P in Indonesia, with which I was involved from January 2010 until August 2011. Section 12.2 seeks to describe the capacities possessed by Indonesia and the Association of Southeast Asian Nations (ASEAN), which could be utilized or even enhanced to promote the implementation of the R2P principle, particularly in terms of the responsibility to prevent. Section 12.3 includes some recommendations for what needs to develop in order to raise the effort into responsibility to react in the future.

12.1 To what extent has R2P been understood in the region?

The R2P principle, which was unanimously adopted by the heads of state and government at the 60th session of the UN General Assembly in September 2005, as expressed in the *World Summit Outcome Document* (WSOD), is supported by three equally important and non-sequential pillars:

1 The responsibility of the state to protect its population from genocide, war crimes, ethnic cleansing and crimes against humanity. This responsibility entails the prevention of such crimes, including their incitement, through appropriate and necessary means (para. 138).
2 The responsibility of the international community to encourage and help states to exercise this responsibility to protect (para. 138).
3 The international community, through the United Nations, also has the responsibility to use appropriate diplomatic, humanitarian and other

peaceful means, in accordance with Chapters VI and VIII of the Charter of the United Nations, to help protect populations from war crimes, ethnic cleansing and crimes against humanity. In situations where a state fails to protect its population from such crimes and should the peaceful means be inadequate, then the international community is prepared to take collective action, in a timely and decisive manner, through the Security Council, in accordance with the Charter, including Chapter VII (para. 139).[2]

There are several points to underline from such elaboration. First, the pillars are equally important; no single pillar is more important than another. Second, R2P specifically stresses the aspect of prevention, rather than reaction. Third, R2P (especially the Second and Third Pillars) merely serves as a "call" or, to some extent, an "invitation", rather than a new legal obligation on states and the international community, in order to implement what they have already adopted. However, there are some dynamics that can be found in terms of its implementation, which are elaborated in the next sections.

12.1.1 Southeast Asian governments' position

Five years ago, head of states and governments showed their general support of the R2P principle. Despite some reservations, the international community has been of one accord in saying "never again" to genocide and crimes against humanity in the civilized world today. In Southeast Asia, the principle has been welcomed even by some that are considered to be authoritarian states. The governments have agreed to the scope of R2P which is limited to the four serious crimes, i.e. genocide, war crimes, ethnic cleansing and crimes against humanity. Therefore, the question of whether R2P is necessary or not is off the table.[3]

Nevertheless, governments in Southeast Asia are still questioning the circumstances when R2P should be implemented and who should be the "whistle-blower" if symptoms of any of the four serious crimes should arise. These problems were revealed during the debate at the UN General Assembly initiated by UN Secretary-General Ban Ki-moon back in 2009 over how R2P should be operationalized. As stated by the Malaysian Permanent Mission to the United Nations, "Collectively, we have not yet reached agreement on the exact parameters of R2P, including how we will conclusively decide when the Responsibility to Protect comes into being in any given situation."[4] Following this, the Singaporean representative raised the concern that R2P is prone to misuse, especially by certain powerful states who might invoke this principle in order to justify intervention into other states' territory for reasons beyond its scope.[5] Moreover, the Myanmarese representative argued that "the norm cannot be used to address all social ills but rather is narrowly focused on prevention of genocide, ethnic cleansing, war crimes and crimes against humanity".[6] Thus, Southeast Asian states remain wary of R2P due to the possibility that a widening of its scope beyond the four atrocity crimes might precipitate unwarranted international attention and intervention.

In a similar vein, some countries favour acknowledging R2P in its prevention aspect, rather than embracing all the components of R2P. While R2P is actually an indivisible "package" – starting from Pillar One which is the responsibility of the state to protect its populations, Pillar Two, the responsibility of the state to assist others to build their capacity to implement Pillar One, and Pillar Three which refers to the responsibility of the international community to protect, if the individual government fails to meet its obligation, by taking decisive and timely action to stop the crimes – countries in the region are still very reluctant to show strong support in embracing Pillar Three. The reason is simply that Pillar Three opens the possibility of the Security Council's authorizing multilateral action under Chapter VII of the UN Charter, which then specifically allows the use of coercive force into another's territorial sovereignty if necessary due to the situation on the ground. There is also somehow an argument that R2P as a whole is not relevant to the situation faced by Southeast Asian countries, and therefore not too urgent to be upheld so far. As explained by the representative from the Philippines, while commending the achievement to take up the R2P principle, it is important that stronger efforts should be made to have more clarity on the use of force to enforce R2P.[7] Then, rather than using the same words, the Indonesian representative came up with the view that "prevention is key" in the implementation of R2P.[8] In this case, the Indonesian government widely believed that R2P is strongly linked to efforts to strengthen the capacity of states in establishing good governance and application of the rule of law, which would eventually assist states to provide better protection for their populations.[9]

12.1.2 Indonesian civil society's position

In the context of Indonesia, the views of civil society are also relevant to be taken into consideration. Large numbers of non-governmental organizations (NGOs) engaging in issues related to human rights, conflict resolution, peacebuilding and inter-religious relations certainly play a significant role in the effort to search for local "R2P champions".

From interviews with several NGO representatives, it can be inferred that there is still a minimal understanding of what R2P is. Little information has been received by civil society, in this case academics, practitioners and activists, regarding the definition, the pillars and scope of R2P.

Only a few have heard about the principle and have basic knowledge of the key elements of R2P.[10] Most admitted that they do not have information about the position of the Indonesian government on R2P, nor on the recent development of R2P.

Regarding the scope of R2P, many do not know that the principle only applies specifically to four serious crimes, i.e. genocide, war crimes, ethnic cleansing and crimes against humanity. When asked whether such scope is sufficient, views are divided into those who propose to keep their focus within this scope and others who would prefer to include other issues such as poverty and natural disasters due to the magnitude of such problems in Indonesia. Furthermore, while some interviewees argued that genocide or crimes against humanity have never taken place in Indonesia, others claimed that those crimes have taken place before, such as in the operation to abolish communist activities back in 1965 and also in Papua and Aceh.

Nevertheless, there is general support for R2P. Some respondents clearly stated that R2P should be implemented in Indonesia due to the incidence of horizontal, i.e. inter-ethnic and inter-religious, conflicts. To a certain extent, many believe that ignorance on the part of state authorities concerning imminent and existing violence is itself a violation of their responsibility to protect. Concerning the potential act of intervention, which has been considered a sensitive aspect of R2P by the Indonesian government, there are mixed feelings among civil society groups. Those in the human rights field boldly stated that they have no objection to the possibility of foreign intervention, and would even invite such action if the government failed to meet its responsibility. They argue that sometimes the intention of foreign authorities to "interfere" would certainly place a certain pressure on the government to do what it has to in terms of protecting its populations. On the other hand, although it is a minority view, there is still a degree of worry that some countries, especially the developed countries, might potentially use human rights concerns as a way to justify their own interests to intervene into other states' domestic affairs.

Nevertheless, what must be highlighted from this exercise is the fact that civil society, without having sufficient knowledge of the R2P principle, has already taken up certain aspects of R2P, particularly the responsibility to prevent and rebuild. Some NGO activists have been heavily engaged in the reconciliation process in Maluku province by utilizing the local movement called BakuBae ("the spirit of peace") where the government seemed unable to deal with the situation (Malik, 2003). The BakuBae movement is basically a civilian movement which mobilized to stop the violence in Maluku that ravaged the area from 1998 to 1999. The movement was initiated by some facilitators, with victims as well as aggressors, including traditional societies, refugees inside and outside Ambon (the capital city of Maluku province), NGOs from Ambon, young people (from Ambon Island, the Lease Islands and Seram Island), college students, even housewives, disabled groups and society leaders in Ambon. There are now over 200 participants (Malik, 2003: 8–9). The activities, which may fall within the category of peacebuilding activities, range from victims' meetings, meetings of local parties, advocacy to parliament, international campaigning, and workshops for intellectuals, religious leaders and local leaders (ibid.: 5–36). Another coalition of NGOs has been active in putting together a draft Act on Managing Social Conflict, which was sent to the government and parliament in 2003 but has not yet received any response.[11] This, then, is a powerful example of civil society activists acting on the responsibility to prevent, illustrating not only the presence of cultural norms similar in theme to R2P, but also the significance non-state actors can have in responding to the need to prevent violence.

12.2 Capacities to implement R2P

Looking at the contexts in Indonesia and Southeast Asia in general, all those R2P ideas seem to fit in, while I might argue that such capacities in the region are pretty much still implicit and unexplored rather than actual. At the level of ASEAN, despite developments toward the promotion and protection of human rights, so far the exact phrase "responsibility to protect" is not to be found anywhere in any ASEAN document. Therefore, I look now at the traces of such capacities which can be found in national legislation as well as regional instruments that might reflect some elements of R2P.

12.2.1 National legislation

At the national level, one indicator to measure the capacities of the state to implement R2P is a package of national legislation that substantially addresses the pillars of R2P. So far, there are only five regulations which contain "traces" of R2P: (i) the Revised Indonesia Basic Constitution 1945; (ii) the People's Consultative Assembly Resolution No. XVII/MPR/ 1998 on Human Rights; (iii) the Human Rights Act No. 39/1999; (iv) the Human Rights Court Act No. 26/2000; and (v) the Presidential Order 40/2004 on the National Plan on Human Rights. However, all of these regulations have simply embraced the first pillar of R2P on the responsibility of the state to protect populations, and none has referred to the other two pillars.

The Revised Basic Constitution, in Section X A on Human Rights, Chapter 28 I (4) stated that "Protection, promotion, enforcement, and fulfillment of human rights is the responsibility of the state, which is primarily the government."[12] Then, the Charter of Human Rights as contained in the People's Consultative Assembly Resolution (TAP MPR) No. XVII/MPR/1998, which laid the framework for the subsequent Human Rights Act 39/1999, firmly stipulated that the protection, promotion and fulfilment of human rights shall be primarily under the responsibility of the government (Chapter 43). The Human Rights Act 39/1999 Chapter 8 emphasizes that the protection of human rights "shall be mainly under the responsibility of the government", while Chapter 71 formulates that "the government is having the obligation and is responsible to respect, protect, maintain and promote human rights as regulated in this Act, other regulations and international law on human rights which have been accepted by the State."

As part of the implementation of this Act, the National Human Rights Commission (Komnas HAM) was then established. It is to act as an independent entity, (yet) under the government, to monitor as well as to promote understanding of human rights.[13] The Commission, as part of its monitoring function, is entitled to make observations and to write an annual report on the implementation of human rights protection in the country and, more importantly, to conduct investigations if there is a strong allegation over the possibility of human rights violation having taken place (Chapter 89 (3)). This special authority of Komnas HAM is restated again in the Human Rights Court Act 26/2000 Chapter 18. It is stated that, if necessary, Komnas HAM may take the initiative to create an ad hoc team, together with other public elements, to conduct certain investigations.

Moreover, the Presidential Order 40/2004 on the National Action Plan on Human Rights 2004–2009 included six programmes for enhancing the promotion and protection of human rights, namely: (i) establishing and strengthening institutions to implement the human rights action plan; (ii) preparing to ratify international human rights instruments; (iii) preparing harmonization of various national regulations; (iv) dissemination and education on human rights; (v) implementation of human rights norms and standards; and (vi) monitoring, evaluation and reporting. The national government also stipulated the establishment of national committees and sub-committees, at both provincial and regency levels, to implement these programmes. It is interesting to note that in spite of recognizing the necessity to "balance" observance toward human rights standards and national conditions, it is firmly stated that human rights is universal in nature where the responsibility to implement lies on the shoulders of every government.[14]

Relating to the scope of R2P, only two national regulations make reference in some way to the crimes that fall within the scope of R2P. The Human Rights Act 39/1999, Chapter 33(1), refers to the rights of every person to be free from being tortured or receiving cruel, inhumane or undermining punishment or treatment. The actual words "gross human rights violations" can only be found in Chapter 104, which is particularly linked to the statement on the Human Rights Court. Then, in the Human Rights Court Act 26/2000, Chapters 7, 8 and 9 refer to genocide and crimes against humanity as serious human rights violations, but do not mention war crimes and ethnic cleansing.

12.2.2 Regional instruments

The evolution of ASEAN, particularly the developments of the past three years, has ideally opened up a chance for the regional institution to accelerate implementation of the R2P principle. The adoption of the ASEAN Charter in 2007 and in force since 2008, the elucidation of the ASEAN Community Blueprint, particularly the ASEAN Political Security Community (APSC) Blueprints as well as the later launch of the ASEAN Intergovernmental Commission on Human Rights (AICHR) have become the modalities for ASEAN to move forward in order to prevent, react and rebuild in relation to the occurrence of mass atrocities in the region. The step taken by ASEAN to incorporate promotion and protection of human rights (Article 1(7) of the ASEAN Charter) certainly links strongly with the spirit of the R2P principle.

In the APSC Blueprint 2009–2015, there are several programmes or activities which can be seen as contributing to the operationalization of the R2P principle, especially in developing regional capability on conflict prevention and an early-warning system. Besides the establishment of AICHR, as well as the ASEAN Commission on Women and Children (ACWC) and the ASEAN Commission on Migrant Workers (ACMW), ASEAN also plans to strengthen coordination between the network of existing human rights mechanisms, other civil society organizations, and relevant ASEAN sectoral bodies, to conduct or enhance exchange of information in the field of human rights among ASEAN countries in order to promote and protect human rights and also to promote education and public awareness on human rights.

Further, as part of promoting peace and stability in the region, ASEAN initiatives are to support poverty alleviation and the narrowing of development gaps. Some programmes are targeted at strengthening the capacity of regional experts in conflict prevention and peacebuilding as well as military capacity, such as developing and publishing an annual *ASEAN Security Outlook*; holding voluntary briefings on political and security developments in the region; developing an ASEAN early-warning system based on existing mechanisms to prevent occurrence or escalation of conflicts; and holding consultations and cooperation on regional defence and security matters between ASEAN and external parties and dialogue partners. Then, under the head of strengthening research activities on peace, conflict management and conflict resolution, there are initiatives to consider the establishment of an ASEAN Institute for Peace and Reconciliation; compile ASEAN's experiences and best practices on peace, conflict management and conflict resolution; enhance existing cooperation among ASEAN think-tanks to study peace, conflict management and conflict resolution; and develop a pool of experts from ASEAN member states as a resource for assisting in conflict management and conflict resolution activities. Under the promotion of regional cooperation to maintain peace and stability, ASEAN intends to establish a network among existing ASEAN member states' peacekeeping centres to conduct joint planning, training and sharing of experiences. Finally, as part of post-conflict peace-building, there are schemes to strengthening ASEAN humanitarian assistance (AHA) and to implement human resources development and capacity-building programmes in post-conflict areas.

Turning specifically to AICHR, in its Five-Year Workplan (2010–2015) there are several planned activities which may contribute to accelerating the implementation of R2P in the region. First, AICHR plans to enhance public awareness of human rights among the peoples of ASEAN through education, research and dissemination of information. Second, AICHR may obtain a copy of country reports submitted by ASEAN countries to the human rights bodies in the UN system. If this is not sufficient, the AICHR may also invite ASEAN member states to share additional and updated information in their country reports. Third, in an initiative to develop common approaches and positions on human rights matters of interest to ASEAN, the initial step is to identify current and potential human rights matters of interest to ASEAN.[15]

All these programmes and activities have the potential to contribute to Pillar Two, with its focus on the international community and regional organizations building protective capacities. However, without political willingness from state authorities, at both national and regional levels, to activate such capacities, they may remain idle capacities. So far, just a few AICHR commissioners have been notably active in engaging in dialogue with civil society to gather inputs on certain issues. If such interactions can be shared by the other commissioners, then there is a good chance of AICHR performing in an effective way. For now, the establishment of rules of procedure that set out specifically how AICHR should relate particularly with non-state stakeholders (i.e. individuals and groups) to address human rights situations is an urgent issue requiring follow-up.

12.3 What needs to be done?

Alex J. Bellamy argued that there are three ways in which the R2P principle can be advanced in order to translate the principle from words into deeds. The first is to clarify the conceptual limitations of the R2P principle, particularly on the prevention aspect where almost all social issues, such as economic inequality, underdevelopment and poverty, can be brought in. Second is to incorporate states and civil societies in developing practical measures, where he focuses on peacekeeping activities. Third is the importance of fostering institutional capacities, particularly non-military measures that might prevent mass atrocities (Bellamy, 2009: 119–124).

In relation to those views, some efforts can be made to enhance or even develop the capacities of state and regional arrangements in implementing R2P, as set out in the following sections.

12.3.1 Raising awareness of the R2P principle

It is crucial to raise awareness of the R2P principle among the public since they may ultimately be the victims if the state fails to fulfil its responsibility to protect. One way, in the long term, is actually through education on the subject of human rights, which is still very much lacking in Indonesia. In fact, the introduction of the R2P principle can be substantially included in this subject. In addition, other parties such as members of parliament and military officers and troops are among those who should also know about R2P.

Particularly in the context of Indonesia, efforts to introduce the R2P principle can be started by addressing existing cases, which perhaps so far cannot be considered as part of R2P's scope but carry the potential to escalate into crimes against humanity if ignored by the government. For example, recent cases where the authorities were unable to deal properly to prevent inter-religious tensions – such as the action of certain groups carrying the Islamic banner to crush the Ahmadiyah sect whose beliefs were claimed to deviate from true Islamic teaching – can be used to trigger discussion about the responsibility of the government to protect. In this case, the media was able to play a role in raising awareness, when one of the biggest national newspapers ran the headline "Negara Gagal Lindungi Warga" (The State Fails to Protect the People) when reporting on the incidents.[16]

Nevertheless, it is well understood that such a step brings the potential to "deviate" from what R2P means. Yet, without the ability to include some of the more contextual issues such as these, it will take a much longer time for R2P to be mainstreamed.

12.3.2 Creating national regulations to implement R2P

While governments have shown support for the R2P principle, as part of the implementation effort it is important to enact the commitment through the creation of legal frameworks at the national level. This is actually the most effective way to ensure R2P is accepted and observed in a real sense. By doing so, the global norm, like R2P, can somehow be internalized into the local context and become more relevant.

In the case of Indonesia, civil society has been trying to persuade the government and in 2003 delivered a draft regulation on managing social conflict; however, there has been no significant response since then as yet.[17] The draft, among other matters, regulates for the setting up of a Commission on Social Conflict Resolution (Komisi Penyelesaian Konflik Sosial; KPKS) as well as addressing how the government should deal with conflict prevention, cessation and post-conflict peacebuilding. It also supports the development of an early-warning system and how to involve different components within the state, both military and non-military resources, to deal with conflict.[18]

12.3.3 Engagement with civil society

Based on the facts above, it can be generally said that states in the region have a good understanding and, more importantly, support the R2P principle. However, the implementation of the R2P principle, stressing the primary responsibility of the state to protect its populations, cannot be realized without the involvement of a larger part of society or for the people themselves to actually invoke such responsibility. In this regard, the state cannot be assumed to be always aware of the need to take up its responsibility to protect the populations; it is certainly too important to be left in the hands of the government alone.

In this case, engagement with civil society is crucial to serve as a "wake-up call" for the government to respond before it is too late, and also as a control mechanism where the government holds the potential for being a perpetrator of crimes. Therefore, it is certainly important for civil society to understand the R2P principle and to know how they can actually collaborate together with their government to strengthen the state's capability to prevent the four R2P crimes from occurring. In Indonesia, since the reformation era in 1998, there is more room for civil society to speak out in putting pressure on and criticizing the government if there is any human rights violation.

At the regional level, ASEAN has announced its vision to become a people-centred organization (ASEAN Charter, Art. 1(13)). Also, in the terms of reference of the AICHR, one of the mandates and functions of AICHR is "to engage in dialogue and consultation with other ASEAN bodies and entities associated with ASEAN, including civil society organizations and other stakeholders, as provided for in Chapter V of the ASEAN Charter".[19] However, ASEAN still needs to prove whether such a vision will become a future reality.

12.3.4 The development of regional peacekeeping arrangements

In relation to establishing the APSC, one of the initiatives put forward by Indonesia, as Chair of ASEAN in 2011, is to "establish a network among existing ASEAN Member States' peacekeeping centres" (APSC Blueprint B.2.2.iii). As this network is expected to facilitate the conduct of joint planning, training and sharing of experiences among the national peacekeeping centres in (so far) Indonesia, Malaysia, Thailand, the Philippines and Cambodia, such activities will undoubtedly contribute to increasing the capacity of the region's armed forces. Despite the fact that the creation of regional peacekeeping forces, as proposed by Indonesia back in 2003, may still be far from a reality due to the concern of several member states that this instrument might be used to illicitly interfere in their domestic problems, yet this network could definitely serve as a basis to form such a regional arrangement in the future. By doing so, it is hoped that any situation that potentially leads to the outbreak of mass atrocities can be responded to in a timely and effective way; such a regional arrangement would reduce the "phobia" about non-ASEAN intervention. The examples of Aceh and Myanmar, when the host country required some degree of "ASEAN face" in the humanitarian missions, have indicated how an effective regional peacekeeping arrangement is important in promoting the implementation of the R2P pillars in Southeast Asia. In the case of Aceh, an Initial Monitoring Presence (IMP) was deployed in August 2005, with the task of monitoring the peace process as well as starting the confidence-building process in Acehnese society after the signing of a memorandum of understanding between the Indonesian government and the Free Aceh Movement. The IMP consisted of 80 monitors from the European Union and ASEAN countries, providing the basis for the creation of an ASEAN Monitoring Mission (AMM) a month later (Bivar, 2005). In the case of Myanmar, soon after Indonesia rejected the French Minister's call for the R2P principle to be applied in the emergency following Cyclone Nargis, Indonesia was able to push for ASEAN to take the leading role in order to gain access from the junta for international humanitarian assistance and then to coordinate the delivery of international aid (Bellamy and Drummond, 2011: 191).

Finally, what is critically important is the implementation and establishment of those various initiatives within the ASEAN framework. Some initiatives have already taken place, such as the establishment of AICHR;

some still need to be strengthened, such as the network between civil society in the region and ASEAN sectoral bodies; but some others are still vague in terms of implementation, such as the voluntary briefings on political and security developments in the region and also the establishment of an ASEAN early-warning system. Although it is clearly mentioned in the Blueprint, no steps have yet been taken to develop this early-warning system.

In conclusion, the word "voluntary" somehow reflects the nature of ASEAN itself which until now still maintains the consensus way in dealing with its internal issues. This mechanism certainly cannot guarantee that a state would be willing to open up a situation within its own country – although the incident might lead to the occurrence of any of the four crimes – to other countries in the region in order that the emergency be tackled as soon as possible through the regional mechanism. Unfortunately, the ASEAN early-warning mechanism would need to somehow work along these lines as well, with monitoring only occurring with the host state's consent. Political willingness from the member states of ASEAN is definitely an important factor.

12.4 Conclusion

R2P as a new – and, to a certain extent, contested – principle has gained traction among the countries in Southeast Asia. In spite of general acceptance of the principle by those countries, however, there are still many challenges to translate the way R2P should be implemented. Since Pillar Three of R2P allows multilateral action in using force under Chapter VII of the UN Charter if all normal procedures to deal with mass atrocities have been exhausted, R2P has been accepted with some caution. In this case, while protection of civilians is considered a well-accepted principle which has strong correlation with the R2P principle, countries in the region have been attempting to divert the focus toward measures of prevention and increasing the capabilities of each state to be able to protect the populations within their jurisdiction. Firm acceptance of the non-interference principle certainly plays a crucial role in shaping attitudes to R2P.

Indonesia, considered to be doing relatively well with its democratic path and human rights implementation, has the potential to advance R2P and even to serve as the R2P "champion" in the region. The progressive achievement in term of developing national instruments related to civilian protection, its keen involvement in pushing for the establishment of an ASEAN human rights body, as well as the existence of a vibrant civil society, illustrate some modalities possessed by Indonesia to support the implementation of R2P, especially Pillars One and Two. Finally, such focus emphasized by Indonesia would certainly enrich the discourse on how R2P can be internalized or contextualized at both the national and regional levels.

Notes

1. "Mainstreaming" here means to have a common understanding of what the R2P principle is and how it can be implemented. This is important since R2P can be understood or interpreted differently by different actors due to the different contexts where some countries, such as in Southeast Asia, do not see immediate challenges from the four crimes under the R2P principle. The fact that R2P is often perceived as similar to an interventionist act makes the effort towards mainstreaming this principle important.
2. A/60/L.1, 20 September 2005, paras. 138–139.
3. As stated by H.E. Ambassador Bui The Giang, Deputy Permanent Representative of Viet Nam, at the GA's Plenary Meeting on Responsibility to Protect (R2P), 24 July 2009.
4. Statement by Mr. Zainol Rahim Zainuddin, Charge D'Affaires of the Permanent Mission of Malaysia to the UN, at the General Assembly Debate on the Responsibility to Protect, New York, 28 July 2009.
5. Statement by Ambassador Vanu Gopala Menin, Permanent Representative of Singapore to the UN, at the Informal Interactive Dialogue on the Responsibility to Protect, 24 July 2009.
6. Statement by U Kyaw Zwar Minn, Deputy Permanent Representative of the Union of Myanmar to the UN, on Agenda Items 44 and 107, in the general debate of the 63rd session of the United Nations General Assembly, 23 July 2009.
7. Statement of H.E. Mr Hilario G. Davide, Jr., Ambassador Extraordinary and Plenipotentiary, Permanent Representative of the Republic of the Philippines to the UN, 23 July 2009.
8. Statement by H.E. Dr R.M. Marty M. Natalegawa, Ambassador, Permanent Representative of the Republic of Indonesia to the UN. "Follow-up to the outcome of the Millennium Summit" (Agenda Item 107), 23 July 2009.
9. Ibid.
10. After being briefed, most of the interviewees tried to link R2P with post-conflict peacebuilding, humanitarian action and human security, or even poverty, where they see the term "responsibility" also includes responsibility in providing for the basic needs of the people.
11. Interview with Mohamad Miqdad, Director of the Titian Perdamaian Institute, 9 November 2010.
12. Indonesian Basic Constitution 1945. This particular section on human rights was amended on 18 August 2000.
13. Elaboration concerning the National Human Rights Commission is in Chapter 75–103 of the Human Rights Act 1999. Based on an interview with a human rights activist, most of the functions of the Commission were referred from the Paris Principles (1991) and to a certain extent also, in terms of its structure, looked at the similar commissions in Australia and Canada. In this case, reflecting on the best practices and experiences of other countries may serve as a good example on how the First and Second Pillars of R2P are being implemented.

14. Attachment 1, Executive Order 40/2004 on National Action Plan on Human Rights, p. 55.
15. Five-Year Workplan of the ASEAN Intergovernmental Commission on Human Rights (2010–2015).
16. *Kompas,* 9 February 2011.
17. Interview with Mohamad Miqdad, Director of the Titian Perdamaian Institute, 9 November 2010.
18. Naskah Akademik Draft Rancangan Undang-undang tentang Penanganan Konflik Sosial (Draft Regulation on Management of Social Conflict).
19. Terms of reference of the ASEAN Intergovernmental Commission on Human Rights, on Mandate and Functions 4.8.

REFERENCES

Bellamy, Alex J. (2009) "Realizing the Responsibility to Protect", *International Studies Perspectives* 10: 119–124.

Bellamy, Alex J., and Catherine Drummond (2011) "The Responsibility to Protect in Southeast Asia: Between Non-Interference and Sovereignty as Responsibility", *Pacific Review* 24(2): 191.

Bivar, Caroline (2005) *Emerging from the Shadows: The EU's Role in Conflict Resolution in Indonesia.* EPC Issue Paper No. 44, December 2005. Brussels: European Policy Centre.

Cotler, Irwin, and Jared Genser (2011) "Libya and Responsibility to Protect", *New York Times*, 28 February.

Malik, Ichsan (2003) *BakuBae: The Community Based Movement for Reconciliation Process in Maluku.* Jakarta: Tifa Foundation and Yayasan Kemala.

Rieff, David (2011) "R2P, R.I.P.", *New York Times,* 7 November.

13

Towards a "responsibility to provide": Cultivating an ethic of responsible sovereignty in Southeast Asia

See Seng Tan

At the United Nations World Summit of 2005, member countries from the Association of Southeast Asian Nations (ASEAN) unexpectedly adopted the "responsibility to protect" doctrine – popularly known as R2P – concerning the protection of populations from genocide, ethnic cleansing, war crimes and crimes against humanity (UNGA, 2005). However, ASEAN states' responses to UN Security Council Resolution 1674 – which reaffirmed R2P and endorsed the use of appropriate measures where necessary to ensure its implementation – were relatively lukewarm.[1] The shared caginess among the Southeast Asians towards Resolution 1674 implied a collective adherence to sovereignty as the right of nations rather than a responsibility to the peoples whom they represent. As a senior official from Singapore once urged his ASEAN colleagues, any deviation from their regional organization's long-standing emphasis on the doctrines of sovereignty and non-interference would prove injurious to the region's stability, since the upkeep of those principles constitutes "the key reason why no military conflict has broken out between any two ASEAN countries since the founding of ASEAN" (Jayakumar, 1997). Arguably, even the academic consensus on ASEAN has continually fostered the impression that Southeast Asian states rarely flout their non-interference principle (Jones, 2010). Indeed, ASEAN's typical rationalizations of its own inaction in the face of domestic crises and intramural disputes within Southeast Asia have encouraged the perception of the Association as an effete organization, irrelevant to regional security other than for its members' own parochial ends.[2]

Norms of protection: Responsibility to protect, protection of civilians and their interaction,
Francis, Popovski and Sampford (eds),
United Nations University Press, 2012, ISBN 978-92-808-1218-3

However, despite their uneasiness regarding R2P, ASEAN states do not reject the idea of sovereignty *qua* responsibility. Recent scholarship has shown that while Southeast Asia, in real policy terms, has neither fully embraced R2P nor shown any willingness to do so in the foreseeable future, there is preliminary evidence to suggest that the region is not necessarily averse to the idea of responsible sovereignty (Bellamy and Beeson, 2010). Intriguingly, the respective positions of the ASEAN member states on R2P reflect an interesting diversity, ranging from democratic Indonesia's ambivalence to the concept to illiberal Singapore's involvement in the "Group of Friends" of R2P (which aims to facilitate dialogue between like-minded states at the level of the permanent missions to the United Nations in New York). Arguably, the region's efforts in response to a growing host of transnational challenges could open the R2P concept to revision in order to fit regional realities (Caballero-Anthony and Chng, 2009; Haacke, 2009a). As such, some ASEAN countries may not be as loath to the idea of responsibility to one's own population – and possibly even the populations of their Southeast Asian neighbours – as some might have (unfairly) assumed.

This chapter argues there is reason to suppose that Southeast Asian countries, some more than others, are cultivating, at least in an instrumental if not normative fashion, a "sovereignty as responsibility" ethic and are actively developing the means to implement it. This ethic is partly embodied in ongoing efforts to establish and enhance regional capacities and modalities to provide, as and when needed, various forms of assistance in response to primarily non-military challenges confronting the well-being of the region's societies. The chapter will examine the regional discourse on and policies of responsible provision at the heart of the region's institutional arrangements, particularly the ASEAN Defense Ministers' Meeting (ADMM) and its embryonic enlarged format, the ADMM+8 (the ASEAN ten plus Australia, China, India, Japan, New Zealand, South Korea, Russia and the United States). Arguably, it is not the responsibility to protect as much as the responsibility to *provide* which most concerns the Southeast Asian states (or most of them at least) for now.

13.1 Southeast Asians respond to R2P

It is worth recalling that variations of the R2P principle adopted at the 2005 UN World Summit and, alternatively, furnished by the UN Secretary-General's 2009 Report on R2P (UNSG, 2009) are somewhat different than the one originally presented in the report produced by the Canadian-sponsored International Commission on Intervention and State

Sovereignty (ICISS, 2001). Although the 2005 version employs the language of the ICISS report, it nonetheless rejects certain features recommended by ICISS, such as criteria to guide decision-making on when to intervene, a code of conduct for the use of the veto, and the prospect for the conduct of interventions not sanctioned by the UN Security Council (Bellamy and Beeson, 2010). The 2009 version contains four key points:

1 All states have a responsibility to protect their own populations from genocide, ethnic cleansing, war crimes and crimes against humanity;
2 The international community is duty-bound to encourage and assist states to fulfil their putative responsibility, including by helping them to build the requisite capacity;
3 The international community ought to employ, through the United Nations and/or regional organizations, diplomatic, humanitarian and peaceful means – and, as a last resort, coercive means – to protect populations from genocide, ethnic cleansing, war crimes and crimes against humanity; and,
4 The UN Security Council is prepared to adopt appropriate measures to achieve those same ends (UNSC, 2006).

Further, with the release of the UN Secretary-General's 2009 Report, the UN had by then identified three key considerations aimed at "operationalizing" R2P, and whose respective developments are not sequentially linked to one another. Rather than diluting the ICISS version as some have observed, others have argued that the 2009 version is in fact "a substantively stronger and more operational version" of R2P (Bellamy and Beeson, 2010; CSCAP, 2010):

Pillar One: Protective responsibilities of states;
Pillar Two: International assistance and capacity-building;
Pillar Three: Timely and decisive response (including military action) (UNSG, 2009: 2).

The Third Pillar, which essentially endorses robust and forceful intervention, if warranted, is particularly worrisome for both ASEAN and other countries (RSIS, 2010a: 8). The issue is further complicated by the UN Security Council's indecisiveness over Darfur and America's invasion and occupation of Iraq in 2003, both of which, among other things, posed significant problems for the conceptual integrity of R2P. As Thomas Weiss has pointedly observed, "Plotting the growing consensus [about R2P] on a graph would thus reflect a steady growth since the early 1990s whereas the operational capacity and political will to engage in humanitarian intervention – like the transformed humanitarian system – would seem to be on a rollercoaster" (Weiss, 2008: 742).

Yet, despite their shared circumspection towards R2P, important nuances and variances exist among the ASEAN countries in this regard. Adapted from Bellamy and Davies (2009: 551), Table 13.1 provides a

Table 13.1 ASEAN states' position on R2P

Advocates	Engagers	Fence-sitters	Opponents
Philippines (2004–2005)	Indonesia Philippines (2006–2008) Singapore Vietnam (2008)	Brunei Cambodia Laos Malaysia Thailand Vietnam (2005–2007)**	Myanmar*

*Myanmar has not explicitly rejected the idea that states have a responsibility to protect their own populations.
**Vietnam was almost opposed to R2P prior to the 2005 World Summit.

sense of the spectrum of regional views ranging from advocacy, engagement and fence-sitting to opposition vis-à-vis R2P.

The Philippines is unique in having openly advocated, at least for a time, R2P during its membership of the UN Security Council in the period leading up to the adoption of Resolution 1674. From a peak in 2004, Manila had, by the end of 2005, significantly reduced its usage of R2P-related language in UNSC debates and even privately resisted attempts to persuade the Council to reaffirm R2P immediately after the World Summit. This abrupt change may have resulted either from the Philippines' departure from the Security Council in 2005, or from growing concern over the potential use of R2P by outside actors in order to criticize the Aquino administration or intervene in the increasingly troubled peace process in Mindanao (Bellamy and Davies, 2009: 555). Be that as it may, the Philippines has consistently expressed initiatives in support of the implementation of R2P, such as capacity-building, interfaith dialogue, creation of rapidly deployable reserve forces for peace operations, and so forth. In 2009, the Philippines joined the Group of Friends of R2P.

Among the so-called "engager" countries, there are importance variations as well. Notwithstanding its reputation as Southeast Asia's only consolidated democracy, Indonesia demonstrated cautious support for R2P, but sought greater clarity on situations whereby the use of force might be appropriate, so as to avoid any misapplication. On the other hand, illiberal Singapore saw fit to join the Group of Friends. (Interestingly enough, both Indonesia and Singapore registered verbal support for the concept at the 2009 UN General Assembly session which debated R2P.) Vietnam started off as a "fence-sitter" with some serious reservations over the idea as a justification for pre-emptive attack against itself. At the same time, it also used the same General Assembly session to signal a significant change of mind (and subsequently evolved into an engager). But just how relevant these shows of support really were, in the eyes of critics, was partially "discredited" by Myanmar, whose political and practical opposition to the idea – without explicitly rejecting it – was "balanced", as it were, by its ostensible support for it in 2009 (Bellamy and Beeson, 2010). Finally, the other ASEAN countries have more or less remained noncommittal.

What could have conceivably triggered the developments in 2009 – Philippine membership in the Group of Friends, Indonesian and Singaporean rhetorical support for the 2009 UN General Assembly debate – was the post-Cyclone Nargis situation from a year before. In May 2008, the regional debate on R2P received a nudge in the wake of that devastating cyclone and the Burmese junta's initial refusal to accept foreign assistance. Dr Bernard Kouchner, the French foreign minister, invoked R2P to legitimize the forcible delivery of humanitarian assistance without the consent of the Myanmar government (Asia-Pacific Centre, 2008: 3; Le Monde, 2008). Others have likewise argued that R2P could be revised to include the provision of humanitarian relief as well as protection (Caballero-Anthony and Chng, 2009; Haacke, 2009a). At the same time, this enlarged understanding of the concept – R2P-plus, according to one formulation – is aimed at rendering it more palatable to Asian contexts.

In response, the concept's original architects have mostly been sceptical about the above efforts. Gareth Evans, a co-principal drafter of the ICISS report, cautioned against any move that might inadvertently unravel the international consensus on R2P by (as he saw it) imprudently linking it to the Burmese junta's post-cyclone blockage of foreign aid (Lee, 2008). Another contributor to the ICISS report, Ramesh Thakur, called for consideration of other avenues and modalities, such as: direct exchanges with the Burmese authorities; encouraging rather than threatening resolutions and statements at the United Nations by the Secretary-General and presidents of the General Assembly and Security Council; engagement of Myanmar by the major Asian powers (China, India and Japan); and engagement by ASEAN and Myanmar's ASEAN neighbours (Thakur, 2008).

Despite the efforts of the UN Secretary-General and the European Union, it was the last of Thakur's options, ASEAN engagement, which proved the most acceptable to Myanmar's generals, if only as a conduit for international assistance – reportedly in excess of US$600 million – furnished by twenty countries and the European Union (ASEAN, 2010). Maligned following the cyclone for its initial inaction, ASEAN consequently became the intermediary between a junta distrustful of foreign participation and an international donor community fearful of the deliberate diversion of aid from their target recipients. As Dan Collison, an official of Save the Children, a humanitarian agency that participated in the post-Nargis relief effort, noted, "ASEAN really stepped into the breach in the third week of May [2008] and provided a really vital bridge, if you like, between two fairly mistrustful sets of stakeholders. In terms of providing some predictable humanitarian space, it has worked very well" (cited in Baldwin, 2009). The ASEAN-led effort ended in July 2010 with the Myanmar government taking over the coordination role of the aid mission.

Notwithstanding the regional disquiet over R2P, the post-Nargis effort by ASEAN arguably reflects the existence of an embryonic responsible sovereignty – as provision, not protection, at least not yet – though clearly neither of a quality nor consistency that would necessarily satisfy the conditions of R2P.

13.2 The sovereign responsibility to provide

The logic of provision is not unique to Southeast Asia, even if regional political, strategic and possibly even cultural factors offer seemingly ready explanations as to why provision has hitherto trumped protection there. ASEAN leaders are neither alone in their guardedness about R2P nor alone in their apparent openness to the notion of sovereignty as a responsibility as much as a right. Despite long-standing criticisms about the region's relative illiberality and preoccupation with the non-interference doctrine, the logic of performance legitimacy typically invoked by ASEAN states – to which, for the most part, they have sought to live up, successfully or otherwise – as the basis of their moral and political authority clearly includes the element of responsibility (Alagappa, 1995). Following the Asian financial crisis of 1997–1998, it became evident that performance legitimacy should not be defined only in terms of a state's ability to maintain and enhance its economic competitiveness, but equally its capacity to provide its population with adequate social protections in times of crisis (Nesadurai and Djiwandono, 2009). Further, the uneven democratic transitions in the region facilitated a partial rethink on democratic legitimacy in Southeast Asia, even though only in the case of Indonesia can it be said with some confidence that democratic consolidation has indeed taken place (Caballero-Anthony, 2009; Case, 2002).

Obviously, all this has quite significant implications for the long-standing ASEAN doctrine of non-interference. As regional experiences have shown, the doctrine is not as sacrosanct as it has been made out to be, no matter the *ad nauseum* claims by Southeast Asian leaders regarding the non-violability of the doctrine. Indeed, under appropriate conditions, the principle has been contravened as often as it has been upheld for self-interested reasons, not least the shared aim to maintain a non-communist social order (Jones, 2009, 2010). Arguably, recent instances, particularly where Myanmar is concerned, suggest that wider collective concerns could have played a role in determining ASEAN's interventionist forays, successful or otherwise. For example, the Association's collective expression of its "revulsion" over the military junta's use of violence against the clergy-led demonstrations in 2007 could be seen as interference (ASEAN, 2007a). The preceding illustration of the Association's role in post-Nargis humanitarian assistance also holds interesting implications for the non-interference doctrine, a situation readily explained by the regional protagonists as non-interventionist because ASEAN was "invited" by the troubled member in question (Myanmar) to assume its role as conduit. Granted, interference by invitation is not really interference at all. When applied to Southeast Asia, however, it appears, at least in some instances, that invitations of this sort require a fair bit of moral and/or diplomatic suasion; as Singapore's former foreign minister, George Yeo, once mused about the ostensible efficacy of "peer pressure" among ASEAN members:

> But little by little, as we took into account each other's concerns, we were able to move forward. While ASEAN may work on the principle of consensus, ASEAN also works on the principle of peer pressure, and peer pressure can be very effective. And it is not easy for an ASEAN member country to take a rigid position when all the other nine countries are in opposition. (Yeo, 2011)

Similarly, at the wider Asia-Pacific level, the readily available conclusion among analysts that the ASEAN Regional Forum (ARF) has hitherto been unable or unwilling to implement preventive diplomacy because of an abiding obsession among the more conservative members of the ARF over the prospect of interference by others, while not incorrect, cannot fully account for why other security-oriented initiatives in the region have been actively engaging in preventive diplomacy-type activities (Emmers and Tan, 2011). Further, the likelihood that Southeast Asian governments will prevail on (and presumably collaborate with) one another to address a growing complex of risks and threats in the transnational security realm – challenges no country can manage on its own – has grown (Drummond, 2009). Drawing on these strands of evidence, it seems clear enough that ASEAN countries are not as bound by their own doctrines as previously thought, but indeed transgress existing conventions with apparent regularity, so long as political conditions prove sufficiently permissive and persuasive.

If not quite R2P, what is the likely understanding of responsible sovereignty among Southeast Asian countries? How, if at all, has such a responsibility been expressed in institutional and political practice? While the ASEAN states may have shown their declaratory support for R2P at the 2005 World Summit, their policy positions on the doctrine, as highlighted in the preceding section, range between advocacy, engagement, ambivalence and opposition. Significantly, as noted, Southeast Asian countries' views on R2P are not that far off the global mark, where implementation of R2P and the constraints that complicate it are concerned. Nor is the region's apparent willingness to countenance sovereign responsibility-as-provision anything close to a regional distinctive relative to the rest of the world.

Arguably, the growing importance of non-traditional security concerns in the Asia-Pacific region, and intergovernmental responses to such, offer a conducive environment for regional expressions of the so-called "responsibility to provide". Non-traditional security issues have emerged as areas most amenable to practical cooperation among regional countries (Haacke, 2009b; Severino, 2009). In the light of the ARF's obvious limitations as a security institution, there is growing appreciation in the region regarding the insufficiency of dialogue alone for dealing with regional humanitarian crises caused by natural disasters such as the Boxing Day 2004 tsunamis and the deadly earthquakes that have rocked Indonesia in recent times, and pandemics such the SARS crisis in 2003 and the avian flu/H1N1 crisis in 2009. It has long been acknowledged that many ASEAN countries are simply unable to cope with such challenges, given their lack of technical expertise and resources for taking on disaster relief functions. Some Southeast Asian militaries lack the requisite doctrine, equipment and preparedness for conducting non-military missions (or what defence establishments refer to as "operations other than war" or OOTW).[3]

Recent discursive and institutional developments in the region point to the existence of an incipient responsibility *qua* provision logic. Not yet a doctrine, it nonetheless underscores an evident readiness among some Southeast Asian governments to ensure the region possesses the requisite capacity to respond to crises of the sort that have blighted it in recent times. As noted, the Cyclone Nargis incident in 2008 elicited a lively regional debate on R2P, notwithstanding the admonitions issued by its progenitors against the perceived risk of conceptual dilution through enlargement (Evans, 2007; Thakur, 2008). Spurred partly by the unfolding humanitarian catastrophe in Myanmar, defence ministers at the Shangri-La Dialogue of 2008, a non-official annual forum for senior defence officials and intellectuals from Asia-Pacific and European countries, verbally agreed that multilateral cooperation in humanitarian assistance in disaster relief could be guided by three principles (IISS, 2008: 15):

1 The responsibility of disaster-hit countries to bring humanitarian relief quickly and effectively to their people;
2 Where necessary, affected countries should facilitate the entry of external assistance;

3 Any external help should have the consent of the affected countries and fall under their control.

In contrast to the appeal by some to broaden the R2P concept to include humanitarian challenges (Caballero-Anthony and Chng, 2009), the defence ministers at the Shangri-La Dialogue, much like Evans, Thakur and other R2P advocates, sought to avoid linking any collective response to Nargis with R2P. For instance, when invited to share what he and his fellow ministers discussed at their private ministerial lunch, the Singaporean defence minister sought to differentiate R2P from what he termed the "responsibility of governments to provide":

> The "responsibility to protect" is different. [R2P] was discussed extensively at the UN World Summit in 2005. That responsibility is very specifically defined to cover instances of genocide, war crimes, ethnic cleansing and crimes against humanity. I think, here, we are talking generally about the responsibility of governments to provide. And in the end, it is the people in the country and in the international community who will be the ultimate judge of whether or not governments of those countries have lived up to their responsibilities. (Teo, 2008)

In other words, while the list of concerns identified by R2P doctrine as rightfully justifying military action remains a highly sensitive matter for ASEAN states, humanitarian emergencies are quite a different kettle of fish altogether. Accordingly, Southeast Asian governments – at least in that minister's view – ought to exercise their sovereign responsibility to provide for their own peoples' security and well-being. However, in the absence of any such ability, regional governments ought to do their utmost to ensure that *other* resources are brought to bear in realizing those same objectives. As Teo Chee Hean (2008), Singapore's deputy prime minister, has put it, the responsibility to provide – the R2Provide, as it were – can be defined as "a responsibility of all national governments to provide for the welfare of the people. If they are not able to provide for it, then it is their responsibility to see what other resources they can garner to help provide for the people." Interestingly, the R2Provide, as understood here, is not couched in terms of the responsibility of *other* nations to furnish what the nation in question lacks in providing for its population. Rather, the onus remains with the latter; it has a *dual* responsibility to provide for its own people, on the one hand, and, failing which, to seek foreign assistance to get the job done on the other. Why so? Because, as should be obvious by now, of the continued discursive primacy of the non-interference doctrine in Southeast Asia, which renders unlikely any prospect for a potentially contradictory doctrine to emerge at this juncture.

Notwithstanding the careful avoidance of unwarranted conflation of the R2Provide with R2P, the preceding elite ruminations on the responsibility to provide have not precluded the appropriation of language with a canny resemblance to the first two pillars identified in the UN Secretary-General's 2009 Report on R2P, namely, (1) protective responsibilities of states and (2) international assistance and capacity-building. The key exception here, of course, is the emphasis on provision rather than protection. That being said, others have argued that the fundamental wrangle Southeast Asian countries have with R2P is not the notion of protection per se as much as that of military intervention as an accepted "protective" response – ostensibly to prevent external interference. According to a report on a regional consultation on R2P, Southeast Asian governments are generally agreeable to protective responsibility and provision of assistance to others, and may even grudgingly accept the need for timely and decisive intervention, but only through diplomatic and not military means (RSIS, 2010a: 3). Conceivably, the R2Provide could, in time, assume the following characteristics (in the form of non-sequential "pillars" analogous to R2P):

Pillar 1: Southeast Asian states have a responsibility to ensure the survival of their citizens in times of natural calamities (floods, tsunamis, earthquakes and the like) by providing them with food, water and shelter.

Pillar 2: The international community and regional organizations have the responsibility to work consensually with individual Southeast Asian states to build capacity to be able to aid their member states when they are confronted by natural disasters.

Pillar 3: When a Southeast Asian state is unable to provide for its citizens in times of natural disasters, and is for whatever reason unwilling to allow international actors to do so, it is the collective responsibility of that state and ASEAN members and regional partners to come to a diplomatic solution, with respect to reasonable security concerns of that state in question, to ensure a humanitarian crisis is averted.[4]

Needless to say, discursive reflections and sentiments alone are not a sufficient condition to presuppose the existence of a responsibility-as-provision ethic in Southeast Asia. On the other hand, despite the general failure of countries worldwide to implement R2P – although military intervention to establish a no-fly zone in Libya in 2011 to prevent Gaddafi's forces from killing unarmed civilians could conceivably fit the bill – some see their declared commitment to the doctrine rendered at the UN World Summit of 2005 as an indication that R2P has evolved unquestionably from mere idea to global principle.[5] Dialogue aside, to what extent Southeast Asian governments are prepared to assume the responsibility to provide for their own populations – and/or those of their regional neighbours – remains to be seen. In this regard, recent institutional developments, specifically the ASEAN Defense Ministers' Meeting (ADMM) and the related ADMM+8 processes, could conceivably become the regional mechanism through which the responsibility to provide can be nurtured as a regularized convention cum practice throughout Southeast Asia.

The ADMM was launched in May 2006 in Kuala Lumpur, Malaysia. At the fourth ASEAN Summit in Singapore in 1992, the decision was taken to upgrade the status of regional security cooperation from an informal and loose enterprise to a sanctioned feature of the Association's official agenda (ASEAN, 1992). Near the end of the Cold War, defence and security relations, for the most part bilateral, among Brunei, Indonesia, Malaysia, the Philippines, Thailand and Singapore – the so-called "ASEAN-6" – were sufficiently thick to merit being described by a top Indonesian general as forming a "defense spider web" (Acharya, 1990: 1). By the time the ADMM – "the highest defense mechanism within ASEAN", according to ASEAN's official website – was established, the leaders of ASEAN had already, in 2003, initiated the process to form the ASEAN Security Community (later changed to the ASEAN Political-Security Community, APSC) with 2020 (later brought forward to 2015) as the envisaged date of completion.

As a key component of the ASEAN Political-Security Community, the ADMM has four objectives (ASEAN, 2006):

1 To promote regional peace and stability through dialogue and defence and security cooperation;
2 To serve as a sort of "top-level management" for extant defence and security cooperation within ASEAN and between ASEAN and its dialogue partners;
3 To promote mutual trust and confidence through enhancing transparency and openness;
4 To contribute to the establishment of the APSC and promote the implementation of the APSC's Vientiane Action Program (VAP).

At the second ADMM in Singapore in November 2007, ASEAN defence ministers approved the concept paper on the "ADMM-Plus", which provides for the ADMM's engagements and interactions between ASEAN and its dialogue partners – the basis, in short, for the ADMM+8. Importantly, the concept paper acknowledged that "ASEAN's future was increasingly intertwined with the developments of the larger Asia-Pacific region, and that the region would benefit from the expertise, perspectives and resources of extra-regional countries" (ASEAN, 2007b). In 2009, a second concept paper, this time on the principles of membership of the ADMM-Plus, arguing that the ADMM "needs to be plugged into the external environment", reiterated the need for the active engagement of "friends and dialogue partners" in ways that would allow ASEAN to draw on "the varied perspectives and resources of a wide range of non-ASEAN countries" in addressing the security challenges facing Southeast Asia (ASEAN, 2009). The inauguration of the ADMM+8 occurred in Hanoi in May 2010 as a formal expression of the ADMM-Plus formula. Specifically, the area of non-traditional security considerations – humanitarian assistance and disaster relief (HADR), military medicine, counterterrorism, maritime cooperation and peacekeeping – were identified at the Hanoi gathering as matters on which ADMM+8 member countries are to collaborate. Non-traditional concerns have been selected, presumably because they are viewed as less sensitive than traditional or hard security concerns (Capie and Taylor, 2010a).

What should not be missed here is the publicly articulated rationale behind these formal defence arrangements. Baldly stated, Southeast Asia's active engagement with the defence establishments of the world's major and middle powers – or at least those among the eight dialogue partners in the ADMM+8 – is aimed at tapping their technical know-how and resources to accomplish complex tasks in maritime security or HADR; in short, drawing on external assistance for (as the euphemism goes) building regional capacity. What the ADMM and ADMM+8 provide, as such, are frameworks for institutionalizing and possibly enhancing the existing but largely informal forms of assistance from dialogue partner countries to the ASEAN members. Significantly, this type of capacity-building assistance is by no means new. For example, since 2000 the Japanese Coast Guard has been providing direct assistance to Southeast Asian states in support of antipiracy operations in a variety of ways, while the United States has been a major benefactor in facilitating counterterrorism and antipiracy activities conducted by several Southeast Asian states (Ho, 2009). Further, as a consequence of Southeast Asia being in the Pacific "ring of fire", the proneness of its landscape to natural disasters has accentuated the role of regional militaries in disaster management (and the imperative to ensure they are empowered and equipped to do so). As Singapore's defence minister has acknowledged:

> Armed forces too have a crucial role to play in humanitarian assistance and disaster relief. They have the resources and manpower to fulfill an important quick response role in the crucial first stages of disaster relief and rescue operations. Armed forces can transport aid to where it is needed most in the affected locality and help in its distribution. It is not the value or quantity of the relief supplies. The question is whether they can be delivered in a prompt and effective manner to the last mile, down to the actual victims who need it, when they need it. Armed forces in turn can pave the way for civilian agencies and

international organizations to follow up in the subsequent phases of disaster management. There is one key objective in such operations – bringing relief speedily and effectively to the victims. (Teo, 2008)

The perceived need to furnish relief for victims of a disaster in a fast and effective manner is a key expression of the responsibility to provide. In this regard, the Three-Year Work Program of the ADMM and the Two-Year Activity Work Plan (2010–2011) adopted by the ASEAN Chiefs of Defense Forces Informal Meeting (ACDFIM) are equally important to the ongoing process of developing standard operating procedures, referred to in this context by the acronym SASOP (Standard Operating Procedures for Regional Standby Arrangements and Coordination of Joint Disaster Relief and Emergency Response Operations). These procedures include things such as a template for the roles and terms of reference for both provider countries and recipient countries that would enhance interoperability among ADMM+8 militaries in disaster management.[6] Indeed, it could even be argued through facilitating reportage – voluntary, at best – of their military assets for disaster management, ADMM+8 countries would actually be contributing to a limited version of a regional arms register. In this respect, ASEAN leaders are seeking to establish a regular submission process via the ASEAN Coordinating Centre for Humanitarian Assistance on disaster management (AHA Centre) and the ASEAN SASOP. Moreover, while these forms of capacity augmentation are mostly concerned with the defence-related assets of Southeast Asian governments, there is growing awareness among regional stakeholders that building local, societal-level capacities is equally necessary to ensure more effective and rapid responses to disasters, while reducing reliance on their national governments (Kuntjoro and Jamil, 2010). As evidenced by the serious constraints in early warning and post-crisis rescue efforts vis-à-vis Indonesia's "twin disasters" in November 2010 – the earthquakes and tsunami at the Mentawai Islands and volcanic eruptions at Mount Merapi – this is a poignant concern for peripheral regions that are difficult to reach.

To be sure, frameworks and work programmes, no matter how impressive, are irrelevant without the concerted and sustained efforts by regional countries and their defence establishments to fulfil their commitments. Arguably, a motivation behind the formation of the ADMM and ADMM+8 was the perception – held by some in regional defence circles – that the ARF was simply not faring as it should. Indeed, some have even hinted that the ARF, with its inability to graduate beyond being just a talking shop, serves as a model of what *not* to do if progress in security cooperation were the goal. Some have also alluded to the likelihood of resentment among some regional defence practitioners for their secondary role and status in the ARF, a regional arrangement initiated and helmed by foreign policy practitioners.[7] Formed in 1994, the ARF was designed to satisfy the need for a cooperative security enterprise linking ASEAN to its major partners in Northeast Asia and North America. The security agenda of the ARF, as conceived by its architects, was ambitious, covering both traditional as well as non-traditional (or, more specifically, non-military) issues (Simon, 2007: 20). But as noted, the general ineffectiveness of the ARF in managing traditional security concerns in the Asia-Pacific is well known. This has conceivably contributed to a renewed interest in the ARF as a regional platform for non-traditional matters with cross-border ramifications (Haacke, 2009b; Severino, 2009).

As institutional manifestations of the R2Provide ethic, the ADMM and ADMM-Plus processes are clearly oriented towards enabling the ASEAN states to collectively provide, for their and their neighbours' peoples, a fair measure of respite from humanitarian challenges. Significantly, it is the defence establishments of Southeast Asia that have taken the lead in this regard. By no means devoid of "sovereignty as right" considerations – memorably, Indonesia's proposal for a regional peacekeeping element in 2003 drew lukewarm responses from several ASEAN members (Bandoro, 2004) – the emphasis on regional capacity-building and assistance vis-à-vis non-traditional concerns has proved sufficiently salient to warrant a collective buy-in from regional stakeholders. In this sense, the contributions of the Shangri-La Dialogue deserve acknowledgement as well, not least as a context for regional debate of R2P and the development of the responsibility *qua* provision ethic, or for that matter, the idea that an annual (albeit informal) defence ministerial in Asia is not as asinine an idea as some might have initially thought (Capie and Taylor, 2010b). But it is early days yet, with little hitherto said about how the ADMM and ADMM+8 relate to the ARF, given that their interests and agendas overlap. Indeed, it is precisely this sort of ad hoc proliferation of regional arrangements with evidently overlapping remits that has led many to question the inherent incoherence of Asia-Pacific regionalism and to advocate the streamlining of the region's institutional architecture.

13.3 Conclusion

Despite their declaratory commitment to the responsibility to protect made at the UN World Summit in 2005, Southeast Asian countries have generally been reluctant fully to accept R2P, largely out of concern over the doctrine's endorsement of the use of military force in its implementation. However, this reluctance has not precluded the development, more generally, of an ethic of responsible sovereignty and, specifically, the logic of responsibility as provision, or R2Provide, in the region. To be sure, that development has been uneven, as implied, say, by the obduracy of Myanmar's military regime regarding the Burmese people's well-being. At the same time, ASEAN's long-standing principles of sovereignty and non-interference continue to be invoked by Southeast Asian governments to ward off potentially intrusive security ideas and practices, not least R2P. But as this chapter has sought to show, those same countries are not averse to circumventing established conventions as and when it suits their respective national – and increasingly shared – interests. As a capacity-building enterprise that significantly enhances regional responses to particular non-traditional security challenges with potentially acute humanitarian ramifications, the responsibility to provide has evidently found a measure of resonance and ready acceptance with and by regional stakeholders. That said, even as stakeholders have taken the initiative to enhance ties between ASEAN and its dialogue partners through innovating regional arrangements that facilitate capacity-building and knowledge-cum-technology transfers, it remains to be seen how these incipient modalities will complement rather than compete with established institutions.

That most Southeast Asian nations – Myanmar is a significant exception – generally accept their lot as responsible providers, but not quite yet as responsible protectors, suggests that the logic of implementing a doctrine by force – the Third Pillar of the UN Secretary-General's 2009 Report on R2P – is still anathema to Southeast Asians out of fidelity to the non-interference principle and concern over their contested territories. And if theorists of "norm localization" are right in claiming the localization of global norms in Southeast Asia through a process of contextualization (Acharya, 2004) – as a recent study has persuasively suggested regarding R2P and Southeast Asia (Bellamy and Beeson, 2010) – then responsibility *qua* provision rather than protection is likely due to the pervasive influence of regional conditions and conventions, particularly the "ASEAN Way", although there have been hints that the ASEAN Way is incrementally evolving (Caballero-Anthony, 2005). Whether the road to R2P in Southeast Asia runs through the responsibility to provide, as understood here, remains at best an intriguing but hitherto ambiguous prospect.

Notes

1. As the proceedings of a recent policy roundtable on the R2P concluded, "ASEAN states are generally agreeable to the principles of RtoP, but some are uneasy about its potential impact on ASEAN's noninterference principle" (RSIS, 2010b: 5).

2. An unpublished review by ASEAN suggested that only about 30% of the initiatives taken over the years have been implemented (Desker, 2008).
3. Indeed, regional armed forces such as the Tatmadaw of Myanmar have historically been focused on counterinsurgency and are, as such, latecomers to force modernization and expansion, which arguably began in 1988 (Maung, 2009).
4. The author is indebted to Dr Hugh Breakey for help in formulating these R2Provide "pillars".
5. At an academic-practitioner workshop on protection of civilians (POC) and the R2P jointly organized by the United Nations University and three Australian universities, held at the Sydney Law School on 17–18 November 2010, a former UN Assistant Secretary-General forcefully defended the *World Summit Outcome Document* as proof that the R2P is indeed a global norm.
6. Author's interview with Singapore defence officials, 14 September 2009. Also see ASEAN (2007b) and MINDEF Brunei (2010).
7. Author's interview with Singapore defence officials, 14 September 2009.

REFERENCES

Acharya, Amitav (1990) "A Survey of Military Cooperation among the ASEAN States: Bilateralism or Alliance?" Occasional Paper 14. Toronto: Centre for Strategic and International Studies, York University.

Acharya, Amitav (2004) "How Ideas Spread: Whose Norms Matter? Norm Localization and Institutional Change in Asian Regionalism", *International Organization* 58(2): 239–275.

Alagappa, Muthiah, ed. (1995) *Political Legitimacy in Southeast Asia: The Quest for Moral Authority*. Stanford, CA: Stanford University Press.

ASEAN (1992) "Singapore Declaration of 1992", 28 January. [Online] Available at: ⟨http://www.aseansec.org/5120.htm⟩.

ASEAN (2006) "Concept Paper for the Establishment of an ASEAN Defense Ministers" Meeting", 9 May. [Online] Available at: ⟨http://www.aseansec.org/19892.htm⟩.

ASEAN (2007a) "Statement by ASEAN Chair: Singapore's Minister for Foreign Affairs George Yeo", New York, 27 September. [Online] Available at: ⟨http://www.aseansec.org/20974.htm⟩.

ASEAN (2007b) "ADMM-Plus Concept Paper", 14 November. [Online] Available at: ⟨http://www.aseansec.org/21216.pdf⟩.

ASEAN (2009) "Concept Paper on ASEAN Defense Ministers' Meeting-Plus (ADMM-Plus): Principles for Membership", 26 February. [Online] Available at: ⟨http://www.aseansec.org/18471-e.pdf⟩.

ASEAN (2010) "ASEAN SG Thanks Friends and Partners for Post-Nargis Support", 27 August. [Online] Available at: ⟨http://www.aseansec.org/25136.htm⟩.

APCR2P, Asia-Pacific Centre for the Responsibility to Protect (2008) "Cyclone Nargis and the Responsibility to Protect", Myanmar/Burma Briefing 2, 1 May, Brisbane: Asia-Pacific Centre for the Responsibility to Protect, University of Queensland.

Baldwin, Kevin (2009) "ASEAN Finds New Purpose with Cyclone Nargis Response", *AlertNet* (Thomson Reuters Foundation), 1 May. [Online] Available at: ⟨http://www.alertnet.org/db/an_art/55076/2009/04/1-125433-1.htm⟩.

Bandoro, Bantarto (2004) "Undesirable Consequences of an ASEAN Peacekeeping Force", *Jakarta Post*, 2 March.

Bellamy, Alex J., and Mark Beeson (2010) "The Responsibility to Protect in Southeast Asia: Can ASEAN Reconcile Humanitarianism and Sovereignty?", *Asian Security* 6(3): 262–279.

Bellamy, Alex J., and Sara E. Davies (2009) "The Responsibility to Protect in the Asia-Pacific Region", *Security Dialogue* 40(6): 547–574.

Caballero-Anthony, Mely (2005) *Regional Security in Southeast Asia: Beyond the ASEAN Way*. Singapore: Institute of Southeast Asian Studies.

Caballero-Anthony, Mely, ed. (2009) *Political Change, Democratic Transitions and Security in Southeast Asia*. London: Routledge.

Caballero-Anthony, Mely, and Belinda Chng (2009) "Cyclones and Humanitarian Crises: Pushing the Limits of R2P in Southeast Asia", *Global Responsibility to Protect* 1(2): 135–155.

Capie, David, and Brendan Taylor (2010a) "Two Cheers for ADMM+", *PacNet* 51, 20 October.

Capie, David, and Brendan Taylor (2010b) "The Shangri-La Dialogue and the Institutionalization of Defense Diplomacy in Asia", *Pacific Review* 26(3): 359–376.

Case, William (2002) *Politics in Southeast Asia: Democracy or Less*. Richmond, UK: Curzon.

CSCAP, Council for Security Cooperation in the Asia Pacific (2010) "Final Report of the CSCAP Study Group on the Responsibility to Protect (RtoP)", First Meeting, 26–27 February. [Online] Available at: ⟨http://www.cicp.org.kh/download/asean-isis%20and%20cscap/CSCAP%20RtoP%20Study%20Group%20-%20First%20Meeting%20Final%20Report.pdf⟩.

Desker, Barry (2008) "Is the ASEAN Charter Necessary?" *RSIS Commentaries* 77/2008, 17 July. Available at: ⟨http://www.rsis.edu.sg/publications/Perspective/RSIS0772008.pdf⟩.

Drummond, Catherine (2009) "Noninterference and the Responsibility to Protect: Canvassing the Relationship Between Sovereignty and Humanity in Southeast Asia", *Dialogue e-Journal* 7(2). [Online] Available at: ⟨http://www.polsis.uq.edu.au/dialogue/articledrummond2.pdf⟩.

Emmers, Ralf, and See Seng Tan (2011) "The ASEAN Regional Forum and Preventive Diplomacy: Built to Fail?", *Asian Security* 7(1): 44–60.

Evans, Gareth (2007) "Gareth Evans Offers Five Thoughts for Policymakers on R2P", 13 April. [Online] Available at: ⟨http://www.responsibilitytoprotect.org/index.php/component/content/article/35-r2pcs-topics/932-gareth-evans-offers-five-thoughts-for-policy-makers-on-r2p⟩.

Haacke, Jürgen (2009a) "Myanmar, the Responsibility to Protect and the Need for Practical Assistance", *Global Responsibility to Protect* 1(2): 156–184.

Haacke, Jürgen (2009b) "The ASEAN Regional Forum: From Dialogue to Practical Security Cooperation?" *Cambridge Review of International Affairs* 22(3): 427–149.

Ho, Joshua H. (2009) "Southeast Asian SLOC Security", in Shicun Wu and Ke-yuan Zou, eds. *Maritime Security in the South China Sea: Regional Implications and International Cooperation*. Aldershot, UK: Ashgate, 157–176.

ICISS, International Commission on Intervention and State Sovereignty (2001) *The Responsibility to Protect*. Ottawa: International Development Research Centre.

IISS, International Institute for Strategic Studies (2008) *Report of The Shangri-La Dialogue: The 7th IISS Asia Security Summit,* Singapore, 30 May–1 June, London: International Institute for Strategic Studies.

Jayakumar, Shunmugam (1997) Opening Statement by Foreign Minister Shunmugam Jayakumar of Singapore, ASEAN Ministerial Meeting, Subang Jaya, Malaysia, 24 May. [Online] Available at: ⟨http://www.aseansec.org/4002.htm⟩.

Jones, Lee (2009) "ASEAN and the Norm of Noninterference in Southeast Asia: A Quest for Social Order", *Nuffield College Politics Group Working Paper*. Oxford: Nuffield College, University of Oxford.

Jones, Lee (2010) "ASEAN's Unchanged Melody? The Theory and Practice of Non-Intervention in Southeast Asia", *Pacific Review* 23(3): 479–502.

Kontjoro, Irene A., and Sofiah Jamil (2010) "Strengthening RI's Disaster Preparedness", *Jakarta Post,* 4 November. [Online] Available at: ⟨http://www.thejakartapost.com/print/286877⟩.

Le Monde (2008) "Burma: Article by M. Bernard Kouchner", Minister of Foreign and European Affairs. 20 May. [Online] Available at: ⟨http://www.ambafrance-sg.org/IMG/pdf/BURMA_ARTICLE_BK.pdf⟩.

Lee, Matthew Russell (2008) "Rebranding Responsibility to Protect, Gareth Evans says Somalia's not covered", *Inner City Press*, 17 September. [Online] Available at: ⟨http://www.innercitypress.com/r2p1evans091708.html⟩.

Maung, Aung Myoe (2009) *Building the Tatmadaw: Myanmar Armed Forces since 1948*. Singapore: Institute of Southeast Asian Studies.

MINDEF Brunei (2010) "7th ASEAN Chiefs of Defense Forces Informal Meeting (ACDFIM)", 26 March, Ministry of Defense, Brunei Darussalam. [Online] Available at: ⟨http://www.mindef.gov.bn/MOD_Brunei2/index.php/news-mainmenu2-92/670-7th-asean-chiefs-of-defense-forces-informal-meeting-acdfim⟩.

Nesadurai, Helen E. S., and J. Soedradjad Djiwandono, eds. (2009) *Southeast Asia in the Global Economy: Securing Competitiveness and Social Protection*. Singapore: Institute of Southeast Asian Studies.

RSIS (2010a) *Report of the Regional Consultation on the Responsibility to Protect (RtoP)*, 8–9 April. Organized by the RSIS Centre for Nontraditional Security (NTS) Studies. Singapore: S. Rajaratnam School of International Studies.

RSIS (2010b) *Report of the Policy Roundtable on Civilian Protection: Issues and Challenges*, 9 February. Organized by the RSIS Centre for Nontraditional Security (NTS) Studies and funded by the Australian Responsibility to Protect Fund and the MacArthur Foundation Asia Security Initiative. Singapore: S. Rajaratnam School of International Studies.

Severino, Rodolfo C. (2009) *The ASEAN Regional Forum*. Singapore: Institute of Southeast Asian Studies.

Simon, Sheldon W. (2007) *Asia and Its Security Offspring: Facing New Challenges.* Carlisle, PA: Strategic Studies Institute, US Army War College.

Teo, Chee Hean (2008) "Plenary Speech by Minister for Defense Teo Chee Hean at the Shangri-La Dialogue 2008", 1 June. [Online] Available at: ⟨http://www.mindef.gov.sg/imindef/resources/speeches/2008/01jun08_speech.html⟩.

Thakur, Ramesh (2008) "Should the UN Invoke the 'Responsibility to Protect'?", *Globe and Mail,* 8 May. [Online] Available at: ⟨http://www.responsibilitytoprotect.org/index.php/component/content/article/172-asia-pacific/1666-ramesh-thakur-should-the-un-invoke-the-responsibility-to-protect⟩.

UNGA (2005) *UN General Assembly Resolution 60/1: World Summit Outcome Document,* A/Res/60/1, 16 September 2005. [Online] Available at: ⟨http://daccess-dds-ny.un.org/doc/UNDOC/GEN/N05/487/60/PDF/N0548760.pdf?OpenElement⟩.

UNSC (2006) *UN Security Council Resolution 1674 (2006): Protection of Civilians in Armed Conflict,* S/RES/1674, 28 April 2006. [Online] Available at: ⟨http://daccess-dds-ny.un.org/doc/UNDOC/GEN/N06/331/99/PDF/N0633199.pdf?OpenElement⟩.

UNSG (2009) *Report of the Secretary-General: Implementing the Responsibility to Protect,* A/63/677, 12 January. [Online] Available at: ⟨http://www.un.org/preventgenocide/adviser/pdf/SG%20Report%20R2P.pdf⟩.

Weiss, Thomas G. (2008) "R2P after 9/11 and the World Summit", *Wisconsin International Law Journal* 24(3): 741–760.

Yeo, George (2011) Remarks by Minister for Foreign Affairs George Yeo and His Reply to the Supplementary Questions in Parliament During the Committee of Supply (CoS) Debate, 3 March. [Online] Available at: ⟨http://app.mfa.gov.sg/2006/press/view_press.asp?post_id=6820⟩.

14

Interaction of the norms of protection

Vesselin Popovski

Norms and laws originate in various backgrounds and traditions, they advance historically in parallel and often overlap and interact. Questions arise as to whether, how and when their interaction is beneficial or counter-productive for international law and for world peace. In editing a major recent volume, Roberta Arnold and Noelle Quenivet (2008) looked comprehensively at this issue. They argued in favour of the complementarity of international humanitarian law (IHL) and human rights law (HRL), but at the same time they acknowledged possible risks. They did not go so far as to advocate a "merger" of the two branches of law, as the title of the book provocatively suggested. They correctly concluded "that IHL and HRL are two distinct categories with their specific aims and fields of application. However, particularly in grey area situations such as military occupation or insurgencies, their complementary application may guarantee the respect of the rule of law" (ibid.: 592). Contributing a chapter for the same volume – on the protection of children as the most vulnerable group in the population – I argued in a similar way, that overlap between IHL and HRL could be problematic, but it could also be beneficial:

> There is a need to identify possible gaps in protection, make sure that children do not fall in these gaps, and that each branch does not over-estimate the other. IHL and HRL should complement each other and, where necessary, interplay with other regimes (refugee law) as to offer full protection and best care for all children, in all circumstances, in all times. (Arnold and Quenivet, 2008: 385)

Norms of protection: Responsibility to protect, protection of civilians and their interaction,
Francis, Popovski and Sampford (eds),
United Nations University Press, 2012, ISBN 978-92-808-1218-3

Turning now to two more specific norms – the protection of civilians (POC) and the responsibility to protect (R2P) – I would like to attempt to discuss in a similar critical way the benefits of interaction and the perils of confusion.

The norms, POC and R2P, originate in similar humanitarian concerns and had a long existence in the history of Just War principles and the norms of war. However, they have often been deliberately ignored by warlords and governments. The recent attention to and development of POC and R2P was triggered by a massive failure to protect innocent people over the last two decades – in Rwanda, the former Yugoslavia, Congo, Darfur, Syria and elsewhere. The norms gained a strong global acceptance and universality: R2P was enshrined in Articles 138–140 of the *World Summit Outcome Document* (WSOD) in 2005. POC, evolving from the 1949 Fourth Geneva Convention, has been strengthened through numerous Security Council resolutions to become a core obligation of UN member states and UN agencies today. The text of the UN Security Council resolutions 1970 and 1973 (on Libya, 2011) illustrated the interaction of the two norms and can be seen as a textbook example of the joint applicability of R2P and POC.

In this final chapter of the book, I reflect on the joint applicability of POC and R2P and argue – contrary to some observers[1] – that the danger of irreconcilability between the two norms is not as great as the benefit of their interaction. In a similar way as for child protection mentioned above, I would argue in this chapter that the mutual reinforcement of R2P and POC is essential so as not to leave gaps in protection and to ensure that all groups of people are protected in all situations, both during and after armed conflict, from all present or potential deadly risks.

14.1 The protection of civilians

POC in armed conflict is an historical norm – its origin goes back to early ethical and religious considerations of just war and was developed by scholars of military history, politics and ethics over many centuries (Popovski, Reichberg and Turner, 2009). The need to protect civilians in armed conflicts has been gradually accepted in IHL, universalized and codified in the 1949 Fourth Geneva Convention "Relative to the Protection of Civilian Persons in Time of War" (ICRC, 2005). The POC norm has evolved as relevant to armed conflicts only. Civilians, in comparison with combatants, are vulnerable: they do not possess weapons, equipment or training to survive the hardship of war and, therefore, they need special care and protection.

This book has demonstrated how POC has been a constant topic in the UN Security Council's discussions, resolutions and documents over the last dozen years. The norm has expanded recently with various UN peacekeeping missions – authorized by the Security Council – accepting POC as part of their mandates. The UN agencies with protection mandates – the Office for the Coordination of Humanitarian Affairs (OCHA), the United Nations High Commissioner for Refugees (UN-HCR), the International Committee of the Red Cross (ICRC) – and humanitarian NGOs interpret POC as one of their core activities and apply it not only during armed conflict, but also in protecting civilians in post-conflict situations. Following these developments, one can certainly consider POC to be a much broader concept today than in the 1949 Fourth Geneva Convention. One warning should be made that expanding POC endlessly is undesirable – no need to equate it, for example, with the protection of citizens (also POC in abbreviation) in time of peace, as this would effectively merge the norm with human rights protection – a much broader regime. POC is a norm with a specific application and should remain focused on civilian victims of warfare or internal disturbances.

14.2 The responsibility to protect

R2P emerged as a norm after failures to protect people from mass atrocities, such as genocide, war crimes and crimes against humanity. These grave international crimes, notorious and universally condemned as such, needed a robust response.

However, similarly to POC, R2P did not suddenly emerge in 1999 out of Kosovo. Kosovo was the trigger indeed, but how to protect people from mass atrocities has been a long historical consideration. One can find roots of R2P in various international laws, such as the 1948 Genocide Convention, the 1949 Geneva Conventions, and in the statutes and practice of international criminal tribunals. R2P inherits moral as well as legal obligations. It is often associated entirely with so-called "humanitarian intervention" (Chandler, 2009); R2P in fact came as a challenge to the inconsistencies in both the doctrine and practice of humanitarian intervention.[2] What R2P does is to shift the focus from the interests of intervening states to the interests of potential victims of atrocities. R2P, in comparison with humanitarian intervention, contains large preventive and rebuilding aspects – it is not a response-only concept. And even in its responsive aspect, it has three pillars and only the third part of the Third Pillar is about intervention, after the other two options of diplomacy and sanctions have been exhausted.

R2P builds on an idea of Francis Deng who, in co-editing a fundamental study *Sovereignty as Responsibility* (Rothchild et al., 1996) on conflict prevention in Africa, challenged the millennia-old concept of sovereignty and argued that sovereignty can no longer be a platform to abuse people, rather it bears a responsibility to protect people from threats to their lives and well-being. The then UN Secretary-General Kofi Annan wrote similarly about this paradigm shift from an old to a modern concept of sovereignty (Annan, 1999).

After the controversial and unauthorized military intervention by NATO in Kosovo, the International Commission on Intervention and State Sovereignty (ICISS) was set up and produced an important report (ICISS, 2001). R2P was globally accepted, when in September 2005 in New York almost 150 world leaders adopted the WSOD (UNGA, 2005).

The UN General Assembly continued to address R2P in several of its sessions, with a strong majority of member states supporting the concept, and very few countries still reluctant to accept it. In parallel the UN Secretary-General encouraged his Special Adviser on Prevention of Genocide and his Special Representative on R2P (now a joint office) to develop the concept (UNSG, 2009, 2010, 2011).

R2P applies to mass human-made atrocities, but it is a narrow concept with clear limits. It does not cover all violations of human rights, nor does it address suffering from natural disasters. When Cyclone Nargis struck Myanmar in May 2008 and the government was recklessly ignorant of the resultant human suffering from flooding, an R2P claim would have been possible under the original scope of the ICISS 2001 Report, but not under what was agreed by the UN General Assembly in the 2005 WSOD.[3] The cyclone in May 2008 in Myanmar is a good example of a situation where R2P does not need to be utilized. It is a narrow concept, but one can utilize other mechanisms – human rights machinery, humanitarian assistance – instead of R2P, and still help people in need.

14.3 Comparing R2P and POC

POC attempts to protect all potential and actual victims of conflict and combat, whereas R2P focuses on particularly evil and criminal practices – such as deliberate targeting and extermination of groups of population.

A short and a simplified distinction would be to say that POC is a norm that protects people in general from a wide spectrum of threats, whereas R2P is a norm that protects smaller groups of people, but from more serious, well-defined crimes.

The two norms can be combined when mass atrocities are committed in a time of armed conflict. The massacre of Armenians in Turkey during the First World War, and the Holocaust of Jews in Nazi Germany during the Second World War, are clearly R2P crimes, but they also represent massive failures to protect civilians in time of war – they effectively triggered the adoption of the POC norm in the Fourth Geneva Convention.

POC addresses the suffering of all civilians in time of war or internal disturbances, whereas R2P addresses only those who could be victims from systematic mass extermination, and not necessarily in time of war. As presented in this book, the two norms share a similar initial humanitarian impulse, but they have different applications. R2P demands the addressing of atrocity crimes that are not necessarily part of an armed conflict; whereas POC demands addressing the vulnerability of civilians during or after armed conflict. The application of the two norms can overlap – yet they remain distinct.

To illustrate – the civilian victims of war crimes, as well as of crimes against humanity committed during armed conflict, would fall under both R2P and POC; in these situations R2P and POC would overlap. An example of a situation that would fall under POC, but not R2P, would be protection of civilians threatened from escalating armed conflict, if mass atrocities are not planned and committed as part of such armed conflict. If the two sides in the war fight by the rules and do not commit crimes against humanity, R2P is not relevant, but POC is – civilians need to be protected from suffering even in purely *jus in belli* situations.

A situation that would fall under R2P, but not POC, would be, for example, ethnic cleansing or crimes against humanity, planned and committed without any link to an armed conflict. For example, the massive massacre of innocent people in Cambodia by the Khmer Rouge regime of Pol Pot in 1976–1979 would fall under R2P, but not POC – the latter norm being relevant only in a situation of armed conflict, or internal disturbance.

The differentiation between R2P and POC is subtle and can be confused, but it is an important one to keep in mind. R2P is narrower than POC; it would not apply to general human suffering in time of war, short of a situation of systematic mass atrocities, planned or committed. But POC could also be narrower than R2P, as it needs the threshold of armed conflict or internal disturbance to be applicable.

A further complication comes from the fact that situations can change and what originally was not an armed conflict can escalate into such and activate POC. To illustrate with Libya – the first Security Council resolution (Res. 1970) addresses violence against peaceful demonstrators (not yet an armed conflict) and activates – in a more preventive mode – R2P (potential crimes against humanity). The second Security Council resolution (Res. 1973) describes the situation as a civil war – a fight between government and rebels, no longer peaceful riots – and accordingly the whole scope of international humanitarian law and POC becomes applicable. The text of Resolution 1973, interestingly, demands POC not only from the Gaddafi regime, but also from the rebels.

14.4 POC and R2P are integral to state sovereignty

One popular myth about R2P is that the norm suggests a contravention against state sovereignty. R2P is easily equated with intervention, or an act against the consent of a state, and accordingly, an argument – unsubstantiated and intellectually confused – is made that POC should be detached from R2P, as the latter is about intervention. R2P, if examined closely, in fact reconciles sovereignty and intervention.

Indeed, sovereignty and intervention have been in tension for centuries, but the two concepts are remarkably integrated in R2P. The major evolution of R2P was exactly in defining a *responsibility*, rather than a *right* of "humanitarian intervention". There is very little about intervention in the R2P norm – many of its demands lie entirely within the sovereignty and the consent of all states. In fact everything in Pillar One, Pillar Two and the first part of Pillar Three is based on states' consent. Even when it comes to the last part of Pillar Three – sanctions and military intervention – these can be activated only through the authorization of the Security Council – a clear and non-disputed constitutional legal choice.

The missing proper understanding of R2P leads to warnings that R2P needs to be "detached" from POC, so as not to "contaminate" it. Instead, what needs separation is R2P from the notion of military intervention. UN peacekeepers and agencies, instead of worrying about R2P, may find in Pillar One and Pillar Two great scope for fruitful interaction. R2P has a massive focus on and scope for prevention, that can be useful for many missions, including those involving POC. For example: exercising successful responsibility to prevent will result in fewer mass atrocities, fewer refugees and internally displaced persons (IDPs), fewer victims and accordingly a lighter workload for UNHCR, OCHA, UNICEF, the World Food Program (WFP) and others. These agencies can regard R2P as a norm that helps them, rather than hindering them.

R2P – in its preventive stage – does a lot of work that helps POC. But I would argue that this is true not only in the preventive stage – the mere option of a robust, last resort, Pillar Three response could be a very important tool for most of what POC aims to achieve. Often it is that last resort, even if not put into practice, that can induce tyrants to consider stopping violence. If the last resort is removed from the choice of options, the diplomacy and the economic sanctions will be less productive. Therefore, I would argue that Pillar Three, with its three sub-pillars – diplomacy, sanctions and military intervention – represents exactly the balanced framework within which POC actors may achieve their goals more easily.

One has to stop equating R2P with military intervention, understand it as a global responsibility for human survival in the face of universally accepted crimes, such as genocide and crimes against humanity, condemn these crimes and undertake measures – individually or collectively – to protect people. R2P needs its robust last-resort option just because genocide and crimes against humanity are not usual human rights violations – they are so extreme that people need a higher level of international protection when domestic jurisdiction fails. When faced with the possibility of genocide, states agree that their sovereignty includes a responsibility to protect people from such atrocities. Therefore, R2P does not violate states' sovereignty – it exists inside it. People are not at the mercy of their rulers,[4] they are under the protection of their rulers.

If a state lacks the domestic capacity to protect, it can invite bilateral, regional or global assistance (Pillar Two) to enhance this capacity, and sovereignty is not affected. Sovereignty remains integral to R2P even in Pillar Three – unwilling to protect – situations. If a state manifestly fails to protect, or engages deliberately in genocidal actions, I would argue that such a state's behaviour, not R2P, renders sovereignty questionable, invites negotiations and diplomacy, and if these are also ineffective, the Security Council – annulling the domestic jurisdiction obstacle (Art. 2/7 of the Charter) – imposes sanctioning measures. The imposition of sanctions is an act of fifteen sovereign states – Security Council members – acting on behalf of 193 sovereign UN member states (Art. 25) who made an original and sovereign commitment to accept and implement voluntarily any resolution of the Security Council. Paradoxically, even the state against which the sanctions are imposed is (under the Art. 25 obligation) required by its mere membership in the UN to implement the decisions of the Security Council. Therefore state sovereignty is fully respected at every level of R2P, and with this understanding states accepted the norm in 2005. There is no tension between R2P and state sovereignty – the R2P norm is part of the sovereignty norm. There is no single situation where R2P should raise any doubt of abusing state sovereignty.

R2P has little to do with military intervention not only in theory, but also in practice. The Pillar Three situations since the R2P was adopted in 2005 include Sudan over Darfur, Kenya for few months in 2008, Kyrgyzstan in the summer of 2010, Côte d'Ivoire and Libya in the first half of 2011, and Syria today.

Libya demonstrated the triumph (see Evans, 2011; Bellamy et al., 2011) and Syria the fiasco, of R2P and POC. In Libya in 2011 the full and deepest scope of the norms' implementation was utilized, for the first time since they emerged. Pillar One, domestic R2P, was demanded in Security Council Resolution 1970. When this responsibility was manifestly ignored, with Gaddafi threatening a rebellious population with massacre, R2P shifted to the international community – and the UN and regional organizations engaged the full scope of Pillar Three measures: negotiations, diplomatic pressure, sanctions and – when all these proved ineffective – authorization for use of force, explicitly for POC purposes. The removal of Gaddafi from power was nowhere stated as an aim in the resolutions and had nothing to do with POC and R2P. Regime change may, indeed, happen at the same time as exercising R2P and POC, but one differentiation is crucial – "Who Did What?" It was the people of Libya who overthrew Gaddafi. If the Libyan people had wanted Gaddafi to stay in power, he would have been in power today, no matter who may have intervened or what the Security Council resolutions may have prescribed. Nothing that happened in Libya in 2011, therefore, should do any damage to R2P or POC. One needs to distinguish between genuine efforts to protect civilians at risk, and actions by the same actor(s) for other purposes. Certainly, not everything that NATO did in Libya should be associated with R2P or POC: supplying the rebels with weapons and munitions – in fact, violating the arms embargo of the Security Council – had nothing to do with R2P and POC.

I would argue that the R2P fiasco in Syria became, sadly, the "collateral" victim of the proper exercise of R2P in Libya. What happened was that Russia and China manipulated the Libyan situation, linking R2P with regime change – in my view entirely incorrectly – and threatened to use their veto continuously in the Security Council, effectively to keep a murderous regime in power and assisting the massacres of innocent people. Russia and China manifestly failed their own responsibility to protect in Syria, at the same time blaming those who exercised responsibility to protect and saved the lives of thousands of people in Benghazi and elsewhere in Libya in 2011. Gaddafi would not have been less murderous than Bashar al-Assad, but he was prevented from committing crimes against humanity.

Many do not like to talk about R2P, and this is not surprising, as it involves the horror of crimes against humanity and the highly politically charged and controversial responses to these crimes. R2P might not be as harmonious and diplomatic as are the other topics in the UN agenda. Talks about R2P will always emerge when innocent people are facing deadly risks, and urgent actions are necessary. These situations, naturally, will not be easy to handle. R2P will be invoked in very critical circumstances, which will always be political, controversial and problematic.

Norms and laws do not necessarily disappear if they are disliked or abused. Despite many violations they progress to stand firm today as opportunities to restrict tyrants' power. R2P similarly will not disappear, though some may not like it or may ignore it. Genocide and crimes against humanity are extreme and controversial situations, and often they cannot be dealt with through consensus.

14.5 Interaction of POC and R2P

This book argues that the two norms, POC and R2P, can coexist in a mutually beneficial interaction. If properly understood, not confused and simplistically associated with military intervention, the interaction between the two norms represents a major conceptual achievement and a strong practical opportunity.

One such opportunity for POC-R2P interaction is the building of regional capacities that can be instrumental for both protection norms. R2P has inherited from the African Union the norm of non-indifference (2000 Constitutive Act, Article 4(h)), under which the African states have agreed that the African Union can intervene in a member state "in respect of grave circumstances, namely war crimes, genocide and crimes against humanity" through diplomatic and peaceful measures and, as a last resort, with the use of force. Article 4(h) allows the African Union to intervene militarily and later to receive Security Council authorization.

The R2P and POC norms have been mainstreamed within various institutions of the European Union (see Helly, 2008) and have been recently advanced in the Asia-Pacific region.[5] Even in East Asia a commitment is emerging to build norms and capacities to prevent mass atrocities and it would be very encouraging to see the R2P and POC norms developed and terminology added in the regional organizations' charters.

Another important task is to produce greater clarity on specific capacities, measures and tools and to ensure policy coherence with efforts related to, but not solely focused upon, realizing R2P and POC. There is also a need to streamline the distinct strategies required for the prevention of violence and effective responses in settings of ongoing violence. More South-South, region-to-region learning would certainly help. Moving R2P and POC norms from words to deeds and ensuring their normative entrenchment is a long-term process, but there are indications that R2P and POC can shift from a rhetorical to a substantive role.

Both R2P and POC contain preventive and reactive measures, but stop short of demanding prosecution of perpetrators of violations. Discussion and analyses of the protection of civilians and the prosecution of perpetrators have hitherto proceeded along separate lines. It would be interesting to foresee a dynamic where international protection and prosecution agendas draw closer together.

In terms of POC-R2P capacity-building, other opportunities would be to identify the needs for enhanced early-warning systems; strengthen regional standby forces; empower additional organs, for example the Peace-building Commission, with mandates and finance; develop national R2P and POC implementation strategies; and increase assistance in developing states' capacities to prevent and protect.

The evolution of R2P and POC from 1999 to the present is illustrative of the difficult road and the many uncertainties experienced between the birth of norms and their transformation into policy. However, this has been an impressively fast normative evolution – an academic formula that turned into a major global agreement on how to protect civilians and respond to mass atrocities.

14.6 Conclusion

The parallel conceptualization and rapprochement of POC and R2P in the last decade saw the universal acceptance of R2P and the increasing presence of POC in peacekeeping mandates. These parallel evolutions created the opportunity for the cross-utilization of R2P and POC in tandem, demonstrated in this book. We, the authors, have attempted to elaborate on the potential for the interaction between R2P and POC and we see this interaction as a crucial factor in ensuring that no groups or individuals remain unprotected in the face of atrocities. Unfortunately, the two norms are often confused and misused; we have warned against misinterpretations and pointed out some gaps. We "protected" the two norms of protection from confusion and looked at how they may interact and reinforce each other.

The two norms are indeed in a dialectical relationship. They have similarities and differences; they can support each other, but they can also be misused. On balance, I do not see much danger of rapprochement between R2P and POC, rather an opportunity for synergy. I find it more useful to elucidate the opportunity for interaction between the norms, to find ways in which they can operate more efficiently. Ultimately, rejecting synergies between the two norms closes the door to a wider pool of normative resources to assess breaches of international law.

States and agencies opposing the interaction between R2P and POC often confuse them and fail to distinguish their specifics. They just take Pillar Three only, and its final, military option, and simplistically argue that the interaction between R2P and POC could be problematic. Such arguments do not recognize the exceptional nature of R2P – dealing with atrocities such as genocide – which makes it inherently contentious. To say that peacekeeping operations will find it difficult to engage in Pillar Three coercion is obvious to all.

These arguments also do not recognize that the major application of R2P is in Pillar One and Pillar Two. Only in a small minority of countries in the world at any time can one confidently define Pillar Three necessity and, in those cases, the scope for consent-based, peacekeeping interventions is more limited. POC as part of peacekeeping missions would be – naturally – more difficult in situations of foreign military intervention; however, only a small part of R2P is about foreign military intervention.

R2P and POC have much in common and the Secretary-General's 2009 Report, *Implementing the Responsibility to Protect*, made this clear by linking R2P to many UN activities, including peacekeeping and conflict prevention.

States and agencies may misinterpret the norms – either to avoid their obligations or to pursue selfish national interests – but this does not make the norms useless. Violating the law should not always make the law disappear. If an aggressor misuses R2P or POC language to justify an intervention, this does not necessarily make the norms problematic. R2P and POC are not originally "imperialist" concepts to justify military intervention; they were born from the horrors of Rwanda and Srebrenica, out of the cries for help by the dying victims of genocide. R2P and POC, accordingly, do not sit comfortably with dictators, aggressors and criminal warlords. And they should not create worries among peacekeepers and UN agencies. If understood and used correctly, R2P and POC can effectively reduce human suffering and eliminate threats faced by civilians around the world.

Notes

1. Respecting Chatham House rules, I will not reveal names but, demonstrating a current fear of associating POC with R2P, some observers went so far as to say that they cannot attach their names to anything that puts POC and R2P in the same sentence.
2. These inconsistencies are revealed in Wheeler (2002).
3. For analysis, see APCR2P (2008).
4. This has been a result of a long evolutionary development of the concept of sovereignty in political theory from the times and writings of Hobbes or Weber – who regarded sovereignty as unlimited absolute power – until the modern understanding of sovereignty as a responsibility that is accepted today.
5. The Asia Pacific Centre for the Responsibility to Protect has been established and it engages in very active promotional and educational work (⟨http://www.r2pasiapacific.org/⟩).

REFERENCES

Annan, Kofi (1999) "Two Concepts of Sovereignty", *The Economist* 8 September, 49–50.

APCR2P, Asia Pacific Centre for the Responsibility to Protect (2008) *Cyclone Nargis and the Responsibility to Protect*, Myanmar/Burma Briefing No. 2 by the

Asia-Pacific Centre for the Responsibility to Protect, 16 May 2008. [Online] Available at: ⟨http://www.r2pasiapacific.org/documents/Burma_Brief2.pdf⟩.

Arnold, Roberta, and Noelle Quenivet (eds.) (2008) *International Humanitarian Law and Human Rights Law: Towards Merger in International Law.* Leiden: Martinus Nijhoff.

Bellamy, Alex, Tom Weiss, Jennifer Welsh et al. (2011) "Libya, RToP, and Humanitarian Intervention", *Ethics & International Affairs* 25(3).

Chandler, David (2009) "Unravelling the Paradox of the 'Responsibility to Protect'", *Irish Studies in International Affairs* 20(1): 27–39.

Evans, Gareth (2011) "Ending Mass Atrocity Crimes: The R2P Balance Sheet After Libya", the Second Renate Kamener Oration, Leo Baeck Centre, Melbourne, 31 July 2011.

Helly, Damien (2008) "R2P, Africa and the EU: Towards Pragmatic International Subsidiarity?", EU Institute for Security Studies, November 2008. Available at: ⟨http://www.iss.europa.eu/uploads/media/R2P_Africa_EU.pdf⟩.

ICISS, International Commission on Intervention and State Sovereignty (2001) *The Responsibility to Protect: Report of the International Commission on Intervention and State Sovereignty.* Ottawa: International Development Research Centre, December 2001.

ICRC (2005) "Convention (IV) relative to the Protection of Civilian Persons in Time of War. Geneva, 12 August 1949", *International Humanitarian Law – Treaties & Documents.* International Committee of the Red Cross. Available at: ⟨http://www.icrc.org/ihl.nsf/FULL/380?OpenDocument⟩ (accessed 22 November 2011).

Popovski, V., G. Reichberg and N. Turner (eds.) (2009) *World Religions and Norms of War.* Tokyo: United Nations University Press.

Rothchild, D., F.M. Deng, I.W. Zartman, S. Kimaro and T. Lyons (1996) *Sovereignty as Responsibility: Conflict Management in Africa.* Washington, DC: Brookings Institution Press.

UNGA (2005) *UN General Assembly Resolution 60/1: World Summit Outcome Document*, A/Res/60/1, 16 September 2005. Available at: ⟨http://www.un.org/summit2005/presskit/fact_sheet.pdf⟩.

UNSG (2009) *Report of the Secretary-General: Implementing the Responsibility to Protect*, A/63/677, 12 January 2009.

UNSG (2010) *Report of the Secretary-General: Early Warning, Assessment and the Responsibility to Protect*, A/64/864, 14 July 2010.

UNSG (2011) *Report of the Secretary-General: The Role of Regional and Sub-Regional Arrangements in Implementing the Responsibility to Protect*, A/65/877–S/2011/393, 27 June 2011.

Wheeler, Nicholas (2002) *Saving Strangers: Humanitarian Intervention in International Society.* Oxford: Oxford University Press.

Index